MARTIN TARBUCK

LIFE OF PIES
IN SEARCH OF PIEFECTION

First published November 2014 by Mudhuts Media

Copyright @ Mudhuts Media

Design by Andy Greenhalgh

Printed and bound by 1010 Printing (China) Ltd

To Emma and Jess

Life began when you came along

Acknowledgements:

Andy G for the design and eternal patience

Migs for the website and technical support

Andy B for the pinstripe and red braces marketing gubbins

Andrew L for printing

Emma for the proof raeding

FOREWORD

"Mrs Tarbuck, I don't think I can help you," said the solicitor. "A pie quest is not a valid reason for divorce."

"How about unreasonable behaviour?"

"No."

"Desertion?"

"No."

"Neglect?"

"No."

"Mrs Tarbuck, why don't you consider an alternative avenue? How about mediation?"

Six weeks later and I have admitted that I feel abandoned, acknowledged that this leaves me lonely and accepted that his love of pies is as well as his love for me, not instead of. The solution? If you can't beat them, join them. My daughter and I embarked on his ludicrous journey fuelled by obsession.

We saw lots of lovely places and enjoyed some pleasant days out, only tempered by my husband's continual frustrations over us not being ready and missing the 12 o'clock pie deadline (that magical time when all the pies suddenly disappear).

It was actually heart warming to see the look of joy and triumph on his face, as he emerged from the shops with his prize in his arms; talking animatedly to himself on his phone; laughing away at his own silly little jokes. And not one to be selfish (ha!) he would always bring a flapjack for me and a gingerbread man for Jessica.

I even became quite addicted to Britain's Best Bakery and was excited when we visited bakeries featured on the show! I even forgave him for the disastrous "holiday" in a freezing, grotty, shack of a caravan in Cornwall.

So on the whole it's not been a bad experience and secretly, I am of course proud of his achievements (although **note to author** the phrase "labour of love" is more appropriate when talking about childbirth and child-rearing, rather than when gallivanting around the country in search of pies).

I only hope that he gives me the same level of support when I embark on my search for Britain's best shopping centre.

Emma Tarbuck

PS. Please look out for my daughter's forthcoming book "Gingerbread Journeys: A three year old's quest to find the perfect gingerbread person".

PROLOGUE

Well hello there dear reader and thanks for accompanying me on my journey. You've probably worked out what this is all about now, so I thought I'd better briefly tell you what it's not about in the form of some very serious disclaimers:

Disclaimer #1: For many decades large swathes of professional and amateur commentators alike have laughed at the town of Wigan and mocked its inhabitants for being pie eating simpletons.

So please don't be too disgruntled if this book is a little biased towards the country's undisputed pie capital and the surrounding region. You started it not me. And now it's payback time!

Nevertheless what I discovered during my research is that pies are not necessarily a Wigan thing. They are a national treasure where each area has its individual intricacies and delicacies. I'm on a voyage of discovery here if you'll bear with me, learning as I go.

Disclaimer #2: Whereas most books of a culinary genre are written by someone in a position of considerable experience and expertise in this field, I am writing this book from a position of COMPLETE IGNORANCE. I literally haven't got a clue what I'm talking about. I just like good pies and will be putting in the miles to seek them out. I am not a food expert. I am not a connoisseur. In fact I am a fussy get. So why the hell am I writing a book about food? Well it's not just about food is it?

Disclaimer #3: This is one man's opinion on one pie repeated several hundred times over. By even being in this book the pie in question must be half decent but as with the pies – a pinch of salt should be added to all content. Don't get shirty about my ratings.

Disclaimer #4: The reviews at the start will be two or maybe even three years old by the time you read these works so prices will have inevitably risen in many cases. All prices were correct at the time of my visit however.

Disclaimer #5: Furthermore, I have made strenuous efforts (sat on my arse and typed words into Google) to ensure that all the establishments featured in "Life of Pies" are still trading. If they aren't, or they have changed name, I have annotated this in the index. All details are correct as of going to print. But with this being one of those quaint old things called a book, that's not to say the details will remain correct in perpetuity. Check before you set out is my advice intrepid pie ramblers!

Disclaimer #6: We all get daft ideas which pop into our heads. However what usually happens is the sensible part of the brain comes along – the part which reminds you to put the bins out or pay the credit card bill – and flicks the maverick part with an elastic band barking "What on earth do you think you're playing at? Pack it in! Right now!" Clearly the sensible part of my brain went AWOL for a couple of years therefore I feel duly obliged to say that pies, brilliant though they are, should only be consumed in moderation.

Disclaimer #7: Furthermore, this book is self-funded, self-published and written by an enthusiastic amateur. There's also nearly 140,000 words in it. I've tried to check them all….honestly….but if you're the kind of individual who is already thumbing through it, gleefully looking for the first spelling mistake, well you're in for a treat. I tried so please go easy on me will you?

Disclaimer #8: No animals were hurt during the production of….oh hang on that's not right.

Enough! Feeling peckish are we?

THE PIE CHART

You know the way Hugh Hefner parades around his Beverley Hills mansion in his dressing gown surrounded by a bevy of poolside beauties? Well that's how I feel when you put pies in front of me. Through my eyes, there's no ugly ones and each and every one of them deserves to be loved equally.

I've not set my stall out to be harsh. I've only set out to eat good pies in this book unless I've been particularly hungry so bad reviews will be few and far between. However, I need to differentiate somehow, so let me introduce the "Pie Chart".

Seven categories marked out of ten to give a total score out of seventy. If it's passed the magical fifty mark, then it's a pie worthy of a repeat devouring. Over fifty-five and it's truly exceptional.

Purveyor: Who produced this beautifully baked creature?

Premises: Where has it come from? This will be the purveyor's base/head office if they are part of a chain rather than the shop or branch visited. There's a full index at the end because I'm geeky like that.

Purchase: The flavour and cost of the purchase.

Place: People and Places might be a slightly dated Trivial Pursuit category but it is essential for getting the great pie adventurer's dining experience off to a flyer. It's all about the service and surroundings you see….

Pastry: See also *portability*. A pie has to be completely encased for a start – otherwise there's no chance of eating it with your hands; and the top crust should be the decorative invitation to the party that lies within. Oh and if that pastry falls apart, then so do I. WITH RAGE.

Presentation: Not withstanding the pastry, was it served warm or cold? How was it parcelled up? What whiff did it giff off? These are auxiliary elements but all contribute to the consumption experience.

Package (Filling): We've all unwrapped a present and found ourselves slightly disappointed with what we've unravelled. So what's inside this parcel then? Is it packed like a rush hour tube train or are there air pockets large enough to fill a hot balloon? Oh and we don't just demand a high quantity of filling, we want quality as well!

Palate: Oh yes: the taste! The proof of the pudding is in the eating! Only if it's a steak pudding in this case mind you.

Price: Or more pertinently: value for money. If you get change from a quid then it's bound to score highly. However, if it's slightly more expensive but packed full of meat procured from the beefiest bull in Bonar Bridge or is an exquisite, gourmet dining experience then it's hardly fair to penalise for that.

Portion: Let's not be crude here but yes, we *are* all size queens where pies are concerned.

The top crust

Part 1: The first 100

Aka: No woman·no pie

DAY ONE: Monday 16th January 2012

I'm sat in my car in a leafy lane near Knutsford town centre. I have carefully assembled a digital camera and have got a white chopping board laid out on the passenger seat, with the box underneath to prop it up level to the seat's curvature. There's a load of white van men working on a big house across the road and a postman has just walked past, whistling. Because all postmen whistle. I lay the pie out on the chopping board and I produce a large shiny carving knife out of my Asda bag, lift the pie out of it's foil tray and proceed to sever it in half with one almighty, glee-filled blow. Just as a pair of ageing pedestrians walk past with their dog.

"Police are trying to trace a man seen acting suspiciously in a silver car in the area at the time of the crime"

Those are the words ringing through my head right now. I'm not right in the head am I, let's face it? This is ODD behaviour; or at the very least OCD behaviour. It makes perfect sense to me though: this is the first stage in a quest I have believed in for quite some time now.

It is the duty of a Wigan man to sample as many pies as is humanly possible from around the world.

I want to find the best there is. It may be in my home town of Wigan, or further afield. I need a plan, a map, an understanding wife and some healthy working organs. Can I travel the UK, albeit ever so slightly skewed towards the North, to find and review the best pies and seek out the ultimate pie? It's time to find out....

My first review is in Hampsons in Knutsford near work. It's posh. The local MP is George Osborne. This might well be where he comes when he wants to rough it and stick a meat pie down his grid. I doubt it though.

It's nearly 1pm when I wander in to break up the chit chat as two ladies turn and stand to attention.

"I'll have a meat and potato pie please"

You'll be hearing me say that an awful lot. It's my staple diet for 700 days, although I'm prepared to mix it up a bit in the interests of research. I mean they do a CHIP SHOP CURRY PASTY in here for God's sake, who wouldn't want one of those?

There are a range of pasties from chicken tikka and cheese and onion but it's the pie I'm after which comes in a Sayers wrapper. Confused? Hampsons are part of the Sayers group and they also own the Pound Bakery (more on them later). They have sensibly opted to retain their prestige brand name for the residents of the Tatton constituency mind you.

1.

PURVEYOR: Hampsons Bakers
PREMISES: Bolton
PURCHASE: Meat and Potato pie £1.05
PLACE: 7 I get a smile which is a start! Attentive and seem genuinely pleased to see me. They offer me a fork which blots their copy book a bit mind you
PASTRY: 7 The pie possesses perfect portability and holds together throughout. The crust edge is a tad thick which often sets the heartburn alarm bells ringing but the whole pie is eaten by hand and there is zero, I repeat zero spillage
PRESENTATION: 7 It's scorching hot like a hand grenade but once the foil tray has been dispensed with, it's almost the perfect room temperature to chomp into
PACKAGE: 8 A deep mix of meat and potato chunks full to the brim with hardly any airspace
PALATE: 7 This lot churn out the pies by the van load so it's a quality, solid performer if a little generic
PRICE: 8 Slightly above average sized pie for a slightly below average price
PORTION: 7 Just about filling
OVERALL: If I had the best pie in the whole wide world first, it would be a very short book. The Hampsons pie is a good, solid performer but not spectacular. It sets a benchmark that some will exceed but many will fall short of and gets a respectable 51 out of 70 marks. Now, I need to get a plan together....

I can be a bit odd and obsessive at times but I think most of us are. Men, in particular once they reach a (cough) certain age get this way. It might be real ale or socks or some lunatics start to do triathlons but essentially we start looking where we are in life and decide that we need to try as many things as possible before we die.

I've had this idea for ages but for the first time in twenty years I got made redundant last summer and decided to put it into action. I walked out of work on the Friday and got another job on the Monday and my dreams of being a Bohemian literary visionary were quashed once more.

I've had a few false starts but I've bought the utensils and started a list now. We cannot function without lists right? My pockets are constantly full of scrunched up post it notes with tasks scribbled upon which never get fulfilled.

House style? That's important right? In my muddled head, I originally wanted it to be a reference book like the Good Beer Guide but for pies. Pies are serious business you see.

I get zero response when I pimp out the idea to my red braces and pin-stripe suit marketing guru Donuts so I ring him.

'I know you. Whenever I put an idea in front of you, you always go into overdrive about it, full of enthusiasm and excitement. I sent you an email about this pie book and you've never text or emailed me back. You think it's a shit idea don't you?'

'How about a good idea not perhaps executed as well as it could be? I know in its present form I wouldn't buy it (OUCH THAT HURT) I'd go more pie adventures in novel/diary form, it worked well in Pies & Prejudice'.

This is Pies & Prejudice, the title of which I thought up in a petrol station forecourt; my 2005 book co-written with Andy Vaughan about Wigan Athletic's rise to the Premier League. Not to be confused with the book with exactly the same title which surfaced several years later written by a BBC radio presenter and fellow Wiganer.

So to the next hurdle: At what point do I speak to the missus about it? Not yet. I'm terrified.

I get home from work to find a chippy tea waiting for me. Sat in the microwave is a Holland's Meat and Potato pie with half a ton of chips piled on top smothered in gravy. I'll have to tell her.

Saturday 21st January 2012

It's highly probable that blood has been spilled over the debate as to who makes the best pies in Wigan. Or pie gravy at least. This is why the question needs answering. There are people who swear by the Muffin Man. Plus it's in my village so giving it a shit review will see me ostracised by my local community and earn me the nickname "that pie wanker".

Keep it simple for now:

"Right darling – going getting my hair cut, then I'm getting some petrol. Fancy a pie for lunch?"

It needs to be a local one given we're going out for the afternoon and I'm still operating incognito but there are some big hitters within the confines of WN6. I don't want to crown a king in the first few pages but I envisage at least one or two Champions League places for Wigan pie shops when judgement day arrives.

The beauty of this land of ours is that you can be anywhere in the country by lunch time if you get up early enough but just for today, my local pie shop will have to do.

When I was a kid growing up in the Springfield area of Wigan, there were at least four pie shops within a few hundred yards of my house. I'm left to lament D&J Wilcock and the Gidlow Bakery, however the Muffin Man remains.

It's a traditional bakers with several branches in Wigan. As the name implies they do lovely, fluffy muffins in packs of six. These are known in Wigan as barmcakes. Known elsewhere as cobs/rolls/baps/teacakes/breadcakes and the source of regional internet arguments everywhere.

There's also pasties, chunky steak pies, breakfast items, and chicken and mushroom pies (the latter of which I often decline on the basis that I refuse point blank to eat anything that grows between your toes). This is a phobia I will have to conquer in the coming months.

For today, I manage to procure the last three meat and potato pies on the shelf.

"Put some more pies in, these have run out"

It's barely eleven in the morning! Only in Wigan!

2.

PURVEYOR: The Muffin Man
PREMISES: Wigan
PURCHASE: Large meat and potato pie £1.35
PLACE: 8 Brisk and brusque, the Wigan pie woman in action is truly an art form to admire
PASTRY: 9 Firm enough that the crust doesn't crumble in any way yet softer than the dulcet tones of the Cadbury's

Caramel bunny. Heavenly
PRESENTATION: 6 Not very warm but this was acknowledged
PACKAGE: 8 Densely packed potato bound with mince in a mash. Heavier on the potato than meat but plenty in there

PALATE: 8 The mince is pinkish but deliciously tender and it is a proper Lancastrian pie with sloppy potato filling oozing all over
PRICE: 8 Two options to serve different appetites works for me
PORTION: 8 I mean who on earth orders a small pie when there's a large one on the menu?
OVERALL: 55/70. I'm parked up at the side of the road talking into my phone like an Apprentice candidate. A paperboy walks past looking at me oddly as I narrate this review Partridge-style. As I said: Pies are serious business. An early contender.

Monday 23rd January 2012

Got to keep up the batting average: now, where can I reasonably get to within my lunch hour without anyone noticing I've disappeared? I do 12 hours days so if I take longer than an hour it's not a huge deal but then there's the side effects. Having a pastry heavy pie for lunch often lays a bit on the stomach; I may as well have six pints I'd be that lethargic. Like the IT developers who go to our canteen and polish off a full curry and apple custard and crumble for dessert. If I did that I'd have my head on my desk all afternoon.

I've no idea how we managed before the internet. Yellow Pages I suppose. A couple of mates of mine used to go on pub crawls in towns and villages armed only with Yellow Pages not knowing whether they'd get a warm welcome or stabbed upon entering each establishment. A great idea indeed possibly even more fun than gallivanting around the country eating pies but I won't be going down that route. Some pubs are great, some pubs are lousy but pubs, like pies, deserve love. I do need to try and push it a bit given the missus hasn't yet OK'd it for me to bugger off to Scotland for the weekend.

I decide on a bakery who are based in Crewe and serve the Potteries. I identify a place called Biddulph and it's just the other side of Congleton, which I know is just a few miles away from work: 25 minutes each way, ten minutes to scoff a pie. Piece of piss. Plus I can probably cut a few minutes off that with a spot of demon driving down country lanes. It's on Biddulph High Street. I've never heard of the place so it can only be a little village and will be a doddle to find once I get there.

Needlessly to say my naivety quickly finds me reversing down country lanes. I've got two SatNavs on my phone but they are both shit. Sheer panic sets in once or twice as I get hopelessly lost in places of Cheshire which I didn't know existed. When I do find myself on the right track I get stuck behind all manner of tractors, salt gritters and gun toting Farmer Palmers in Land Rovers. Not to mention four Police motorbikes flying past just as

7

I am studiously waving the map about on my phone in front of my seriously agitated little face.

Forty minutes and I'm still nowhere near and I consider that this might have to be an abortive mission. However at that point the roads veers upwards to a viewpoint giving me a scintillating view of the whole of Staffordshire. I still haven't a clue where I am but it's a real Planet of the Apes moment.

Biddulph is massive and upon parking up in Sainsburys I discover the High Street is at least half a mile long. Now to ascertain which way to walk: I'm looking for the big orange sign of Wrights but nothing jumps out at me. I then see a lad walking down the street with a couple of brown wrappers with writing on them: he's been getting the pies in – GOOD LAD – and I trail his recent path. It's only as I get closer that the truth is revealed by virtue of a large POVEYS OATCAKES sign above the window. I'm in Stoke country and I've just been had!

Some other time perhaps. I head back the other way past a Wetherspoons with a few likely lads hanging about outside and it crosses my mind to ask them. I don't and it's just as well as I can't tell a word they're saying as one shouts his head off to the other in that daft Potteries brogue.

I still can't smell pies but keep walking. Just as I look close to getting to the other end of the High Street, I find it. Except it's not – it's another pie shop, called bizarrely New Cooks. This is an interesting development and I'm torn. What now, do I go to both? Have I got time to do both? Pie shops like gift horses should not be looked in the mouth, their products should be placed in the mouth.

Maybe I just go to New Cooks, as it's less of a chain than Wrights with their fifteen shops across Stoke and more likely to produce a better, more independent pie? Is it fair to represent two bakers from such a confined area only for me to possibly miss out a large city completely later down the line like Bristol or Portsmouth if I can't find anywhere to procure a decent pie from?

These early moral dilemmas will shape my mission and my instinct tells me to stick to Plan A in order to fully absorb myself in the Wrights Pie experience. I make a note of the other one in my pie master spreadsheet as one for the future. Time is on my side.

I eventually find Wrights another hundred or so yards down the street right at the far end. Pie procured, tempted though I am by the offer of Staffordshire lobbies (hot pot) with peas and gravy and on my way. The pie is raging hot. If Art Garfunkel walked in here he'd probably sing "Wrights Pies, burning like fire"

Sorry. By this point I need a wee and pop in the bogs by Sainsburys, a very sleek cylindrical affair. As if I didn't have enough of a phobia already about public conveniences, there's grunting coming from one of the cubicles and a bloke with a flat cap comes and has a slash next to me, immediately initiating conversation about the weather. Get me out of here!!

3.

PURVEYOR: Wrights
PREMISES: Crewe
PURCHASE: Meat and potato pie £1.30
PLACE: 7 **PASTRY:** 6.5 **PRESENTATION:** 8 **PACKAGE:** 8
PALATE: 7 **PRICE:** 7.5 **PORTION:** 8
OVERALL: 52/70 An above average size pie with a crust which has a lovely feel to it but wastes no time introducing me to Mr Heartburn. A delightful, powerful aroma comes off it which veritably stinks my car out. A fine mix of fresh, almost green potato and generous meat content with a distinct flavour to it which retains its heat superbly. Slight amount of airspace at the top giving it an aircraft hangar type effect but overall a valiant effort.

Tuesday 24th January 2012

"Do you sell pies?"

A fairly innocuous request. It might get you a funny look if you walk into a bakers in Wigan and ask that question, as you are likely to be confronted with a shop full of the blighters. The pie lady – and it is a lady 99% of the time – might think you're being a sarcastic get. You'd have to offer some variation along the lines of

"Got any pies left?" or a more genteel

"What flavour of pies do you have available for immediate consumption to warm my cockles on this crisp winter's afternoon?"

Both acceptable, albeit the second can show you up to be something of a pie novice in the jungle that is a North West pie shop if you can't spot a pie type on sight.

It's a bloody stupid question to ask in a bakery in the North West of England. Yet it also garners an equally profound "have you just been beamed down from outer space sunshine?" type expression should you venture that query forward in certain other parts of the country.

I'm in Poplar, officially within the sound of Bow bells. It's freezing, there are polar bears wandering freely up and down the tube. I get off at All Saints and wander through Chrisp Street Market in search of a Percy Ingles bakery, famed throughout East London and Essex. I actually walk past a pie and mash shop to get there.

I find it easy enough, it's striking green fascia illuminating the precinct and wander in. It's a baker's right, just like thousands of others up and down the country – they MUST sell pies?

THREE TIMES I ASK.

It might be my accent but each time the Eastern European girl serving laughs a little louder and repeats the last word "Pies?" until she's cackling manically like one of those Russian girls in Bond films.

"OK I'll have a steak bite then"

A sheepish retreat but I need summat to eat. It's bizarre. She looks at me like I'm some kind of escaped lunatic. You know – a pie? They're flogging them with mash around the corner?

It seems that in the East End of London there are rules: bakers sell bread, cakes and a selection of pasty type pastry products. If you want a pie, you go to a pie and mash shop. Never the twain shall meet. They then go and put eel liquor instead of gravy on it and put their potatoes on the outside. I'm learning I suppose and I will come back and try your famous Cockney pie and mash soon. In the meantime, I settle for scoffing this steak slice/bake/bite/pastry whatever they call it.

4.

PURVEYOR: Percy Ingles
PREMISES: Leyton
PURCHASE: Steak bite £1.39
PLACE: 7 She's frostier than an Eskimo's nose but it's not her fault I'm a simple minded buffoon
PASTRY: 6 Puff pastry. More air than ex Byker Grove poplet Donna
PRESENTATION: 6 As per my initial reception upon entering, it's a touch lukewarm
PACKAGE: 7 Steak, gravy with no bulking agent
PALATE: 7 Surprised me this, it is actually steak
PRICE: 7 Not bad for London prices
PORTION: 8 None too deep but a good size, like a pastry iPad
OVERALL: 48/70 Just as you can't compare apples with oranges, you can't compare pies with pasties/slices/bakes/bites.

Saturday 28th January 2012

Fat Boy Slim once sang a song about a Crumpsall Brother. For a while, Hampsons in Wigan used to do four pies for a pound when I worked in the centre. The first two slipped down easily, the third presented a bit of resistance and by the time I got to the 4th my stomach was aching. Today I went to Crumpsall and ate four pies which makes me a Fatboy.

My sporting persuasion is such that although I am not a Man Utd fan I was only too willing to become a member of fan owned FC United of Manchester. Our lot (the Mudhutter mob) have mates there and they always look after us and ply us with real ale and pastry products.

I have often marvelled at the deep dish "tater hash" served up in their infamous pre match irreverent gathering "Course You Can Malcolm" and decided to seek out a few recommendations from the custodian of the tater hash, Mr Maurice Twomowers of Openshaw. I imagine if you're going to ask anyone where to get the best pies in Manchester, then a gentleman called Maurice Twomowers is a good place to start. He comes up trumps immediately.

I come off at Bury and below the "Welcome to Manchester" sign I see another which says "Slatterys – World class bakers and confectioners". I head through the predominantly Jewish area of Prestwich before the long drag into Manchester becomes more urban and continental, with kebab shops and curry houses now lining the streets. I'm not actually sure where I am until I spot the Police station (which ALWAYS has the location on the front) and I can see I'm in Cheetham Hill now; a dearth of pie shops, save for the ubiquitous Greggs on the main drag. A couple of left turns and I'm driving through a ropey area where I spot a lad selling drugs to a girl in broad daylight shortly before spotting me watching him deal drugs in broad daylight. Car inconspicuously locked.

I'm on Cleveland Road, supposedly the home of Slatterys Bakery but all I can see is a big church. On closer inspection, crouched behind it in a corner terrace is this little gem of a place.

There's huge plate pies and pasties and sandwiches but I'm further taken aback by the cakes, which look so sweet they can make your teeth drop out by just looking at them.

5.

PURVEYOR: Slatterys
PREMISES: Whitefield
PURCHASE: Meat and potato pie £1.50
PLACE: 8 If Willy Wonka made crusts not chocolate it'd look like this place
PASTRY: 7.5 A glazed top crust with a little porthole and a large crack running through the middle giving a seductive peek at the delights which lie inside
PRESENTATION: 7 Authentic aroma and of good temperature
PACKAGE: 8 Upon attempting hand based consumption, gravy spills down my sleeve. This is indeed a wondrous experience!
PALATE: 7 Slight lack of seasoning but this enables the individual components to come through

PRICE: 7 £1.50 Feels like a "value ceiling" in the meat and potato market
PORTION: 7 Average size devoured in record time
OVERALL: 51.5/70 An impressive pie and an impressive start to the day.
It appears that the man in possession of both a Flymo and a Qualcast
knows his stuff pie wise.

Sat in a retail park making a proper mess of the wife's car here so I wander
over to B&M Bargains and get some binbags and air fresheners. More accessories carried around by mass murderers basically.

On to Ancoats and the irony of Man Utd lads sending me to one of their
hidden treasures situated in the shadow of the Etihad isn't lost. Though
technically this is where Manchester United started off back when they
were just a bunch of workshy railwaymen who'd rather kick a ball about
than stoke a steam engine with no grand designs on global domination.

I drive through part of the "Shameless" estate, finding it relatively genteel after having gone through much gentrification in recent times and
arrive in Beswick Street. The Crusty Cob sits in a secluded row of shops,
perched on a hill which runs down to the stadium.

It's well kept and I'm queuing up trying to ascertain the menu. Manchester is firmly meat and potato country. There's meat pies and potato
pies and meat and potato pies, all of them look homemade and delicious
as I tune in to other people's orders. The fella in front orders 12 (twelve)
meat and potato pies and six cream horns.

6.

PURVEYOR: The Crusty Cob
PREMISES: Manchester
PURCHASE: Meat and potato pie £1.22
PLACE: 6.5 Queuing system a bit of a mess
PASTRY: 9 Home made impeccably soft short crust pastry made to
perfection. The crust is the first thing you see and I can't take my eyes
off these beauties from the second I walk into the shop. A quite simply
stunning uneven top crust
PRESENTATION: 9 A real looker, highly distinct. More importantly,
it's piping hot with more steam coming off it than an irate Popeye
PACKAGE: 9.5 Fantastic dark gravy spilling out and wrapping up
a crowded filling of meat and potato chunks
PALATE: 9 Dark, mysterious and opulent gravy coating steak and
potato which has a remarkable freshness about it
PRICE: 8 I endorse the fact it's £1.22. It implies they are resisting the lazy
option of whacking the price with all their might. Putting the customer's
pocket before their own ball-ache of handling masses of coppers

PORTION: 7.5 Average size but great volume
OVERALL: 58.5/70 Equally as suitable for an Arab sheikh or a humble railway worker.

Wow! I'm beaming away like a small child in Openshaw Matalan car park, being observed closely by a fag toting security guard who is probably wondering what the hell I've got to be so pleased about on a drab Saturday morning.

But there's more! I make for the Openshaw/Droylsden border down a side street which is tail to bumper with erratically parked white vans full of blokes stuffing their faces. Hello hello, what have we here?

Westwells, home of previously mentioned Tater Hash is a corner plot and very rustic inside. Sandwiches, pies, two pans of peas and gravy and a fridge full of cans. No price list and when she orally presents the bill for my purchase I am inclined to clean my ears out…

7.

PURVEYOR: Westwells
PREMISES: Droylsden, Manchester
PURCHASE: A meat and potato pie for EIGHTY FIVE PENCE
PLACE: 8 I'm kept waiting a while as the hi-viz gentleman in front orders his sides of peas and gravy. However the old girl behind the counter quickly shouts her co-worker for assistance in a lovely Mancunian accent so deep it makes Barry White sound distinctly soprano
PASTRY: 8 A bit crumbly but again distinctly home made with a teasing little peephole in the middle
PRESENTATION: 8 The foil tray is so furnace like it appears to be burning a hole in my hand but the smell of gravy emanating from inside means this pie is destined for a quick larruping
PACKAGE: 8 Intensely full inside, easy on the eye with potatoes that are so sodden with gravy they're dark brown in colour
PALATE: 7 The spectre of the tater hash rears its ugly head again (on a previous trip to FC United, world renowned food critic Orrible Ives of the Norley Hall council estate in Wigan decreed the tater hash "dry and tasteless" – nor did he pay for it the ungrateful bounder!) It was a touch dry in parts, however the divine softness of the filling compensates for a slight lack of flavour
PRICE: 9. I repeat, EIGHTY FIVE NEW PENCE

PORTION: 7.5 Slightly raised in the middle in order to accommodate more content
OVERALL: 55.5/70 A splendid price and a great looking pie but the (arguable) lack of seasoning only enforces the suggestion that you might want to team up this little cracker with some peas and gravy.

That really should be my lot for the day but unfortunately I spot a Martins Bakery on my way to Westwells. Despite feeling more than a little punch drunk after ingesting enough pastry to sink an aircraft carrier I cannot resisting indulging in one last exhibit.

I park around the back of the main drag in Openshaw by the health centre and wander into Martins to be confronted by organised chaos in front of and behind the counter. There's no queue of any fashion at all and I get called forward before some old boy who looks like he's been stood there for around 12 years. Every man for himself.

8.

PURVEYOR: Martins Bakery
PREMISES: Manchester
PURCHASE: Meat and potato pie £1.15
PLACE: 5.5 **PASTRY:** 6 **PRESENTATION:** 6 **PACKAGE:** 7
PALATE: 7 **PRICE:** 7 **PORTION:** 6.5
OVERALL: 45/50 The pie is presented in a raging hot foil tray yet the ample serving of meat and veg is only moderately warm inside.
How does that work? It has a glazed, buttery lid which is always welcome yet the crumbly exterior soon falls part in my hands, causing heartbreaking scenes on an emotional day. It tastes adequate with all the ingredients coming out. The sort you'd expect from a major baker. I didn't set out to be harsh. I suspect I'm just a bit pied out today as I look wistfully at a bin at Birch Services whilst contemplating throwing up into it.

Pie and chips waiting for me on the table for tea when I get in FFS!!

Tuesday 31st January 2012

Forgive the parochial nature but much is made of the rivalry locally between St Helens and Wigan. Not just in rugby league terms but also in pie eating with many notable St Helens bakeries rating themselves up there with their Wigan counterparts. Nobody ever mentions Warrington for some reason. Is this fair? Time to find out!

Well I'm heading to Lymm actually which although technically part of

Warrington may as well be a different planet. Home of footballers and soap stars, as evidenced by me spotting Eileen off Corrie walking hand in hand down the road with her beau on my approach.

A village square with cobbled streets lined with cafe bars. Lots of well heeled types pottering about. Plus the inevitable young dickheads wearing tight t shirts, shorts and flip flops showing off their shit tattoos and shit haircuts when it's about minus five outside.

Unfortunately for me, there's also double yellows everywhere and the entrance to the car park is gridlocked. I can't quite see what's going on up the hill. A bloke goes past walking his dog and tells me "You wanna turn around pal they're all fucking scrapping up there!".

And as my car creeps up I can see that there does indeed appear to be two blokes fighting: shoving and grabbing and then throwing punches while a blonde bimbo in a white fur coat appears to have pulled one of her high heels off and is goading the larger, burlier gentleman. From what I can glean the big bloke in the Audi has been crashed into by the white Beetle (owned by the WAG type bint) and her hubby is squaring up to him with some reticence, whilst onlookers shake their heads in disgust/encourage them mischievously.

The rabble disperses and I seek out my pie at Sextons. It's double fronted with a sit down café attached to it and my biggest concern on arrival is that there are no pies on display. I'll be looking to hit someone if the delay caused by that altercation has meant that the last pie has gone but after a short wait my booty is delivered.

Lost in Lymm afterwards where for the first time in my life I go under the Thelwall Viaduct three times and admire the spectacle of cars bombing over a huge flyover. The serene Lymm dam set aside a splendid looking church is charming but I need to get back to work and the smell of my dinner is torturing me.

I've had a good feel and smell of the pie and it's feels a bit like a Galloways, Wigan's premier pie maker. The foil tray is thirty degrees hotter than the sun and the base is tapered off and it comes in a branded paper bag.

9.

PURVEYOR: Sextons
PREMISES: Warrington
PURCHASE: Meat and potato pie £1.28
PLACE: 7 **PASTRY:** 9 **PRESENTATION:** 8 **PACKAGE:** 8
PALATE: 8 **PRICE:** 7 **PORTION:** 7.5
OVERALL: 54.5/70 The temperature is powerful and the crust is sublime; a touch of puff pastry yet light and soft in the mouth. The filling,

consisting of ringlets of pink meat and mushy slabs of potato comes oozing out like a lazy river rolling out to sea. This is a pie which packs a real punch. Much like the patrons of nearby car parks.

Friday 3rd February 2012

The Friday night Booths booze cruise. The opportunity to get matriarchal glares off semi-retired check out girls as I pass a dozen bottles of beer through their counter and nothing else. If you beamed an alien down from outer space and put them in a supermarket at Friday teatime, their research would lead them to conclude that human life forms can live solely off a diet of alcoholic beverages – all noted down in their little alien iPads. I suppose I'd better put some food in there then.

I peruse the whoopsie section while the locals pour scorn upon me. By contrast there's open warfare by the whoopsie counter in the Wigan Asda when they release the half price chickens at 8pm every night. Here, I Just look like a vagrant.

Booths do brilliant food – and wine and ales and cheese and lots of other things that matter and for seekers of obscurity, like myself, they seem to rotate their suppliers regularly. It's expensive mind and you wouldn't want to do a big shop here. Consequently they play up to their target demographic by only situating their stores in posh Northern market towns.

Lancashire bakers, Greenhalghs and Clayton Park, are their core producers but as I move on to the pie shelf I spot the pork pies: Vale of Mowbray – actually in Yorkshire?? Dickinson and Morris, definitely authentic Melton Mowbray; and Philip Baker pork pies. Appropriate name you've got there Philip old bean, now let's see what your produce is made of:

10.

PURVEYOR: Philip Baker
PREMISES: Exeter
PURCHASE: The ultimate pork pie £1.49
PLACE: 8 Delightful as ever in Booths, maintaining a pleasant demeanour throughout. Even though my basket contains eight bottles of cider, a pork pie, a bag of crisps and sod all else
PASTRY: 7.5 Solid and reliable; a thick, dense base and hot water pastry crust
PRESENTATION: 8 I heated this up in the oven and whereas the smell wasn't overpowering, once the pie gets close to my mouth it hits me like a steam train
PACKAGE: 8 Nice outer layer of jelly encasing lots of thick, juicy fine sausage meat

PALATE: 8.5 It's so rich I feel a bit drunk as I consume it, although that could be the accompanying Kingston Press cider on special offer at a quid a bottle. As the jelly comes sliding out I'm hit with an explosion of sage and sausage with hints of bacon and pepper

PRICE: 7 That's Booths' prices too!

PORTION: 8 Big enough plus they have larger ones for sharing. I don't share pies

OVERALL: 55/70 He may look like a bit of a toff on his website but this is a growler and a half. Philip has earned his stripes here with an enticing pork pie bursting with flavour.

I have a gander on his website which states "we use meat from happy animals raised on farms". This is just what I want to hear when I'm eating one of them. Although Philip himself looks way too posh to be stunning piglets with electrodes, as he waxes lyrically about the captivating rapport he encountered between buyer and vendor in downtown Paris. They also do a pork pie with juniper and crushed acorns. Acorns? I used to go to school with a lad who used to eat acorns.

Saturday 4th February 2012

Wigan is snowbound and gridlocked. I've got 500 copies of the Mudhutter fanzine which we sell at the football in the boot of the car and there's a blizzard outside. Hailstones, sleet, ice and with a sick wife and child at home, I'm sat in the car weeping openly.

I manage to get out to Waterstones in Wigan to drop some magazines off and whilst crossing the Market Place, I go unceremoniously arse over tit and pull my hamstring. It is then that it appears like a golden vision, an oasis in the desert:

THE POUND BAKERY

A pie for a pound is a headline grabber. However, when you discover that it's actually TWO pies for a pound, or pasties, sausage rolls or whatever, well the cap is well and truly doffed.

I dust myself down and wander in. The range of pies isn't too extensive, (or at least what's available) but the chip shop chicken curry pie does enough to arrest my attention.

It's as you'd expect: a pie filled with chip shop curry. And a bit of chicken. I team it up with a meat and potato and get stuck in.

11.

PURVEYOR: Pound Bakery

PREMISES: Bolton

PURCHASE: Chip Shop Chicken Curry Pie 50p
PLACE: 6 Quiet for Saturday lunchtime and the staff carry on yapping when I walk in
PASTRY: 8 A tad too flaky for my liking but redeems itself by having an extra piece of pastry on top. No idea if it's by accident or design but it earns an extra mark
PRESENTATION: 7 A tepid offering only compensated by the moderate whiff of curry. It comes in doubled up foil trays and if they've done that to protect the heat then they have failed I'm afraid
PACKAGE: 7.5 Some airspace at the top but still a reasonable portion of tender chicken pieces wrapped in a deep yellow curry sauce
PALATE: 7.5 As it says on the tin albeit the curry is a touch mild for me
PRICE: 10 Not cheap and nasty just cheap
PORTION: 7 Circular shaped with tapered sides
OVERALL: 53/70 Because we can all afford a novelty pie at those prices!! After this, I devour the meat and potato which is passable too. Large slabs of potato and juicy mincemeat. Again there is a heinous amount of airspace towards the roof of the pie and it arguably smells better than it tastes but whaddayawant for ten bob?

12.

PURVEYOR: Pound Bakery
PREMISES: Bolton
PURCHASE: Meat and Potato Pie 50p
PLACE: 6 **PASTRY:** 7 **PRESENTATION:** 7 **PACKAGE:** 7
PALATE: 8 **PRICE:** 10 **PORTION:** 7
OVERALL: 52/70 Two pies demolished in exactly four minutes. Probably not the best I will consume during the course of this book but the cheapest? I think so.

Tuesday 7th February 2012

There was a quote in today's paper from Karren Brady about her impending diet. It read "I cannot imagine a future without pie and mash" You and me both Kazza. You and me both. Actually, mash I can take or leave but I've got a conveyor belt of pies as long as the Channel Tunnel heading in my direction with no let up in sight.

The quote is highly appropriate given I've been sent to London today with work. London is a city of eight million people so it's a fair bet that there will be something in the region of four million shops. I've no idea how many of these are pie shops and whether they meet my ever so strict criteria but I have heard about Square Pie. Best make sure I have some money on me as £1.30 won't buy a Mars Bar in that London so I hear.

After much aimless wandering around the underground shopping malls entrenched within the bowels of Canary Wharf, I find my target at 5.45pm on a Tuesday evening. I get my pie and sit on a ledge to eat it as thousands of power dressed, serious looking folk walk past glaring at me with a look of utter contempt for eating in public. It's as if I've got a large neon sign above my head with the words 'NORTHERN TRAMP' flashing away.

13.

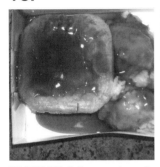

PURVEYOR: Square Pie
PREMISES: London
PURCHASE: Steak & Cheese pie (£4.70) with mash and gravy (£6.80 in total)
PLACE: 8 Very attentive, no queue, explained the deal and selection of extras. Served in a cardboard box
PASTRY: 8 Good quality, nice and soft and fully encased
PRESENTATION: 7 Warm enough

PACKAGE: 8 Composing of semi melted cheese on top of a decent quantity of steak with two big dollops of potato on the OUTSIDE. It'll never catch on!

PALATE: 8 I'll level with you: the cheesy mash is outstanding and the content itself is richer than some of these banker toffs swanning past me in pinstripe right now

PRICE: 7 (insert stereotypical moan about things being so much dearer down south) Well I'm not going to – as this was a full meal and a highly satisfying one to boot!

PORTION: 7 If I was using callipers and protractors in my research then a square pie would have me flummoxed

OVERALL: 53/70 Passionate about pies? It's clearly hip to be square lads!

Thursday 16th February 2012

There's nowhere quite like internet message board forums if you want to see a group of men (and it's usually men) act like a bunch of bickering kids. I've been planning a lunchtime sortie and chanced upon a Macclesfield Town FC website. A "Best pies" thread has been started by somebody who I presume to be the proprietor of the Treacle Town Pie Company and he is being viciously rag dolled about by the other board users, all submitting their own pie vendor of choice and arguing over their individual virtues.

Fittons, Spearings, Belfields and Broadhursts are all the popular choices and most of them are butchers. It's a bit different to Wigan where the bakers do the pies and the butchers do the meat. Maybe a butcher is better as they know their meat. It's a pie puzzler: which came first, the meat or the pastry?

The road to Macc is a snarling, sprawling one but upon arrival I am greeted with well kept streets and lots of little shopping areas, set against a backdrop of green patchwork quilt rolling hills leading out to the Peak District.

I can't get to the Treacle Town gaff as it's down a back street so I pull over and park opposite a pub, where I can hear the throaty cheer of drinkers sat outside on a balmy February afternoon. To my right is a butchers. This is a turn up for the books and I quickly establish above the bright red and white canopy that this is Marshall Spearings, whose pies were the subject of some consternation from Macc Town fans earlier today.

I'm fiddling with my phone trying to find out where I am and I notice a lad stood in front of me leaning on the church smoking a fag. He's been staring at me for some time. All in black, hoodie wearing, waiting outside court and eyeing me up intently.

Fortunately I can leap from car to butchers in two paces. I have a nosey around: Joints and sausages and lamb chops and chickens. It's thrown me a little to be honest.

"Can I help you?"

"Pies?"

The old dear in the familiar red stripey apron waves her hand over the tray of baked goods like she's the most glamorous gameshow assistant in the world – and to me – she is!!!

"Warm pies?"

"Yes just one"

I get a return sneer off the chav in black, deposit pie number one, lock the car carefully and set off for Charlotte Street. It's down a side street and I spot the luminous card in the window advertising its wares and stroll in. The Treacle Town Pie Company. Just down from The Silktown Snooker Club and opposite Silvertown Taxis. Macclesfield: a town of many talents.

Treacle Town might sound all razzamatazz and Americanised but the reality is somewhat different as I walk straight into the kitchen where a series of small, household type ovens stand. I'm transfixed. I think I like it. Small scale and as home made as they come. There's a fella downstairs wearing an apron and he grabs a kitchen towel to dry his hands. I can't help thinking that despite the big sign, if I've not walked into the wrong place, I've definitely walked into the wrong part of the right place.

"Can I help you?" I am greeted by a broad chirpy Mancunian with cropped greying hair and arms full of tattoos. He reaches into the oven and pulls out what looks like a large pork pie but is in fact a meat and potato. I'm a tad disappointed; it's the smallest one I've ever seen.

14.

PURVEYOR: Marshall Spearing
PREMISES: Macclesfield
PURCHASE: Meat and Potato pie £1.50
PLACE: 7 **PASTRY:** 9 **PRESENTATION:** 7 **PACKAGE:** 9
PALATE: 8 **PRICE:** 7 **PORTION:** 8
OVERALL: 55/70 Despite sounding like an American rapper, Marshall Spearing produces a divinely proficient pie. The pastry is crisp and glazed on the outside with a soft doughy interior. The filling is light and moist with a real authentic feel to it. It's a Bobby Dazzler.

15.

PURVEYOR: The Treacle Town Pie Company
PREMISES: Macclesfield
PURCHASE: Meat and Potato pie £1.40
PLACE: 8 A one man band
PASTRY: 6.5 Thick, ominously dark hot water pastry which falls to bits but is still rather unique in texture
PRESENTATION: 8 Served straight out of the oven with no foil tray, a little pocket rocket
PACKAGE: 8 The cuts are quality and it's nice and packed inside
PALATE: 8 Almost casserole like. Every pie made fresh that day is their claim and it shows in every bite
PRICE: 6 A well crafted effort with one major evident flaw to it....
PORTION: 5 Tiny. Sadly. Of party sized pork pie dimensions
OVERALL: 49.5/70 The old adage of a good little 'un always beats a good big 'un doesn't always apply to the pie eater's prescription.

Tuesday 21st February 2012

Lidl in Wigan. The only thing missing is a sign above the door saying "Abandon hope all ye who enter here"

I'm not sure eating half a kilo of pork in my dinner hour constitutes good brain food but I have targets to meet so I find myself wrestling a medium pork pie off the shelf for the price of just 99p. This is (they claim) the UK's best selling pork pie. They also have some whopping pasties next to it for a mere 59p and steak and gravy pies in the freezer chests.

I'm also impressed by the giant pretzels on the bakery counter, which could only be more spectacular if they were being chased around the store by a giant Pac Man. I team it up with a cheapo Apple energy drink to recharge my soon to be tranquillised-by-meat torso and head for the till.

The reasonably smartly dressed woman in front of me at the checkout is also buying something fruity. It's just gone mid-day on a Tuesday and she's purchasing a three litre bottle of own brand pear cider. She then proceeds to open it and starts glugging away before she's even walked out of the shop. Lovely.

I've got to declare an interest here: I applied for a job at Pork Farms in Nottingham in the summer of 1995 and I still haven't heard back from them. Not that I hold a grudge against the unresponsive bastards.

16.

PURVEYOR: Pork Farms
PREMISES: Nottingham
PURCHASE: Pork pie 99p
PLACE: 7 Having the patience of a saint is a pre-requisite to being a Lidl check-out girl I'd imagine
PASTRY: 7.5 Dark and moody considering it had been out of the oven a while but acceptable
PRESENTATION: 7 Just chilling on the refrigerator shelf
PACKAGE: 8 Mass produced but plenty of fine, well-seasoned sausage meat insulated by a generous layer of tangy jelly
PALATE: 7.5 Consistent if not spectacular
PRICE: 9 Let's face it, you could buy one of everything in Lidl and still have change from £20
PORTION: 9 The nutritional information suggests it is supposed to serve 4. Oops!
OVERALL: 55/70 Despite this company's policy to refuse to give gainful employment to impoverish students, as a budget pie (likely to be consumed by impoverish students) it nevertheless hits the mark. I recommend you compliment it's peppery flavour by teaming it up with a large bottle of Lidl own brand cider.

Tuesday 27th February 2012

Reids of Middlewich in a lunchtime raid. That familiar hue of browny /beige under a canopy next to a butchers. Piles of pies, pasties and cakes stacked up in the window; the place looks a little sparse but the old dears are quick to attend to me. I order a meat and potato, which feels very steak pie in shape i.e. oblong not round and sans foil tray.

17.

PURVEYOR: Reids
PREMISES: Middlewich
PURCHASE: Meat and potato pie £1.10
PLACE: 7.5 Attentive and courteous, I'm thinking "Acorn Antiques"
PASTRY: 7 Soft and supple crust
PRESENTATION: 7 Faintly alluring
PACKAGE: 6.5 Half seems to consist solely of one bright pink piece of steak
PALATE: 7 Rich and meaty
PRICE: 7 Small but cheap
PORTION: 5 Another tiddler of a pie, is this a Cheshire thing?
OVERALL: 47/70 It's no wonder there's no fat people around here.

Hey I'm not done yet Tuesday! As I play five a side, I eat alone on Tuesdays so I pick up a Pooles Pie from next to the cigarette counter at the Asda. I eat quite a lot of Pooles Pies and you could even say they're the inspiration behind this book.

As a youngster I remember the little café Pooles had opposite the train station, where little old ladies wearing pinnies doddered around serving up pies and peas to hungry punters. And as for the pies, my word....they were smaller than they are now but they were amazing! Pastry hand rolled by angels and the kind of sloppy, mouth watering filling which simply by-passed anything I'm likely to taste during the course of this tome. Sadly it's a good 10-15 years ago since they existed in that form. Despite local reclusive sports magnate (and one-time broken leg sufferer) Dave Whelan buying Pooles Pies several years ago, it appears he didn't pay for the recipe.

The shops don't exist anymore but they do have them on the shelves down at th'Asda (84p) and they sell them at the DW Stadium (a somewhat less frugal £2.30)

18.

PURVEYOR: Pooles
PREMISES: Wigan
PURCHASE: Chunky steak pie 84p
PLACE: 7 You think I'm going to give a Wigan Asda counter assistant a bad mark? More than my life's worth.
PASTRY: 6 I don't rate the pastry: crumbly, heartburn inducing and breaks

up easily. The old pastry was 11/10.

PRESENTATION: 7.5 Hot, hot, hot

PACKAGE: 7.5 Very well filled with a good mix of succulent meat and potato

PALATE: 7 The minced beef one tastes of dogfood. However the meat and potato and chunky steak which I have just consumed are infinitely more palatable

PRICE: 9 At the Asda, 6 at a football match

PORTION: 7 Portable and portly and perfectly formed

OVERALL: 51/70 They may be the public face of Wigan pies since 1847 but they've not been the force they were since at least 1987 I'm afraid.

Saturday 10th March 2012

I am pleased to report that Mrs Tarbuck is now officially "in" and I can stop skulking around whilst mysteriously getting fatter. This calls for a road trip and with my good lady literally on board I hit the M6 South-bound to get out of the North West, in my admittedly sluggish bid to audit every corner of the UK for pies. This has been sold to her on a "having a family day out" basis.

What I am quickly learning is that my original theory (that Wigan is the home of the pie) is met with resistance wherever you go. People, towns, cities and counties are proud of their pies and love to make and eat their own regional variations of them. The pie may be a different flavour but the sentiment is as strong as ever.

We're heading to Shropshire – no idea why – although I seem to spend the morning repeatedly driving around the same roundabout in Stafford, before heading through eighteen hamlets all of which proudly claim to be the "Best kept village in Staffordshire 2011".

Due to this navigational mishap, we barely make it as far as Telford with the imperiously conical Wrekin in the background before the baby has started crying and the missus needs a wee.

We stop completely randomly in the village of Donnington on a precinct and I quickly lock eyes on Lynn's Bakery. Rome may not have been built in a day but I suspect Donnington was from the look of it, as packs of lads with trackie bottoms and shaved heads sporting freshly laid Friday night shiners emerge from the council estates to mooch about the shops.

It appears to be home to an MOD site. I wander in to Lynn's Bakery to find that oft found awkward semi-circle of people half queuing, half waiting and staff having to politely ask "who's next" as customers shrug their shoulders and turn inwards. There is a small child running riot and a lad with a skinhead giving me the 'you're not from around here' look, which is confirmed with a knowing nod from him the second I open my mouth.

The carvery is centre stage and there's just a small tray of pies inside one of the display counters. I receive my calling and point to the pies: Meat and potato, Cottage pie, Steak and Kidney and some pasties; I wait a few more minutes while she warms it up in a microwave and the locals take it in turns to glare aggressively at me.

19.

PURVEYOR: Lynn's Bakery
PREMISES: Telford
PURCHASE: Meat and potato pie £1.40
PLACE: 6 All that's missing is a slow hand clap
PASTRY: 7 Much like several residents of Donnington this sunny Saturday morning, it has a very thick lip on it
PRESENTATION: 7.5 Warm as toast
PACKAGE: 8 A reasonable abundance of fluffy mince and well seasoned potato
PALATE: 8 It's remarkably invigorating but then the first pie of the day usually is
PRICE: 7 Average
PORTION: 7 Top crust almost transparently thin not helped by having it warmed up in the microwave
OVERALL: 50.5/70 A run of the mill pie, probably bought in. Call it a warm up for the delights of Much Wenlock and Ludlow....

So to Much Wenlock via the villages of Homer and Wig Wig whilst encountering some of Shropshire's finest lunatic drivers. The purpose is to visit A Ryan & Sons Butchers, who allegedly make the best pies in the UK. I will get used to this claim no doubt. We park up and I immediately stumble into Catherine's Bakery, while the missus disappears off into a nearby market to look at trinkets and other expensive shit. Do they name all the pie shops after women around here?

Their pie selection is limited but they sell chicken tikka pasties and two varieties of "Oggies" which I later learn is a Welsh pasty with leeks in it, that miners used to chomp on after a hard morning down the pit. Neither the old girl or young girl behind the counter seem particularly fond of serving me until I fake a coughing fit.

They've got steak pies but the pork pies are beasts so I part with £1.90 and the weight of it nearly makes me fall over.

20.

PURVEYOR: Catherine's Bakery
PREMISES: Much Wenlock
PURCHASE: Pork pie £1.90
PLACE: 6 They were going to carry on sweeping that floor even if Elvis himself had just entered the building
PASTRY: 7 The base is a touch hard on the old gnashers but still a good hand raised effort. Murderous heartburn later
PRESENTATION: 7 Cold and crisp
PACKAGE: 8.5 Lots of coarse tough meat. Concerns about lack of jelly are quickly addressed upon seeing a big layer of it inside
PALATE: 8 Splendidly rich with salty jelly only complimenting the meaty flavour
PRICE: 8 Nearly two quid but as big as a bag of pies
PORTION: 9 It's a big lad
OVERALL: 53.5/70 They like their growlers big and cold in the Midlands and this was both; capable of satisfying the most hearty appetite.

So through the idyllic Much Wenlock we saunter; there's no snarling chavs here – a place so agreeable that even the traffic wardens are smiling. We nip to the bogs in the pay and display to change the baby's nappy and they're so clean you could sleep in there.

A Ryan & Sons is easy to locate from the lingering queue spilling out on to the High Street. I gaze disbelievingly through the window at the amazing range of plate lasagnes and cottage pies. There's meat from floor to ceiling within its low roof confines, with wall to wall pies of every description – including game and duck pork pies, venison, chicken and leek and the omnipresent steak and kidney.

As the snake of people start to slither indoors I see there's another ten people queuing inside and five butchers rushing around like ferrets fulfilling orders. They lock me in as soon as I get through the door, as they're closing for lunch and after much deliberation I procure a steak and onion pie and a beef and red wine.

21.

PURVEYOR: A Ryan & Sons
PREMISES: Shropshire
PURCHASE: Beef in red wine pie £1.90
PLACE: 8 They call me sir despite working their meat cleavers off and the bustle of this place is quite something

PASTRY: 8 What's not to like about a top crust covered in decorative pastry leaves?
PRESENTATION: 7.5 It's smell does not excel but it has considerable weight to it
PACKAGE: 9 Simply loaded with the most succulent cuts of beef
PALATE: 8 Bit of a shocker this, but you can actually taste the red wine – and it complements the beef perfectly
PRICE: 8 Forget the price and savour the quality
PORTION: 7.5 Deceptively deep
OVERALL: 56/70 Ryans = the meat eaters paradise. Seconded after I wolfed down the steak and onion a day or so later.

We nip next door to The Copper Kettle tearooms only after Emma vetoes the offer of a Pie & Pint for £6.95 in the George & Dragon (dogs welcome). We both devour a gorgeous Malthouse toasted ham, cheese and mustard sandwich and upon exiting we walk straight into a huge queue outside Ryans Butchers five minutes before it is due to open again at 2.

I have further explorations to be carried out in Shropshire and thus I corral the girls back into the car and head west to Ludlow, driving straight through the racecourse and golf club as we go. I'm also desperately disappointed to find out that Craven Arms is not in fact a massive pub.

Ludlow is another posh little town, steeped in history, with beautiful dwellings restored from medieval times including The Feathers Hotel, a modernised working hotel from the year 1619. Not to mention a castle and a church with bells ringing to the sound of "There's no place like home".

But this is pottering with a purpose and I soon demand we drive out to the Ludlow Food Centre to sample a local delicacy. The food hall smells divine from the second I walk in. I can almost hear the strains of 'Land of Hope and Glory' playing in the background such is their proud boast that 80% of the fayre on display is produced locally. Farm Shops are fucking ace and in no time at all I find myself leering at the lush cheeses and dribbling over the real ales.

I know what I want and I order two, ignoring the sizeable pork pies and sweet potato pasties to procure myself a brace of Shropshire Fidget Pies.

22.

PURVEYOR: Ludlow Food Centre
PREMISES: Ludlow
PURCHASE: Fidget Pie £2.25
PLACE: 7 A cheery old dear bolts towards me with considerable aplomb and pleasantry

PASTRY: 7 Mashed potato top crust, only slightly hardened in the oven but still possesses good portability despite not being fully encased
PRESENTATION: 7.5 Looks every inch like a savoury Mr Whippy
PACKAGE: 7 Despite being 50% mustard mash, it's remarkably satisfying
PALATE: 8 A refreshing and intriguing challenge to the tastebuds with mash and mustard amongst a ham and gammon cheesy base, although I can't taste apples
PRICE: 6.5 Bit pricey
PORTION: 7 The fluffed up potato bouffant musters it up to an acceptable size
OVERALL: 50/70 Although it's very much the lunchtime norm around these parts for hungry farmers, to me, it almost has the feel of a breakfast pie given the amount of pork and cheese to munch on during a long day ploughing the fields.

Note to Salopians reading this book in Waterstones: you may as well put it back now because that's your lot done.

Thursday 15th March 2012

Enough flouncing around rural Shropshire, it's time to head to Wythenshawe in South Manchester. I've been here before when I worked in Didsbury and it's no surprise to see that the roadworks which closed the road down that Allison's Bakery is situated on are still there 12 months' later, throwing my plans into chaos.

So I'm careering around the back streets of one of the biggest estates in Europe. Or possibly going around in circles. There do seem to be a lot of women putting their bins out in their dressing gown on a Thursday afternoon.

Allison's is situated on Hollyhedge Road in Benchill, home of the infamous Benchill Mad Dogs, whom David Cameron once tried to embrace in his short lived "hug a hoodie" phase.

It's deprived around here but I don't see a notorious, crime ridden estate. There's a lot of folk roaming about considering it's the middle of the day, but they don't look particularly shifty. A touch weather-beaten, no doubt let down by successive governments and the lack of opportunities flung their way.

I admit to flapping a bit as a gang of half a dozen youths all in black head towards me and keep my head down, resisting the urge to give them all a big manly hug. I walk past a bookies where a large Jamaican gentleman appears to be smoking something the government haven't quite got around to taxing yet. Before you know it the waft of marijuana is giving way to the even sweeter smell of baked pastry as I reach the end unit, looking a lot smarter than I recall.

Allisons is bright and bustling with that typical yellow hue. The pie choice is limited with only meat and potato and steak and kidney, which they're out of. There's some pasties and what I think is a veggie pie but turns out to be a mini quiche. I wouldn't have thought there'd be much call for quiches in Wythenshawe but I'm always learning new stuff like that.

23.

PURVEYOR: Allisons
PREMISES: Wythenshawe
PURCHASE: Meat and potato pie £1.25
PLACE: 7 "Who's next?" and she buggers off before serving me....arghh! Rough and ready
PASTRY: 7 Nice texture and smashing glaze to it but the crust lid falls away as I am chomping into it
PRESENTATION: 8 Foil tray hand scorcher and a fantastic aroma
PACKAGE: 8 Bursting out of the seams and filled top to bottom
PALATE: 8 Very gravy based, lovely and moist
PRICE: 7 Average
PORTION: Size 7 A wee bit on the small size
OVERALL: 52/70 A little cracker.

Saturday 17th March 2012

My worst nightmare upon completion of this book is when I tot up the final scores I find that all the Wigan pie shops occupy the Champions League berths. It may turn out that the best pies in the country are made in Wigan which would be great news but it would undoubtedly result in allegations of nepotism and throughout the process, I would be surreptitiously thinking that maybe I am inherently giving the "home team" better grades than they deserve because they are the pies I am most familiar with.

I could understandably have the accusation levelled at me that I can't walk past a pie shop by now but it's not true. The Rolling Pin Bakery in Wigan has eluded me for all of my 39 years. As I enter I can see that it's two shops in one. They have been opened out into a splendid little emporium containing the sort of fayre you usually find in a more general grocers such as soups and cereal and stuff along with jars of Kola Kubes and Uncle Joes Mint Balls. There's a deli counter serving up paninis and piri piri chicken while staff slice up meat for butties. The place is a hive of activity.

There's little confusion over why most people visit this establishment however, as the bloke at the front of the queue orders four meat and potato pies. His efforts are then gazumped by the next fella who orders 12 meat and potato pies. (TWELVE) in football videoprinter speak! I order merely one paltry pie.

24.

PURVEYOR: Rolling Pin Bakery
PREMISES: Wigan
PURCHASE: Meat and potato pie £1.25
PLACE: 7 An above average wait but then customers will go buying box loads of pies
PASTRY: 7.5 Distinct and delightfully soft yet still of a regimented shape
PRESENTATION: 7.5 I burn my gob on this mainly because it smells so lush I can't wait to get stuck into it. Eaten by hand without too much spillage
PACKAGE: 6 There's a half inch gap between the top of the filling and the crust. Unacceptable levels of airspace are a particular bugbear of pie eaters
PALATE: 7 Good mix with succulent chunks of potato boulders which come tumbling out
PRICE: 7.5 Bulk discounts might be an idea?
PORTION: 7 Average size but great definition to it
OVERALL: 49.5/70 A good if not exceptional pie. Indeed, a good way better than some of the rubbish I've had but I suppose I was harbouring a feeling they were going to be phenomenal. Not Champions League standard, perhaps just above mid-table with a chance of Europa League qualification.

Saturday 24th March 2012

St Helens. I've been here before. I used to work here. I like it, it's salt of the earth. Despite the rugby league rivalry, it's very similar to Wigan in many ways and yes they like their pies.

It was here where my derisory idea all started five years ago, I got the Yellow Pages out one lunchtime and set up a spreadsheet of pie shops. Today I'm going to go back to the very first one: Greenalls on Duke Street.

I also did this trip a few weeks ago, however a phone based "accident" (i.e. I fell over drunk and smashed it) meant that I lost my notes and photos. Along with basic human integrity as two teenage girls helped the drunken old man back to his feet and rang his wife up to collect him.

Another time I went to Greenalls, I found a piece of paper on the window telling customers they'd be shut for six weeks while the proprietor was having a hip replacement. Clearly this is a man who doesn't trust anyone else to make his pies for him.

It feels like the first day of summer today. The girls walk around with cropped tops while St Helens yoofs play football bare shirted in the park and there's an en masse scooter rally heading down the East Lancs Road to the seaside.

I've got a one year old guest reviewer in tow today. She's not currently a big pie eater but is a useful foil all the same and as we step into Greenalls she immediately makes a beeline for the kitchen. The lady escorts her out and says 'aw she's gorgeous'. The chief baker is probably in his sixties and has got a big white pork pie hat on. Colin Greenall is his name I believe, no relation to the former Blackpool, Brighton and Wigan centre half. He takes my order and his female accomplice goes back into the kitchen and returns with a meat and potato pie on a silver tray. It's like a big pastry Ferrero Rocher!

25.

PURVEYOR: Greenalls
PREMISES: St Helens
PURCHASE: Meat and potato pie £1.15
PLACE: 9 An exemplary personal touch displayed both for coping with my roaming little girl and bringing the goods out on a silver platter
PASTRY: 8 Soft lid but firm crust edge
PRESENTATION: 8 Hotter than the sun and smells fantastic
PACKAGE: 8 A generously proportioned, well filled pie
PALATE: 8.5 Heavenly fluffy potato intertwined with small chunks of mince
PRICE: 8.5 Great value for quite a large pie
PORTION: 8 Above average size
OVERALL: 58/70 An absolute delight of a establishment with a wide range of pies and pasties, not to mention some appetising looking jam tarts and scones and fresh bread on display. A great traditional bakers with brilliant pies.

On to Blackburns just half a mile away from Greenalls on a long terraced street of shops in the Newtown area of St Helens. I park outside a butchers and I'm having a nose in the window whilst parking trying to establish whether there's any pies on show as the butcher inside is keeping his watchful eye on me ensuring I don't reverse into his Jag.

The pie stall looks sparse but as I stand there fretting another tray of hot ones is gloriously delivered. They only do steak and meat and potato but there's also a huge plate meat pie out on display, the size of Jodrell Bank. I don't know how much it costs but I'm slavering like a Rottweiler here. They also have some sausages and cold meats in there which is possibly a bit naughty given there's a butchers a few doors down, albeit a Jag driving one. Tons of cream cakes, a deli counter too and a few pasties. The pies aren't the biggest but are priced accordingly at 95p a chuck. It comes in a foil tray and is raging hot.

26.

PURVEYOR: Blackburns
PREMISES: St Helens
PURCHASE: Meat and potato pie 95p
PLACE: 7 **PASTRY:** 7 **PRESENTATION:** 7 **PACKAGE:** 8
PALATE: 8 **PRICE:** 8 **PORTION:** 6
OVERALL: 51/70 The top crust is thin, almost translucent, and has a pork pie type feel to it. There's lots of stringy stewing steak giving it a rich, succulent meaty taste. A great price although it is unfortunately a touch on the small side.

On my way back I pass through Rainford where I know there is another bakers of repute called Samuel Lievesley who serves pies with peas and gravy from a large vat, making a delightful combination. It was always a bit sparsely populated though both in terms of customers and products so it's no surprise as I drive through Rainford eighteen months after I finished working here to find Lievesley is now a financial services firm. Hat trick spurned.

Wednesday 28th March 2012

The coalition government have delivered a bombshell which has caused anger in the (burning) heart of every pie eater across the land. The UK is already awash with the threat of a petrol crisis: now there is a pasty crisis with talk of adding VAT to hot takeaway food. BBC News is broadcasting live on the crisis from a Galloways in Wigan, which is flanked by schoolkids shovelling pies down with their hands. If you think the Miner's Strike was violent Mr Cameron, you ain't seen nothing yet!

Thursday 29th March 2012

Bradley's bakery in Ashton Under Lyne claim to make the UK's best pork pie. The only problem with that is so do about 700 other places. They do have a headstart, given they have nabbed the website URL www.bestporkpie.co.uk however.

I always find East Manchester and Tameside a bit grim and dark and dismal. I've maybe seen a few too many episodes of the League of Gentlemen. However, today the sun is beaming and it's a positively radiant day. Ashton is a big place, it's perhaps off people's radars as their football teams are dwindling around in the non leagues and it just gets subsumed by Manchester but the Ikea in Ashton is bigger than most market towns. The roadworks are appalling and there's also gridlock at petrol stations due to another shortage scare. You'd have to question the wisdom of someone driving 30 miles down the motorway when there's a petrol shortage just to eat a pie.

I turn into Kings Road. A large tattooed geezer with a string vest on is sat outside his off licence swigging a can and onto a long, sprawling road with row after row of terraced houses which leads to the suburb of Hursts Cross. Hey the sun is out so we'll let him off. Eventually I reach Bradley's Bakery which is bookended by terraced houses and only distinguished by the long queue coming out of the door and the surrounding double parked vans.

Below the bold, brown fascia is a large painted sign "Home of the UK's best pork pie". I'm expecting good things here. The huge board with the price list on behind the counter is telling me that this is Pie Heaven with a multitude of flavours and sizes on offer. There's paninis, cakes, jars of chilli jam and there's barms, baps, rolls, muffins or whatever they call them around here galore but other than that the pie range has me taken aback. The one that catches my eye as unusual is the steak and cowheel pie. I'm intrigued as to what a cow's heel tastes like. Much the same as an ox's tail I'd wager, although I've only knowingly had that in soup form. It may be a delicacy or in reality, these animal parts may feature regularly in any form of processed meat.

The range doesn't stop at chopped up cow's feet. They've got pork and black pudding, pork and stilton, cheese and onion pies and a pie of the month which is a special recipe steak and Guinness pie. The queue moves quite quickly considering the number of people in, all blokes wearing industrial clothing which is always a promising sign. The meat and potato I order comes straight out of the oven but so does the Pork pie. There's no tray as both feel hot and a little soft in my hands in a Bradley's branded bag.

27.

PURVEYOR: Bradleys Bakery
PREMISES: Ashton-Under-Lyne
PURCHASE: Pork Pie £1.15
PLACE: 7 Brisk and cheerful
PASTRY: 8 Lovely, light crust with great shape to it

PRESENTATION: 8 The perfect temperature for a growler
PACKAGE: 8 Generously crammed in juicy, succulent cured sausage meat
PALATE: 9 It blows me away, it's as if I've never had a pork pie in my life before until this point. A totally authentic and full blooded taste
PRICE: 7.5 Not a wallet emptier by any means
PORTION: 8 Decent size for a pork pie
OVERALL: 55.5/70 This is a must visit emporium of pastry products for every discerning pie eater. If you take it as seriously as they do, you'll be in for a treat.

28.

PURVEYOR: Bradleys Bakery
PREMISES: Ashton-Under-Lyne
PURCHASE: Meat and Potato Pie £1.15
PLACE: 7 **PASTRY:** 8 **PRESENTATION:** 8 **PACKAGE:** 8
PALATE: 8 **PRICE:** 8 **PORTION:** 8
OVERALL: 55/70 Another cracker from East Manchester's finest. A splendidly thick velvety crust, rich and thoroughly meaty and served fresh out of the oven. You need this pie shop in your life.

Friday 30th March 2012

Foodcraft might sound like a bit of a generic name but this is no ordinary shop. You see, it's a chippy that makes pies and batters fish. I've seen glowing reviews on at least three different websites. Folk waxing lyrically at the mouth watering prospect of these pies described as "First Class" by my new fave site, the Cheshire Pie Society.

I've never been to Winsford before but I've been led to believe from some work colleagues that it's a rough Scouse overspill town. This is only likely to improve the quality of pies if my working class equation holds true. I find it difficult to believe anywhere in Cheshire is dead rough though. The pies are coming thick and fast now and if you're getting concerned about my weight, I ran ten miles this morning with some workmates who are doing a marathon so I've certainly made room for a pie. I am however walking like John Wayne right now.

You've heard of the film 28 Days Later, we'll I'm now up to 28 pies later since I first sunk my teeth into a Hampsons in a leafy country lane in

Knutsford, although I've munched my way through ten or so more which I haven't formally reviewed. It's that time of the month: like a salesman I've got targets to hit, keen to hit thirty by the end of the month, hence I'm upping my run rate with today's trip. I pass the huge Roberts Bakery in Northwich and my mind drifts off as I start to wonder whether there's a factory shop. They're certainly knocking out the bread as loaf after golden brown loaf flies past on the production line. Shame I've not got my window down to take in the smell of freshly baking bread.

Twinned with Deuil Le Barre, Winsford has an unusual dual carriageway High Street. I pull up and am greeted with a ginger specky lad in a trackie, who is glaring at me in a familiar hands down his trackie pose but hey – it's Friday so I'm almost as dressed down as he is!

So Foodcraft, what to make of it: it's a pie shop and a chip shop. Another bashful proprietor with no qualms about stating they are the "Baker of the best home made pies" The trumpet blowing continues as soon as you step inside when greeted with a sign which states "When we say steak pie, we mean steak pie. Our pies are made to a very high standard." Smells to me like someone has had the odd complaint about charging nearly two quid for a pie! Yet from what I have already cast my eye over they do look to be heifer sized. The meat and potato pie is £1.80 and the steak and chicken and mushroom varieties are over the two quid mark. The meat and potato is £1.49 cold or £1.80 hot. A new phenomenon to me a few weeks ago, now I can't get away from it.

Another sign proclaims the minimum meat content to be 25% for steak, 12.5% for the other meat ones. Another states "we bake our pies fresh every day", there's clearly a lot of pride on display here but the proof of the pudding is in the….well you know the rest. I was expecting a bigger shop, at least a double fronted one to reflect the two separate businesses but it's just like a chippy but with most of the inside given away to an open plan kitchen with hygiene signs up everywhere.

It's a tad confusing purchasing a pie whilst the lovely overpowering aroma of fish and chips fills the air. No fish, no chips, no gravy: just a pie. Respect the pie. Upon closer inspection both customers and staff only appear to have a slight Scouse twang and are gloriously cheerful. Although the bloke who comes in behind me is actually Rafa Benitez! Or a very professional lookalike masquerading as a driving instructor.

29.

PURVEYOR: Foodcraft
PREMISES: Winsford
PURCHASE: Meat and potato pie £1.80
PLACE: 8 Friendly efficient and a clean open kitchen

PASTRY: 8 Superb crust, however I struggle to hold the casing together when I pick it up

PRESENTATION: 8 Hot, although smells a little bit of....yeah you guessed it – fish!

PACKAGE: 8.5 Impressive dark coloured gravy filling with delicious chunks of potato and what looks considerably higher than 12.5% meat content

PALATE: 9 Richer than Roman Abramovich. A proper meaty treat!

PRICE: 7 A touch pricey but with an opulent quality to it

PORTION: 9 Very, very heavy and you know what that means

OVERALL: 57.5/70 The pride in their output is certainly not without substance! This is a great pie for a chip shop. Wonder what their chips are like?

Starting to miss fish and chips. And pasties.

Saturday 31st March 2012

Fourth pie in three days. There's a pie shop on the main A49 drag into Wigan called Grimshaws, which I'd never heard of before, so I went out last month to investigate before the "Phonegate" incident. I recall the pie disintegrated in my hands with filling slopping all over my fingers, a heinous crime indeed so you could say they've had a get out of jail card.

It's a small shop with a bright green front and has two counters with tons of scrumptious home made cakes in the window. Two totally unconnected fat lads separately barge in front of me as I walk through the door and the first one orders four pies. Bastard! Incredulously, the second large chap simply asks "Have you got any French baguettes?" Ooh la la my rotund friend, I wouldn't have predicted that! They haven't as it happens but the old girl serving pulls out the biggest, shiniest loaf you are likely to ever see. She needs a fork lift truck to lift it!

I get a meat and potato but there is a good selection of alternatives including chicken and mushroom, cheese and bacon (what?) peppered steak and the normal steak and pork varieties. They've also got some large plate hot pots and a range of pasties including an exotic chicken tikka flavour. The staff, resplendent in green overalls, are a tad slow but thorough and pleasant enough. The pies are mad hot and smell deliciously buttery so let's get stuck in.

30.

PURVEYOR: Grimshaws
PREMISES: Wigan

PURCHASE: Meat and Potato pie £1.30
PLACE: 7 PASTRY: 6 PRESENTATION: 8 PACKAGE: 7
PALATE: 8 PRICE: 7 PORTION: 7
OVERALL: 50/70 Everything about this pie is wonderful except for its
propensity to fall to bits. Get a plate or suffer a messy fate young pie Jedi.

Tuesday 3rd April 2012

I wasn't looking for pies but today they came to me. I work at a large IT
Centre in the Cheshire countryside and once a month there happens to
be a Farmers Market featuring a feast of culinary delights. There's meats
and curries and sweets along with things you don't eat: trinkets and books
and plants and scarves (Pashminas!!) and with it being Easter I should
really look to buy something nice for my wife and daughter. Thankfully
they are fully aware what a selfish tit I am and know full well that I am
likely to make straight for the pie stall. I've seen these pies before and
they look a touch on the exotic side, not to mention exotically priced at
three quid.

I'm showing myself up as a dullard here by opting for the meat 'n' tater
when there's offerings such as chorizo and red pepper in pie form but I'm
consistent if nothing else. There's steak and ale, chilli beef, chicken and
ham, there's about 10-15 types in all including my old chum from Shropshire the Fidget Pie.

I have questions to ask which can't be googled so I am forced to fire
questions at the aging couple sat behind their stall:

"Who are you? Where do you make these pies? Where's your shop?"

"Wales" – yeah great help.

"Whereabouts in Wales".

"A farm shop".

"And what's this farm shop called?"

They give me a look which says "We sell pies love, we don't expect an
interrogation".

31.

PURVEYOR: Harvies
PREMISES: Mold
PURCHASE: Meat and potato pie £3.00
PLACE: 7.5 PASTRY: 6 PRESENTATION: 7 PACKAGE: 8
PALATE: 8 PRICE: 6.5 PORTION: 7
OVERALL: 50/70 It might be my standard pie but this is very different.
An appetising prospect packed with tomatoes and shallots and a cheesy
mash top which perhaps makes it feel more like a cottage pie.

Consequently it gave way a little in the oven due to not being fully encased but the extra ingredients make it a worthy if alternative pie.

Saturday 7th April 2012

Not sure about the wisdom of buying food from a place called Mold if I'm completely honest. Despite another technological mishap which sees me delete twenty minutes of razor sharp narrative that would have Bryson, Whicker and Palin cowering I managed to salvage the remnants of my pie run to Wales.

My post Tuesday pie research led me to a good tip off on a fly fishing forum of all places, said establishment being Hulsons butchers of Mold. It's just over an hour away from me and I can take the girls to the North Wales coast for the afternoon. They'll throw stones in the sea while I throw pastry down my gullet. Fair deal.

Anyway, Mold: smart, bustling town with an undercover market and if the striking black and gold frontage of Hulsons doesn't get you, the queue out of the door at 11am on a Saturday morning is a sure-fire indicator. They're queuing all the way around the counter and back again. This is a butcher where the pies and pasties are in the front window and the meat is around the side.

There's racks of jams and sauces on the back wall and a shelf full of (Scottish) crisps and Mackie's (Scottish) ice cream. The queue moves fast as I clock my first Welsh dragons of the day, generating smoke from their heels as they scuttle around. Hey, who isn't a sucker for Welsh girls serving up pies?

I get a hot pork pie for £1.05 and a meat and potato pattie for 89p. I'm not quite sure what a pattie is. I reckon it's a cross between a pie and a pastie, the wife thinks it's some kind of savoury cake. In reality given the way the crust comes apart it seems to resemble some kind of "pieburger".

32.

PURVEYOR: Hulsons
PREMISES: Mold
PURCHASE: Pork Pie £1.05
PLACE: 8 **PASTRY:** 7 **PRESENTATION:** 7 **PACKAGE:** 7
PALATE: 7 **PRICE:** 7 **PORTION:** 7
OVERALL: 50/70 A proper little hive of activity with lovely staff serving up a cute little growler at room temperature. The crust is crunchy and golden brown with a thin layer of jelly lining the inner casing. The meat is cured and not overly seasoned letting it's natural porky goodness shine through with every mouthful.

We drive out up into the hills and are confronted by a sign telling us that we are entering an area of natural beauty with an unpronounceable name. On first inspection, it just seems to be a series of closed pubs, their names alternating from Welsh to English. Yet as we climb further the landscape opens out into the most stunning, green, lush Welsh mountains towering over Ruthin, nestled deep within the valley below. All the while 'Baa Baa Black Sheep' is blaring out of the car stereo to keep a one year old amused. How very Welsh!

We get plenty of time to admire the view as one or two of the drivers in front are a touch *araf*. We drive through a corridor of trees like the closing credits to Sesame Street glaring enviously at rooftop villas offering panoramic vistas before making the long descent into Ruthin. We park up on a hill and look back at the breathtaking backdrop of snow capped peaks.

In addition to all this jaw dropping scenery, there is an establishment in Ruthin which produces a jaw dropping pie. Leonardo's is a Deli and a producer of award winning pies, (not to be confused with the ninja turtle of the same name). Turn that cynicism detector off – there's a big sign outside proclaiming that they are winner of the 2010 Pie of the year: a chicken, leek and laverbread* variety no less. I haven't got the foggiest idea what laverbread is but let's not worry my little head about that right now. I scrutinise the product list, including the by now omnipotent Oggies but in the end I plump for their award winner. A little pricey at £2.95 but looking every inch a gourmet pie.

One subsequent Google later confirms this is seaweed.

33.

PURVEYOR: Leonardo's Deli
PREMISES: Ruthin
PURCHASE: Chicken, leek and laverbread pie £2.95
PLACE: 7 In no rush whatsoever to serve me but the place has that quirky feel about it. A proper little shrine to good food
PASTRY: 8 Well glazed and decorative crust
PRESENTATION: 7 Fresh, even after a re-heat
PACKAGE: 8 Big strips of seasoned chicken with soft carrots sat on a bed of leeks. A surprisingly moist and juicy pie considering the absence of gravy which is replaced with some dark green stuff recently washed up from the beach
PALATE: 8 Rich and appetising pie of gourmet standards
PRICE: 7 Priced according to the diversity of its content although it must have at least half a chicken breast in there
PORTION: 8 Well filled with high quality ingredients

OVERALL: 53/70 To borrow a Welsh phrase, it was lush. Or as we call it in England, lunch.

Not that I'm done here as I also manage to sniff out a second pie shop of repute, which goes by the name of the Village Bakery, a small Wrexham based chain. Just around the corner from the contemporary Leo's, it's distinguished by large Hovis-style lettering built into the front along with the more modernised Village Bakery logo above the doorway. A traditional looking building in keeping with the nostalgic feel which even the Barclays Bank seems to adhere to in a touristy town like this.

Inside it's a spacious affair with a decent selection, sandwich counter and carvery plus a small café area for diners.

I'm taken aback by the huge Welsh Oggie gently cooling in the display unit, taunting me mercilessly. It's at least twice the size of anything else in there but I know if I take that out of the shop with me, I'll not be eating for a week. It's the size of my head!

34.

PURVEYOR: Village Bakery
PREMISES: Wrexham
PURCHASE: Meat and potato pie £1.35
PLACE: 7 **PASTRY:** 7 **PRESENTATION:** 7 **PACKAGE:** 7
PALATE: 7 **PRICE:** 7 **PORTION:** 7
OVERALL: 49/70 A remarkably run of the mill affair I'm afraid.

We potter around admiring the delightful charms of Ruthin. Its biggest let down the hair dryers in the public bogs which sound so much like an air siren they make me hit the deck. Next stop on this pie rally is the grand Victorian resort of Llandudno. Traffic is heavy as the sun bursts through the clouds and cable cars emerge from the skyline and it seems everyone else has the same idea too as we drive through Llandudno for a good half an hour before finding a parking spot right outside Marks & Spencers. I fancy them cable cars but the missus won't let me on one let alone our daughter. Clearly, she's the brains of this operation.

Llandudno reminds me of Southport with its elegant, canopied shops only disturbed by the sound of some idiot playing a bagpipe. Are you sure we're not in Scotland? Are you selling crisps as well by any chance? I've driven past the place I'm looking for once – the Hambone delicatessen – but it's not there. Seriously. Well it's about time I was thrown a rubber bone! I'm tracking the door numbers on both sides of the road on Madoc Street where it is meant to be and all I see is a Chinese chippy. Bah! An hour stuck in traffic for nothing more than a spring roll. Well not even that because it's shut! Sooner or later I was going to turn up somewhere and they'd be closed, shut down, moved on or turned into a Chinese takeaway in this case. Get over it and move on.

Primitive natural instinct kicks in and I follow my nose and fire up my phone. Even if they've gone bust, there must be somewhere else around here. It would be a shame to waste a good journey just to spend quality time on the beach with my daughter watching her chase gulls and eat pebbles (when you do get old enough to read, that's a joke Jess!) I'm Googling like mad dodging eager shoppers and it does appear to still exist. While I'm deep in thought looking at my phone, it appears like a golden oasis right in front of me.

I first see a posh dining bit and then realise it's split into half and I'm transfixed on a fascinating range of pies under the counter. After walking in, I am ignored for at least ten minutes, despite there only being a few customers in the shop. They don't seem that pushed and when they do come to me, there's no 'sorry about your wait'. At the risk of sounding deadly serious, those four words are just common courtesy and easily resolve all frustrations.

35.

PURVEYOR: Ham Bone Delicatessen
PREMISES: Llandudno
PURCHASE: Meat and potato pie £1.80
PLACE: 5 Slower than a funeral cortege
PASTRY: 8 Flaky with an egg beaten glaze, here comes the heartburn but very rich
PRESENTATION: 8 All the pies have ornate leaves and pastry marks on top which is a nice touch
PACKAGE: 8 Packed to the rafters with prime meat and potato
PALATE: 8 Has a strong, rich savoury taste to it
PRICE: 6.5 A little pricey but on the large side to compensate
PORTION: 8 Man sized pie
OVERALL: 51.5/70 If I had been greeted with even an insincere smile and some kind of appreciation for walking into their shop, it could have been up there but hey…great pie, lethargic staff.

After a brisk stroll along the prom, prom, prom (where my toddler also decides to eat seaweed) we head to Conwy; a historic town dominated by its castle and medieval walls, Chester by the sea.

One thing you can always say about Welsh people is that they do like a good oggy. I said OGGY!! Nevertheless in Edwards there are a veritable orgy of oggies gratuitously out on display. I've had a long day out in Wales and I finally succumb into having a one man oggy.

There doesn't seem to be a definitive style, essentially it seems Oggie/Oggy is just the Welsh word for pastie, be it semi circular, square or Cornish style. The one in the Village Bakery earlier was a monster, the size of Jodrell Bank albeit it at three quid a go, others are squared off, the sort of thing you'd call a bake or a slice in other parts of the (English) country.

Edwards, the classy butchers on Conwy's main street do it Cornish pasty style so I opt for a Welsh Lamb Oggie.

"You do know it's got lamb in it" says the girl behind the counter

"Yes that's why I asked for a Welsh LAMB Oggie!" As if I would....

36.

PURVEYOR: Edwards
PREMISES: Conwy
PURCHASE: Welsh Lamb Oggy £1.55
PLACE: 8 For humouring the English idiot standing before her
PASTRY: 8 Thick and shiny outer shell but also soft and crispy at the same time
PRESENTATION: 7 Perfectly defined goodies and a smashing little shop
PACKAGE: 8 Carrots, peas, leeks and fluffy potato with minced lamb mixed in
PALATE: 8 Nice and spicy and plenty of variety
PRICE: 8 A big 'un with a good filling
PORTION: 8 A hefty size – when I cut it in half it looks like two pasties
OVERALL: 55/70 Controversy here as a pasty scores highly. What can I say m'lud, it was a belter!

I had my eye on a visit to the Ponty Conwy Bakery but there's nowt left. The Tan Lan Bakery does have a few baked comestibles residual to its shelves. I'd originally snubbed this one as I thought it was a patisserie. Patisserie! Indeed!

37.

PURVEYOR: Tan Lan Bakery
PREMISES: Conwy
PURCHASE: Meat and potato pie £1.80
PLACE: 7 PASTRY: 7 PRESENTATION: 7
PACKAGE: 7 PALATE: 7 PRICE: 6
PORTION: 7
OVERALL: 48/70 It's main redeeming feature is an accidental smiley acid house face on the top crust. Either that or I'm hallucinating after eating too many pies

today. It has a perfect spherical shape to it but is a bit Pooles-like to stand out as anything special.

Beaches, castles, mountains and pies all in one day. Today at least, I appear to have balanced a wealth of pie procurement with a bit of family time.

Wednesday 12th April 2012

I'm not saying that Wienholts Bakery in the footballer's abode of Alderley Edge is posh but I heard off a mate that they call a sausage roll a HAM ROLL, so I am expecting the pricing policy to be slightly out of kilter with the Pound Bakery. Let's hope they take credit cards.

George Wienholts are something of a local treasure and it's also possibly safe to assume that this is where the WAG's get their steak bakes and sausage rolls from.

Down the country roads linking Knutsford to Alderley Edge, it feels like every house is a mansion with long, gated driveways flanked by lush, green fields. You can smell the affluence be it sportspeople or stockbrokers but the little town itself caters to its market with a main street chock full of swinging boutiques, jewellers, pavement cafes and those specialist shops that just sell daft shit that only rich people can afford. There are some normal people with normal sized houses as well but they are a touch in the minority and probably aren't too welcome at Panacea – the elite nightclub next to Alderley railway station frequented by Rio and the Rooneys amongst others.

The main drag is gridlocked with nowhere to park. I drive the full length and double down a warren of side streets and eventually find a tight spot to reverse my car into. For all the picture I've painted, I end up outside a boarded up house on my right and a dodgy looking block of flats opposite, with a few youths loitering around looking for something to steal. Oh well, the cars I've squeezed in between are worth ten times mine.

I walk into a chemist for some paracetamol as I've not been feeling too chipper and even the counter assistant is unbelievably glamorous. She must be pushing 50 and has got a broad Nottingham accent and I am left to speculate which 1980's footballer she was married to. Sent out to do a few hours to fund the kids college fees now the wages have dried up.

Back on to the main road and what to make of Wienholts. Or more pertinently what do they make out of me? A mug, that's what! They let me stand there for ten minutes fuming like an industrial chimney while they serve random people. I can't quite work out what's going on but it's definitely a case of "if your face fits" amongst the aristocracy of haughty Cheshire. Until I suss out that you have to take a token from the dispenser behind me to get served in turn. Well how was I to know that! What a dickhead!

I could have had half a dozen pies from here they all look so appealing. They've got little pork pies, big pork pies and enormous ones the size of a dustbin lid for around a fiver; chicken, stilton and leek; turkey and mushroom, a tad small but good variety. The infamous ham roll is on display but they also have party sausage rolls behind the counter so let's give them the benefit of the doubt and assume it's something slightly different. Curiously, the pasties are shaped exactly like the sausage rolls. The "what shape should a pasty be?" debate. Well these look like rolls, cylindrical and open at both ends, a new one on me and I'm eager to try. They also do some proper enticing looking steak pies – so one of each I reckon.

Not that it's all about the pies. There are little cheese savouries and luxurious looking potato cakes on offer and the most marvellous looking gateaux at £15 a pop. I'm not sure what a crystallised fruit gateau is but I know I can't take my eyes off it while I'm aimlessly waiting to not get served.

The usual protocol upon entering a shop is to establish which way the queue is going, if there is one I usually seek the back of it being a polite and patient upstanding chap. There's only three people in there when I walk in but before you know it another ten have walked in and been served while I'm still stood there. It must be great for the locals when a docile outsider is left stood there like a plum, unaware that he has to take a token with a number on it off a hook on the wall and wait for the call.

I eventually cotton on and order a steak pie for £2.35 and a meat and potato pasty (roll) for £1.50. They look and smell so good I'm tempted to review them both. Whether you are a sweet or savoury fan, this is truly a dream of a bakers with so many luscious items it's easy to forget to pick up your token when you walk in. Ahem.

38.

PURVEYOR: Wienholts
PREMISES: Alderley Edge
PURCHASE: Steak pie £2.35
PLACE: 7 Hey I can't penalise them for the fact I am a rampaging simpleton
PASTRY: 8 Delightfully soft, flaky pastry
PRESENTATION: 8 Bit weird this. They take it off the shelf naked and only then put it in a foil tray before serving it to you
PACKAGE: 8.5 A gravy tsunami but bountiful chunks of steak in there too which come tumbling out like little bouncing bombs. All that's missing is the Dambusters theme tune

PALATE: 9.5 If Barry Davies was to have this pie he'd opine that you have to say that's magnificent. An astonishing taste sensation. The most sumptuous gravy you will ever encounter and lashings of it. It's heavily seasoned with a raging peppery kick to it which positively explodes in my mouth

PRICE: 7 When your product is this good you can get away with extortion

PORTION: 7 Circular and tapered off but a reasonable diameter

OVERALL: 55/70 Wayne Rooney's local pie shop produces a pocket rocket of the highest order. The unusually shaped pasty served as a useful accomplice, priced at £1.50. It's drier than the steak pie with no gravy to speak of but jam packed full of meat and potato, mashed together with little flecks of carrot and an almost curried element to the seasoning. Wienholts, it's been a pleasure, despite your flummoxing queuing arrangements.

Saturday 14th April 2012

I'm not doing very well with my long haul ambitions, I concede this much. I was actually in London yesterday and was hoping to get to a pie and mash shop but all I could manage was a cold Cornish pasty from the Sainsburys at Euston which tasted like a dried out Moccasin filled with dogshit.

Jess has been up half the night screaming, as toddlers do so I'm forced to rein in my plans, keep it local and head to the fine city of Preston. Stop sniggering.

Seriously, my parochial view is that Wigan is the pie capital of the world and everything expands outwards from it so by default Preston must have some pretty decent pie makers. I actually once went for a job at Preston pie makers Ashworths years ago and didn't get it. How my career path and indeed empathy towards pies could have changed had I spent all these years surrounded by them, watching them get made, counting them and determining how much margin they make. Sadly, Ashworths are no more. As is the man at Deepdale who used to wheel the trolley around the perimeter of the plastic pitch serving fans through the metal fencing.

I get a couple of decent recommendations however and the consensus of Prestonians is that an establishment called Ted Round & Sons is their go-to pastry vendor. I find it on one of the main thoroughfare's into Preston and park carefully down a side street despite the surfeit of cars dumped on double yellows outside.

It's deceptively busy in that there's no queue outside the door but once inside the queue snakes around all four sides of the shop. It's traditional and bustling and everyone seems to know each other; chatting away in that lovely soft Preston accent.

THEY WRAP THE PIES IN NEWSPAPER!! This is a revelation, why hasn't anyone else thought of it? Like they used to do down the chippy. In addition, they have bread and cakes showcased in those traditional blue written "Fresh Cream" wrappers and lots of groceries but only the kind you'd have with your pie: salt, pepper, red and brown sauce, gravy and mushy peas.

They call the meat and potato "potato and meat" and also do butter pies – a speciality in this part of Lancashire along with some tiddler meat and pork pies for a measly sixty pence. It's a little cracker!

39.

PURVEYOR: Rounds
PREMISES: Preston
PURCHASE: Potato and meat pie £1.20
PLACE: 7 Busy but fast moving
PASTRY: 8.5 A messy looking crust yet it is deliciously soft and tender and evidently has been nowhere near a machine
PRESENTATION: 8 I can smell them before I get around the corner
PACKAGE: 8 As advertised, predominantly potato with a small layer of mince on top. The sort of pie where you suck the filling out rather than bite into it. Lovely
PALATE: 9 Although more like a butter pie than a meat and potato, it is nevertheless sumptuous
PRICE: 8 Cheap and comes with free newspaper (yesterday's)
PORTION: 7.5 Compact with airspace only on the outside
OVERALL: 56/70 An impressive effort from Preston's premier pie candidate.

Of course I'm not done yet and I meander through the back streets of Preston over-populated by a disproportionate amount of young men swigging cans until I establish that North End are at home.

If you're looking for positive indicators, there's a big sign on the door of Gornalls which says "6 unbaked pies for £5". It's on the edge of town in a working class area and it's a hive of pastry related offers; with daily deals involving butter pies, peas and gravy, corned beef hash, home made soups and sandwiches and teacakes (substitute whichever word you use to describe a circular piece of bread cut in half). Pork, meat and steak pies are on offer along with cheese and onion and meat and potato pasties – which look huge causing my pasty cravings to return. The now ubiquitous "STOP THE PASTY TAX" posters are up everywhere again and rightly bloody so: bakeries are fighting this tooth and nail! "You should charge people the VAT if they refuse to sign it" I tell them – you can have that nugget of advice for free.

This one is just called a potato pie so it may not have meat in it at all but it is competitively priced at £1.10 and comes straight out of the oven. Again, it's wrapped up like a bag of chips but in plain paper this time.

40.

PURVEYOR: Gornalls
PREMISES: Preston
PURCHASE: Potato pie £1.10
PLACE: 7.5 Large queue dealt with proficiently
PASTRY: 7.5 Light colour and paper thin middle with thick outer crust
PRESENTATION: 8 A wave of steam hits me as I bite into this beauty giving off a marvellous aroma
PACKAGE: 8 Limited meat content yet more than ample overall
PALATE: 8.5 Salty and potato heavy but lovely sweet smell
PRICE: 8.5 Smart price for a smart pie
PORTION: 8 Thick, deep and well formed
OVERALL: 56/70 The two Preston pies end up neck and neck. This feels fair as I'd say Rounds pies have the more thorough taste but Gornalls offer slightly better value.

Saturday 21st April 2012

I continue my North West tour by planning to hit Blackburn. However, just as their famous football team appears to be in crisis the town also appears to be suffering a chronic shortage of pie shops. I have nevertheless found a shedload in the nearby town of Haslingden, including one of some repute going by the delightful name of Cissy Greens.

Close by is the factory of Hollands Pies, one of the biggest hitters in pieland, sold at football games, in freezer aisles and nearly every chip shop in the North of England. The one thing you can't do however is turn up at their factory and buy one. Another lesson learned.

No factory shop or even a serving hatch despatching hot pies from a side window. Surely a missed trick? Anyway, my mood is lightened after passing under a motorway bridge with GOURANGA written on it. The next motorway bridge on the M65 has a more conventional "I MISS YOU XXXXXXXX" with the name painted over. That time honoured symbol of unrequited love painted in six feet high emulsion. I come off the motorway and hit the West Pennine Moors, with glorious sunshine glimmering off a reservoir nestled in ochre coloured rolling hills with large wind turbines perched atop them. No matter whereabouts in the country you live, you're always within an hour of somewhere that can really take your breath away. We don't half take our own country for granted sometimes.

I park up between a Greggs (no thanks) and another bakers called Mannings. First stop is Cissy Greens however and my first view is of a kaleidoscope of lovely cakes in the window and then the sign: Meat and potato pies and mushy peas for £1.80. There's no menu to peruse so I have to ask the time honoured question. Potato pie; meat and onion, meat and mushroom, cheese and onion, Cornish pastie, steak pie. There's one huge one but I don't have the foresight to simply say "I'll have that massive one please".

Do I want anything with it? she asks. Well I usually have another pie with it. Mushy peas perhaps? Not only mushy peas but they have salt and vinegar on the counter, plus a condiment which goes by the name of Lancashire sauce. Cricket commentator David 'Bumble' Lloyd, a native of these parts is a firm champion of this as an accompaniment to his cottage pie* It's like Worcester Sauce but with a few more curried spices. I bought some once, it was ace but the missus moaned that it stunk the house out.

*Not a real pie, unacceptable under any circumstances.

41.

PURVEYOR: Cissy Greens
PREMISES: Haslingden
PURCHASE: Meat and Potato pie £1.30
PLACE: 8 Top banter with the old girl behind the counter as I only had a twenty. Warm and polite
PASTRY: 7 A crispy outer but soft overall
PRESENTATION: 8 Complimentary condiments, as ever a vote winner
PACKAGE: 6 I was perhaps expecting a bit more given its reputation and what I got was considerable airspace
PALATE: 8 A splendid traditional effort and despite being advertised as a potato pie quite a high ratio of meat within
PRICE: 7 Team up with mushy peas for under two quid
PORTION: 7 Big on diameter not depth
OVERALL: 51/70 Did I eat the right pie here? I'm thinking perhaps not.

I move on to the green fronted Mannings, also on Deardengate. I'm like a pig in muck here. I can't help think how fortunate the residents of Haslingden are to have such a triumvirate of top class bakers within a few hundred yards. Oh and a Greggs.

Mannings are big on bread, it's everywhere but in addition to this they also have a raft of pies hot and ready to go.

42.

PURVEYOR: Mannings
PREMISES: Haslingden
PURCHASE: Meat and potato pie £1.25
PLACE: 7.5 You know when you stand there like a dick waiting for your change when you've actually given them the right money? Yeah, that
PASTRY: 8 Soft, uneven with an undeniably home made feel to it
PRESENTATION: 8 The scorching hot tray burns a pie shaped hole in the palm of my hand
PACKAGE: 7 Every last millimetre occupied
PALATE: 7 A predominantly fluffy potato based feel to it
PRICE: 7.5 Do I detect a bit of competition with the neighbours?
PORTION: 7 Of shallow depth but considerable plate pie style dimensions
OVERALL: 52/70 A pie fit for a portly racist comedian of the same name. Except he's dead.

Just time to find the third one on my list. I survey the scene by a large pub at the junction flanked by what appears to be thirty women in pink in full on hen party mode, making a ridiculous racket for a Saturday morning. There's MEN on it too, what's all that about?

I give up looking for Billingtons the second I espy the vision of "DT Law – Butchers and Delicatessens" across the road and if that isn't several trays of pies I can see in the window? The selection looks promising so time for an impromptu change of plan. I step inside and I am greeted by the kind of selection of quality meats that renders a carnivore speechless: sausages, lamb chops, steaks, kebabs. They're doing hot peppered steak baguettes for £2.25 with the meat sizzling away on a griddle right in front of my eyes or sweet chilli chicken if you prefer and they're doing a roaring trade in that long forgotten delicacy: tripe.

Despite there being only three people in the shop I am the poor relation here. Left standing and unattended to for at least ten minutes, while some posh cow barks orders at her poor, beleaguered hubby, loud enough to be heard on the other side of the Pennines "ooh we must get some chorizo and do we need more chicken skewers?"

A quick "be with you in a minute" wouldn't have hurt? Especially seeing as the half a dozen staff seemed to spend ample time yapping to the other high net worth customers in the shop.

Eventually a lady comes through from out the back and says "Who's next?" A bit unnecessary really. THERE'S ONLY ME LEFT. I eventually get a courteous "be careful, it's hot, it's just come out of the oven".

43.

PURVEYOR: DT Law
PREMISES: Haslingden
PURCHASE: Meat and potato pie £1.20
PLACE: 5 I grew a beard whilst waiting to be served
PASTRY: 8 Solid crust with a dried pool of gravy nestling in the rim
PRESENTATION: 8 It was still cooling down 24 hours later when I ate it
PACKAGE: 9 Deep and abundant
PALATE: 8 A rich, meaty flavour
PRICE: 8.5 Big pie, small price
PORTION: 9 Deep and thick, the size of a brick
OVERALL: 55.5/70 A tragedy really as this was one of the best pies I've had in a long time. Fantastic establishment, amazing pies but their ignorance has cost them in my book. Literally.

I head back through Accrington, Hollands pie spotting and bewitched by the glorious brown slate Thwaites pubs enticing me in to enjoy a few pints and scoff my pies but unfortunately my rock and roll lifestyle means I have to get to Argos to pick up a trampoline. I'm also tempted to veer off and head to the village of Church home to darts legend Rocket Ronnie Baxter, purely so that I can sing that old terrace classic "In Church, it's just like being in Church". I've been stuck in sprawling traffic so long, purely because I wanted to go past the Hollands factory that by the time I get back to the M65 I weep openly and give a chorus of Hallelujahs.

Tuesday 1st May 2012

Funny sounding place Congleton, I can't stop saying it: CON GUL TON, CON GUL TON. Might be a Congle – Jungle – Bungle type word association. It's the Cong bit it I think, sounds a bit like conk, apparently even the locals call it Congy. Do they do the Conga a lot in Congy? It's a shame it's not in a sub-tropical area as you could have a troop of Conger eels doing the Conga in Congy. Now there would be a spectacle! Albeit a little tricky as eels don't have legs. Anyway, I'm lost: as I'm narrating this drivel the SatNav has guided my car into a ditch.

My initial assertion that CON-GUL-TON or (CON-GLEY-TON as my SatNav calls it) is a small village couldn't be more wrong, there's enough new build apartments to house the population of Beijing. It's bigger than MACC-LESS-FIELD!

I arrive at Brook Street Bakery to find said establishment with white washed windows and a noticeable lack of pastry smell. Bloody closed down hasn't it? Or being refurbished under new owners. I envisaged this

nightmare scenario would take place at some point but when it does happen it's still dejecting: a crushing blow of emptiness in my heart, only matched by the one in my stomach.

All I can do is head into Congleton and follow my nose. Brook Street Bakery appears to be shut but somebody must eat pies around here. I bob my head in a Kel's Patisserie but they're out of pies and there's not much else other than sausage rolls and the odd pasty left. I'm looking with my eyes and looking on my phone in tandem and pass another deli style place called Bread and Basil, they sell pies but looks a bit posh.

I've managed to get on the Yellow Pages site and look up a place called Arthur Chatwins on Bridge Street. You're the one for me fatty: you can definitely trust a man called Arthur to make good pies, of that I am convinced. It's either that or Greggs or the Bread and Basil gaff. Yet I can't find Chatwins anywhere either. I'm now completely bloody lost, aimlessly stumbling around Congleton fish market trying desperately to find a local who isn't completely doolally to ask for directions.

This is highly frustrating, as evidenced by the sweat patches forming under my arms after careering around a market town for half an hour. It's called Bridge Street for God's sake. How hard can this be? How many fucking bridges can there be in Congleton? I ask a few older people (because I don't trust younger people, they're BOUND to send me the wrong way for a laugh) but this is descending into a farce.

My SatNav kicks in again and I pin it down to its very spot: the bins around the back of some nursing home and I still can't smell pies. It's only then I realise that the apartment block next door is called Bakers Villas. Oh thanks a lot, very amusing you bastards!

I disconsolately head back to the Bread & Basil gaff. I could always have an oatcake I suppose which seem to be prominent around here perched, as it is firmly on the Manc/Stoke border if the replica shirts on display are anything to go by. I wonder at what exact geographical grid reference to people stop supporting City and United and turn in to Stokies? And why do so many of them bypass Macclesfield or Port Vale? Oh don't get me started on that, it's another book in its own right that topic. Anyway, I've got my pie now after the girls in the shop kindly break off their conversation to bother serving me. It looks suspiciously like a Wrights which I had way back in January but I'm past caring.

They've got leek and lamb, cheese and onion and meat and potato but either way I've got a distinct sense of déjà vu that I've had this one before.

I might have put down half a century or so of pies already this year but I still remember them all, each one was like a son to me. An edible son.

44.

PURVEYOR: Bread and Basil
PREMISES: Congleton
PURCHASE: Meat and Potato pie £1.30
PLACE: 7 **PASTRY:** 7 **PRESENTATION:** 8 **PACKAGE:** 7.5
PALATE: 7 **PRICE:** 7 **PORTION:** 8
OVERALL: 51.5/70 A good solid pie but then I knew that already.

It turns out Chatwins are a chain based in Nantwich so my quest was not in vain. I doubt I will ever return to Congleton again. Therefore I can't resist sticking a petulant two fingers up at the "Thank you for visiting Congleton" sign on my way out in disgust at it's complicated pie purchasing arrangements.

Wednesday 2nd May 2012

After yesterday's debacle, I use the fact I had a 6am start to take an early lunch and head to Marple to a place I've seen frequently listed; one of those "you won't get a pie after 12" type establishments. I thought Marple was by Stockport but it's fucking miles away. Indeed it feels like another world as I hit the stunning village of Prestbury, a place so snooty the locals ride around on penny farthings wearing top hats and monocles. It's like a Mancunian Monaco. You could sleep at the side of the cobbled streets around here they're so clean. I head through Adlington home to the Swizzles Matlow factory, just down Candy Lane. Then on to Poynton where the A6 goes all pedestrianised and the lamp posts lean in scarily like Triffids. The Lib Dems are popular around these parts for some reason as it's council election day tomorrow, trouble is I keep mistaking the big orange signs for speed cameras.

I find Archers, opposite a big Co-Op where I pay thirty pence to park and wander in under its grand burgundy and gold canopy. It's traditional with big loaves and a variety of pies, difficult to tell which pie is which but they're all big uns. Turkey and mushroom, urggh. And a lamb one. Plus the usual steak and meat pies, sausage rolls and pasties.

45.

PURVEYOR: Archers
PREMISES: Marple, Stockport
PURCHASE: Meat and potato pie
PLACE: 7 **PASTRY:** 8 **PRESENTATION:** 8 **PACKAGE:** 8.5

PALATE: 8 **PRICE:** 6 **PORTION:** 7
OVERALL: 52.5/70 A delightful dark brown casing populated with masses of sloppy filling and gravy which smells divine made in a flat, almost plate pie style. An exquisite if a trifle pricey submission into the pie archives.

Tuesday 8th May 2012

I've been plotting. I'm off work today and I was told if I didn't get too drunk at the football match I went to last night we can have a "family day out". Options are Sheffield (ideally), Huddersfield (probably), Blackpool (emergency option).

We've got family in Holmfirth near Huddersfield so that's a doddle and it does seem a bit of a pie hot bed. I've set up a perfect pie hat trick after a bit of Googling: a butchers, a bakers and a farm shop are all lined up.

You can cut the tension with a knife as every two minutes I ask the missus "are you ready yet?". In fact if she had a knife, she'd probably stab me given how irascible I am this morning. This is what comes to be known as Pre Pie tension (PPT) in our house. I give up on Sheffield once ten o'clock passes but there'll be no pies left anywhere at this rate. We should be where we need to be now and we've not even left the house.

It seems that lot from over the Pennines prefer to get their provisions from the butchers rather than the bakers and are fond of a hot pork pie over a meat and prater. I discover the Pork Pie Appreciation Society whilst searching (*www.porkpieclub.com*) – a gang of hardcore growler aficionados from Ripponden and the site provides a great insight, although appears to be even more parochial than myself thus far as every one of its top ten pies comes from Yorkshire. Thankfully the numero uno is in nearby Holmfirth where I've got my hat trick planned.

First to lay a frustration to rest: Just for once I pull off the M62 and see the big yellow sign for Hadfields for the hundredth time, but this time instead of looking on wistfully I stop and I pull into a side street. What I also notice for the first time ever is 'AR Jones – Butcher & Pies' 100 yards further up the road. Off to a flyer!

Hadfields is a touch disappointing with relatively few pastry products on display: a pork pie, a pasty, a few sausage rolls and some kind of vegetarian slice. I go to walk out in disgust and go to AR Jones instead but then skulk back in and order a pork pie. They probably think I'm a bit of a nutter but they're friendly enough.

46.
PURVEYOR: Hadfields
PREMISES: Huddersfield

PURCHASE: Pork pie 95p
PLACE: 7 **PASTRY:** 7 **PRESENTATION:** 7 **PACKAGE:** 7
PALATE: 8 **PRICE:** 8 **PORTION:** 7.5
OVERALL: 51.5/70 The problem with heating this up at home is that jelly, which serves as a layer of insulation, melts in the oven and the meat becomes loose. Thus resulting in me suffering the ignominy of chasing a scoop of sausage meat after it has jumped out of the pie and is rolling around the kitchen. That aside, it's a good size for a growler and a splendid aperitif for today's proceedings. Except I had it the day after.

To AR Jones, champion butcher and pie maker. Sounds promising. There's meat on one side and stacks of great looking pork pies on my left including stilton and pork. Fidget pies! They've got plate cottage pie and meat and potato slices on the counter as well. The tall, pleasant, young man in front of me is not fazed by my pissing about and incessant dawdling and is very civil once I get used to his Yorkshire brogue.

47.

PURVEYOR: AR Jones (NB now Dukinfields)
PREMISES: Huddersfield
PURCHASE: Meat and potato pie £1.30
PLACE: 7.5 **PASTRY:** 8 **PRESENTATION:** 7 **PACKAGE:** 8
PALATE: 8 **PRICE:** 8 **PORTION:** 7
OVERALL: 53.5/70 The meatiness cranks up considerably once you enter the White Rose county and this is a stunningly beefy affair. A glazed, crispy crust with considerable gravy sodden contents inside. A real cracker.

Onwards to Holmfirth and I feel I should arrive in the traditional manner – by rolling down a hill in a tin bath with two equally cantankerous chums. However, the girls prefer a Peugeot 307 chugging into a pay and display as a more conventional method of ingress.

My first port of call is Sharlands Butchers. Smack bang in the middle of Holmfirth by the river and the picture house across the way from the Last of the Summer Wine cafe. It's a small, compact shop with its bold blue logo everywhere with an impressive selection of pies and meats. There are huge pork pies here but I've just had one so I try a meat and potato. The girl behind the counter asks me if I want a small or large one and possibly for the first time in my life, I opt for the small one for the princely sum of £1.18. It might be advertised as small but it's bigger than 90% of the pies I've eaten thus far and even though the large ones are only £2.34 they look like they would put me out of action for three days.

48.

PURVEYOR: Sharlands
PREMISES: Holmfirth
PURCHASE: Meat and potato pie £1.18
PLACE: 8 A no-nonsense "what can I get you" upon arrival
PASTRY: 7 Spot of controversy here. On first inspection it looks an amazing crust but I can't help noticing the bottom of the foil tray is a touch uneven. I attempt to lift the pie out of the tray and realise why: the crust stops halfway down the side. There's no pastry base, it's just filling! This makes it messy eating it the traditional way (i.e. with your hands) but is a novel approach regardless. The lip of the crust is quite heavy and heartburn inducing despite an impressive curl and sheen to it
PRESENTATION: 7 Too hot to handle
PACKAGE: 9 Massive chunks of prime steak enveloped in thick gravy flanked by soft potato cubes
PALATE: 9 Oh my word, this is fantastic, dark gravy and juices permeate down through the thick meaty portions and moist potato keep me dribbling. It's a winner
PRICE: 8.5 Big pie, big filling at a knockdown price
PORTION: 8 Maybe a bit deceptive when you discover the crust situation but still plenty to it
OVERALL: 56.5/70 Call the Salivation Army! This one is in the running!

I head to (Rick) Parfitts, less than a hundred yards away next to a kebab shop. It's shelves are a little sparse considering there is page after page of menus on the wall. Nice looking cakes mind you. Pasties, pork pies and pizza slices seems to be their lot according to the three young girls stood around the counter looking at their phones so I plump for another pork pie at £1.08 and am disappointed to find it smaller than the one I had earlier.

49.

PURVEYOR: Parfitts
PREMISES: Huddersfield
PURCHASE: Pork pie £1.08
PLACE: 7 **PASTRY:** 6 **PRESENTATION:** 7 **PACKAGE:** 7
PALATE: 6 **PRICE:** 6 **PORTION:** 6
OVERALL: 45/70 I've no idea how long this pie has been out there but I nearly broke my bloody teeth on the crust and it is a touch small and

fragile. In summary I'm a tad disappointed that Parfitts aren't capable of maintaining the Status Quo. What??

My last port of call is Hinchliffes Farm Shop. Up in the hills above Hudds, the farm shop scene around here is bob on. It's an impressive marquee type building; half shop selling fine cuisine and toxic looking 8% cider by the flagon and half posh restaurant. There's a well stocked meat counter with racks of pies at the back including a breakfast pie and a steak and Guinness which looks more like a pasty. I go for one of their infamous growlers and a steak and potato and pay a measly £2.40 for the pair.

50.

PURVEYOR: Hinchliffes Farm Shop
PREMISES: Huddersfield
PURCHASE: Pork Pie £1.10
PLACE: 7 Can't get my head around this "order at the counter, pay at the till" lark but no waiting time
PASTRY: 8 Golden brown, regimented well formed crust
PRESENTATION: 8 Taken home and heated up but it absolutely seduces me as it came out of the oven
PACKAGE: 9 Filled to the brim. You wouldn't believe there is a crust on it if it wasn't perched atop of a large, shoehorned in, clump of prime pork
PALATE: 8 Succulent sausage meat with rich jelly pouring out of every corner
PRICE: 8 A generously proportioned growler for the price
PORTION: 8 Big for a porker
OVERALL: 56/70 I took this home and warmed it up for a private dining session. There's something impressively seedy about eating a pork pie with greasy hands as jelly spills all over your person. Sheer heaven!

51.

PURVEYOR: Hinchliffes Farm Shop
PREMISES: Huddersfield
PURCHASE: Steak and Potato Pie £1.30
PLACE: 7 **PASTRY:** 7 **PRESENTATION:** 7 **PACKAGE:** 8.5
PALATE: 8 **PRICE:** 8 **PORTION:** 7.5
OVERALL: 53/70 Another pie with lots of pure steak in there, wonderfully rich and meaty although the pastry is a touch crumbly in parts this is a highly satisfying feed.

THE TOP CRUST. PART ONE: THE FIRST 100

In summary, farm shops don't piss about.

Saturday 12th May 2012

I'm out in Wigan doing magazine deliveries. Back on home turf and seeking savouries. With Greenhalghs (of Bolton) having a strong presence in the town and the Bolton based Pound Bakery never far away, it sometimes feels that the Wigan pie is under threat. Although we are really known for eating them not necessarily making them. Residents of Leigh are known locally as "lobby gobblers" for their preference of consuming their Lancashire Hot Pot without a top crust. Not that the lobby gobbler nomenclature offers any helpful clues to this logic.

On the pie front they've got Waterfields so I head from Waterstones to Waterfields to sample their wares. I don't recall their pies being any good but I always remember the fantastic gingerbread men which I often had foisted upon me as a child and which I recently foisted upon my young nephew to keep him quiet for a few minutes. Highly recommended and I can't wait to treat my own little one to the same.

Today they've got lots of beef and steak pies and a "Big One" for £1 which appears to be a foot long sausage roll.

52.

PURVEYOR: Waterfields
PREMISES: Leigh
PURCHASE: Meat and potato pie £1.37
PLACE: 8 **PASTRY:** 7 **PRESENTATION:** 7 **PACKAGE:** 6
PALATE: 7.5 **PRICE:** 7 **PORTION:** 7
OVERALL: 49.5/70 Delightful staff mainly because as I left I got a cheery, synchronised chorus of "BYYYEEEEEEEEE" back off all three of them. Lovely. Even if they were just glad to see the back of me. However, there is a fundamental flaw with the pie as it is quite hollow inside with a ray of sunlight passing through it. A decent crust and doughy potato and mince filling only partially compensating for this faux pas.

Friday 18th May 2012

Whilst women around the country go crazy for a man called Christian who ties them up and inserts various objects into them, I'm only gutted my own offering into the publishing world isn't quite ready with thousands of red blooded males getting equally aroused at the seductive tale of some simpleton travelling the country inserting countless pies into his gob. It could be quite the antidote.

I've been despatched to London again and I've just got enough time to sneak off to Greenwich Village – sorry I mean Greenwich, UK. I can't ever see this reading Kindles and iPads business ever catching on upon public transport in Wigan, the feral local youths would have it off you before you could say "Angry Birds". I'm sat on the tube across from a short pug faced girl who's reading Fifty Shades of Grey. Her chubby face isn't flinching but her legs are going like the clappers!

A minor epiphany occurs when the DLR goes under the Thames and emerges in this improbably chic enclave of South London, having come from the residual less salubrious parts of the Isle of Dogs. The second I walk out of the station I am greeted with a cacophony of noise and bustle along with the majestic sight of the Cutty Sark, the magnitude of which is impossible to comprehend until it's imposing build is floating right there in front of you. Once that white, heavily dreadlocked Big Issue seller moves out of the way.

I wander though the bohemian covered market (which I swear is the one they always feature on The Apprentice) and past the inevitable throng of tourists admiring the Cutty Sark. It's also the first time I've ever seen a Ben & Jerry's store but then again it's probably just catering for the masses of large Americans wandering around with huge cameras.

I head to King William Walk to locate the emerald green façade of God-dards, who sell traditional pie and mash and jellied eels to tourists and lo-cals alike. It is a grand building but also slightly secluded tucked around the back facing the park and naval college. I peruse the menu: they've got steak and kidney, cheese pies, chilli beef, proper veggie with Soya meat and a Banks veggie pie. They also serve ale if you're looking to eat, drink and be merry. All served up with mash, peas, gravy or eel liquor if you prefer. I carry out a steak and ale pie and try to find a spot amidst the grandeur of the gardens of the Stephen Lawrence building. I walk through the grounds of the naval college, with its pristine whitewashed buildings and find a tramp-free bench to sit on and consume my wares.

53.

PURVEYOR: Goddards
PREMISES: Greenwich
PURCHASE: Steak & Ale pie £2.20
PLACE: 7 Sprightly service and always a pleasure to hear an actual Cockney accent in this tourist over-run corner of the capital
PASTRY: 7.5 I'm a sucker for a pattern on the top. Although in traditional London style the crust extends way beyond the base making it look deceptively large

PRESENTATION: 7.5 Served warm and a cultured meaty whiff about it
PACKAGE: 7 High meat ratio but feels more mincemeat than steak and
also a load of dark jelly. In a pork pie yes, but I'm not sure about it in a
steak pie
PALATE: 7.5 Rich, dark luscious gravy and mince although I can't taste
much ale in there
PRICE: 7 An excellent price given the surroundings
PORTION: 8 Circular and tapers off underneath but of good overall size
OVERALL: 51.5/70 A sure fire winner which just about gets the balance
right in its attempts to cater for both Londoners and pie-starved
Northerners stuck down south.

I head home with a full belly and the platform on the Cutty Sark resembles
downtown Tokyo at rush hour with millions of Japanese tourists rammed
onto the DLR station. It's only when I check my train ticket that I realise
I have another hour before my train goes and I could have had a sit
down job.

Saturday 19th May 2012

My shoes have got holes in them so I'm off to Colne to procure footwear,
via one or two catering establishments in East Lancashire of course. I first
went to Boundary Mill over twenty years ago and cleaned them out of
Timberland. Now it's more likely to be practical Clarks and a reconnais-
sance of the Pendle valley for pastry.

I was looking to get a pie from Blackburn but the only name that keeps
coming up is Jasat Halal Pies. Sounds intriguing even though in my cultural ignorance I thought halal was vegetarian meat until I caught up with
the world. I plug their address in my SatNav and it takes me all the way to
their doorstep. IN THEORY.

In practise, I end up driving around a half derelict business park staring
at wasteland and boarded up units; something has gone a tad awry here:
no pie shop, no factory, nowhere even open. I cruise around three vast,
vacuous business parks to no avail. I roll across a dual carriageway to scrutinise a large map, nearly crashing the car and running over two lads who
give me the universal sign for "you're fucking mental". Safe to say this one
is a fail.

I head further up the M65 and come off at Burnley where row after row
of grey slate flanked terraced houses are angled into the hillside like teeth
on a comb. This time the big burgundy canopy of Oddies Bakers appears
almost immediately.

I walk in to find the usual confusing scrum of customers huddled in no particular order. The menu has a few exotic "non-pie" choices including Pork & Pepper rolls and Moroccan Veg Rolls but upon spotting a solitary potato pie I nab it for my research.

54.
PURVEYOR: Oddies
PREMISES: Burnley
PURCHASE: Potato pie £1.27
PLACE: 7 PASTRY: 7 PRESENTATION: 7 PACKAGE: 8
PALATE: 7.5 PRICE: 7 PORTION: 7.5
OVERALL: 51/70 A rich, herby potatoey filling, exactly as it says on the tin (foil) with the occasional piece of mince in there. Nevertheless, a solid, traditional bakers. Incidentally, the owner if you haven't guessed is called – Bill Oddie!

Burnley town centre and Haffners is smack bang in the middle surrounded by some rough looking shut down boozers underneath a block of flats. Established 1889, and I immediately spy a raft of pies under the window: the big chicken curry pie takes my fancy a bit but I get my meat and potato in, a big 'un for the princely sum of just £1.10.

55.
PURVEYOR: Haffners
PREMISES: Burnley
PURCHASE: Meat and Potato pie £1.10
PLACE: 7 A polite young lass
PASTRY: 8 Crispy, dark outer top crust and firm base but softer interior
PRESENTATION: 7.5 A prize winning waft hits me upon pulling this out of the oven and the pie was still warm when I bought it
PACKAGE: 7 Not as overcrowded in there as I thought at first inspection
PALATE: 9 Yorkshire pies are very meaty and Lancashire pies are very potato heavy; yet with Burnley being close to the border, this pie fuses the two perfectly with the optimal meat to potato ratio and harnessing the best all round qualities you'd find either side of the Pennines
PRICE: 8.5 Cheap as chips, not that they sell chips
PORTION: 9 A whopper of a pie
OVERALL: 56/70 A big hitter from Burnley that hits the mark in more ways than one.

We head to Boundary Mill and find this shopping lark is hungry work not to mention dangerous given the heaving masses that descend on this part of East Lancashire at weekends, so after an hour scouting around we go

THE TOP CRUST. PART ONE: THE FIRST 100

upstairs to feed the nipper and what should be on the menu but pork pies. Pork and apple pies in fact!

56.

PURVEYOR: Boundary Mill
PREMISES: Colne
PURCHASE: Pork & Apple pie £1.59
PLACE: 7 **PASTRY:** 7 **PRESENTATION:** 7 **PACKAGE:** 7
PALATE: 7.5 **PRICE:** 6 **PORTION:** 6
OVERALL: 47.5/70 Eaten cold, this is a dinky looking pie whose filling sadly fails to make it all the way to the top although I do like the introduction of apple into the mix. Despite being a tall pie, it only succeeds in filling me because I've already eaten. Twice.

Monday 21st May 2012

The missus is at her sisters and I'm on my tod. I have no option but to take pity on that Fray Bentos Boozy Steak and Ale pie which has been festering in the cupboard for months. "Tender pieces of steak drenched in a delicious real ale gravy topped with our signature puff pastry"

See that's not bad? For all the bad press that a Fray Bentos pie gets predominantly as the flagship meal for home alone sad bastards who are either incapable or can't be arsed cooking (not that I'm stereotyping), it actually smells alright. I'm greeted with a solid, stodgy looking pastry with a mere ribbon of gravy oozing out of the edges. For the uninitiated, it is a pie with a top crust only cooked in the oven still in its tin. Twenty-five minutes later out it pops with its big bouffant crust and gravy spilling all over the baking tray like an angry tributary from the River Nile.

Would this book be complete without a Fray Bentos? I doubt it. The first thing to say is that considering the ubiquity of this Argentinean spherical (erratum number one: Fray Bentos actually originates from Uruguay) the task of eating the bugger can be remarkably contrived. It's practically impossible to eat one with your hands unless you like scooping up hot gravy with them but the crust by now an average height of three feet does not always detach cleanly from the can it has been baked in. So you are left with a load of puff pastry, which disintegrates into a million flaky pieces and a bit of soft, suet-type pastry which remains welded to the tin, that you have to scrape and spoon out along with the rest of the filling. You can of course eat it directly from the tin but plastic cutlery is preferred as metal on metal scraping often grates.

Upon dismantling this beast, I feel slightly underwhelmed at the lack of meat content and quickly up-end the lid onto a plate to find out where it is hiding, (burning my hands on the casing and spilling gravy all over the tea towel as I go). Eventually I get it all on a plate and it manages to adequately cover the surface area despite my concerns over low meat content.

57.

PURVEYOR: Fray Bentos
PREMISES: Leicestershire
PURCHASE: Steak and Boozy Ale pie £2.18
PLACE: 7 Delivered to my door by th'Asda man
PASTRY: 6 Top crust only (BOOOO!!) with crisp outer layers and a soggy interior
PRESENTATION: 7 A messy affair
PACKAGE: 7 Skimpy meat levels and hardly "boozy" but passable
PALATE: 7 Delicious gravy AOTS
PRICE: 6.5 Over two quid and you have to cook it yourself!
PORTION: 7.5 An ample meal for one not two unless chips and peas are added to the equation
OVERALL: 48/70 A-Frayed I've had better.

Tuesday 22nd May 2012

Bollocks to it, I'm going after Arthur Chatwin again, you won't escape me this time you wily old fox! My big hooter can sniff out decent pastry products and I'm getting the smell for it. They are a small Cheshire chain based in Nantwich with a handful of branches. I've only been to Northwich once before and I ended up driving around the periphery for hours like an airplane circling without ever establishing where the centre actually was. Even if you can see the centre, you can't always get to it and end up in Sainsburys car park.

I'm stuck in temporary traffic lights outside a pub called The Slow and Easy, it's just like being in downtown New Orleans until I hesitate briefly as the lights turn to green and a pensioner overtakes me with his window down shouting gratuitous abuse at me.

Fruitlessly searching for a space in three separate car parks, I dump my car outside a Wetherspoons already fronted by several slightly swaying gentlemen. No sign of Chatwins but I pass Webb's Butchers on the main pedestrianised street: a double fronted outlet – one full of meat, the other full of – hang on – PIES!! I can't resist and go in and order a meat and potato pie for £1.86. It's a big old unit. There's grotesquely sized pork pies for £3.00 and I am obliged to ask what the big brown one is, indeed it's almost black: a rich, dark crust which screams GAVISCON at you. It's a pork and apple job but around eight times the size of the one I had on Saturday.

58.

PURVEYOR: Webbs
PREMISES: Northwich
PURCHASE: Meat and Potato pie £1.86
PLACE: 8 The lady serving deals expertly with my many questions plus they have sawdust on the floor!
PASTRY: 7.5 Glazed and so dark
PRESENTATION: 7 Sawdust on the floor though!
PACKAGE: 8.5 A big, sturdy, robust pie, a butcher's pie basically.
PALATE: 8 Big lumps of glistening potato combined with smaller chunks of braised beef, a bit unlike a butchers pie in this respect but it is nevertheless a corker
PRICE: 7 Big but not cheap
PORTION: 8.5 Heavy enough to knock a featherweight boxer out with
OVERALL: 54.5/70 Yet more evidence that butchers don't mess about.

I scurry around the partially covered precinct. I know I'm heading somewhere but I haven't a clue which way's north in this rabbit warren of shops. I eventually find Chatwins next to the Northwich Victoria club shop, only for them to tell me they have no pies left but come back in five minutes. The second time I walk into Chatwins they still don't have any pies out but when I ask, the other woman behind the counter recognises me and says "ooh we've got one in the oven warming ready for this gentleman". Now that's service!

59.

PURVEYOR: Chatwins
PREMISES: Nantwich
PURCHASE: Meat and potato pie £1.40
PLACE: 9 For baking me my very own personalised pie
PASTRY: 7.5 Light and airy pastry
PRESENTATION: 7.5 Jumps straight out of the oven into my sweaty palms
PACKAGE: 8 Very soft creamy potato filling complimented with very, I mean very, light pink chunks of beef. Is it beef or ham/pork/mutton?
PALATE: 7.5 A wave of creamy, fluffy potato hits you when you bite in along with that meat (which I'm still not sure about)
PRICE: 7 Average
PORTION: 7.5 A big round plate pie raised in the middle
OVERALL: 54/70 Excellent service but just like Reid's before it, the case of the unknown meat rears its ugly head again….

Sunday 27th May 2012

I call in at Spar on the way home from a weekend away and I'm a tad peckish. They have Clayton Park pies on the shelf. One of those and a bottle of Pinot Grigio for the wife. Pielife never ends.

I need cheering up after spotting a large lorry coming over the Pennines, with GH Sheldon finest bakers emblazoned on it, only for me to later check and find out they only make Lancashire oven bottom muffins (baps, barms, teacakes etc). Still, what's not to like about a bottom muffin? Probably a good wrap around for an infamous Wigan pie barm. A Pie barm? Yes it's exactly as it says – it's a pie; on a barmcake (roll, cob, breadcake – you get the picture by now)

When I was a young office lad prowling the streets of Wigan on my dinner hour, this was one such occasion where I would usurp a pie and always opt for a pasty instead. The dimensions dictate that a pasty, (unless Cornish), is flatter, thus reducing spillage and making an all-round tidier handheld meal. Even though pasty barm isn't quite the same headline grabber.

We also hear about pie kebabs in Wigan, essentially three pies on a stick but this is something of an urban myth, no-one actually prepares and eats such a thing. Do they?

You could stack them up on a plate I suppose but putting a skewer through them would just be plain odd wouldn't it?

Back to the matter in hand and along with Hollands, Clayton Park are one of the big hitters on the Lancashire pie manufacturers scene so it's one I have to tick off, preferably in a sober review manner not half cut at a football match.

60.

PURVEYOR: Clayton Park
PREMISES: Accrington
PURCHASE: Potato and meat pie £1.10
PLACE: 7 PASTRY: 7.5 PRESENTATION: 7 PACKAGE: 8
PALATE: 8 PRICE: 8 PORTION: 8
OVERALL: 53.5/70 A layered potato filling, well seasoned and peppery. Heavily glazed, sticky top crust with a well defined crimp to it. "Creating true British masterpieces" it says on the wrapper. Might be stretching it a bit there but it wasn't bad for a quid.

Thursday 31st May 2012

There's a very well put together nostalgia website called Wigan World. A real hive of information, great pictures and memories. Some of the old boys who post on the messageboard probably don't like me much as they are all old school rugby men who spent fifty years down the pit and think football is a game for jessies.

The one area where I will defer to their superior knowledge is of Wigan past. I generally enjoy reading their opinions, especially on the topic of pies. The long lost original recipe of Pooles Pies is as lamented as Indiana Jones' lost ark, (along with a whole plethora of great pie shops lost in the realms of time). One or two speak very highly of the pies of Crewe, with a place called Finigans mentioned in passing. You can tell when it's a traditional bakery because no matter how much you try to use Google you still can't figure out how it is spelt, where it is, and there's definitely no website for it; at best you might be able to source an address from one of the myriad of ubiquitous business directory websites plastered with shitty adverts.

So I find an address and set off into the unknown. Is it still going to be there? Best find a Crewe back up option just in case and jot it down on my scraggy Post It note. Always got to have a back up; I'd hate to end up salivating with nothing to stick my gnashers into.

I head into Crewe through the village where the car steering security device was invented, Wheelock, past the station and the football ground and on the edges of the grotty Nantwich Road with its ropey nightlife. The Olympic torch is touring the area and signs are up everywhere but the only hot thing I'm interested in is a burning package of meat wrapped in short-crust pastry.

Down Gresty Road, Crewe and it's only second time around I spot Finigans, a small corner terraced shop with a green painted front. Given its proximity to the football ground, I'm amazed I've never heard of it before; I've certainly frequented the blinder of a chippy behind the home end. There are people queuing outside, not ideal as it's pissing down. As I join the queue I realise that there are only actually two people inside the shop, yet four queuing outside. The woman stood just inside the shop is a rather large lady, in fact I'd go as far as to say that she's fucking enormous; about six foot four with the girth to match. The long lost illegitimate daughter of Giant Haystacks.

The queue is a good indicator backing up the sign which says "Pies are baked here fresh every morning for 50 years". So I get a little bit drenched whilst waiting but when I get inside, I find a very small counter and a bustling butty shop with just one woman serving; taking phone orders, dealing with customers and making sandwiches all at the same time. They've got meat and potato, steak, steak and kidney, chicken and mushroom pie. They also sell Oggies. We're not THAT close to the Welsh border – unless I'm missing something about the immigration patterns of Crewe's population.

61.

PURVEYOR: Finigans
PREMISES: Crewe
PURCHASE: Meat and Potato Pie £1.40
PLACE: 8 The poor lass is run off her feet. Hardly her fault if hungry punters haven't got the brains to shuffle up a bit and let those getting soaked cower in the doorway
PASTRY: 7.5 Proper sticky glaze to bite into
PRESENTATION: 8 I can certainly smell this hearty beast coming my way
PACKAGE: 8 A mash of potato with small chunks of beef in there to chomp into
PALATE: 8.5 Bursting with flavour. Strong seasoning but a highly traditional taste, like a pie from yesteryear before people saw fit to continually scaremonger over salt content
PRICE: 7 Benchmark pricing
PORTION: 8 Of above average size and density
OVERALL: 55/70 Potentially one of the finest Southerly staging posts of meat and potato pies in the North West before you traverse into oatcake and faggot (pardon?) country.

Saturday 2nd June 2012

Got work to do and left my laptop power lead at the office. A 70-mile round trip seems a waste for a cable so I decide to take a circular detour over the Wirral, even though it's straight down the M6.

Liverpool is not generally considered a pie hotbed. Sayers are The Sopranos of the Scouse bakery scene and quickly muscle out any competition. A quick yellow pages search just brings back page after page of the buggers along with the occasional Waterfields, the omnipotent Greggs and the fast emerging Pound Bakery. There must be some independent craft bakeries in a city the size of Liverpool? Even though they revel in calling Wiganers woollybacks and pie eaters, they must have some pastry shaped skeletons in their closet? Yet even the infamous Scouse Pie, which a few miles east becomes known as a Lancashire hotpot tends to be a home cooked dish rather than one sold in shops.

I find a few on the outskirts: Crosby, Formby and Prescot but otherwise the best chain seems to be Hursts of Birkenhead, or the Wirral peninsula to give it it's posh name. I don't know much about that side of the river, I've been to Tranmere Rovers a few times but it was always dark, unsurprisingly given they were the pioneers of Friday night football.

As I drive through Liverpool I start to get twitchy, eyes glancing left and right, nothing in sight. I can find nothing other than the standard fayre of Sayers and Greggs. I even pass a pub called the Bakery Inn but there's no bakery to be seen. Then, over the roundabout and under the fly-over by Walton Church on County Road, I spot my prey: Phil Manion's Bakery.

I walk in without acknowledgement, the woman behind the counter engaged in deep discussion with the only other customer who reassures her with an "At least you finish early today giiiiirrrrllll!" All I can see are a few loaves of bread and some cheeseburger flavour quarterback crisps. Mmmm. I can see some empty trays but not many pies, it is only just gone 12 o'clock so I ask her what she's got (attempting an absolutely diabolical Liverpool accent in the process). I get a steak pie for 80p which she pops in the microwave.

62.

PURVEYOR: Phil Manions
PREMISES: Liverpool
PURCHASE: Steak pie 80p
PLACE: 7 **PASTRY:** 7 **PRESENTATION:** 7 **PACKAGE:** 6
PALATE: 7 **PRICE:** 8 **PORTION:** 6
OVERALL: 48/70 It's small and sparsely populated with meat inside, however it is remarkably cheap with a soft oblong shaped crust.

I get back in the car and spot another Phil Manion bakers around the corner on Carisbrooke Street. Maybe they'll have a better range in there? Get a grip Jimmy lad and keep driving. Down on to Scotland Road, or rather what's left of it. Older relatives tell me there used to be thirty pubs on this stretch and a proper thriving community, most of it now is derelict and what gets re-built is sterile and lacks much of the character of yesteryear. There's just one shop which looks like it has potential with low counters despite nothing on display but it could be a taxi office or low grade escort agency for all I know. Keep moving. The Radio City tower is up ahead and my favourite pub in the world, The Ship & Mitre is on the right. Before you know it, the tunnel just appears and swallows me up like the Great Pit of Carkoon in Return of the Jedi.

I can't remember the last time I went through the Mersey tunnel and it surprises me just how long, undulating and well maintained it is. I can see why the toll price is £1.50 and therefore I maybe shouldn't have gone through it with a mere £1.40 in my pocket. I try it on with the booth operator and he seems warm to the idea of giving me a discount, until I check and find I'm actually 26p short "Aw eh are kid" he says in a frustrated and comical manner, as I reluctantly fish a tenner out from my other pocket.

Birkenhead centre is a write off: gridlocked, heavily pedestrianised and no Hursts Bakery in sight. I re-route to another branch whilst keeping my eye out for suitable alternatives. All I can find is the imaginatively named Norman's Buckets & Bowls as I head up the wonderfully named Balls Road. All of a sudden it turns very Knutsford-esque with huge houses, the size of my entire street set back from leafy lanes. They take me uphill to Oxton Village which has a Hursts bakery amidst a row of shops, situated on a swish residential street which smells of money not pastry.

The big red grilles are making me nervous that maybe they're closed. The café is but the bakery is still open. Hurrah ! Again, it's not brilliantly stocked but they've got steak and pork pies and a few pasties. She's not the friendliest girl in the world, only young and no doubt focussed on her forthcoming Saturday night on the piss rather than being pleasant to some fat middle aged plonker mithering for pies and following the briefest of exchanges I part with £1.50 for an reasonably large pork pie.

63.

PURVEYOR: Hursts
PREMISES: Birkenhead
PURCHASE: Pork pie £1.50
PLACE: 6.5 **PASTRY:** 8 **PRESENTATION:** 7 **PACKAGE:** 8
PALATE: 8 **PRICE:** 7 **PORTION:** 8
OVERALL: 52.5/70 I am presented with a thick, juicy pork pie which is hand raised with an almost regal looking crown on top. I don't detect a lot of jelly in there but it's meaty and succulent enough to get away with it.

Tuesday 5th June 2012

I woke up this morning and my missus told me she was dreaming that I had bought her an expensive ring. Coincidentally (or not) when I woke up I was dreaming that I was hunting for pies down the smoky, hilly back streets of Sheffield in a bygone era. I went past butchers and chippies as the "Greasy Chip Butty" song rang through my head desperately searching for the holy grail of that amazing back street shop with pies the size of dustbin lids. We both snap quickly out of these fanciful notions as we are off down South for a few days. Yes I'm leaving the North West! Needless to say I've been scouting for pie haunts for weeks under the cloaked facade of "days out" while we're down there.

As a stop off on the way down I've put forward Banbury but it all depends upon how the baby's sleeps. I envisage Banbury as being the home of nursery rhymes, fluffy clouds, maidens and Little Bo Peep wandering around the town centre looking for her missing flock. Turns out it's a reasonably functional, normal town with chimneys and industrial estates and ring roads and roundabouts. Sensibly, I've driven straight through to the quaint village of Deddington where there's a place called The Crown and Tuns where they do real ale and "truly exceptional" pies (their words obv.) A magical combination – (for me at least), and I'm doing the driving so I get to choose – right girls?

"KEEP CALM AND EAT MORE PIES" reads the sign outside. I'm like a rat up a drainpipe…

We're greeted warmly as we work out the formalities. They've got a wide selection of real ales on offer and a menu on the blackboard consisting almost wholly of pies. They are quite prescriptive in that they won't serve you one to share between two people (unless you've got a child with you) even though their pies are large enough for two. And this is a problem because?

I survey the scene whilst quaffing a pint of Old Hookey ale from nearby Hook Norton. It's an eye opener for me; deep in Morse country surrounded by snooty ladies in blue rinse shovelling pies down their grid, a very different clientele from the Pound Bakery. The whole country loves pies you see but in subtly different ways. Up north you just walk down the street and scoff it with gravy dribbling down your shirt but once you're past Birmingham, you're more likely to be sat at a table in a gastro pub with a napkin tucked under your collar to absorb any spillage.

Furthermore, the pies in here are all priced at around a tenner but you get what you pay for and when they come, they are both huge with a crust lid the size of a Goodyear Blimp.

They've got around twelve different varieties and I opt for the Steak and Old Hookey Ale pie whilst Emma goes for the turkey, sage and onion pie which looks equally delicious and voluptuous.

64.

PURVEYOR: The Crown & Tuns
PREMISES: Deddington, Oxfordshire
PURCHASE: A steak and Old Hookey Ale pie with chips, veg and a jug of gravy for £11.95. A new record? I think so!
PLACE: 8 Extra mark to the girl behind the bar for being dead sweet with my daughter whilst she rampages around the place pulling all the tablecloths off
PASTRY: 7 I'm not the biggest fan of puff

pastry given it's generally 80% air but I concede that this is a mighty lid. Top crust only so certain to upset the pie purists though

PRESENTATION: 8 As you'd expect, piping hot when served in a pot

PACKAGE: 8.5 Masses of rich steak with the odd bit of veg mixed in; carrots, leeks and a hint of garlic, all swimming in luxuriant gravy, and served up in a Betty's Hotpot style dish

PALATE: 9 Heavenly steak chunks, dark divine gravy with enough real ale in it to make me think I'd spilled my pint in it. A truly sumptuous dining experience. They say they know their pies and yep, they do, (flat) cap well and truly doffed

PRICE: 6.5 Quality pie, quality ingredients but not cheap. Northerners; your jaw is over there on the floor if you wish to pick it up

PORTION: 9 A monster portion and a monster crust

OVERALL: 56/70 These pies are hot property, a real class act and exceedingly filling.

Hang on, was that a deli around the corner? More importantly, can I nip in before the missus gets seriously pissed off and demands that we hit the road again? It's called Eagles Deli and there's a big life sized porcelain butcher outside. Why, it's almost as if I planned it!

I'm the only person in the shop along with two young girls on the counter and a bloke out the back carving up carcasses. It's bright, sparklingly clean and spacious with a number of display counters which quickly get bewildering for me. There's a lot of big fish laid out everywhere, sole and halibut and I'm literally having to follow my nose to find what I'm looking for. There's uncooked pies galore but I'm away for a week and not likely to go anywhere near a kitchen. I plump for a cooked pork pie which is described as a small one but even this looks a bit much for me in my current state of pastry based intoxication.

65.

PURVEYOR: Eagles Deli
PREMISES: Deddington
PURCHASE: Pork pie £2.15
PLACE: 7 **PASTRY:** 7.5 **PRESENTATION:** 7
PACKAGE: 7.5 **PALATE:** 7
PRICE: 6 **PORTION:** 7
OVERALL: 49/70 Delicately cased with a lattice top crust and plenty of jelly in the lining of the pie. The sausage meat is slightly coarse but very soft, perhaps a little bit dry when eaten at room temperature but a half decent, if slightly pricey growler.

Thursday 7th June 2012

Funny folk around these parts. Imagine calling a bakery after the act of trumping in bed whilst placing your wife's head under the covers.

I'm not saying it's wet in Yeovil today but Noah's Ark just went floating past. This is not the sunny South I had sold to me. It's so bad that I take a turn down a country lane and my car nearly ends up floating. The forecast says it's going to clear up and get better the further west we go so an afternoon in Weymouth awaits.

I'm perhaps being a tad ruthless in ticking off Somerset by venturing just over the border to Yeovil to visit a place going by the marvellous name of the Dutch Oven. I'm hoping that their goods are more savoury than the outcome of this particular playful act.

The tables outside are just about sheltered from the torrential rain by the concrete overhang of the shopping parade and are occupied by a youthful family smoking and loudly jabbering away. In summary, it's not as grand as it sounds, if indeed it does. However, they do have about eighteen types of pasty and three types of pie: Meat and Potato, Chicken & Mushroom, Steak and Kidney.

66.

PURVEYOR: Dutch Oven
PREMISES: Yeovil
PURCHASE: Meat and Potato pie £1.50
PLACE: 8 Attended to straight away by two pleasant Pam Ayres type ladies on a grim day giving it a 'what can I get you my luv?'
PASTRY: 7 Firm and sturdy crust
PRESENTATION: 6.5 Not very warm. After toiling hard to keep my pie dry while I get soaked, I feel a bit cheated here
PACKAGE: 6 Considerable airspace between the roof of crust and filling
PALATE: 8 Large chunks of potato with a bit of meat in there, wrapped up in tasty gravy
PRICE: 7 With cost of living adjustment this is acceptable
PORTION: 8 Biggish
OVERALL: 50.5/70 After initially fearing the worst this was more than acceptable.

I can't really wax lyrical about the many endearing qualities of Yeovil and its environs as a storm of biblical proportions ensures it is a flying visit. And I can only apologise to the gentleman stood smoking outside Wetherspoons, whom I almost knock flying whilst sprinting back to my car in a race to keep my pie dry.

The next stop is picturesque Sherborne with its imposing castle and narrow cobbled streets. The plan to go for a potter around is abandoned given it is absolutely wellying it down. I'm left to leg it around on my own while Emma and Jess sit in the car like a disgruntled pair of mini Queen Victorias.

Not to be deterred although I'm getting drenched sprinting past posh little delis and gift shops until I find Sabins Deli down a side street. Your intrepid reporter kicks the door down, throws himself with two forward rolls, then standing upright and doing a "dah-dah", throwing his hands in the air all the while looking a sorry, sodden mess. Really? A bell rings as I gently push the door ajar and a solitary drop of rain falls off my nose as a polite young gentleman sympathetically addresses me.

67.

PURVEYOR: Sabins Deli
PREMISES: Sherborne
PURCHASE: Pork Pie £1.75
PLACE: 7.5 **PASTRY:** 7.5 **PRESENTATION:** 7 **PACKAGE:** 8
PALATE: 7 **PRICE:** 7 **PORTION:** 8
OVERALL: 52/70 The crust is hand raised and beautifully formed with a lovely softness to it whilst the filling is succulent and intense; a real fillip on a particularly shitty day.

Both these reviews are carried out under the shadow of a man's large penis. A chalk one that is, carved into the hills at Cerne Abbas. It's not intentional, it just appears and feels very apt. We have a drive through the small centre of Cerne Abbas which has a gift shop full of items paying homage to said chalk man and his enormous white outlined erect appendage. Whatever do you tell the kids eh?

We head through Dorchester, it's smart looking football ground the only landmark of note and on to Weymouth. I'd been tipped off about The Handmade Pie and Alehouse in Weymouth but upon arrival it's clear that I have absolutely no concept as to how big Weymouth is. Plus the wife is moaning that she doesn't want a pie for her tea.

We roam the streets of Weymouth's seafront and the harbour behind it as the sun fights to break clear from the showers. It's sort of like Blackpool would be if a) they actually bothered to clean Blackpool occasionally; b) hundreds of hen parties and stag dos didn't turn up every weekend and trash the place; and c) there weren't drunks and drug addicts on nearly every street corner.

As the clouds disintegrate we're left in awe at a stunning beach which feels continental in every respect, until the sun showers start up again and the beach clears once more.

A game of cat and mouse ensues as our four older relatives are in town looking for us whilst I am looking for the pie house. "We can come back tomorrow" Emma says, "But I have other places to visit then!" I reply with typical only child mentality. Meanwhile, my actual child is now hungry and needs her stinky nappy changing so we retire to a seafront pub. In a day of considerable frustration, I spot at least four pie shops amidst the back streets of Weymouth and visit absolutely none of them. Not fucking happy.

Friday 8th June 2012

Still grumpy, I should have gone to Weymouth first. We could have done an all day pie session down there such is the plethora of bakeries. More cat and mouse as I attempt to evade family duties while Em's mum and dad ask numerous questions about my intended whereabouts. I'm trying not to piss Emma off, who is the only one who does know what is going on but is getting increasingly irritated herself.

I sneak off to Bennetts the Bakers in Broadstone, Poole, the best I can find locally. I am somewhat hampered by the fact that when I Google for pies in Poole it inevitably comes back with Pooles Pies.

I initially spot a Greggs across the road. Shit, they've been bought out! – thankfully Bennetts appears on an opposing street corner looking all sweet and seductive.

It says on the shelves they have steak pies but I can't see any and it's barely ten to eleven in the morning so I'm left with a choice of pasties. She's dead nice with me so I ask the question. She confirms not and starts to talk up their wonderful pasties. Sold, I suppose.

68.

PURVEYOR: Bennetts
PREMISES: Poole
PURCHASE: Cornish Pasty £2
PLACE: 7 **PASTRY:** 8 **PRESENTATION:** 7 **PACKAGE:** 7
PALATE: 8 **PRICE:** 6 **PORTION:** 7.5
OVERALL: 50.5/70 Consisting of a shiny puff pastry crust you could argue that ingredients such as carrots, swede and onion are mere bulking agent padding things out but they also add a lot of flavour to the extent that when peppery mince is thrown in, I larrup this in seconds.

We head to Bournemouth and a ferocious argument ensues en route as to whether it is a town or a city. I'm firmly in the town camp, whereas Emma maintains it's a city because there is a Bournemouth City College. As always, I'm right. Unless it has become a city in the last twelve months since I've written this. Next stop is Idah's Patisserie which is slap bang in the middle of Bournemouth's city centre, (er I mean business district) and is doing a roaring trade this Thursday morning. The window display is piled high full of Danishes (for business types) but there's also a vast array of savoury pies and pasties. The choice of pies is stunning including a chicken tikka and a sausage and bean pie. Yet probably out of complete shock that they sell them so far down south, I go for a meat and potato. Poor show by me this.

69.

PURVEYOR: Idah's Patisserie
PREMISES: Bournemouth
PURCHASE: Meat and Potato pie £1.55
PLACE: 8 **PASTRY:** 7 **PRESENTATION:** 7 **PACKAGE:** 7.5
PALATE: 7.5 **PRICE:** 7 **PORTION:** 7
OVERALL: 51/70 Speedy service plus I get a fork AND a serviette for just £1.55. The sort of pie best eaten upside down. With a dense top crust and a floppy base, this tactic just about keeps the pie intact. The filling consists of fluffy mash and ringlets of mincemeat although tastes a little bland in parts.

Whereas yesterday's pies were eaten underneath a man with a giant chalk cock, today's are eaten overlooking the luxurious and salubrious surroundings of Sandbanks beach. Sat in the richest square mile in the country eating pies in front of exclusive flats watching windsurfers glide by. I half expect the Redknapps to stroll past walking their very wealthy dog. You can tell there's money around here because the old boys playing bowls have got proper whites on like cricketers.

We stroll along Bournemouth beach then through its genteel gardens, only polluted by the lesser spotted student knobheads on stag dos, all sporting matching t-shirts personalised with "dickhead" and "wankface" on the back. We then pay a visit to Poole Asda for provisions. Whereas you might think an Asda is an Asda I do manage to notice some subtle differences between Poole and the Wigan Asda:

There is no wetsuit aisle in Wigan Asda.

There are no Pooles Pies on sale from a hot display cabinet for under a quid in the Poole Asda (surely having no Pooles in Poole they are missing a trick here?)

I've not seen a man called Norman careering around Poole Asda in a motorised scooter with a Warrington Wolves tracksuit on.

You do not have to pay a quid to use a trolley in Poole Asda.

I have not seen two middle aged men fighting over a discounted half roast chicken in the Whoopsie section of Poole Asda.

Saturday 9th June 2012

Oh my word, I'm off again. I'm doing the wife's nut in. Again, on the flimsy premise of a bit of sightseeing we're off to Corfe Castle for a drive while the baby sleeps in the back. I have however researched that there is a general store there called Clealls* who stock Bridport Gourmet pies. I can't drive to Bridport, even within the constraints of Dorset it is, by my mate Andy's admission, "Way out West" and the roads are shit.

Corfe is as pretty as you like and as we drive past quaint postcard cottages we both remark about how amazing it would be to live here, as the sun is beaming and the ruins of Corfe Castle look on majestically. Then we turn into the main square and find it absolutely teeming with people. The whole area is totally swamped with tourists and backpackers, circling the big hill, plucking up courage to make the long ascent to the ruins of the 11th century castle.

I head the other way, nipping through a churchyard and slaloming past gravestones while there is a wedding going on. Yes that was me in your photos!

As I wander into the store, a geriatric in front of me is buying enough ale to sink the General Belgrano: a full bottle of Vodka, a bottle of Bells, eight cans of cider, four cans of Stella and a couple of bottles of Rioja for good measure. It's twenty past eleven in the morning! I shouldn't be so judgemental, he might just be hosting a party. He does seem to be swaying already mind you.

The girl politely sends the local alcoholic nutter lovingly on his way. Next up is a non-local nutter who proceeds to buy up all her stock of pies. She's having one of those days.

The Bridport pies are on display and they are huge: chicken and mushroom, steak and kidney. They cost £3.50 but they are definitely pies for two and in that sense reasonably priced. Me, I opt for a more conservative Dorset Pork and Blue Vinney pie for £1.40. I also point at another little sausage based treat. "Oh that, that's a Purbeck Smokey". I'm in.

Clealls is now closed. A local man was said to be "devastated" (slurring his words slightly).

70.
PURVEYOR: Bridport Gourmet Pies
PREMISES: Bridport

PURCHASE: Dorset Pork & Blue Vinney Pie £1.40
PLACE: 8 PASTRY: 8 PRESENTATION: 8 PACKAGE: 8
PALATE: 8 PRICE: 7 PORTION: 7
OVERALL: 54/70 That's more like it! A decorative oval shaped pie with a map of Dorset in the top crust. The cheesy bit is a touch subtler than I'd expected and takes a while to register but it gets there in the end and when it does, it lingers as I chomp through the filling which is so porky it oinks as I bite into it. Complimented with a generous helping of jelly and a fair old wedge of sausage meat encased in a hot water pastry, this is a little stunner of a pie.

71.
PURVEYOR: Purbeck Smokeys
PREMISES: Purbeck
PURCHASE: Purbeck Smokey £1.50
PLACE: 8 PASTRY: 7.5 PRESENTATION: 7
PACKAGE: 7.5 PALATE: 8 PRICE: 7 PORTION: 7
OVERALL: 52/70 Essentially I've no idea what this is and haven't been able to find anything about it subsequent to publication. However, it twirls around and folds in like a gift wrapped present of cooked meat. Very soft and flaky in the mouth, almost puff pastry like. Tastewise, there's something in there, possibly even a bit of game judging by the dark colour pigment and toughness to it with jelly both on the inside and out. Upon inspecting the wrapper, it is almost two months out of date. Live life on the edge, me.

Monday 11th June 2012

Gone too far this time. It didn't look too bad on the map. I might have gotten away with it if Emma didn't have a stinking headache and we weren't driving through torrential rain. We're on our way back up North and of course my brainwave involves taking a slightly different route so I can pick up a couple of pies. She ain't impressed in the slightest and as we're stuck behind a multitude of lorries and farm vehicles all the way up the A303 through Wiltshire well, if looks could kill then my car would look like the inside of an abattoir.

We go through Salisbury with its stunning, dominating cathedral but it's too wet and tortuous to give it any more than a cursory glance. Even the million and one identikit thatched cottage villages are starting to tire us out now. We make it as far as Tesco at Marlborough by 1 o'clock for a weestop. My chances of getting to Cricklade for my pie are diminishing, if she doesn't kill me first.

We eventually get motoring as roads and weather both improve. Emma keeps asking why we're not on the motorway "We will be in a bit, this is just a more direct route" – factually true but she's not having any of it. Somehow, we get to Cricklade – a 9th century Saxon town – hopefully they'll have 9th century prices then – oh and it's still pissing down like you wouldn't believe.

It takes me another hefty soaking to establish that the numbering on the High Street in Cricklade isn't the usual "odds on one side of the road and evens on the other". Basically one side of the street is numbered 1 – 50ish and then all the way back down its 51 – 100ish so having just walked past 1 – 50 I realise that number 99 is back where I started. Fucking Anglo-Saxon smartarses and their confusing 9th Century ways.

Sprinting down the deserted high street like a drowned rat, I can take no more until the front of Michael Hart – (his shop not him personally) appears in front of me on my left.

It's more than worth the effort though as there are pies by the bucket-load inside and I take a second to imbibe in the spectacle. There's four or five varieties of steak, including the very tempting steak and stilton. They've got huge Cornish pasties and Scotch pies as well and some big plate pies. However I decide to choose something different and plump for a venison pie. Is that a calf or a deer? I don't actually know! Hey as if I couldn't be even more in Emma's bad books I'm now going back to the car to tell her I'll be eating Bambi for my tea!

72.

PURVEYOR: Michael Hart & Son
PREMISES: Cricklade
PURCHASE: Venison and Burgundy pie £2.20
PLACE: 7.5 Served by a cheerful chap with a large moustache who comments about the awful weather
PASTRY: 9 Superb: split into several layers, crispy on the outside gradually getting softer with an appetising glaze
PRESENTATION: 7 A delightfully fresh aroma to the pastry
PACKAGE: 7.5 Not quite packed to the brim but plenty of large, high quality chunks of meat
PALATE: 8 Pretend it's steak! Pretend it's steak! Pretend it's steak! In truth I probably have had venison before, I just can't remember. It is just steak under another name; the meat is quite dark but a lot softer and I can clearly taste the red wine
PRICE: 7.5 There's no such thing as a free lunch in Cricklade
PORTION: 8 Large, oblong shaped and heavy
OVERALL: 54.5/70 Glad I ate this when I got home rather than wolfing it

down there and then in the shop as it could have quite possibly sent me over the driving limit given the abundance of red wine coming through. A delightful little find. Just don't tell the missus I took an hour long detour to get there....

If you're going to say the word Cirencester you've got to say it with a West Country twang otherwise it simply doesn't work. Just like when I was in Corfe Mullen, a Northern accent just doesn't cut it. Sadly, we won't be hanging around to listen to the locals saying it.

We're in the middle of a five hour journey, the missus has a banging headache, the baby is crying and even I want to get home as soon as possible as there's an England game on at five o'clock. I double park in the middle of the capital of the Cotswolds, leaving them both in the car and head for the Castle Stores. I leg it down the cobbled streets looking for it to try and ensure I don't get a parking ticket to round off the day. I feel like Anneka Rice, except I don't possess a yellow jumpsuit, nor have I ever won Rear of the Year.

I'm looking for Viners Bakery, part of Halls Bakers but my brain isn't computing and I just end up running around in circles to no avail. Loads of shops down identical narrow, pedestrianised alleys but not the one I'm looking for. Castle Stores, Castle Street, I can't even see a Castle?

After ten minutes of headless chicken behaviour my salvation arrives in the form of Jesse Smith's; a butchers who also appears to have pies in the window. Bollocks, this will do instead. There's some big pasties in there with huge folds on them and a selection of pies including lamb and apricot, chicken and mushroom, steak and kidney. I opt for a Wychwood pork pie, not sure of the relevance of the Wychwood bit but it looks like a belter.

73.

PURVEYOR: Jesse Smiths
PREMISES: Cirencester
PURCHASE: Wychwood Pork Pie £1.69
PLACE: 7 **PASTRY:** 8
PRESENTATION: 7 **PACKAGE:** 8
PALATE: 7.5 **PRICE:** 7
PORTION: 7
OVERALL: 51.5/70 Low on jelly
but lots of reasonably cured pork meat
encased in a tough water based pastry
that was very dark even before I warm it up. It's a hefty pie and
a growler with a proper bite.

Saturday 16th June 2012

Back home. I don't know what is going on with the water on the South Coast but my teeth have been chattering like a Glaswegian bingo caller for days. Hopefully it hasn't affected my taste buds.

Apparently, Boltonians have been known to sing "I'd rather have a pastie than a pie" when visiting the nearby town of Wigan for football based excursions. Paddy McGuinness's home town does actually export a lot of pies to Wigan via Greenhalghs and the Hampsons/Sayers/Pound Bakery cartel but even so, the suggestion that Boltoners actually prefer pasties to pies purely because they don't like Wiganers is a ludicrous one. I could insinuate lots of similarities between Bolton and Cornwall at this juncture but I'd best not. Let's just say the Bolton pasty obsession is not completely without foundation, given the town is home to Carrs Pasties and Ye Olde Pastie Shoppe which are both apparently superb.

It's a tough matter for a Wiganer to concede but there are absolutely shitloads of quality independent bakers in Bolton which makes it hard to select a target. I end up feeling ever so slightly dirty browsing Bolton Wanderers message boards, but even that isn't conclusive as pies are second only to football in the list of things that people love to argue about.

There's enough positive feedback about Tony Mayoh's to give that a go. It's situated on the marvellously named Plodder Lane in Farnworth, which evokes images of shit footballers but in reality possesses more than one decent eatery.

So welcome to Bolton, twinned with Le Mans. I'm sure Bolton is associated with many things but high octane world class motorbike events isn't usually one of them. I walk into Tony Mayoh's, let's assume the H is silent otherwise it's impossible to say without sounding like one of the tailor's out of the Fast Show. They have party sized meat pies starting at just 60p but back on home soil, I return to my trusty meat and potato in this busy little bakers.

I park up around the corner to eat my booty and get strange stares from a family of Mark E.Smith lookalikes: a dad, a mum and four lads aged roughly 10-16, all drinking cans and it's still morning. They're so gaunt looking I'm tempted to give them my pie, as they peer into my car window watching me stuff my face.

74.

PURVEYOR: T&M Mayoh
PREMISES: Bolton
PURCHASE: Meat and potato pie £1.20
PLACE: 7 PASTRY: 8 PRESENTATION: 7.5

PACKAGE: 7.5 PALATE: 8
PRICE: 7.5 PORTION: 7
OVERALL: 52.5/70 It's jam packed with some huge slabs of spud in there smothering juicy knots of mince meat. The crust is thick but gentle with a soft, not soggy, bottom as potato based runny gravy comes spilling out of this piping hot little stallion of a pie.

Time waits for no man on Plodder Lane and neither do the proprietors of Pollards Bakery further down, as it's closed this fine Saturday morning. Frustrating but I plod further along Plodder Lane and head to the centre of Bolton in search of the highly rated Ye Olde Pastie Shoppe.

I meander through the traffic, chugging through the Saturday morning retail park scrum before a vision appears on the left: it is the famous Burnden Park Pie Shop. I'm having some of that!

Regardless of sporting antipathy when there's signage plastered across the front stating "95p a pie or 3 for £2.70" all bets are off. With its high blue walled front and big neon OPEN sign, it looks more like a bookies or, ahem adult shop yet this only serves to add to its allure.

I pull up in the car park at the rear and spot a rather large middle aged couple sat in an old Mondeo communally tucking into their pies. Now there's a chap who knows how to treat a lady!

I assume they shared the third one.

Astounding. What a treasure. It's like stepping back in time, a real gem! There's hand written signs all over the place, badly spelt and written in coarse markers and random bits of paper all over the shop. It looks like it's probably seen better days and no doubt got hit hard when the football club upped sticks to Horwich a few years back but nevertheless it is over-flowing with earthy home made charm and ambience. They do meat and potato, pork pies, chicken curry (madras) – their brackets not mine, steak and kidney and dinky pies. And all they sell is pies; hand delivered from out the back on a silver tray. Oh and cans; I get a can of 7Up as well "I don't drink it myself" he says "I'm a Lilt man me" and he gives me a know-ing glance.

Proper pie craic in here lads!

75.

PURVEYOR: Burnden Park Pie Shop
PREMISES: Bolton
PURCHASE: Meat and potato pie 95p
PLACE: 8 Gent, scholar and pie maker extraordinaire in spite of this place's supposed "Sweeney Todd" reputation
PASTRY: 7 Bit thick and stubbly for my liking

PRESENTATION: 8 Sublimely aromatic and warm as Caribbean sunshine
PACKAGE: 8 Juicy gravy and loads of stock soaked meat and potato inside
PALATE: 9 A terrific fusion of potato, gravy and mince, a touch peppery on the seasoning front but carries it off perfectly
PRICE: 9 What's not to like about a full sized pie that costs less than a quid?
PORTION: 7.5 Deep and crisp and uneven
OVERALL: 56.5/70 The secret is out! For many years a trip to Burnden Park was met by hostility towards away fans. All they were trying to do was protect their pies!

Burnden Park itself is all houses now and as I drive through Bolton town centre it's like a ghost town. The shopping areas are derelict and devoid of people, the out of town flight to Middlebrook has had a devastating effect. A shame as I used to have many a good night out here.

A small, pedestrianised part of Churchgate has a distinctly retro feel about it however. There is Ye Olde Winche and Trinkets Hardware Shoppe, Ye Olde Man & Scythe Pub and of course Ye Olde Pastie Shoppe. I'm only surprised that the late night eatery on the corner hasn't joined in by calling itself Ye Olde Kebab Shoppe but you can't have everything.

However, I am making light of a DISASTER here, as you see Ye Olde Pastie Shoppe is closed! I can't work out whether it's closed for good or just closed on Saturday but the shutters are up and no-one's home. I can see from some paper stuck inside the window that they sell mini meat pies for forty pence mind you. Have they been shut for twenty years?

I'll be back for this, like a pretty girl flirting across the dance floor, they're just playing hard to get with me. I don't give up that easily.

Sunday 17th June 2012

I first noticed these little buggers in Poole last week but elected not to buy whilst subconsciously thinking "I wish they sold these up North". Sauntering along the deli counter in my local Asda and what should pop up again but a trio of Bells mini steak and gravy pies. I don't think they are any relation to the whisky distillers but I'm sure thick chunks of steak will nevertheless be enough to intoxicate me.

According to THE INTERNET, Bells are Scotland's number one pastry brand who do a wide range of pies and at three pies for a quid I figure they might be worth a wee punt in the direction of my mouth.

76.

PURVEYOR: Bells
PREMISES: Lanarkshire
PURCHASE: 3 mini steak and gravy pies £1
PLACE: 7 **PASTRY:** 8 **PRESENTATION:** 7
PACKAGE: 7 **PALATE:** 8
PRICE: 9 **PORTION:** 6
OVERALL: 52/70 Whereas the content is low the quality nevertheless is high with a real strong steak flavour coming through in every mouthful. The crust feels more deep fried than baked and I recommend approaching it with caution, as it's sharp enough to take your front teeth out if you bite into it from the wrong angle.

Tuesday 19th June 2012

Working in London this week so time to seek out some traditional pie and mash. So what awaits me as I peer down from the 26th floor of my ivory tower in Canary Wharf: Well I'm looking for G.Kelly – no relation to R.Kelly I assume – situated on the Roman Road in the heart of the East End. Although it's only a couple of stops away I can see the meandering DLR line disappearing deep into the smog and sprawl upstream into the metropolis.

It says on G.Kelly's website that Bow DLR is a mere ten minute walk but it feels like ten miles on one of the hottest days of the year. Trekking over rough terrain. Run down flats and every third car blaring out drum and base. I've got a suit on like a twat and suspect everyone who passes by is considering mugging me. Hey, twenty years ago I'd probably have mugged myself!

I get a little lost somewhere near Bow bus station, which must have been the set for On the Buses judging by the exterior and find myself walking down surreal city streets: plush, gated apartments on one side of the road; grey, run down tenement blocks on the other. Nouveau riche Olympic influx yuppie flats versus long standing semi-derelict shitholes where a youth appears to have just flicked his still lit cig butt at me from the 4th floor balcony.

Roman Road itself also looks familiar (if a little daunting to a daft Northern monkey) down at ground level. It's cordoned off and totally pedestrianised with market stalls running down the road, in a scene last spotted in the opening credits of Only Fools and Horses. Here, the posh looking twats in suits have REALLY dried up. I'm clocking the door numbers ferociously looking for 526 whilst dodging angry pram pushing Cockney birds and cheerful rotund Jamaican ladies.

I dive in and Kelly's is quiet, save for a few Londoners tucking into a dish of jellied eels: "Pie and mash please love" in my bestest fake Cockney accent. It's £1.50 for the pie and another quid for the mash. I get some liquor in the absence of gravy for another 55p. The serving wench is friendly enough, although she sees straight through my hopelessly inept fake accent. She hands me a bag and sends me back out into the sweltering market place. It's only when I'm walking back I realise I've not got a knife and fork.

After a tortuous wait for the DLR where I am looked up and down by shell suited youths and placid but mean looking Afro Caribbean gents I eventually get to the sanctuary of Canary Wharf (back where I am the underclass) and find a quiet spot to consume my haul. I fit in a treat with the city slickers scooping up mashed potato with my fingers I can tell you. Even eating a pie with my hands brings on looks of disdain, especially when I keep dunking it in the tub of liquor. I struggle to ascertain much taste out of the liquor and just end up drinking it and it's perfectly palatable, verging on bland. Vinegary hot water really.

77.

PURVEYOR: G.Kelly
PREMISES: London
PURCHASE: Minced Beef pie £1.50
PLACE: 8 **PASTRY:** 6 **PRESENTATION:** 7
PACKAGE: 8 **PALATE:** 8 **PRICE:** 7 **PORTION:** 8
OVERALL: 52/70 The filling tastes cheap but then that's the whole idea, so nothing wrong with the ample layer of mince inside. The pastry, however, is char grilled in parts and the top crust gives way to a much shallower base. This may be a traditional pie, however it is also black and burnt to a crisp.

Wednesday 20th June 2012

Now this is more like it, although Emma will kill me. I'm swanning down Oxford Street, thronging with tourists and shoppers, on an early Wednesday evening on my way to meet a mate of mine from Wigan. He's taking me to the Windmill in Mayfair, a pie house smack bang in the centre of London. I hear the throaty swill of city geezers boozing outside on a summer's day. Having lugged my case from Bond Street tube station I'm a tad sweaty and respite comes in the form of an ice cold beer and an enticing walk up two flights of steps to the imaginatively named Pie Room.

We're too busy catching up and yapping to order but when she comes around Phil asks what the special is: a breakfast pie!! Sausage, bacon, mushrooms and beans. She hasn't tried it but says it's selling well. These are the questions I should be asking if I was any kind of professional!

They've got a great range and plenty of pie extras. They even have a pie club. I'd love to tell you more about it but the first rule of pie club is that you do not talk about pie club.

Anyway, it's not a difficult choice, given that the first option is their three times champion steak and kidney pie. Phil has a healthy cabbage dressing while I go for the mash and mushy peas on the side, all washed down with a few pints of Peroni.

It takes a while to arrive but is well worth it as two pastry coated steak and kidney flavoured door stops are placed on our table with us half expecting them to go crashing through the table, the floor and the ceiling below followed by a shriek of pain from a gentleman underneath who's innocuous post-work pint ends in tragedy as he is knocked out cold by a shot putt filled with meat.

They are weighty portions indeed; all that's missing is a pair of horns coming out of the top, Desperate Dan style. There's an interesting mix of characters in here, pride of place going to a couple of tiny Chinese fellas who appear to be devouring about five plates each. But the diversity is no surprise as this place is a rare treasure for exiled Northerners and pie lovers alike. Plate cleared in minutes and no mention of a dessert menu from either party.

Roll out the barrels? Roll me down the stairs back to the tube station more like!

78.

PURVEYOR: The Windmill
PREMISES: London
PURCHASE: Steak and Kidney pie £9.35
PLACE: 8 Nice cold Peroni's delivered to our table and an extra jug of gravy after a bit of gentle prompting
PASTRY: 8 A rich, thick yet delicate golden crust
PRESENTATION: 7 No problems here, the perfect temperature
PACKAGE: 8 Wholesome chunks of steak and even my nemesis kidney was sufficiently well cooked so as not to cause offence
PALATE: 8 Three times award winner and vindicated for once
PRICE: 7 NINE QUID!!
PORTION: 8 So round and heavy it would fit nicely under Geoff Capes' chin
OVERALL: 54/70 Proper pies, proper boozer.

We go our separate way with Phil's parting advice: "Go easy on the pie and mash shops won't you?" Erm yeah about that….

Sunday 24th June 2012

That irresistible Sunday morning moment when you walk to the shop for a paper and get a faint whiff of pastry coming from the hot food display. Then you find out that they're half price at just 50p. A funny Sunday lunch but I'm not going to pass this one up courtesy of my local Co-Op.

79.

PURVEYOR: Co-op
PREMISES: Manchester
PURCHASE: Meat and Potato pie 50p
PLACE: 7 **PASTRY:** 7 **PRESENTATION:** 7 **PACKAGE:** 7
PALATE: 8 **PRICE:** 10 **PORTION:** 7
OVERALL: 53/70 Unbeatable value for a pie which does leave a little airspace and has a crust that's a bit thick and crumbly. Yet tastewise it leaves little to be desired and is digested in minutes. All hail the whoopsie shelf!!

Tuesday 26th June 2012

During my prestigious career in amateur football, there was always a long standing tradition of providing and sampling the post match grub. With pies always high up on the agenda, we used to give them all a rating, (along with the barmaids of course) the outcome being that some away trips were much more anticipated than others. Now it's a mere Tuesday night ritual as whenever I go to play 5 a side Emma invariably ends up asking me to nip to the chemist or Asda after, which is a bit annoying as when she goes out shopping, I don't ask her to accidentally backheel a football into her own net as I did earlier tonight.

So drugs procured and wandering around Asda in stinking football kit, I check the deli counter and spy two Hollands' meat and potato pies for £1.40. I'd be surprised if anyone reading this hasn't heard of Hollands, even before my failed attempt to break into their factory a few weeks back. You don't have to work hard to get a Hollands' pie as they service most of the chippies, football grounds and supermarkets throughout the North of England and beyond before the Pukka heavy mob muscle in on their turf as you head east or south. The filling is generally consistent and adequate, with a distinctive creamy texture that I'm confident I could pick out amongst twenty other pies with a blindfold on.

80.

PURVEYOR: Hollands
PREMISES: Accrington
PURCHASE: Two meat and potato pies £1.40
PLACE: 7 **PASTRY:** 7 **PRESENTATION:** 7.5 **PACKAGE:** 7
PALATE: 7.5 **PRICE:** 9 **PORTION:** 7
OVERALL: 52/70 At supermarket prices, the Hollands pie was always going to muster up a respectable score. It's flavour is distinct but not exceptional, with soft potato and chewy little rings of mincemeat, and the crust is perfectly defined.

Wednesday 27th June 2012

A seminal moment as I will be eating my 100th pie of the year. I've only reviewed 80 in the league but I've had 99 in all competitions, therefore the next will be my hundredth unless we get really silly and start counting the cottage pie me mother-in-law made me last week.

My mission will only expand further now, much like my waistline. Although there was just one pie I didn't finish. Maybe it was just the way it had been baked, or the gravy, or jelly seeping through the crust. But no, it was mould. I'm sure of it. A mouldy pie.

No names, no pack drill – let's assume it was a one off.

To today's sojourn and you hopefully get the flavour by now: sometimes I go looking for the pie, sometimes the pie finds me. Sometimes it's a shop recommendation, sometimes I just hit a particular town or city and see what it has got to offer. Sometimes I'll be on a treadmill in the morning watching BBC News and the pie will appear in front of me on a plasma causing me to yank the earphones blasting early 90's Italian House music out. When the pasty tax was kicking off they did an interview in Devonshires Bakery and I quickly established that it's in Weaverham, wherever that is.

A sleepy drive alongside the Trent and Mersey Canal leads me to languid Weaverham where it's bin day: green, black, brown, red and small green bin day to be precise. As I've put a G instead of an E in my SatNav (because I can't read my own writing) I end up in yet another farmer's field. It is a town full of falsehoods however. I drive down a Beach Road yet we're 30 miles inland. There's a row of shops and a pub with the name Castle in it, but no castle to be seen, not even a bouncy castle. I'd still pay a few bob to see a boat chucked up in the air at the Anderton Boat Lift mind you.

I eventually find Devonshire's at the end of a small precinct. I'm the only customer in this large outlet and the old bird serving acknowledges me with a slight grunt. I can't see too many pies on display; what they have looks disappointingly small. I'm ready for the question: they have meat and potato; pork; chicken, ham and leek pies along with sausage rolls and Cornish pasties and rolls but yes, that miniscule thing there is a meat and potato pie and to add insult to injury I get charged £1.86 for it.

81.

PURVEYOR: Devonshires
PREMISES: Frodsham
PURCHASE: Meat and potato pie £1.86
PLACE: 6.5 **PASTRY:** 7 **PRESENTATION:** 8 **PACKAGE:** 7
PALATE: 7.5 **PRICE:** 6 **PORTION:** 6
OVERALL: 48/70 A compact effort, well filled but of scarce diameter. Plenty mince and potato, little flecks of carrot and a peppery kick to it and served red hot. Just a wee bit too small.

I trudge back to the car and I am almost barged out of the way by some scrawny lad bawling at his bird in the chippy next door. I can't tell what he's saying but he definitely has something long and pastry like in his hands. It's only when I walk back down the precinct I spot a Sayers. Ah yes, Sayers, the Liverpudlian institution – ideally I would visit one in the heart of Liverpool but, as the pie I have just purchased wouldn't satisfy a malnourished sparrow, my hand has been forced here.

I move my car around the back where people stand outside their flats smoking with their washing fluttering in the wind. I go past a Bargain Booze and a bookies but before I reach Sayers, a mirage appears in front of me: GEORGE'S BUTCHERS – FAMOUS FOR IT'S HOME MADE PIES. Change of plan again then! Sayers won't be the same without the renowned Scouse shop assistant banter anyway. So George, whoever you might be, you have just laid down a gauntlet in my direction and I'm dragged in by an invisible forcefield. That and the trays of huge pies in the front window priced at £1.40.

A happy double act wave their hands aside at the pies with lamb, pork, beef and steak on offer but the meat and potato are huge and hand crimped to a tee.

82.

PURVEYOR: Georges
PREMISES: Weaverham
PURCHASE: Meat and potato pie £1.40
PLACE: 7.5 A charming couple and a great find
PASTRY: 7 Different. A great crust but the lid is uneven and part of it sticks to the foil tray. This makes it difficult to eat with my hands forcing

me to scoop the filling out manually. Hey, at least my hands smell of lovely pie all afternoon!

PRESENTATION: 8 Foil tray and pie so hot I should have gone to A&E to get my hand bandaged

PACKAGE: 8 Maybe deceptively deep looking as the base is uneven but a good quantity of peppery potato and meat with lashings of gravy

PALATE: 8 Maris Piper potatoes is my guess and thick, rich meaty juices prevailing in every mouthful

PRICE: 8 A feisty beast at an affordable price

PORTION: 8.5 Butchers' pies nearly always seem to be huge. Solid

OVERALL: 55/70 The wildcard sweeps aside my original target with considerable disdain.

I sit in my car munching pies while people walk by with Sayers wrappers. A touch demoralising when it's flanked by two independent pie makers but the public gets what the public wants and as this town's residents possess three decent bakers within a precinct of a dozen or so shops; well you lucky, lucky Weaverhammers.

Saturday 30th June 2012

A lad I play football with works for the Council so gets to visit such far flung places as Leigh, Atherton and Tyldesley; which are technically part of the Metropolitan Borough of Wigan but whose residents would punch you enthusiastically in the face if you ever suggested they were Wiganers.

He comes up trumps by offering forward Dawsons and Whittakers of Tyldesley which are both situated on the same street. I follow up his suggestion with a quick search on the net and lo and behold: DAWSONS ARE THE WORST PIES I'VE EVER HAD, THE SERVICE IS SHOCKING AND THERE'S NOTHING IN THEIR PIES. Meanwhile someone from that Bolton Wanderers forum I was on the other day claims they are the best pies in the world. Another is extolling the virtues of Whittakers. Either way, these are old school bakers and don't have a website telling you how good their pies are, I can barely even find an address for them.

Dawsons Bakery first and it's perched on the corner of a particularly savage one way street, which cars screech around with all the finesse of negotiating a hairpin at the Monaco Grand Prix. I find out later that they have a shop in Hindley which is much closer. This pisses me off as I've driven through the full expanse of the Wigan Metropolitan Borough whose motto is "Our roads are shit" stuck behind a W reg Vauxhall Astra for twenty minutes with a BABE ON BOARD sticker in the rear window. I think a baby is doing the driving given the erratic state of it.

The pies look like big 'uns and the fruit pies look highly appetising as well. Their peppery meat and potato are rumoured to be something special however.

83.
PURVEYOR: Dawsons
PREMISES: Tyldesley
PURCHASE: Meat and potato pie £1.15
PLACE: 7 **PASTRY:** 8.5 **PRESENTATION:** 8 **PACKAGE:** 9
PALATE: 9 **PRICE:** 8.5 **PORTION:** 8
OVERALL: 58/70 Oh my word! It's peppery pie perfection!

Sometimes you just know when you've got a winner on (in) your hands and this was it. A delightfully soft crust perfectly formed with a firm base, whilst inside there is a ferocious tsunami of sloppy potato and fiery, peppery mincemeat. Occasionally it recedes but there's pepper lurking all over this beast, circling like a shark in potatoey waters ready to bite. I only stop short of giving it a 10 for taste as some might consider over-seasoning as cheating.

I greedily devour a meat pie as well which is swimming in meaty juices so abundant that they wriggle out and spurt all over the sleeve of my jumper. I tilt it back and more juice sneaks out and burns the palm of my hand. Oh well it is an occupational hazard for pie eaters I suppose. Dentists deal with bad breath, Firemen suffer smoke inhalation and pie eaters scorch their hands on escaping pie juices. As I take the final bite a bolt of lightning strikes my car, in an impromptu thunderstorm sent from the pie gods to seal their approval.

Dawsons, a pie shop with fire in its belly (and yours).

I return to the car between visits. I imagine the worst thing you can do to a baker is walk into his shop carrying someone else's pies. Back across the road, this time narrowly avoiding getting hit by a bus and around the corner to the green fronted "Laura's Pies" aka Whittakers. It is remarkably sparse inside with two emerald green tiled walls, a little bakery out the back and a bell which rings when you enter. All they sell are meat pies and meat and potato for £1.20, that's your lot save for some dishy looking cakes and obscure bottles of pop in the fridge, available for the princely sum of fifty five pence.

84.

PURVEYOR: Whittakers
PREMISES: Tyldesley
PURCHASE: Meat and potato pie £1.20
PLACE: 8 **PASTRY:** 8 **PRESENTATION:** 8
PACKAGE: 8 **PALATE:** 8
PRICE: 8 **PORTION:** 8
OVERALL: 56/70 The residents of Tyldesley are indeed fortunate to have two such wonderful yet different pie shops in their environs. I withstand a solid attempt to upsell to me ("Are you just having the one pie then?") and receive a large plate style pie with a shallow filling but wide diameter which rises to a more than acceptable level in the apex of the pie.

In complete contrast to their neighbours it's very sweet tasting with presumably a fair old sugar content and a highly unique taste to it.

On another day, this product would blow me away but it has to suffice with a very close second place. Kind of like a Ray Clemence to Dawson's Peter Shilton.

Tuesday 3rd July 2012

"At a mechanics and 20 yards away there's a van for Peter Herd's bakers of distinction. Strangely 'no pies left in this vehicle overnight' sign to be seen".

It starts with a tweet from Oldham mate of mine Neil and ends with me stuffing my face in a lay-by. This time scooting down Noah's Ark Lane in Wilmslow, which is barely wide enough to ride a bicycle down it. The kind of road whereby if I turn around a blind bend and a car is coming the opposite way we're both immediately dead. Still if you don't take risks you don't live do you?

Peter Herd's is situated on a back street with a few surrounding shops and they have a full on wedding cake showroom attached, including fetching pink Gucci and Louis Vuitton emblazoned ones.

The service is awful with a long, agitated queue heading towards the door although it's not the staff's fault that the two pinstripe suited arseholes at the front are taking forever to place their order and ringing back to the office to tell Sandra they've no red onion and is she OK with plain onions on her tuna baguette? Oh Kevin's just got back has he? Hey find out if he wants anything as well. Just piss off you twerps. There's the obligatory gaggle of logo-shirted workmen and directly in front of me, a spotty student who looks like Viz's Mr Logic. He orders a steak baguette in a snooty voice, only to find they don't sell them so he changes his mind to a pork pie. We'll make a man of you yet lad!

I have to go for a pork, seeing as they are the best in Cheshire (their words) and a meat and potato. Although the odd cheese and baked bean pie sticks out like a sore thumb, we'll have no kinky business around here....

85.

PURVEYOR: Peter Herds
PREMISES: Wilmslow
PURCHASE: Meat and potato pie £1.65
PLACE: 8 Yeah I was queuing ages but get this: they have complimentary sausage rolls along the length of the counter to munch on. Presumably to stop people picking the marzipan off the wedding cakes
PASTRY: 7.5 Brown and golden and just a little bit flaky
PRESENTATION: 7.5 The buttery flaky pastry gives off an amazing smell
PACKAGE: 7.5 No room in here with tons of diced potato interjected with slightly pinkish meat
PALATE: 8 A mildly seasoned classic
PRICE: 6.5 A bit Katie Pricey for what it was
PORTION: 6 A wee bit wee
OVERALL: 51/70 A pie of distinction? Well it was OK I suppose. As for the pork pie, it probably rates about the same: great jelly content and healthy quantities of pork but not exceptional.

Not that I'm finished for the day as I tuck into a post football Pukka pie. They were always the staple diet in the chippies of Nottingham (where I used to live) and of course are a regular feature at football matches – I always associated them with Rotherham's Millmoor more so than anywhere else. They do a multitude of flavours including their most popular Steak & Kidney and Chicken & Mushroom. I pick up a steak pie for just a quid in Tesco.

86.

PURVEYOR: Pukka Pies
PREMISES: Leicester
PURCHASE: Steak Pie £1
PLACE: 7 Comes with free clubcard points and a customary "unexpected item in baggage area" warning
PASTRY: 7 Multilayered, tough and flaky on top then doughy. As the crust lid is stronger than the base, it's probably best eaten upside down
PRESENTATION: 7 Just about edible with the hands as the steak oozes everywhere and the crust maintains its shape
PACKAGE: 7 What there is in it is rich, chunky slithers of steak but I can't

fathom these pies out due to their bouffant puff pastry lid, it perhaps
makes them look deceptively deeper than they actually are
PALATE: 7 Rich and juicy and full of gravy with a bit of a kick, almost
spilling over into the boundaries of peppered steak territory
PRICE: 8.5 Supermarket prices
PORTION: 7.5 Feels weighty but half of it is pastry
OVERALL: 51/70 Pukka = appalling word, decent pies.

Wednesday 4th July 2012

The past weekend saw every male under 50 in the North West at Heaton
Park watching the Stone Roses reunion. Me, I'm on a half day as I'm going
watching Roxette later with the missus. There's got to be something in it
for me though right? I decide to divert on the way home in a bid to crack
Bolton's Ye Olde Pastie Shoppe. I now know it doesn't open Saturdays but
weekdays they're open till 2.45pm, giving me ample time to get over and
hoover up any remaining pies or pasties.

It's pissing down like last time and I park in exactly the same space in
the same car park as last time. There's no such thing as bad omens though
is there?

BASTARDS! I'm fuming here! This is Bolton's revenge on Wigan. As I
approach Ye Olde Pastie Shoppe I see the familiar sights: Originals clothes
shop, the kebab house, the man talking to himself and gesticulating wildly
outside Ye Olde Man & Scythe pub. Then I see a couple turning away from
the black (no longer red) grill shaking their heads. Don't tell me they close
on a Wednesday as well?

They don't but there is a sign on the door written in crude marker pen
"CLOSED TILL 16TH JULY FOR REDECORATION" Well that just puts
the top hat on it. If I ever do get my hands on these pasties they had better
be good!

I've got the appetite now though, so a quick Google and I'm driving
through Halliwell in Bolton barely paying any attention to the road. Time
is not on my side any more. The steak grills are opening up but the bakeries
are closing. I've found one on my phone called Hunters but if I see anywhere open then I'm in. Carrs Pasties – closed. Mandy's Bakery, also shut.
I find Hunters Bakery down a secluded hilly back street overlooking
Bolton through a warren of terraced houses. I can smell pies and it's open,
you'll do for me as a famous Bolton dweller once said. They're as pleased
to see me as I am them. You can question the authenticity and popularity
of an establishment who still has pies left in the mid afternoon, but not
me, not this time....

The pie raises the temperature of my palm and the unmistakable aroma of pie invades my nostrils like a soothing lullaby. I'm like Malcolm the Mountie but instead of always getting my hands on much lamented Labatts, I scoff pies and I always get there in the end.

87.

PURVEYOR: Hunters
PREMISES: Bolton
PURCHASE: Meat and potato pie £1.25
PLACE: 8 **PASTRY:** 7.5 **PRESENTATION:** 7.5 **PACKAGE:** 7.5
PALATE: 8 **PRICE:** 7.5 **PORTION:** 7.5
OVERALL: 53.5/70 Big chunky meat pieces and a sweet gravy taste to it. The crust rim is a touch crumbly but the rest of the pastry is re-assuringly soft and golden.

Right time to plan tea in Manchester. Maybe we can go to Kro Bar where they serve up a "Pint of Pie", literally a puff pastry lidded pie served up in a ceramic pint jug! Though they have to pour it out for health and safety reasons. Nah she'll batter me.

Friday 6th July 2012

Another post work booze run to Booths. A bit low on cash if I'm honest but I can stretch to a bottle of Cava and some Minstrels for the missus along with a selection of craft ales for myself before I undertake the inevitable audit of pie stocking repositories.

I do the usual lap to see what beautiful British delicacies they have on offer today and come across Laverstoke Farm pies on the whoopsie shelf, reduced from £5.98 to £2.49. They've got steak and ale, lamb and mint and buffalo peppercorn. By process of elimination I rule out the steak and ale and then conclude that I don't really like mint in a pie any more than I like kidney in an After Eight mint, so I'm left with the buffalo peppercorn denoted by the BP letters embroidered on its top crust.

I remove the packaging at home and find it wrapped in a wedding cake style braiding. Does that go in the oven or not then? Thirty minutes later and there's absolute carnage as I attempt to peel off the paper banding and it takes half the crust with it. Not only that but the bottom crust doesn't want to detach itself either from something that resembles cardboard underneath and I have to get some scissors on the case to get a cross section picture. This is just not cricket, why are they making it so bloody difficult?

Yet as I lick the scissors the rich, spicy filling tantalises my tastebuds and serves as an enticing little teaser to the contents of what lies in front of me...

88.

PURVEYOR: Laverstoke Farm
PREMISES: Basingstoke
PURCHASE: Buffalo and peppercorn pie £2.49
PLACE: 7 The usual Friday night Booths hospitality
PASTRY: 6 Sadly ornate pastry lettering can not detract from the messy packaging situation. I even take a bite out of the bottom crust to check. Yep it's cardboard. The sides fall to pieces in the oven and the shortcrust lid caves in soon after
PRESENTATION: 7 Put together well but equally as quick to fall apart
PACKAGE: 8 Proper big chunks of buffalo meat coated in melted peppercorns married with onions, leek, carrot and garlic. Lovely
PALATE: 8 Slightly tougher meat but the peppercorn comes to the rescue, marinated with the buffalo meaning you don't miss a mouthful
PRICE: 6 And that's at half price
PORTION: 7 Reasonably sized meal for one
OVERALL: 49/70 There's no buffalo stance here. Despite a great taste this was unfortunately the amazing disintegrating pie.

Tuesday 10th July 2012

I was working till 1am this morning and I'm back in at 7am getting beaten up for impossible deadlines I cannot meet. Time to fight back and get a bit of this work/life balance people keep insisting we should have and come good with a promise to return to Biddulph. I know the way this time so it won't take half as long. I'm duty bound to seek out the Three Cooks/New Cooks (whatever it was called) bakery I walked past right at the start of my adventure.

Ah Biddulph, how I've missed your earthy charms! Straight on the big Sainsburys and I walk down the main street which is as previously, full of random people shouting at one another. It's a dour day only coloured in by a young 'un driving down Biddulph High Street in a lime green BMW, blasting out gangster rap. On the plus side, it's stopped raining and I manage to get myself in and out unscathed this time with a pie from New Cooks, well part of a pie at least. You see outside they're offering home made meat and potato pie or home made corn beef pie with mushy peas and gravy but when you step inside there is nothing on display. Technically there is pie but it's one big school dinner style tray sized pie at £1.20 a slice. It'll do.

89.

PURVEYOR: New Cooks
PREMISES: Biddulph
PURCHASE: Meat and Potato Slice £1.20
PLACE: 7 Poor service but as she said "bye duck" I'll forgive her
PASTRY: 7 Not completely encased but nice doughy texture to it
PRESENTATION: 6 Not too warm but a lovely aroma
PACKAGE: 8 Chunky and bulging out of the three sided crust
PALATE: 8 Melt in your mouth potato and sweetly seasoned large chunks of steak
PRICE: 7 Not expensive but this is just a piece of somebody else's pie isn't it?
PORTION: 7.5 Deceptively large although as it's served on a slab by slab basis, questions should be raised about consistency
OVERALL: 50.5/70 A novel way of approaching matters, I nevertheless get to consume a slab of pastry roughly the size of a house brick for just over a quid.

Saturday 14th July 2012

With weather more unhinged than Pete Doherty, we decide against a long walk out somewhere and hit the more sedate localised charms of Blackpool. More noted for piers than pies along with stag dos, donkeys, illuminations and a garish football kit I'm not expecting spectacular things but I do manage to pull together a hit list.

Laines is my first stop off. A mate tells me it's a blinder which he comes to when the cricket's on around here. THE INTERNET differs: "Bit of a drab, dreary looking place. Needs an overhaul and to sort out staff handling food in an unhygienic way. Didn't taste as fresh as it should have done". Yet elsewhere on THE INTERNET it is being praised to the hilt. The best pies in Blackpool however are apparently Gigli's, a butcher in Lytham and their website looks slick. Also nearby is Kevin Barry Quality Pies who have secured the website URL *www.quality-pies.co.uk* although it appears to have been designed by a five year old.

No sooner than we join the M6 we overtake a hen party bus from Wigan: pink clad t-shirts aplenty, clearly stating their intentions on the back by imploring folk to "Jump On Jackie" and "Ave a go with Angie". Eventually, onwards to Blackpool North Shore where we turn into a ropey looking council estate with a pristine windmill in the middle. We hit the busy Devonshire Road where Lainés Bakery appears on the corner, complete with a cute indeed acute accent plonked on the é of the delightfully fonted signage. Traditional and quirky.

Seagulls squawk overhead as I join the queue outside the door – that's mainly as the till is right next to the door; there are only actually three old people in, who are having the usual lengthy conversation, giving their order in between listing their ailments. Tons of scrummy looking cakes. No beef pies left, (I gauge that from an earlier customer) but they've steak and kidney, cheese and onion, chicken curry along with a potato and meat which I obtain for the competitive price of £1.20.

90.

PURVEYOR: Lainés
PREMISES: Blackpool
PURCHASE: Potato and meat pie £1.20
PLACE: 7 **PASTRY:** 8
PRESENTATION: 8 **PACKAGE:** 7.5
PALATE: 7 **PRICE:** 7.5 **PORTION:** 8
OVERALL: 53/70 A big, shallow plate pie with a raised centre and exceedingly hot. There's some colossal spuds within – although as it's advertised as a potato and meat pie I can't complain if there's a full five kilo bag of King Edwards in there.

We head south through the back streets of Blackpool passing the famous landmarks on our right: the Tower, The Big One, Bloomfield Road and a sandwich shop called Big Butts. I swerve to overtake a scruffy gentleman in a motorised wheelchair which he is steering with one hand whilst merrily swigging a can of Kestrel Super Strength in the other before the terrain gives way to the greenery of Lytham St Annes.

Lytham is smart and very liberal if the two butch lesbians walking an equally butch dog and the two gay gentlemen holding hands outside the fish shop are an indicator. The Open is on here next week so there's also a large quantity of sweater wearing middle aged American blokes pottering around with their implausibly tall and attractive younger wives. I double park the car and leap down the long, main canopied street with an obligatory busker playing the accordion adding a touch of joie de vivre to proceedings on the not so sunny Fylde Coast. Ooh Tom Tower's Cheese Shop – I like the look of that! Pies, Cheese, Ale are my holy trinity of temptation as you've probably ascertained by now but let's stay focussed.

I'm looking for Kevin Barry's Quality Pies which I spot right at the end of the main drag, shadowed by a big blue van with a pie in front of it. It's white and airy like a butcher's shop, much smarter than I'd expect a shop called Kevin and Barry's pies to be. I was anticipating Sweeney Todd's

Burnden Park Pie Shop Mark Two but it's spick and span and a pleasant Lancastrian lady serves me up a bulky meat and potato pie. It comes straight out of the oven with a scalding hot foil base for the princely sum of just £1.10. Ooh they've got butter pies as well. More on them later.

91.

PURVEYOR: Kevin Barrys
PREMISES: Lytham St Annes
PURCHASE: Meat and Potato pie £1.10
PLACE: 8 **PASTRY:** 8 **PRESENTATION:** 7 **PACKAGE:** 8
PALATE: 8 **PRICE:** 8 **PORTION:** 8
OVERALL: 55/70 Service with a smile and as soon as I tuck into this deep, sturdy handsome beast I'm smiling as well. A lovely dark glaze on the top crust which possesses an outer crunch and inner softness whilst inside rich, heavenly seasoned potatoes interspersed with vivid meaty chunks give great satisfaction.

I walk past a deli where they are selling kangaroo, ostrich, wild boar and venison meat….hmm I wonder? Stick to the plan, Jimmy. Onwards to St Annes, and whilst I'm trying to find out where I'm going, my resolve is broken as I drive past the Upper Crust Bakery for the second time. Presumably no relation to the national chain who specialise in extortioning hungry commuters for a five pound baguette which would cost about ten bob in Asda. Next door, there's two kids having a toy sale on their front garden. Emma's cooing at their entrepreneurial spirit and is out of the car buying off them.

The hotplates are a little bare and perfunctory. Please let there be a butter pie, I'm regretting not getting one from the last gaff. Sadly not.

92.

PURVEYOR: Uppercrust Bakery
PREMISES: Lytham St Annes
PURCHASE: Steak and Kidney pie £1.45
PLACE: 7 Abrupt, getting ready to knock off I reckon
PASTRY: 7 Dark, crispy texture in an oblong shape
PRESENTATION: 8 Keeps its temperature well
PACKAGE: 7.5 Chunky steak with kidney and is that mushroom? I never can tell but it's drenched in rich gravy
PALATE: 7 Look I'm not a massive kidney fan. This is going to be a problem isn't it?
PRICE: 7 The quantity of steak is a saviour and a triumph
PORTION: 7 Let down perhaps by a big dint in the underside

OVERALL: 50.5/70 A speculative but valiant effort from the Uppercrust.

Right, where was I going? Oh that's right Gigli's Pies. Award winning pies. Christ, they must give out a lot of awards in the pie world. I park up next to the YMCA (Join in and do the actions if you like) as the sun breaks through, reflecting off the re-assuring sight of a crafty butchers in a Clifton Meats van unloading at the rear. It's a hive of activity down a quiet suburban street with the familiar red and white overhanging canopy and wide open frontage. For the whole time it takes me to go in and out, and old boy is sat on a bench facing the car, staring vacantly yet contently at me and the girls, watching the world go by in his idyllic St Annes retirement heaven.

More plate pies to feast over: cheese and onion, steak and Guinness; chicken, ham and leek along with some sturdy looking pork pies. There's meats and cheeses galore and I only snap out of my dreaminess due to some arse of a fella asking for almost everything in the shop in a highly shouty manner.

I get a meat and potato (£1.10) but my eyes are also diverted to the generously topped pork and apple pie (£1.30) which is too cute to ignore

93.

PURVEYOR: Giglis
PREMISES: Lytham St Annes
PURCHASE: Meat and Potato £1.10
PLACE: 7.5 Admirably affable considering some of their customers
PASTRY: 7.5 A heavily glazed top crust half of which is still stuck to the roof of my mouth this very day
PRESENTATION: 8 A palm singer
PACKAGE: 7.5 Light, creamy gravy comes oozing out at me
PALATE: 8 Sweet mash flavoured mixture with meaty overtones
PRICE: 8 A superb price
PORTION: 8 Big pie, titchy price
OVERALL: 54.5/70 Giglis, like Giggsy are a timeless classic.

With today's tasting session successfully negotiated it's off to Lowthers Gardens in Lytham, where they pipe music through the trees using loudspeakers and the elderly gents clad in whites participate in crown green bowls. A lush park full of Victorian grandeur which also does home made pies in it's caff – at six pound a go. But I'm full. It also possesses the oldest cash register still in use, so much so that the girl behind the counter needs a mallet to press the keys down. Apparently the Pavilion is playing host to former X Factor finalist Andy Abrahams in a few weeks.

After Jess charms the old ladies in the park, we wander back through

Lytham and discover the street organist goes by the name of Doctor Hotfingers. The missus browses gift shops and the continental aura is only disturbed by two drunken, shirtless lads running down the street, the second of which is shouting "I'll kill you, you c***!!" Two coppers follow in hot pursuit. Life in a Northern (seaside) town.

Anyhow I have another pie to eat....

94.

PURVEYOR: Giglis
PREMISES: Lytham St Annes
PURCHASE: Pork & Apple Pie £1.30
PLACE: 7.5
PASTRY: 8 Hot water based pastry smothered with apples on top yet I still manage to eat with one hand and no spillage
PRESENTATION: 8 After a 20 minute reheat the apples on top remain cool and crunchy yet the pork inside has steam coming off it
PACKAGE: 9 A double whammy of tons of sausage meat crammed in with a sublime external topping of sweet apples to take the edge off
PALATE: 9 The sweet and savoury mix challenges the tastebuds and is pulled off perfectly
PRICE: 8 A cut price fine dining experience
PORTION: 7.5 A real looker
OVERALL: 57/70 Giglis came with a reputation and certainly lives up to it, be it their standard fayre or something with a little twist to it.

Friday 20th July 2012

I've had a long week and was going to see what I could find in Chester today however after considerable searching, all I can find is a website that makes dog pies. That's pies for dogs – not pies with dog in them. I am a fussy eater but I am prepared to suffer for my art, however I'm just thinking of you dear reader when I say that there is little artistic merit in my eating a dog food pie. I mean if you want me to wolf down little Fido's can of Pedigree Chum wrapped in pastry I will do, but you don't right? Phew.

So instead to Frodsham, Cheshire's very own Cape Town, shadowed as it is by its very own table top mountain, always a dominating sight as you head towards Wales. I wander down the main street which is clad with fading Union Jack bunting earwigging on a middle aged gentleman having a very public row with his wife. I soon find Cowards with its meats out the front and big neon sign stating "Home of Sue Coward's home made pies" hanging above. As I walk in, two coppers walk out armed to the teeth with pies. Crime won't crack itself lads! I've seen a few folk raving about this place on forums. It's been going 80 years apparently and people flock miles for the pies of Cowards Butchers. I am greeted with a scrum of bodies the length of the shop but I can see pies galore all for around a quid. There's the obligatory deli counter although curiously perched atop of it, there is a bucket of what appears to be dog's offcuts and bones. That's bones for dogs not actual dog's bones. It's what all proper butchers used to do.

I order my pie – can't tell whether it's hot or cold, I suspect it's a "cooling on the counter" job to avoid the VAT charges. Goods purchased and I exit Frodsham.

95.

PURVEYOR: Cowards
PREMISES: Frodsham
PURCHASE: Meat and Potato Pie £1.00
PLACE: 7 **PASTRY:** 7.5 **PRESENTATION:** 7.5 **PACKAGE:** 8
PALATE: 7 **PRICE:** 8.5 **PORTION:** 8
OVERALL: 53.5/70 A deep, oblong shaped pie populated with slide rule square cubes of potato and mince sprinkled with liberal amounts of gravy. The pastry is a little dry but the top crust is adorned with a small star on top. Fantastic value for just one English pound. Team it up with a bag of dog bones for another 15p if you like. FOR YOUR DOG!

Saturday 21st July 2012

I've been craving a butter pie since I went to Blackpool. I won't be going far today as Jess isn't well but they do sell them around this neck of the woods too. To cover the history bit, I understand that the Lancastrian preference for a meat and potato pie evolved from the austerity of not being able to afford a full meat based dinner. When times were really hard they would have to forego the meat completely. It's also a Catholic thing, just like going to the chippy on a Friday: the butter pie was devised to be a belly filler on the days that the good traditional pious types were forbidden to eat meat.

After being up half the night with our sickly little cherub I am delighted to be greeted with a fine selection of savouries at gone 2pm at my local Greenhalghs. Pies in the window, pies behind the counter, pies on the shelves and of course pies in the oven. The top sellers sit in the front window looking seductive, like a crispy pastry red light district: beefsteak and meat and potato. Speciality products like scotch pie and cheese pasties are under the counter along with a beef madras pie that has a bright red angry looking sauce peeping out of the top. Big plate pies, steak and ale hand crimped, uncooked steak puddings and on a slight tangent, the infamous crumpet loaf. It's a crumpet – but in loaf form. It's not a loaf nor a crumpet – it's crumpet and a loaf. Yes a CRUMPET LOAF!!! A CRUMPOAF!!! A LUMPET!!! You just have to try it. A potato cake loaf, that's what I'd like to see next....

The order is a butter pie (£1.35), a meat and potato pie (£1.40), another for the missus and a cheese pasty for the baby asleep in the pram. From cradle to grave.

96.

PURVEYOR: Greenhalghs
PREMISES: Bolton
PURCHASE: Butter Pie £1.35
PLACE: 8 They do a great line in "Saturday girls" at Greenhalghs
PASTRY: 8 Solid shortcrust pastry with a soft almost lattice top crust
PRESENTATION: 7 Steady stream of hot pies throughout the day here
PACKAGE: 8 Big slabs of potato laced with butter, seasoning and a bit of onion in there
PALATE: 8 If the butter pie has a flaw it's that it can be a bit sickly but this is a buttery beauty
PRICE: 7 A fair price for what is usually a large pie
PORTION: 8 They don't do things by halves
OVERALL: 54/70 The best compliment I can give here is that it didn't feel like there was something missing....

Easy for me to say that as I quickly move on to devour the meat and potato.

97.

PURVEYOR: Greenhalghs
PREMISES: Bolton
PURCHASE: Meat & Potato Pie £1.40
PLACE: 8 **PASTRY:** 7 **PRESENTATION:** 8
PACKAGE: 8 **PALATE:** 8
PRICE: 7 **PORTION:** 8
OVERALL: 54/70 Consisting of generous slabs of soft, yellowy potato interspersed with beads of mince, the pastry is soft but a tad heartburn inducing at times. Nevertheless this is a large, satisfying pie. Finally, Jess awards her cheese pasty a 7/10 judging by her only throwing half of it all over the floor.

Tuesday 24th July 2012

Ever get that feeling of Déjà vu?
Ever get that feeling of Déjà vu?
Ever get that....oh you get the picture.
Early morning dentist visit today – and you know what kids get if they're good at the dentist? That's right – a treat!!
So I'm off to Bolton in search of a pasty from the highly elusive Ye Olde Pastie Shoppe. There's a bloke called Tom Bridge. He's a proper chef who has done a recipe book and in the process he ate 600 pies and voted these pasties the best of the lot, so you'll understand my perseverance here.
I park up (again) behind the now familiar establishment called Diamond's lapdancing bar and wait. It opens at half nine, (the shop not the strip club). It's not even half eight and I'm sitting in a Bolton car park waiting for a fresh pasty to emerge. I've already had a quick drive past and let out a gleeful "Yippee" craning my neck to spot that the now infamous metal grills appear to have been removed from the front. I may yet march in and shout Partridge like "Give me one of ye olde bloody pasties, ye olde bloody pastie shoppe!" Will they have pies ready at half nine on a Tuesday morning? Who the hell eats a pie at that time?
The door is open, the lights are on and I am confronted by a women who is actually baking pasties right in front of my eyes, glazing a tray of uncooked ones before bunging them in the oven. Arrive early and you get to see the magic!
They really do sell mini pies and pasties for FORTY PENCE. Elsewhere they have large plate fruit pies including Whimberry & Apple. I note that they've been baking here since 1667. That's some shift! To think that someone could walk in here 350 years ago and get a pasty to accompany their gallon of mead. Has the recipe changed? Did they used to throw any old shit in it? Who knows? Maybe I need to learn. It's all a bit humbling really. Today's output has a delightful aroma, is scorching hot and as you'd expect couldn't be any fresher.

98.

PURVEYOR: Ye Olde Pastie Shoppe
PREMISES: Bolton
PURCHASE: Meat and Potato Pastie 90p
PLACE: 8 A Bolton accent so broad she makes Sarah Cox sound like Princess Anne
PASTRY: 9 In stark contrast to the usual flaky, messy pasty crust this is as soft as a baby's bum. Thin yet satisfying; you could wash your face with it, it's so clean and pure. Individually hand crimped and delicately folded over

PRESENTATION: 8 Impeccably fresh due to my impeccable timing (third time lucky) **PACKAGE:** 8 Not the biggest size but thanks to the thin, soft crust it has plenty of finely chopped meat and potato stuffed into it **PALATE:** 8 A luscious, stodgy meat and potato pasty filling. Somehow I was expecting it to blow my mind given the high esteem many Boltonians hold it in so perhaps expected a little more....

PRICE: 8.5 No debit card required

PORTION: 7 I imagine it's usually a place where you buy in threes

OVERALL: 56.5/70 This is a triumph which shoots straight to the top of the pasty leaderboard! There may be pasties in Cornwall which can kick it's arse but I doubt you'll get change for a quid.

Wednesday 25th July 2012

You might think where you live is a bit congested. But you don't know the meaning of the word congested until you've walked through the streets of South London on a hot, humid day. I am a frail shadow of a man who feels like he has been walking for an hour from London Bridge tube station to Manze's Pie shop. I can see the Shard in the distance but the area around me is smoky council flats and grimy buildings wedged tightly between one another. There's a moody edge around here that you don't need senses to pick up on but I quite like that. What I can't cope with is that it's about thirty degrees and I'm about to walk into a furnace of pie production.

It's sweltering; my shirt is dripping and my head is fuzzy, each passing vehicle breathing steamy smog all over my feeble form. I call at a corner shop on Tower Bridge Road and down a litre and a half of water in about ten seconds flat. Still sweating profusely, I'm sat in a bit of shade at the side of the road, I want nothing more than to go and sit in an igloo for an hour and cry tears of happiness.

Got to push on. I could get used to city life, the people watching element is unsurpassable, but this is like wandering through the Sahara desert. There's a Barclays cycle hire rank over there. Now, why didn't I think of that? Mind you I'd be even hotter after ten minutes pedalling me knackers off on a pushrod in this heat.

Manze is all dark green Victorian marble inside and out and is full of folk tucking into bowls of jellied eels. Or "sushi for scrubbers" as I like to call it. It's a genteel environment but there's also an aura about the place which alludes to a moody past: the dark tiled walls and white Formica tables; old school South London gangster chic.

All they sell is the one variety of pie or so it seems but you can have mash with it, gravy, the traditional eel liquor or some kind of chilli vinegar. I have to repeat myself due to her not being able to understand my pathetic snide Cockney accent.

Christ, I've got to walk back now! There's an Albert Square doppelganger of a park in the middle of some flats. It's gentrified enough for me to contemplate a sit down but I'm simply too hot to consider eating a pie right now. I could always drink the eel liquor I suppose.

I make it back to Borough tube station, get the lift down and when a searing wave of heat hits me as it reopens below ground I come close to passing out. I stumble back on to the tube and get to Canary Wharf. I proceed to pull the goods out of my Manze branded bag, making me look a proper tourist in front of all the bankers and spivs that inhabit the place.

Like Kellys, the pie is filled with very cheap meat but they're just staying true to their roots. I need to apply a consistent benchmark but if they started doing Aberdeen Angus and Rioja pies, then it wouldn't be Cockney pie and mash any more, it'd be gourmet shit.

I pull out the vat of liquor which is so big you can float the pie in it. I take a sneaky swig and find it inoffensive, the faintest hint of fishiness but also watery with a whiff of parsley.

99.

PURVEYOR: M.Manze
PREMISES: London
PURCHASE: Minced beef pie (£1.65)
and tub of liquor (65p)
PLACE: 7 PASTRY: 7 PRESENTATION: 7
PACKAGE: 7.5 PALATE: 7.5
PRICE: 7 PORTION: 7
OVERALL: 50/70 The pie itself is full
flavoured and is essentially mince, mince
and more mince, not that the descriptor in
the shop described it as anything other than just PIE. The crust is dense
and of the standard oblong shape, with a big wide rim and thinner, tapered
base. If I was permanently exiled down South I'd be slavering over these.

My day is not done with an hour to pass at Euston on a cooling evening and with me not feeling particularly sociable I decide to dine al fresco with a product from the West Cornwall Pasty Company. Anything David Cameron can do, so can I. Although he's richer than me. Which is important when the sum of the medium pasty I procure is £3.70. The last of the large ones (£4.60) has been devoured by some big boned student just in front of me. The medium is hefty enough to knock out a passing pigeon anyway.

100.

PURVEYOR: West Cornwall Pasty Company
PREMISES: Buckinghamshire (yes I know!)
PURCHASE: Steak Cornish Pasty £3.70
PLACE: 6.5 "No I don't want any drinks or wedges to go with it, not at them fookin' prices"
PASTRY: 7 Traditional or not, I can't say I'm a huge fan of the large roll of pastry with nothing in it brought on by a side crimp
PRESENTATION: 7 You can almost smell the West Country! That might just be the 18.32 from Penzance arriving though
PACKAGE: 7.5 Ample chunks of chuck steak and lots of veg, although the potato slices have dark edges, is this gravy stock or is it actually mushroom? Ambiguous
PALATE: 8 Well seasoned and the meat is complimented beautifully with carrots and swedes
PRICE: 6 A double hit of London prices and train station concourse extortion
PORTION: 9 And this wasn't even the biggest!
OVERALL: 51/70 Yes I know the Penzance train would arrive at Paddington.

And with that opportunistic hit he waves his bat skywards and wipes the sweat from his brow to milk the applause.

I suppose at this point I had better garner some feedback but unfortunately I'll have to guess what abuse you're flinging at me, reader, given the somewhat antiquated nature of this periodical.

You want me to stop eating so many meat and potato pies?

Not a chance! I will however cut down and mix it up a bit more, how's that?

And you want me to get out of the North West a bit more?

Understandable. Although this approach is primarily driven by budget constraints, I am pleased to report that trips to Leicestershire, Sheffield, Cornwall, Norfolk and Scotland have all been pencilled in for the forthcoming months.

I intend to seek out excellence on your behalf, dear reader. Let's start with a trip to the Midlands...

VARIETY IS THE PIES OF LIFE

Rabbit & Red Onion Pie
from Parkside Farm Shop

Scotch Pie from Boghall Butchers

Pauls' Christmas Pie

A Bedfordshire Clanger from Gunns Bakery

A Ludlow Fidget Pie

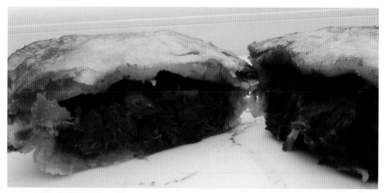

Venison & Red Wine Pie from Harts of Cricklade

It's the infamous Pie & Ale Horse Pie

NZ Gourmet: Mike's Chilli Beef Pie

Boxing Day Turkey Curry Pie
from the Great North Pie Co

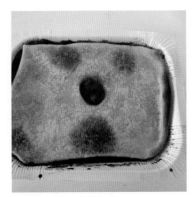

Gents Lancashire Hot Pot

Burbush's Pork & Gooseberry Pie

"The Publican" by Legges of Bromyard – A Steak & Stilton Pie

Macaroni Pie by Murdoch Brothers Butchers

A Game Pie from BW Deacons Butchers

A gigantic Steak Pudding served up by The Mill at Conder Green

A Vegetarian Mexican Cheese & Chilli Pie from Sakers of Hebden Bridge

Greenhalghs' Chicken Tikka Pie

The Bakewell Tart Shop's Dales Lamb & Leek Pie

A Minced Beef Bridie from Mhor Bakery

A Proper Yorkshire Growler: Percy's Pork Pie

A Proper Yorkshire Growler: Percy's Pork Pie – The inside view

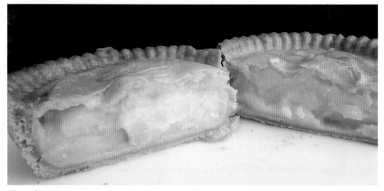

Glovers' Butter Pie

Gourmet pub dining: Steak & Guinness Pie
from the Farmers Boy Inn (Gloucester)

A classic Meat & Potato Pie
from Foodcraft of Winsford

A sumptuous looking Steak Pie from Wienholts of Alderley Edge

The meaty filling

Part 2: 101-200

Aka: These pants are getting tighter

Oh – you want to know which pie is leading don't you? You really sad ones will have worked it out already. Well I'm not telling you. Don't get a COB on with me!

Saturday 28th July 2012

I'd never stoop so low as to use a shit "sent to Coventry" joke but it's hardly surprising it is a common metaphor given my inability to locate a decent pie within its environs.

The pressure to uncover something original and tasty means before I head anywhere unknown, I like to Google my little arse off. After much pissing about, I get all giddy upon discovering that the big thing in Coventry is triangular pastry parcels filled with mince called Godcakes. They've started re-selling them in the transport museum cafe and they're baked using a secret 200 year old recipe. This is exactly the sort of quirky shit I'm looking for!

Oh hang on, it might be shaped like a pasty but contains sweet mince. Bollocks to that then, it isn't even Christmas! I suppose the clue should have been in the name really i.e. CAKE you dozy get. Well thanks but no thanks Coventry. The search goes on.

I find a baker called Carl from Bedworth, who's submitted a pie to re-place Betty's hotpot for a competition but he doesn't have a shop, he appears to just be a man called Carl who lives in a house and bakes pies. At the other extreme I find Aubrey Allen, butcher to the stars (well celebrity chefs) but it appears to be a meat only butchers. When I try looking up bakers in Coventry I end up on the Wikipedia page for ex Stockport now Coventry forward Carl Baker. I don't get these problems when I trundle up the road to Bolton!

After a good hour of searching through the minefield, I clap eyes upon John Taylor Butchers. Splendid, I'm on me way!

For Birmingham itself I find a link reviewing the country's top ten pork pies and Walter Smiths is prominent. But beyond that I'm getting re-directed to Birmingham, Alabama. And when I Google local chain Braggs it turns out it has been bought by Greggs and rebranded. There's a West Indian bakery in the centre of Birmingham, although they sell jerk chicken they don't appear to put a lid on it. I decide I will head to Urban Pie in The Bullring and have a gander around the market to see what I can sniff out.

Nevertheless the journey down is seamless apart from a Sikh gentleman nearly ending it all by swerving across all eight lanes of the M6/M42 section of the toll road in his white van. Off the A45 into Coventry and it's surprisingly rural with no urban landscape magically rising up in front of me, even when the sign appears: Welcome to Coventry – home of peace and reconciliation. Aww, that's nice! I assume it refers to World War Two and not the Eighties riots. Nor The Specials, the car industry or Lady Godiva.

I get to Earlesden and find John Taylor's butchers perched on the corner of a long dipping street of terraced houses which winds all the way down into the city. I am greeted by a gentleman who calls me "Young man", always a vote winner. It's early yet, still only half ten and I can hear chopping and slashing going on in the back room.

They've got loads of chicken and steak pies, sausage rolls and Earlesden pasties: not even named after a county now but being named after a district of a city – audacious! Why do they do this? IT'S A CORNISH PASTY!! They've got plate pies and whopping pork pies and black puddings. Plus a big bowl of faggots for the connoisseurs; they look like chocolate truffles although I suspect they don't taste like them.

101.

PURVEYOR: Taylors Butchers
PREMISES: Coventry
PURCHASE: Chicken Pie £1.50
PLACE: 8 Smiling away from beneath his hat and butcher's clobber
PASTRY: 7 Thick semi-flaky shortcrust
PRESENTATION: 7 Comes in a polythene bag sealed with blue tape
PACKAGE: 7 I know I asked for this but it's just chicken!
PALATE: 6 A bit bland and in desperate need of seasoning
PRICE: 7 High meat content
PORTION: 7 Circular and deep
OVERALL: 49/70 I feel dead harsh, I think my pie decision making let me down here. It would go well as part of a meal I suppose with a sauce and veg to compliment it. Sorry John. Go visit him if you're in Coventry and buy a pie. Don't listen to me, I'm a meanie.

I drive on past a boarded up Subway, schadenfreude eh? There it is: majestic Coventry with tower blocks, office blocks, a huge Ikea and the maddest roads I've ever encountered. It's like being at the airport with ramps, underpasses, flyovers, ring roads, roundabouts, six lanes of traffic weaving left and right and all manner of crazy stuff going on. I'm shitting myself.

Coventry was one of the first football grounds to sell the famous Chicken Balti pie and a quick look at www.famouspies.com tells me they are made by Shire Foods in nearby Leamington. They claim to sell them in supermarkets across Birmingham so it should be a doddle right?

Not right! I end up back in residential sprawl, parked outside some rough boozer painted all sky blue at a bakery called Stoke, (which for clarity is in Coventry not Stoke). It's exceptionally clean in green and white marble, with staff buzzing around and cooking out the back. But where are the pies? There are no pies on sale in this shop! Disaster!

So what do you have then? Sausage Rolls plus deliciously soft looking, hand crimped Cornish pasties and a series of "slices". Slices? Slices? This is not cricket! Slice is what I do when I play golf. Given a choice of chicken, peppered steak and cheese and onion I go for the West Midlands aligned Chicken Balti slice.

102.

PURVEYOR: Stoke Bakery
PREMISES: Coventry
PURCHASE: Chicken Balti Slice £1.35
PLACE: 6 For a) making me walk to the till at the end to pay rather than coming to me and b) warming up my "slice" and completely forgetting about it until prompted by myself. She did apologise
PASTRY: 7 Layered puff pastry
PRESENTATION: 8 Stunk me car out good and proper
PACKAGE: 7 A flimsy thin layer of meat and sauce
PALATE: 8 Rich, spicy balti marinade and onion
PRICE: 7.5 Thin but a weighty slab
PORTION: 7.5 As square as an Apple employee
OVERALL: 51/70 Yep, I'm a sucker for a curried pastry product.

A battle of wits with the bin wagon ensues as I attempt to escape Stoke (Coventry) and make it out on to more dual carriageways, flanked by retail parks and new build estates. The whole infrastructure is so Americanised, no doubt having been re-built so much after the war. I exit Coventry past the space station sized Ricoh Arena and head back on the M6, with the massed banks of Birmingham tower blocks emerging in the distance. I've something of an obsession with these, I had a couple of great aunties who lived in Scholes flats in Wigan and I used to love visiting them and looking down and spitting (sorry Mum). Me Auntie Florrie who lived on the 11th floor of Mannion House was always preferred to my Auntie Nellie who lived on the 2nd floor of Crompton House. But you can't fail to be impressed by the Birmingham skyline though, even if like most places the old tenement flats are being knocked down in favour of plush new apartments.

Heading to Erdington first, which sounds like toxic German lager but I come off the M6 on the wrong side and quickly find myself heading towards Handsworth, Lozells and Aston, all places I remember for being in the news for the wrong reasons back in the Eighties.

I double back and find myself on the other five of the ten lanes on the A38 up Gravelly Hill and onto Erdington High Street. It's a never ending road full of bustle and colourful stalls with a throng of people going about their daily business. Poundland. B&M Bargains. Betfred. Greggs. Looking for Walter Smith, as it happens, and not the former Rangers and Everton manager.

Brummie girls yelling at their kids, West Indian ladies talking with accentuated drawl, Hijab clad women pushing prams, callow youths smoking in shop doorways and sixth form students munching on doughnuts. Is that a bakery? Yes, it's a Firkins, well known across the Midlands but there's no pies. Elsewhere there's a shop called the Silly Lemon (which sells nothing other than lemonade) and an Anglo-Danish catering shop (which just sells bacon and Carlsberg surely?).

Walter's gaff has meat and sausages down one side, pies down the other. I spot the pork pies too late: they're nearly three quid with a dark crust. But I want something to eat now which won't fill me up so I go for a steak pie instead. They've got steak and ale, steak and kidney, sausage rolls and big Cornish pasties. They have cheese, potato and onion pies, but I rebuff the latter due to it looking too much like a cottage pie with potato masquerading as top crust.

Shit. I just bought a Pukka pie! Walter's sold me a pup! The Irish drawl of Loyd Grossman pops into my head....the clues were there....the puff pastry lid....the black foil tray....the "WE SELL PUKKA PIES" sign. I'm regretting my choice as those pork pies were huge with a deep menacing pastry screaming "heartburn" at me but still too good to resist. Ho hum....

103.
PURVEYOR: Walter Smith
PREMISES: Birmingham
PURCHASE: Steak pie £1.50
PLACE: 7.5 **PASTRY:** 7 **PRESENTATION:** 7 **PACKAGE:** 8

PALATE: 7.5 **PRICE:** 6 **PORTION:** 8
OVERALL: 51/70 See previous Pukka Pie review. Walter, I'll be back!

Not to be perturbed I head back into the colossally intimidating centre of Brum, through an area called Millennium Point which is impressively shiny and new but also completely devoid of life. I park up on the Bull Ring market. Never under-estimate the power of a multi storey car park if you're looking for a cheap panoramic view of a city: Tower blocks and Travelodges in abundance, the new Selfridges Bull Ring with its metallic chain metal exterior and a large flock of seagulls who have made it a long way inland to loiter over the fish market.

I wasn't quite sure what the Bull Ring is. In my formative years when I visited, it just seemed to be one ropey looking shopping precinct but it has subsequently been modernised and converted into a vibrant multi-level swish retail paradise. Rejuvenated architecture sits alongside fountains, greenery and the old St Martins' church. Yet still it has traditional indoor and outdoor markets bolted on to its perimeter. I spot a pie stall on the market. See you in a bit pal. First up though it's Urban Pie on the third floor. I get there eventually, after doing three laps of the ring and circling a million designer clothes stores and walking into a mirror at one point.

Handmade gourmet pies: deep filled with the best ingredients, fresh mash, wine and beers. Table for one please, or can I take out? Ooh nice flavours: Aberdeen Angus, Steak and stilton, chicken and mushroom, chicken and gammon, lamb and potato, lamb and mint and so on and they're so deep they look more like steak puddings. They also do sides of Yorkshire puds and wedges along with the more traditional peas and gravy. It's bloody roasting in the Midlands today so I'll pass on the gravy. I enquire about take outs and get a pie in box with the foil tray dispensed with.

104.

PURVEYOR: Urban Pie
PREMISES: Birmingham
PURCHASE: Steak & Stilton Pie £4.15
PLACE: 6 If I'd known they were going to take that long I'd have ordered a beer....but I couldn't as they didn't want to appear to serve me. Shame as it looks a great place for lounging outside watching the well heeled Brummies sauntering in and out of the Hugo Boss shop
PASTRY: 7.5 Bit flaky on top but an edible Urban Pie logo to munch on adds a nice touch

PRESENTATION: 7.5 It comes in a nice heat retaining box which you can organise into a plate, unless you're a Neanderthal like me who prefers to eat food with his hands. A great venue for having a beer and an outside pie whilst watching the world go by

PACKAGE: 8 Deep rather than wide but with generous portions of steak

PALATE: 8 You can't see it or even smell it but as soon as I bite into the jelly-like braising steak the overpowering stilton flavour is mesmerising as my mouth is invaded by some of the cheesiest steak ever produced

PRICE: 7 I'll let them off given it's city centre prices. Well packaged, borderline gourmet pie etc etc

PORTION: 7.5 Deeper than Loch Ness after a month of continuous rain

OVERALL: 51.5/70 McService with a "do you want wedges with that?" Lovely pies mind.

I brace myself and enter the mayhem that is the Bull Ring market and I am immediately hit with an avalanche of smells, sights and sounds. They're selling fruits here I've never heard of, from paopu to araza, meanwhile across the road a couple taking a photo of the church knock over a drunk man eating a peach. The sound of hollering pierces the air as I pass by Mick the Meats van, who sadly does not encase his meats in pastry then I gingerly approach Chilly Billys stall. Market stall prices, market stall value: you can have two chicken and mushroom or mince and onion for a quid, or two Cornish pasties for the same price or just the one family pie. Four continental cheeses for a quid from Emmental to Camembert, blimey.

Pork Pies, three for a quid. Bollocks to it, let's get a big one for a whole pound.

I suspect we're all guilty of paying a visit to a supermarket and doing a big shop but I hope the trusty old fashioned market never loses its presence. Full of energy, vibrancy, bonhomie and a mild amount of aggression and suppressed violence. All forms of life exist here, long may it thrive! Sikh lads in England shirts, Asian ladies in Burkhas and drunken Harold Ramps, Birmingham has it all. If I have one criticism, it's that people don't seem to understand what a car is, given their penchant for stepping in front of mine. I will run you over make no mistake about it. I'm such a pedantic twat I'll do it solely to make my point.

105.

PURVEYOR: Chilly Billys
PREMISES: Birmingham
PURCHASE: (Very) large Pork Pie £1
PLACE: 9 Rude, noisy, abrupt and impersonal. I love it.
PASTRY: 7 Dense and hand raised, you'll pay more for less.

PRESENTATION: 7 Served and eaten cold
PACKAGE: 8 On volume alone there's a huge romping ball of (possibly cheap) sausage inside
PALATE: 7 A bit bland really, I think I was seduced by the size
PRICE: 9 No sting in the bull ring
PORTION: 9 Bigger than an actual pig
OVERALL: 56/70 I'll be honest, I always had Birmingham down as something of a non-entity but in the last half hour it has charmed the arse off me.

I exit the city centre via the De La Tour Hotel named after Frances of Rising Damp fame, a noted Brummie. Before you know it, I'm back on the A38 driving the wrong way through a tunnel whilst my SatNav tells me to do a U turn on what is probably the second busiest road in the country. I hit some lights and a heavily pregnant Asian girl chucks a bottle of water over my car and gets the squeezy out. Shite!!! Nothing to do but give her a couple of quid; feels a bit sad, firstly because I'm a cheapskate but secondly because I've just passed a five star hotel and a handful of rich bastards in this country are making poor people suffer by forcing them into doing shit like this. Luxury and poverty always did sit very closely to each other no matter where I've lived.

Back into Birmingham again. This time past the Fiveways Shopping Centre, where the once white building is almost black with grime and then something of a theatrical quarter as the contrast continues. It's simply impossible to navigate the roads in Birmingham unless you've had a frontal lobotomy or you are absolutely certain of where you are going and are prepared to wildly veer left and right at breakneck speed to get there. On through Perry Barr, where the shops are so multicultural that even Greggs haven't moved in and the Crown & Cushion pub advertises chips and patties rather than pies.

I roll up at Aston Expressway Tesco in search of nothing more exotic than a chicken balti pie to round off the day. THERE ARE NO FUCKING CHICKEN BALTI PIES TO BE SEEN! Absolutely bugger all, the best I can muster are Jamaican patties costing a trivial 70 pence.

What's a pattie? Well, according to the wrapper it's tender pieces of meat marinated in the vibrant flavours of traditional jerk recipe including spices, onions and scotch bonnet peppers. For the last bit alone: BRING IT ON!!

Or as Paddy McGuinness might say: let the jerk see the chicken!
Except it's beef.

106.

PURVEYOR: Island Delight
PREMISES: Birmingham
PURCHASE: Jamaican Jerk Beef patty 70p
PLACE: 7 Picked off the shelf
PASTRY: 8 A very different type of crispy, all-shortening, tantalising texture
PRESENTATION: 8 If you mean that kind of heat....
PACKAGE: 7 Not much depth to it but lovely content
PALATE: 9 Beef. Spices. Chillies. Socks well and truly blown off
PRICE: 8.5 A paltry price
PORTION: 7
OVERALL: 54.5/70: It should come with a health warning as it appears to blow torch a hole in my nose through the roof of my mouth as I chomp into it. The cheeky buggers have only given it two out of three chillies on the front, crikey!

So I exit Tesco and exit Birmingham past Uncle Brum's pawnbrokers (Slogan: "Need some money? Ask your uncle!")

I follow my nose. Lost again before you know it: Perry Barr, Perry Common, Perry Groves, Kevin & Perry, I give up. Then through Great Barr which despite its name looks distinctly average. One last hideous roundabout to negotiate and I'm safely homewards on the M6.

Saturday 4th August 2012

Staying local this weekend, I may just nip to Galloways who incredulously weren't even on my pie list, a shocking omission given their inspiration towards this book.

I don't think Galloways have been around that long but you can barely visit a shopping precinct in Wigan now without seeing the garish turquoise header, black Galloways lettering and their ubiquitous little baker man piccy assigned to a shop front. Walk out of Wallgate station and you more or less walk into one. They've filled some of the void left by the shutdown of several fine Wigan bakers and much more importantly than that, they make amazing pies. Generally regarded to be the best in Wigan (although I may find one or two to challenge that theory), and a real force to be reckoned with, yet despite their success and growth, they're still a very localised brand.

As I arrive in Standish, every third person seems to be carrying their uniform green bag of goodies; be they glammed up yummy mummies wearing wraparound shades fresh from their spray tans to doddery pensioners. As I turn the corner the queue is spilling out into the High Street.

Waiting time is around three minutes, just enough for me to survey the scene and Galloways is always a very open kitchen with doors almost as wide as the shop itself. In front is a wide expanse of pie display including several racks of potato and meat pies (called meat and potato in the meal deal above – stuff the EU regulations) but anyway what that means is you can get pie, peas and gravy for £1.79. You can have cheese and onion, chunky steak, minced steak, party meat, pork pies, chicken and mushroom, butter pies, pasties, turnovers, sausage rolls and on it goes. There's an impressive range of sandwiches and cakes including a Bradley Wiggins gingerbread man complete with novelty sideburns.

I get served and as I walk out past the dry cleaners, the owner is stood outside his sweltering shop and spots my beaming little face with a pie in my hand.

"You're going to enjoy that pie aren't you lad?"

I am my friend. I am.

107.

PURVEYOR: Galloways
PREMISES: Wigan
PURCHASE: Potato and Meat Pie £1.35
PLACE: 7 SHE ASKS ME TO REPEAT MYSELF!!! Shocking! I expect that if I'm down south but in Wigan?? My Wiggin accent is hardly the broadest but if anything that should help. Mildly offended here
PASTRY: 9 Beautifully soft but never soggy, with the trademark peepholes in the top which dried gravy and filling gently oozes out of. Despite this flexible exterior they can usually be adeptly eaten by hand without the contents slopping out
PRESENTATION: 8.5 An orgasmic smell and a volcanically hot foil tray
PACKAGE: 9 Rammed full of mashed potato and mince which attacks me head on as I bite into it
PALATE: 9 An explosion in the mouth of peppery meat and potato mush which never disappoints. You just have to try this pie once in your life. I've been told to give Galloways a shit review, as my mate's brother owns them, but I can't do it
PRICE: 7.5 Not cheap but a quality offering
PORTION: 8 Deceptively large in that it's a semi-plate pie wider at the top than the bottom

OVERALL: 58/70 Bar well and truly raised. Galloways simply produce a winning formula which is simply adored by the ravenous locals. Britain's best? We'll see!

You've probably established by now that I'm something of a fussy eater but I'm positively adventurous compared to Emma. So it comes to pass that I have to go to Greenhalghs in Shevington as well, as she will only eat cheese pasties, not cheese and onion pies. She's letting me run wild on a pie trail for a good two years or so, therefore it's my duty to keep her happy with her savoury of choice. For me, this calls for a "bonus pie".

So what's new? This time they've gone for Olympic donuts with different coloured icing in tribute to the Olympic rings, which are as ornately decorated as the tattoo on the back of the woman's neck in front of me, which appears to state her date of birth. She's still going to need at least two mirrors there if she ever forgets it.

They've got large hand crimped steak and ale pies, doughy and tempting potato cakes and at least four types of pork and whist pies and there in front of me I spy a chicken tikka pie. Intriguing. Maybe I didn't have to go to Birmingham after all....

108.

PURVEYOR: Greenhalghs
PREMISES: Bolton
PURCHASE: Chicken Tikka Pie £1.35
PLACE: 8 A most amiable young lady
PASTRY: 8 The crust lid is almost sunken into the filling beneath it but this gives it a real unique handmade feel to it
PRESENTATION: 7 From hot plate to hand in seconds
PACKAGE: 8 Sizeable chunks of chicken flavoured in a fruity tikka sauce
PALATE: 9 I like to tackle a vindaloo and can often be seen with sweat pumping out of my head, eyes and ears when attempting to navigate one. But when I cut this open and lick the knife, I have to say it's got a respectable kick to it
PRICE: 7.5 Standard
PORTION: 6.5 A touch small but compensated by the densely packed filling with not a square millimetre wasted inside
OVERALL: 54/70 A pocket rocket and an enjoyable distraction!

Tuesday 7th August 2012

Once more into the breach; well the gridlock that is Macclesfield town centre and on to the village of Bollington on the edge of the Peak District.

Any pie based almanac would remain sorely incomplete without sampling a pie known colloquially by the Cheshire Pie Society as a "Bellfields Bollington Belter". An indicator to the rough terrain ahead is in evidence as the rain starts to pour and signs for sheepdog trials emerge. I pass a cotton mill with a big chimney, a chippy, a butcher's and a conservative club (well we are in rural England I suppose) and just before the road leads all the way up to the sky, I spy Bellfield's village bakery and convenience store opposite a picture postcard church.

It's much more than a bakery, it's a proper village store with wall to wall cans of beans and dog food whilst the windows are taken up with community announcements and adverts for home helps. Oh, plus a tabletop display of pies, with a range of rich looking cakes including Bakewell tarts which catch my eye.

109.

PURVEYOR: Bellfields
PREMISES: Bollington
PURCHASE: Meat and potato pie £1.50
PLACE: 8 "What can I get you me darling?" says one of the old girls as she sees me peering around in a shifty manner
PASTRY: 8 Dark and soft
PRESENTATION: 8 Aromatic and spicy hue
PACKAGE: 7 Not quite full and an interesting addition of onion and little orange flecks of carrot in there, complimenting the staple brown mince and potato chunks
PALATE: 9 Does the job. Heavily seasoned with salt and pepper and the carrot bolstering the flavour further. Spicier than the chicken balti I had the other day in fact
PRICE: A borderline 7
PORTION: A borderline 7
OVERALL: 54/70 La la la....let's put our fingers in our ears and not worry about salt and pepper levels and say that this is a great pie!

Friday 10th August 2012

Sheffield at last!! We're up against the clock as it's quarter to ten and Emma's nothing like ready. A lot of these places close at 1 o'clock! Pies are the food of the working man and the working man has usually concluded his dinner by 1pm. Plus any baker worth his proportionally added salt has usually sold out of pies by lunchtime, it's the law! And anyone who hasn't worked up an appetite to eat a pie by 1 o'clock simply doesn't deserve one. My answers come courtesy of *www.sheffieldforum.co.uk* with a pie thread returning loads of good suggestions along with some cracking country walk recommendations.

Soon after we start to traverse the beautiful, rolling desolate green hills which envelope the Snake Pass, the petrol light flashes on and we're forced to nervously meander the contours and hairpins in neutral to save fuel. I have the foresight of an amoeba. This is irritating the boy racer's convention going on judging by the dozens of young men teararsing around the Peak District with their shit hashtags like #fastroar and other charming slogans such as "NO SMOKE NO POKE" emblazoned across the back of their fat exhausted penis extenders. They sit uneasily alongside walkers plodding along the main road, sheep perched halfway up cliffs ready to topple in front of a lorry at any point and cyclists who have bitten off more than they can chew in their bid to emulate Wiggins, peddling backwards up hills, sweating like pot bellied pigs in ill-fitting lycra. Just a standard British summer time!

The sight of stunning, radiant fir trees lining the road above the Lady Bower Reservoir, shimmering in the reflection of glorious sunshine, helps to ease concerns that the needle is now horizontal. We eventually spot rooftops of houses peering out until a mile or so later we land slap bang in the centre of Hillsborough, where trams and cars jostle on the same tracks as I locate my prey.

Lilys: big, bold, double fronted, set back off the main road with a large car park at the rear. Doing brisk trade and full of the familiar swagger of football casuals, though I've no idea if there's a game on. They're all stood in a huddle which makes it hard for me to ascertain the queuing system and are slowing me up by asking for daft shit like a pork crackling sandwich and a sausage, egg, tomato, bacon and mushroom baton – surely quicker to say "give us the works love"?

110.

PURVEYOR: Lilys
PREMISES: Sheffield
PURCHASE: Steak and potato pie £2.25
PLACE: 7 Big queue quickly resolved
PASTRY: 8 Splendidly encased shortcrust
PRESENTATION: 8 Served cold but in a delightful wrapper: "God bless Lily's for real bread and taste!!"
PACKAGE: 9 For a flat plate pie, there's some gigantic chunks of meat and spud packed into it and plenty gravy swilling around too
PALATE: 8 The individual components do the job but combined it feels in need of a bit more oomph and flavour

PRICE: 7 Not cheap but you'd struggle to eat two
PORTION: 9 Like a golden meat filled flat cap
OVERALL: 56/70 Big place, big pies, impressed with everything apart from possibly the price.

Happy to get out alive given some of the ruffians knocking about, I leg it for petrol, where they sell the Green 'Un on the counter, the Yorkshire Football Pink and from there I spot Bere's Pork Shop! The official pies of Sheffield Wednesday no less.

Wonder how you pronounce it? Is it Beers, Bears, Ber-ries or Be-rets? I walk in and around six women jump on me (a position I frequently find myself in) but first I need to digest what is in front of me: Pork, lots of it. I've seen parts of a pig I didn't know existed in here. They've got large pork pies, pork dripping and black puddings on display, along with a huge joint for pork rolls. I get a cold steak and a monster of a sausage roll for the missus (which I ate).

111.

PURVEYOR: Beres
PREMISES: Sheffield
PURCHASE: Steak and potato pie £1.29
PLACE: 8 Bold and brassy staff yet as efficient as German railway workers
PASTRY: 7.5 Rugged crust lip and dark, lardy glaze
PRESENTATION: 7 The wrapper advises to exercise caution as it contains crackling, only recommended for people with strong teeth. This evokes visions of numerous gummy Sheffield folk wandering around the streets looking for their missing gnashers because they had too many pies
PACKAGE: 7.5 An almost wholly meat and jelly based filling with the odd lump of potato lobbed in
PALATE: 7 Rich and meaty. Definitely steak and potato around here compared to the weedy potato laden version we have over in Lancashire
PRICE: 8
PORTION: 8
OVERALL: 53/70 As I take it out of the oven the dark pigment of the gravy refuses to dislodge from the foil tray and I have to get a knife on the job. Not a problem here, however, I can't see that producing a knife from the pocket to do the same at a Sheffield Wednesday match and then walking around with the serrated edge of a pie foil tray would go down too well.

As I walk out of Bere's on Middlewood Road I am confronted by three more bakeries all within my eyeline: Brook bakery, Helen's bakery and Staniforths bakers and confectioners no less. "Right love, you don't mind sitting in the car a bit longer do you?"

It's a pie strip – you know like they have in Magaluf or Kavos but a succession of bakers instead. Helen goes flat on the pie dimensions as well. It's 24 hours later when I heat this one up. I get it out of the oven and oh Helen, what are you doing? We've got a collapser! When I remove it from the tray, the crust disintegrates. It expires in my fingers into a dozen pieces. Just as well it was sold cold as there could have been serious repercussions had I attempted to eat it with my bare hands.

112.

PURVEYOR: Helens
PREMISES: Sheffield
PURCHASE: Steak and Potato Pie £1.35
PLACE: 7 **PASTRY:** 5 **PRESENTATION:** 7 **PACKAGE:** 8
PALATE: 8 **PRICE:** 7.5 **PORTION:** 7
OVERALL: 49.5/70 Crust disaster aside, this was errmm....different.
A load of cheesy mash in one half of the pie and two whopping chunks of steak in the other, giving it an almost cottage pie type feel to it.

I cross the road to Staniforths where a courteous lady tells me their product range and I'm off again procuring the one solitary steak and potato pie left.

113.

PURVEYOR: Staniforths
PREMISES: Rotherham
PURCHASE: Steak and Potato Pie £1.08
PLACE: 8 **PASTRY:** 7.5 **PRESENTATION:** 8 **PACKAGE:** 7
PALATE: 8 **PRICE:** 8 **PORTION:** 7
OVERALL: 53.5/70 The only hot pie I manage to procure in Sheffield all day. Again it has a high meat ratio, sweet gravy and a dark, devious, flaky crust.

Knowing my luck, the one I didn't visit will turn out to be a blinder but to find so many outlets in such a small space is indeed pie heaven. The residents of Owlerton and Hillsborough are truly spoilt.

Onwards into Sheffield down Penistone Road dodging trams left, right and centre and taking care not to get distracted by the thirty foot tall picture of Jessica Ennis on a wall, we head south of the city with Bramall Lane and Wards brewery emerging in the distance.

To Ecclesall Road, another notable thoroughfare, a little more bohemian and studenty than the north of the city. Café bars, gastro pubs, Nandos and a gunsmiths – WHAT?!?! No matter how vibrant, I wouldn't like to walk it mind as it's a good two miles uphill before I spot the big green canopy of Sean's bakery. I'm served by a cheery Irish chap. I don't know if he's Sean himself but like everything else he's also totally green. At least wearing a big green apron to match the big Irish cartoon font on the signage and generally green paint and decorations that have been festooned all over the premises. So long as the pies aren't green!

114.

PURVEYOR: Seans
PREMISES: Sheffield
PURCHASE: Steak and Potato Pie £1.75
PLACE: 7 **PASTRY:** 8 **PRESENTATION:** 7 **PACKAGE:** 9
PALATE: 8 **PRICE:** 7 **PORTION:** 8
OVERALL: 54/70 A big oblong, pie (served cold again – do people not eat pies on the fly around here?) it's substantially packed in flavour – rich potatoes and hearty slabs of meat with a tasty savoury gravy flowing through. Ideal teamed up with a homemade Scotch egg.

I give up on one last target – O'Reillys on Mansfield Road as it's too far away when I've two restless girls in the car and although I land upon a totally red establishment called Rosies, they have no pies left, just a cheese and onion roll and a wedding cake.

I call the competition to a halt for the day and we make for Bakewell to spend the afternoon pottering by the river looking out for tarts. We head through beautiful, undulating valleys, flanked by gastro pubs and scary speed cameras which look like shit Star War droids, as I nearly kill the lot of us when I crane my neck to look down a street where I suspect there's a pie shop.

It's a rare balmy, sunny day. We spend the afternoon feeding the ducks by the River Wye and Jess runs about in the playground with an outdoor splash area.

Bakewell is a quaint, picture postcard Peak district town only polluted by the fumes of a thousand motorbikes pummelling the A6, destroying the calm. There's a wedding going on too, the attendees consisting of around 500 almost exclusively Afro-Caribbean ladies and gentlemen who are now wandering around this pretty little town in sharp suits, bling and shades, dancing along to a busker playing jazz on his saxophone, creating quite a spectacle.

It doesn't take long before my head gets turned however and The

Bakewell Tart Coffee house appear to be selling pies, so DJ let's play one more tune. They've got a raft of pasties and a range of pies including a Huntsman's pie (lamb, turkey and stuffing), spinach and feta cheese pasty (no thanks), award winning steak pies and the ubiquitous pork pie. I opt to purchase a traditional Dales lamb and leek pie for £2.25 along with a whopper of a Bakewell tart – not a Bakewell pudding; its predecessor which usually comes without icing.

115.

PURVEYOR: Bakewell Tart Shop & Coffee House
PREMISES: Bakewell
PURCHASE: Lamb and Leek Pie £2.25
PLACE: 7 I'll assume she's not being sarcastic when I ask how much the big Bakewell tarts are and she says "£6.95 they've all got the prices on" Dickhead
PASTRY: 8 Sturdy, dense and with a flower on top. Not that sturdy though as a trusty knife and fork has to come out
PRESENTATION: 7 Cooked to perfection by myself with brilliant moistness inside
PACKAGE: 8 A spot of subsidence but a good inch and a half deep with tender chunks of lamb, luminous green slices of leek and a hint of mint
PALATE: 8 Once I've acclimatised to the flavour contrast it grows on me considerably
PRICE: 7.5 For a gourmet pie, this is not a bad price. The Bakewell tart on the other hand....
PORTION: 8 A robust door stopper of a pie
OVERALL: 53.5/70 As the old nursery rhyme goes: Mary had a little lamb, until some tit from Wigan ate it.

Saturday 11th August 2012

It's 25 degrees outside and whereas it might be splendid weather for a jaunt around middle England, there's no bloody way I'm sitting in a car for four hours with the family in tow.

So I'm checking out Bowens of Adlington. I chanced upon them mainly because I saw a van go past me the other day and also that they were the suppliers for last year's World pie eating contest (held in Wigan obviously!) Their website features gratuitous, full frontal, minced beef and potato pie photos with no 9pm watershed and they also do their own steak puddings, another fine Lancashire delicacy. I need to refrain from making any disparaging comments about Adlington or its natives however as my wife teaches there.

A brief jalopy up Chorley Road past the infamous Duxbury Park golf course, where I once shot an impressive 120 taking so long to go around that they'd shut the place by the time I finished and I had to get a taxi home wearing my golf shoes. Wouldn't mind but I'd cheated on a number of holes too. It's heavy going on the roads due to the sheer volume of middle aged fat wankers wobbling down the road on racers. It's as if a local lad has just won the Tour de France or something!

Bowens is across the road from Babylon Lane, not on it and hence ruining my attempts to do a poor gag about Babylon Lane being paradise. Nevertheless it's bright blue sign draws me across the busy road like a tractor beam. A little girl playfully blocks my way and refuses to let me gain ingress to the premises, until a big fat fella with protruding teeth (presumably her dad) tells her to "gerrout road!!" I blame the teachers myself!!

There is a huge, high, silver counter dominating the shop containing a myriad of products and a handful of staff in aprons wearing pork pie hats beavering away. Service is brisk, just as well as I'm on double yellows. Lots of pies and as a giddy compliment I partake in the rack of Lancashire crisps on display, including Salt and Ellseys vinegar – an old traditional Wigan vinegar company and Bumble's favourite Lancashire sauce flavour crisps.

The pie? Oh yes, it's a blinder!!

116.

PURVEYOR: Bowens
PREMISES: Adlington, nr Chorley
PURCHASE: Meat and Potato Pie £1.19
PLACE: 8 Polite and brisk
PASTRY: 8 A sturdy, solid shortcrust
PRESENTATION: 8 Even with the window down full, it still smells lush in my car and is piping hot 30 minutes later when I tuck in
PACKAGE: 9 Huge uncompromising slabs of golden spud concatenated with lots of flowing meat and juices
PALATE: 9 Hits the spot from the first bite with a hint of pepper but natural flavour pouring out too
PRICE: 8.5 Good price and great value
PORTION: 9 Possessing both width and girth, I mean depth
OVERALL: 59.5/70 Exceptional, we are truly spoilt around these parts. At the risk of sounding parochial, whoever's written that "top 10 pies" article on the MSN website is talking out of their arse and needs to spend the day around the North West scoffing a few of these beauties. A truly phenomenal pie and the crisps were fantastic too.

Chorley next and after tweeting a piccy of my Galloways pie the other week, not only was I unfollowed by @PoundBakery who got the hump because I made some derogatory comment about them but I was also inundated with alternative suggestions from fellow pie lovers.

A Blackburn Rovers fan who buys the mag comes straight back with a Halls "pie barm". I check them out and find their website proclaiming they are "the proper pie shop" (so beware all those fake ones out there) and the owner Joe Hall has got a blog on there going under the ingenious title of Joe Blogs. They've just employed a new driver!

I pull onto Eaves Lane next to a Police car. Halls has a deli feel to it with a big sandwich and cafe area, set aside from the pie racks and a visible kitchen at the back. Yet it also has a community feel with ads and a noticeboard telling patrons about all the riveting stuff that's going on in Chorley.

I plump for the potato and meat again (£1.16) although mull over teaming it up with a mini "whist pie". They wrap my pie up like a bag of chips and send me on my way. As I return to the car I spot what looks suspiciously like a discarded adult magazine in the bushes next to it. A rarity indeed in these times! Have we got some explaining to do officers? No it's just one of those cheap tabloid TV guides you fool, shut up and eat your pie!

117.

PURVEYOR: Halls
PREMISES: Chorley
PURCHASE: Potato and Meat Pie £1.16
PLACE: 8 **PASTRY:** 8 **PRESENTATION:** 7.5
PACKAGE: 8 **PALATE:** 8
PRICE: 8 **PORTION:** 7
OVERALL: 54.5/70 Another great pie where the meat juices fusion perfectly with the potato, and there's possibly a bit of swede in there for good measure. Perhaps room for a little more filling mind you within its soft, seductive crust.

Today's job done as I nip to the chemist to get the missus some headache pills and try not to mow down too many cyclists on the way. Turns out there's a clay pigeon shooting event going on in West Lancashire today. Odd hobby that. Says the man travelling around the country scoffing pies.

Friday 17th August 2012

I can be a reet devious get when I want to be. You see we're off to a wedding in the Lakes this weekend and Emma needs something for her outfit.

"Why don't we get up there early and get it when you're there?" I helpfully suggest.

"There's no shops in the Lakes is there?" she replies.

"Yeah good point, but there's a Next in Barrow, that's *near* the Lakes".

The plan hasn't just been hatched, there's been a yellow fluffy chick chirping away inside my head for weeks.

The next step is a novel one: having to ring through to secure your order. This, however is no ordinary pie shop. It is the baked product vendor of choice of none other than Dave Myers, 50% of the Hairy Bikers. It is where the chefs get their nosebag no less.

Looking at a picture of it, it's a 70's throwback, with white letraset on a green sign perched above the top of the shop at the end of a row of a terraced houses on a council estate. Looks right up my street, indeed evokes romantic memories of the sort of pie shop that you'd find on every street corner during my childhood in Wigan.

Google sends me onto a deep journey into Barrow pie making history. It seems that the meat and potato version is an abundant delicacy in this corner of the world with many, many independent bakers which of course introduces a healthy rivalry, not to mention high standard but low cost pies. Thomas' and McLeys seem to be all laying claim to a better pie than the biker's fave. I can see this one's going to merit a re-visit. It might have been derided by Mike Harding as being the longest cul-de-sac in the world but if it's pies you're after it seems well worth the trip!

I ring through and there's the usual accent babble not helped by a lively cacophony of background noise and I arrange to pick up my pies at half twelve. It's barely half nine and I'm ready but I'm adding an hour "wife time" before we hit the road.

The grim wet and windy approach to Barrow is only illuminated by the stunning Furness Abbey and the Chequers Hotel, until the vast fading beige BAE Ship building yard towers above the skyline, nothing beyond it but the Irish Sea. Perhaps an indicator as to why it's hungry servants require such a diverse calibre of pie shops, full of hungry navvies desperate to get their gums around meat clothed in pastry.

The outskirts are spacious and green considering it's peninsula form and it's only when you get deep into the heart of Barrow that it gets claustrophobically compact, as we weave through an old council estate waiting for Bath Street and Greens to magically appear in front of us.

It's completely unchanged from the photos complete with people queuing out the door and the oldest moped in the Northern Hemisphere parked outside, adorned with huge wing mirrors and shopping basket. The corner plot is no different from any of the houses around it: red brick walls and white pebble slate; street names on the corners. Time for the Greens experience then!

The fella in front of me looks three days older than Moses and I suspect is the proprietor of said motorcycle. The big white crash helmet and Morrisons bag gives it away somewhat. He asks for steak and kidney but they've all gone. Should have ordered old boy!!

Soon after the local constabulary walk in – coppers seem to eat more pies than me! They wait in line whilst jovially cracking funnies as everyone calls them by their first names.

Greens sell nothing else other than pies, cakes and a few bottles of pop and it really is like a step back in time as working class Barrovians wait for their lunch. There's a polite sign on the wall informing customers that they will be putting the price up by 10p shortly to cover the increased cost of ingredients, along with a sign asking that if ordering more than 20 please collect after 12.30. They've got steak and ale, pork, dinky meat pies, the aforementioned steak and kidney, meat and potato and cheese and potato, the latter, which are sold out. Sorry Emma!

I'm getting twitchy here, especially when the staff are scurrying everywhere trying to locate their elusive pies but I need not worry, mine are reserved, hot and fresh. It's £1.15 for a meat and potato pie so I collect a couple; large, weighty and no foil tray.

As I drive onwards, I spot a chippy (closed) on the next street corner and indeed you can tell from the fascias that every corner terrace used to be a shop a few years ago. The only actual other bakery I see goes by the frankly terrible title of Baguette-Me-Not. I park up in Morrisons, facing a restaurant on a boat and the huge BAE building looming behind. I'm as giddy as a puppy about to cut new teeth into a table leg.

118.

PURVEYOR: Greens
PREMISES: Barrow-in-Furness
PURCHASE: Meat and Potato Pie £1.15
PLACE: 8 Splendidly colloquial and friendly but they give me a quizzical look upon realising I have pre-ordered which says "He's not from around here, must be one of those fancy pants writer types"
PASTRY: 8.5 Tender shortcrust softer than an angel crying on your tongue
PRESENTATION: 9 My car reeks of heavenly pie
PACKAGE: 9 Externally it doesn't look at all spectacular but once I open it up I'm left in awe as to how they pack it all in. Layer after layer of thick spud slice expanding like a concertina. It looks like one of those penny

drops at the fairground where the chutes zig zag. There's meat in there as well and juice running all over the show giving a hot pork pie effect when you reach the lower part of the casing

PALATE: 9.5 Yes! Yes! Yes! Absolutely amazing! That's what I'm talking about! This is what I've been searching for!! Dee-lish-ious. Fresh and generously soft Maris Piper potatoes (I believe) complimented with little nuggets of minced beef and gravy running wild inside

PRICE: 9 Even managed to get in before the highly apologetic price rise

PORTION: 8 Deceptively deep and well compressed

OVERALL: 61/70 I've seen the 8th wonder of the world, Greens be thy name. While the girls are still in Morrisons I take the opportunity to devour the second. In terms of reviewer's objectivity, when I only buy a singular pie from a shop, there's always that chance I get a particularly good or bad one. Well this one's even better! Absolute pastry perfection. I'm in love.

Sunday 19th August 2012

Sunday morning. In Keswick. Hung over and need petrol. Even the natural beauty of the Borrowdale pass and the invigorating calm of Derwent Water isn't clearing my head. There's a pie on the shelf. A Cranston's potato and meat pie. I can even put it on the joint account while I'm paying for petrol.

119.
PURVEYOR: Cranstons
PREMISES: Penrith
PURCHASE: Potato and Meat pie £1.09
PLACE: 7 PASTRY: 7 PRESENTATION: 7 PACKAGE: 7
PALATE: 7 PRICE: 7 PORTION: 7
OVERALL: 49/70 Velvety top crust filled with pork rather than beef, though I barely notice at 8am on a Sunday morning with a stinking hangover. Anyway, now I've just bought a pie from a petrol station, I'm off to the butchers for a gallon of unleaded.

Friday 24th August 2012

A Sainsburys Friday night ale run and of course sourcing a pastry based treat. On my left is the Pieminster Shamrock pie containing tender beef-steak, famous Irish stout (YOU CAN SAY WHICH ONE PIEMINSTER, I THINK WE'VE ALL GUESSED!!) and rich gravy with 26% beef content. On my right a Higgidy Spinach and Pine Nut Pie is on offer. Yeah I know spinach was good enough for Popeye but on this occasion Higgidy you can stick your pine nuts up your arrrs....

....anyway, as you may know, Pieminster are two blokes from Bristol who love pies and have built up a cult following with restaurant stockists and stores publishing books with recipes in and good luck to them. The world needs passionate pie makers otherwise fat bastards like me would have nothing to eat. They promise heaven and perfection on the box so I'm dreaming of big things during the twenty five minutes it takes to blossom in the oven.

Upon removing it I cut it in half and I am viciously assaulted by the sublime waft of flavour and filling which jumps onto the plate. Hearty chunks of beef and carrot, it feels like a beef casserole yet perfectly encased in pie form. I wasn't expecting the volume of carrots but they add plenty of variety to the bite. I don't think this is a pie you can eat with your hands, the way the filling comes seeping out like an erupting volcano, although I do manage half by following the trusty method of keeping the open filling facing upwards.

120.

PURVEYOR: Pieminster
PREMISES: Bristol
PURCHASE: Shamrock (steak and stout) pie £2.09
PLACE: 7 **PASTRY:** 8 **PRESENTATION:** 8 **PACKAGE:** 8.5
PALATE: 9 **PRICE:** 8 **PORTION:** 8
OVERALL: 56.5/70 Rich and rewarding with a mesmerising mix of ingredients (40 listed on the box!) plus a delightfully firm, crispy top crust sprinkled with oats, which is a new one on me. The Pieminster offering throws up opulence personified in every mouthful.

Saturday 25th August 2012

Going to drive all the way to Southampton for a football match. I'm fairly sure that I wouldn't be arsed if it wasn't the opportunity to try a different pie. I had designs on going to Sweeney & Todds in Reading but my mate, who's from round there, doesn't feel too well so we push on to Hampshire. My grand idea of nipping to Portsmouth as well looks a bit daft as the two cities are a fair ride away. My passengers aren't arsed so long as they're kept fed and watered. Just substitute monkey nuts for cans of Strongbow and they're happy. But I can't be arsed either, so it's bye bye Portsmouth pie as I just haven't found enough of note to justify paying it a visit, there looked to be one half decent butchers and that's your lot.

Plested Pies in Shirley appear to be open for business in Southampton so that is where I head to. Shirley has a long, wide shopping street which leans down all the way into the city centre. Plesteds is Southampton's Premier Pie Shop – traditional savoury and fruit pies. For a shop which seems so big on pies, they don't seem to have an awful lot of variety. They've got steak and kidney, chicken and mushroom, chicken curry. That's your lot. Cheese and onion slices, the ubiquitous steak bakes and sausage rolls and Cornish pasties with lots of sugar coated apple and cherry pies.

121.

PURVEYOR: Plested Pies
PREMISES: Southampton
PURCHASE: Steak and Kidney Pie £1.60
PLACE: 7 Polite despite my teenage strop at the lack of choice
PASTRY: 7.5 The decorative flower on the top crust is it's saving grace rather than it's crowning glory I'm afraid. Some of the crust refuses to detach itself from the foil tray as well
PRESENTATION: 6 Purchased at half twelve and barely lukewarm
PACKAGE: 7.5 An innovative touch with the layer of gravy sat on top of the meat filling so that it soaks its' way down, but that aside the filling is nothing spectacular
PALATE: 7 Excellent gravy but the meat is as tasteless as Frankie Boyle
PRICE: 7 Sneaks into a 7
PORTION: 7 Traditional oblong shape
OVERALL: 49/70 In a word, passable.

I go to meet my compatriots who I had earlier dropped in a Wetherspoons, and eat the second half of the pie walking down Shirley High Street to open mouthed stares of astonishment from the locals. Even the old boys sat outside the Brightwater, one of whom is in his 70's and sporting a Burberry's cap looks at me like I've just been beamed down from Mars, less so the gaggle of tramps sat on a bench drinking cans outside the police station.

I order a pint from a member of staff with a "back in the big time" red t-shirt, as it's Southampton's first home game in the Premier League and the place is buzzing. Then it's my turn to get gobsmacked as we drive down to the ground past the biggest boats I've ever seen; as tall as tower blocks and about half a mile long, making the Ikea across the road look like a corner shop. How do they ever stay afloat?

Saturday 1st September 2012

The phrase "I'm just nipping to the Gents" might sound like a funny thing to say in your own home, however, Gents is also the name of a storming pie shop up the road.

It doesn't look much of a place, you wouldn't even know it was there unless you were looking for it. There's no signs or advertisements, just a few cakes and loaves stacked in regimented fashion in the dimly lit window. It seems to be shut a lot of the time, probably because it's owner managed and they famously only bake a limited number of pies, meaning you've no chance of getting one after 12pm. Yet Pepper Lane pie shop (or C&G Gent to give it it's proper name) is rumoured to be the best in Wigan. At the risk of sounding like a cliché riddled football manager, I'm expecting a big, big performance today. Anyway – shit! It's twenty past eleven, as Jose Mourinho might say.

I'm flapping like a crisp packet in the wind as I can visualise that last pie being dispatched from the shelf. There's three people in the shop, each of them using a walking stick. I generally see this as a positive as old people generally know their stuff, despite their penchant for taking forty minutes to fulfil a two minute transaction.

I'm barged out of the way by the first of them, complete with his tartan shopping bag full of goodies and I'm reminded of one of the bakers where I grew up off Gidlow Lane, Wigan. I used to run chores for the old woman across the street who was in her nineties bless her. She used to give me the exact same bag and a list of cakes, loaves and pies to buy along with a little treat for myself.

The window is festooned with all manner of colourful tarts and macaroons organised in linear fashion and although the rest of the shop is a touch sparse, you could easily fill a tartan trolley here.

The woman serving apologises that the pies aren't that hot. However, I am equally mesmerised by the stunning hot pots racked up behind. They're the size of house bricks, they might not technically be a pie but they look too good to resist. Their butter pies are spectacular as well.

122.

PURVEYOR: Gents
PREMISES: Wigan
PURCHASE: Meat and Potato Pie £1.10
PLACE: 8 Superb, authentic, traditional baker with lots of endearing touches, for example, they still work out your bill with pen and paper (My total order = £3.05 including a can of dandelion and burdock)
PASTRY: 8 Delicious, delicate and delightful with rigid, uneven edges complimenting the softer centre and semi-dried gravy seeping out of the

top gently bubbling away
PRESENTATION: 9 Despite what she said it's red hot and emitting
a truly heavenly scent. I put them in the boot of the car while I get my
hair cut and I'm hit with a wall of lovely pie smell when I open it again
ten minutes later
PACKAGE: 9 Packed to the absolute brim and although advertised as a
potato and meat pie, the meat content ratio is high with both braised and
minced beef seemingly present, complimented by large uneven blocks of
golden stock soaked potato
PALATE: 9 Not overly seasoned so you can really savour the individual
components with every mouthful offering something different and
a vibrant Lancashire hot pot stock soaked ambience to it
PRICE: 8 Splendid
PORTION: 7.5
OVERALL: 58.5/70 Breathtaking. Simply perfectly made pies. Just get
there early!

Round two and it's the hot pot up next which comes in a big square paper
tray, a crust which just about covers the top and a plastic table spoon to
eat it with

123.
PURVEYOR: Gents
PREMISES: Wigan
PURCHASE: Hot Pot £1.30
PLACE: 8 **PASTRY:** 7 **PRESENTATION:** 8 **PACKAGE:** 8
PALATE: 9 **PRICE:** 8 **PORTION:** 9
OVERALL: 57/70 From what I can tell the official differences between a
hot pot and a pie are that hot pot is supposedly made with mutton, lamb
or occasionally corned beef and that the ingredients are soaked in stock
longer giving a richer casserole type flavour. Either way this is splendid
again and it makes me sufficiently obliged to get the tape measure out for
the first time since starting the book, so here are this little teaser's vital
statistics: Length 6"/Width 4.5"/Depth 1.5".

Friday 7th September 2012

I'm in Booths, as we're on a mini break in a static caravan at Kirkby Lonsdale, and they have Higgidys: Chicken pot pie with ham and leek and a
steak and ale too. See I just needed to find a different Booths! They've got
Wigan's Pooles pies in the freezer with Hollands, Upper Crust and Denby
Dale. The deli counter has Mrs King's Pork & Stilton pies and there are

some proper posh Charlie Bigham ones, £7 for two in the ready meals aisle. Booths = pie heaven. I'll be filling my boots in here a few times between now and Tuesday.

I appear to have developed a spot of animosity towards the slightly poncey Higgidy pies. They irk me further by calling them "pot pies" – supposedly because it has a lid on it – a top crust is a core requirement of a pie so there is simply no need to add the pot prefix. A pie should be fully encased with a top crust, pastry all around it's circumference and a solid base as you don't want a nasty accident when lifting it out of the tray. Basic rules these.

Higgidy are one of those boutique, niche manufacturers like Innocent smoothies who plaster their packaging with fluffy slogans designed to give the consumer a warm inner glow thus distracting them into overlooking the heavily inflated price.

A lot of their pies seem way too twee for me to even consider but this one has potential, a decent size and I bung it in the oven. What comes out is an absolute delight. I can see leeks, ham, chicken and little red mustard seeds ripe to ping open in my mouth. Even without tasting I can tell aesthetically that the contents are going to assault my tastebuds like a pack of wild teenage ASBO's.

124.

PURVEYOR: Higgidy
PREMISES: Shoreham-by-Sea
PURCHASE: Chicken, ham and leek POT pie £2.69
PLACE: 7
PASTRY: 7.5 Puff pastry is (literally) a waste of space but redeemed somewhat with a pastry love heart on top. Perfectly edible with the hands although the pastry is unwieldy and flies off everywhere
PRESENTATION: 8 Excellent packaging full of words of wisdom and a cute tray, complete with recycling message and warming statements about the chicken and ham – raised on RSPCA approved farms apparently. Great news just as I'm just about to eat the little buggers
PACKAGE: 9 Packed full of goodness: meat, veg all encapsulated in a rich, creamy sauce. Lush
PALATE: 8 A class act or a real teaser? Either way it's fabulous
PRICE: 7 I didn't notice as I was reading about the cute animals
PORTION: 8 Meal sized
OVERALL: 54.5 Sorry Higgidy I was wrong, you can make proper man pies as well, just lay off the pine nuts eh?

Saturday 8th September 2012

Time for an ambitious road trip over to the North East coast: Stockton, Whitby and a day on the farm. Stage one is Kirkby Lonsdale to Kirkby Stephen, neither of which remotely resembles Kirkby Liverpool. I take the A-road upwards rather than the M6 which is a big mistake as the M6 doesn't generally contain the following:

Sheep in the road refusing to move

Beautifully ornate, but ridiculously slow, horse pulled gypsy caravans on their way to Appleby horse fair. Bonus points if the caravan is parked up at the side of the road whilst shirtless youths drink cans.

Fog so dense it could pass as a reality TV show participant

Hopelessly lost fell walkers perusing a map IN THE MIDDLE OF THE FUCKING ROAD

And of course the obligatory farm vehicles. The only time you ever don't see farm vehicles on the road is when you see a sign saying "Farm Vehicles".

Eventually after a lot of bobbing, slamming and weaving, which does Emma's head no good we hit the A66 and head over to the imaginatively named Scotch Corner. As a small child, well a gullible teenager of 14 actually I went to watch Wigan Athletic away at Sunderland and a programme collector called Derek spent the whole journey telling me "wait till you get to Scotch Corner, it's amazing, you'll never have seen anything like it". It's a pile of bricks and a petrol station. Cheers Derek.

The missus ain't the most geographically astute but offers the following commentary "Middlesbrough's a bit rough isn't it?" True but Stockton is very passable and the village of Norton, which we descend upon, is radiating as the sun beams over it in late summer. I even drop my change on the floor of the shop and nobody nicks it.

I park up off the village green with lakes and fountains, and head through the green chainmail entrance to Blackwells. The pies come in two forms, small, round porky ones and oblong beefy versions with a variety of flavours. I plump for a plain old pork pie for £1.35 which feels pleasantly warm in my hands.

125.

PURVEYOR: Blackwells
PREMISES: Stockton-on-Tees
PURCHASE: Pork pie £1.35
PLACE: 7 I'm in and out in 2 minutes 50 seconds. I know this because I left the tape recorder running and I am currently listening to the muffled sound of my phone squelching away in my coat pocket.

PASTRY: 7 Uh-oh detachable crust time, the lid comes off in my hand thus necessitating a two handed job
PRESENTATION: 8 Served warm and re-heated again later with pockets of steam bursting through the funnel in the top
PACKAGE: 7.5 Doesn't look that deep from the top but from the cross section there seems adequate volume to it. The pork is chewy in texture offering a bit of resistance but still easy enough to throw down the old gullet
PALATE: 7.5 The crust redeems itself due to the melted jelly making it splendidly moist
PRICE: 7
PORTION: 7
OVERALL: 51/70 Solid Smoggie growler.

We skirt through the perimeter of the 'Boro with the obligatory transporter bridge shot amidst cranes and cooling towers. Make no mistake we are in the heart of industrial Northern England, despite me following a road sign which says A19 THE SOUTH in large font. My previous jaunt to Middlesbrough was for an England game. We sampled the delights of the long since demolished Club Bongo International, around the back of the station where the women seemed very friendly (possibly because they were prostitutes) and the nearby Glass Bottle which we quickly dubbed the Broken Bottle as the patrons scared the shit out of us and that was just the women.

"Welcome to Redcar in Cleveland". Cleveland? Cleveland, Ohio? I didn't imagine it, it used to be a county right? So is this place Teesside, Cleveland or Yorkshire? I've no idea but just as Ikea has its own multi storey car park in Southampton, the same can be said of the Redcar branch of Primark.

We meander around the coast without actually seeing any houses or people just scrapyards and steelworks and dockyards with the Tata Steel factory in particular seemingly going on for miles. "WE'RE PASSIONATE ABOUT STEEL" states a joint Corus and Tata banner upon entry to the town centre. Me too but about pies pal, so where's the bloody pie shop?

As Redcar contains a beach and a racecourse it has presumably been criminally undersold as a stag do location over the years. The shopping area is low level and terraced and I get scuppered by a descending level crossing as I head seawards to Ellisons of Redcar. Mohawks seem to be the order of the day in the Clip Joint barbers as a fella walks a fierce looking pitbull across the road. This is more than offset by the generosity of a chap in the car park who slips me his unexpired pay and display ticket so that I can nip to get pie number two. Ellisons has a big blue canopy next to the Standard pub and as I saunter in, a woman with close cropped hair picks up on me immediately. She enthusiastically goes through the full range and tells me how hot each of them is despite some linguistic difficulties. I give the game and rabbit pies the swerve and go for a plain old steak.

126.

PURVEYOR: Ellisons
PREMISES: Redcar
PURCHASE: Steak Pie £1.20
PLACE: 8 **PASTRY:** 8
PRESENTATION: 8 **PACKAGE:** 8
PALATE: 7.5 **PRICE:** 7 **PORTION:** 6.5
OVERALL: 53/70 Featuring a large pastry S on top so you know what flavour you're eating, it isn't the biggest of pies but it's contents are pure steak wrapped in some seriously tasty gravy. You need two of them to do the job properly. If my small sample size is reflective, the pies in Middlesbrough are a touch on the diddy size in proportion to their gigantic industrial landmarks.

As we move on to Whitby we get an elevated view of the whole of the North Sea shimmering away on our left and the desolate yet enticing North Yorkshire Moors on our right. The Moors in particular are vast and unforgiving with every colour represented from lush green to chocolate brown, while the sun reflects favourably on what appears to be a space station sat on top of a gently crested peak, views only partly obscured by a slovenly Co-Op lorry chugging away in front of us. If all three of us weren't so sweaty and in need of a wee, we'd be truly enchanted by it all. Well, technically speaking one of us has already been for a wee, and maybe a number two as well if the smell coming from the back is anything to go by.

Four miles off Whitby on the A169 and again we're blown away by the views of Whitby Abbey, both sides of the harbour encased in sheer cliffs and the secluded coastline beneath. I pull over on the main Whitby to Pickering road to spot a middle aged serving wench with a hat on and shelves stacked with jams, breads and pastry products. Bothams of Whitby, famed for their pork pies; of which they have none.

As I wander in, the woman being served is spending thirty four quid. There's also a copper next in line. I survey the situation and admire the flat gingerbreads and parkins but precious little savoury stuff. The officer asks what she has left and she murmurs off a list of items which don't exactly arrest my attention. Oh apart from prawn sandwiches. I hate prawn sandwiches. Quiches and sausage rolls, cheese and onion pasties and a Yorkshire pasty. Please don't choose Yorkshire pasty, please don't choose

Yorkshire pasty. He doesn't so I obtain one for the non wallet troubling sum of seventy pence.

"A pasty please".

"A Yorkshire pasty?"

"No just a pasty please".

"You mean a Yorkshire pasty don't you?".

"Yes of course I do, I'm just being a facetious twat to make a point that this is just a normal pasty and there is nothing distinct about it to make it a Yorkshire pasty other than the fact it was probably conceived in this fair county"

As if I would....

127.

PURVEYOR: Bothams
PREMISES: Whitby
PURCHASE: Yorkshire pasty 70p
PLACE: 7 **PASTRY:** 7 **PRESENTATION:** 7 **PACKAGE:** 7
PALATE: 7.5 **PRICE:** 9 **PORTION:** 8
OVERALL: 52.5/70 Puff pastry encased in a semi-circular form with dark meat, potatoes and carrots inside and a distinctive almost *Yorkshire like* taste.

I attempt to stir the wounded beast that is Emma by driving back towards Whitby to the riverside village of Ruswarp as there's a decent butchers. Despite her needing a wee and me being in full possession of the knowledge that the road out of Whitby is forty miles of desolate moors, I am still trying to cram another pie in. She hates me right now and I don't blame her. Jess is asleep thankfully. Oh and it's shut.

Sunday 9th September 2012

Pottering around gloomy Grasmere I chance upon the Croft House Bakery with more cakes and pies that you can shake a shitty walker's stick at. Grasmere 1 Whitby 0.

Uh oh the phone's ringing. "Are you looking for pie shops again? Get back here now!!"

Wife 1 Me 0.

Monday 10th September 2012

Even though I'm the one who probably deserves it, Emma developed a chronic vomiting bug in the magnificent Orange Tree pub last night (before she'd even touched her food) while we were scoffing our huge burgers and I was going down the pumps quaffing all the real ales, so I'm in the chemist awaiting patronising questions. Still it's lunchtime so I nip in the Lunesdale Bakery where baskets of crisps and wholesome bread sit out alongside steak and kidney, chicken and mushroom, cheese and onion and Scotch pies. The fella serving is Scottish yet I order a cheese and onion pie.

SHIT! It's a pasty. He said pie! Well you're here now pasty and that's all that matters!

128.
PURVEYOR: Lunesdale Bakery
PREMISES: Kirkby Lonsdale
PURCHASE: A Cheese and Onion PASTY £1.50
PLACE: 7 PASTRY: 6.5 PRESENTATION: 7 PACKAGE: 7
PALATE: 7.5 PRICE: 6.5 PORTION: 7
OVERALL: 48.5/70 It's cheesy and colourful with flecks of orange and red inside, like a "Four Cheese pasty" including Lancashire I reckon, or maybe it's Scottish. Is there such thing as Scottish cheese or do they just eat the whole cow? Aside from that it's all puff pastry. All pastry and no filling makes Jimmy a sad boy.

Thankfully whilst out drinking last night I spotted Dales Butchers: "Home made pies, sausages and bacon." IN THAT ORDER. They're the 2011 North West Black Pudding and speciality pork pie champion: pork and haggis. Haggis you say? Best not mention it when I get back while the missus is sat at home with her head in a bowl waiting for her devoted husband to bring her tablets.

Two blokes serving (possibly a dad and lad combo) both wearing white aprons splattered with blood. A skinned, dead animal lies prone on a large block table behind them with its innards hanging out. A bit of blood and guts going some way to recompense for the fact I went all veggie on yo' ass in the Lunesdale Bakery before.

There's a curious range of flavours including damson and Mr Vicky's chilli. However, there's an award winner in the house so I'm duty bound. The lad is dead courteous only getting offended upon finding out I just want a solitary pie. Can't see Emma wanting one somehow.

129.
PURVEYOR: Dales Butchers
PREMISES: Kirkby Lonsdale
PURCHASE: Pork and haggis pie £1.20
PLACE: 7.5 PASTRY: 7.5 PRESENTATION: 7 PACKAGE: 8

PALATE: 9 **PRICE:** 7.5 **PORTION:** 7
OVERALL: 53.5/70 It's not a huge pie but consists of a pure meat filling save for a little air pocket where the jelly has nestled in. The spicy variety of several different kinds of sausage meat is quite pleasant, let's just not discuss what it's comprised of.

I'm not one to court controversy. If a pie vendor has a reputation, I've tried not to be skewed by it and given it a favourable review out of respect. I've tried to maintain impartiality throughout, whether I actually like it or not.

Mrs Kings' pork pies have a huge reputation. One of my mates in London swears by them; people have been known to fight over the last one at Borough market. Well, I'm not impressed.

I pick up a big 'un from Booths which costs £3.50 with a posh blue label stuck to the top, take it home and put it in the oven.

What's going on here though? Is it wrong to expect the inside of a pork pie to be pink, given that is the colour of a pig? The meat is discoloured throughout: pink, grey, brown, even greeny coloured. It's been in the oven for a good half an hour, maybe I should have eaten it cold? A cold pie, I don't get it. The variation is scaring me a little, that maybe I've not cooked it right and it tastes a little rubbery as well. What it does have in its favour is oodles of tasty jelly swimming around it. For whatever reason though I can't quite take to this, the Haggis one was miles better.

130.

PURVEYOR: Mrs Kings Pork Pies
PREMISES: Nottinghamshire
PURCHASE: Melton Mowbray Pork Pie
PLACE: 7 The girl on the deli counter seems barely arsed but hey it's a Monday morning
PASTRY: 7.5 Splendid hand raised shape, well packaged and the interior nicely softened up by jelly
PRESENTATION: 7 No noticeable aroma to it
PACKAGE: 6 Sorry, lots of it but I just can't get my head around it
PALATE: 7 Relying on jelly to get it over the line is a dangerous strategy, the meat is a touch bland and tough and my teeth resemble a crossword puzzle after biting into it
PRICE: 7 Family sized to be fair
PORTION: 9 Of monstrous dimensions
OVERALL: 50.5/70 I've bollocksed something up here haven't I? Oh well,

if you're from Melton Mowbray then please feel free to write a book telling everyone that Wigan pies are a pile of shite.

Wednesday 19th September 2012

The wife's birthday tomorrow and whatever did us tragically disorganised blokes do before the Trafford Centre? I also feel that whereas it may be her birthday, we are a partnership and it's also my birthday as well hence I've one eye on any posh pies I may come across.

The A34 is wedged with United fans as they're at home and I am forced to pull off into Handforth Dean after thirty minutes of standing traffic and leg it to M&S for a piss.

The place has a touch of Stepford Wives about it, situated as it is deep in the South Manchester stockbroker belt. Everyone is immaculately groomed with happy, cheery faces young or old and cannot do enough to help one another.

This is further amplified as I exit the toilets whilst looking at my phone and I accidently dry hump a middle aged woman, who is bent over picking up some loose change, and SHE turns around and apologises to me!

Rampaging through their genteel and icy cold food hall I spot a wide range of produce in the usual locations: Fish pie? Shepherd's pie? Cumberland pie? Not in my name pal! Move on. Gastro pies with steak and ale and Portobello mushrooms for SEVEN QUID!! I eventually settle upon a shortcrust West Country Steak pie (£1.59) and get a pocket sized Melton Mowbray pork pie for a quid. The overall range is great and it's always a pleasure to see a space hopper sized steak pudding beaming back at me from the counter.

After thirty minutes in the oven mini-tributaries of gravy are seeping out across the baking tray. Not from the top though, but from the middle, which means it falls to pieces when I attempt to remove it. It's a rich, wholesome, scorching hot pie with golden puff pastry, lashings of gravy and only 515 calories!

131.

PURVEYOR: Marks & Spencers
PREMISES: Chester
PURCHASE: West Country Steak Pie £2.29
PLACE: 7.5 **PASTRY:** 8 **PRESENTATION:** 7 **PACKAGE:** 7
PALATE: 7 **PRICE:** 6 **PORTION:** 7
OVERALL: 49.5/70 Not that the price is an issue but I did expect a more premium product. It's a touch watery and could do with a bit more meat in it with the crisp and golden crust its main redeeming feature.

132.

PURVEYOR: Marks & Spencers
PREMISES: Chester
PURCHASE: Melton Mowbray Pork Pie £1
PLACE: 7.5 **PASTRY:** 7 **PRESENTATION:** 7 **PACKAGE:** 8
PALATE: 8.5 **PRICE:** 8 **PORTION:** 7
OVERALL: 53/70 As I'm still haunted by my Mrs Kings' faux pas I devour this at room temperature. It's highly portable with ample meat and glistening jelly present throughout, making it a powerful and alluring pie as well as a cheap and potent lunchbox filler.

Adjoined to Marks is a Tesco and it would be amiss not to pop in while the traffic subsides. As soon as I walk through the main door there is a hot display rack with a two for £2 offer on Hollands, right next to the Angling times complete with endless shots of grinning portly fishermen on the front, their knees buckling under the weight of the whopper they've just landed.

As I hit the freezer aisle I spot Pukka's latest gimmick: CRUMBLY SHORTCRUST THREE AND A HALF MINUTE PIE. HEAT FROM FROZEN. What madness is this? I don't know whether to be appalled or delighted: you can pull a pie out of the freezer, bung it in the microwave and it can be in your mouth four minutes and thirty seconds later (including one minute cooling time)

133.

PURVEYOR: Pukka Pies
PREMISES: Leicester
PURCHASE: Steak Pie £1
PLACE: 8 **PASTRY:** 7.5 **PRESENTATION:** 7.5 **PACKAGE:** 7.5
PALATE: 7 **PRICE:** 8 **PORTION:** 7
OVERALL: 52.5/70 Served by a young, spotty checkout girl who is nevertheless as sickeningly pleasant as a chocolate gateau. As for the pie: well it's warm, contains steak, bountiful gravy and is quite crumbly and crisp with no freezing bits. Better than expected, not that I expected much.

While I'm there I bung a pair of Tesco's finest chicken, leek and bacon pies in my basket for good measure.

134.

PURVEYOR: Tesco
PREMISES: Hertfordshire

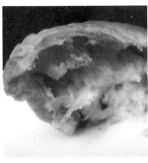

PURCHASE: Chicken, Leek & Bacon Pie (2 for £1.24)
PLACE: 8 Procured from aforementioned finishing school girl
PASTRY: 7 The puff pastry lid elevates itself in the oven until it's floating above the pie like a golden halo
PRESENTATION: 7 Purchased frozen but the box paints a vivid picture of its content
PACKAGE: 7.5 The luxurious, cheesy filling comes tumbling out just like it does on the box and is very diverse in both colour and contrast. The leeks in particular are greener than a newly purchased Plymouth Argyle kit
PALATE: 7 Arguably looks better than it tastes, although contains a welcome injection of cheesiness
PRICE: 9 Sixty two pence each for this pie shaped ice lolly
PORTION: 7.5 Of no mean size and takes forty minutes to cook.
OVERALL: 53/70 If this is Tesco's finest, I wouldn't like to eat their worst! ONLY JOKING – DON'T SUE ME!!

Must get to the Trafford Centre otherwise it's going to be "Here's your birthday present darling. It's the finest pie in Tesco's"

Still stuck in traffic and emptying a family bag of M&S full flavoured Sea salt and malt vinegar crisps down my gullet.

Selfridges: home of the garish yellow bag, plenty I can get Emma from here. In the mean time: FOOD HALL!! It's a tad disappointing; all franchised: Yo Sushi, Prêt A Manger and a patisserie featuring nothing other than cubes of little Turkish delight type treats which look virginally sweet. Then I head around the other side....

The pies are unbranded but what flavours: ham hock & pea (that's a soup isn't it?) Chicken, leek and thyme; Steak, turnip and horseradish plus one with whiskey in it which costs nine quid. I choose my exotic poison, a lamb, chickpea and chorizo pie. You can't beat a bit of chorizo, it's become a firm favourite in our kitchen despite probably not having a fucking clue what it was a couple of years ago.

I'm forced to modify my Selfridges opinion as I wander into the spirits section where you can help yourself to single malt straight from the barrel or they have a stream of multi coloured liqueurs for the younger generation. I could walk in here and get merrily carried out, if only my wallet would withstand it. I whizz around "The Traff" until I've got more presents than pies albeit the pies are a bit cheaper..

So I end up with a yellow Selfridges bag of my own with a pie in it, but whose pie is it? After a spot of searching, I pin it down to a company called Tom's Pies from Devon. I end up having a delightful conversation with Tom himself who does indeed verify that they provide stock to Selfridges. Lovely chap, although I haven't the balls to mention that the name in his email account appears to be "Tom's Piss" not Tom's Pies. Oops.

135.

PURVEYOR: Tom's Pies
PREMISES: Devon
PURCHASE: Lamb, chickpea and chorizo pie £2.44
PLACE: 7 Polite and nonchalant, just how the upper classes like it
PASTRY: 7 A perilously daintily thin shortcrust, almost Scotch pie like
PRESENTATION: 7
PACKAGE: 8 The chickpeas grate a little when biting into them like uncooked beans but there is a great mix in here with plenty of minced lamb and sliced chorizo along with a few other little extras I can't quite place
PALATE: 8 Dashingly different. Although the chorizo isn't too prominent, the lamb is captivatingly succulent
PRICE: 7 To be fair, it's been knocked down from £3.99
PORTION: 7 Good diameter and depth to it
OVERALL: 51/70 Team it up with one of the £10+ malt whiskeys from the spirits aisle at Selfies for the ultimate dining experience.

Saturday 22nd September 2012

They take debit cards in Greggs, I've no idea why. Imagine spending so much in a pie shop that you need to get your card out. They also do gift cards. The perfect way to tell someone you think they're a fat bastard.

I've possibly been a tad harsh on Greggs thus far. I suppose they represent the mainstream: the evil pantomime villain; a corporate giant in a world where I'm seeking out exclusivity, a land where time forgot and the pies are restored from a bygone era. There's nothing wrong with their food or their prices and they have become a by-word for a fast food nation purely by being the market leader, a colossal player in a sector where craft is still prized, swallowing up the competition and swamping every High Street in this fair land. There's probably a multitude of reasons to put the boot into them but for the purpose of this tome, the much maligned Greggs will be judged purely on their pastry output.

The first misconception about Greggs is the belief that they sell pies. Generally they don't: you can get steak bakes, pasties, the infamous baked bean melt, plus sandwiches, cakes, maybe a sweet pie at a push but this aside, no pies. The exception is in the North West of England, where they stock the humble meat and potato, bowing to regional pressure to cater for the locals' avaricious tastes.

In conclusion, I suppose no research of this nature could be considered complete without a trip to Greggs, and as I have a one year old in tow, the three gingerbread men for a pound offer is a vote winner.

I head for Wigan market to Greggs where the waft of ciggie smoke gives way to steak bakes sizzling on a rack and collect my pie while Jess ferociously bites the head off her gingerbread man. I potter back to my car behind four big Wigan lasses with matching Primark bags ready for a night on the town, when one of them utters the immortal line "Save us on that cig will you Shaz?"

136.

PURVEYOR: Greggs
PREMISES: Newcastle
PURCHASE: Meat and Potato Pie £1.20
PLACE: 9 She actually says "ten going in" as I hand her a note. Trust me, we were joking about this in Wigan long before Peter Kay brought it to the nation's attention. Lovely stuff!
PASTRY: 6.5 Crumbly and heartburn inducing on the outer crust albeit a softer, doughy inside
PRESENTATION: 8 I'm given two options in terms of temperature: not so warm or inferno-like straight from the oven
PACKAGE: 7.5 Plentiful if a little sloppy to eat
PALATE: 7 A bit non-descript and watery but a white horse arrives midway through to rescue it in the form of a peppery gravy kick
PRICE: 8 A competitively priced purchase, no doubt possible as a consequence of the vast economies of scale Greggs have managed to accumulate over the years
PORTION: 8 Deep and wide
OVERALL: 54/70 See, that wasn't too scathing was it?

Sunday 23rd September 2012

It might be evident that I've been a bit skint and grounded this month. Fortunately I discover a bevy of Peters Pies in th'Asda. Big in Swansea I recall. I'd been mulling over the fact that I may have to drive there to sample them, and quite frankly it's fucking miles away. I went there for the football last year and spending twelve hours on a coach with a load of intensely flatulent blokes for the sake of a pie doesn't appeal right now. I suppose it would compare favourably to my first visit to the Vetch Field in

1989 when four young lads walked into a pub, ordered a pint in our English accents and promptly got chased several times around Swansea by forty irate Welshmen like a scene from a Benny Hill sketch.

Anyway, they're actually from Caerphilly and I opt for steak rather than steak and *cough* bulking agent kidney. They also do a roast chicken variety but roast chicken belongs in a Sunday roast in my opinion, preferably served alongside an insufficient amount of stuffing, plentiful roast potatoes, carrots and turnips all swimming in gravy so plentiful it's drips off the edge of the plate onto the table cloth.

Peter's Premier Pie is prime tender steak in classic beef gravy (classic always conjures up a Partridge-esque "classic intercourse Sonya" moment) with light golden puff pastry. Looks like a Pukka pie to me but with a shallower, perforated crust lid.

137.

PURVEYOR: Peters
PREMISES: Caerphilly
PURCHASE: Steak Pie £1
PLACE: 7 **PASTRY:** 7 **PRESENTATION:** 7 **PACKAGE:** 7.5
PALATE: 8 **PRICE:** 8 **PORTION:** 8
OVERALL: 52.5/70 It certainly delivers on its gravy promise as the dark stuff comes flying out of the traps like a rabid greyhound as soon as I bite in and I quickly end up pulling the old Bruce Forsyth face trying to keep the pie intact, with the molten lava filling spilling everywhere. It isn't overly blessed with steak and what there is seems a little fatty but the other half ups the meat quota with plenty to keep a hungry fellow occupied.

Friday 29th September 2012

Listen, I feel I owe Mrs Kings' Pork Pies an apology. So with a view to rectifying last week's shambles I procure another from Booths. I've only just realised with my Mr Magoo eyesight that there's another deli counter around the corner. I'm going to eat this one cold. Right now. In my defence, I only froze the last one because the wife got dragged into hospital.

In a nutshell: it's chilled and in possession of a very decadent inner blanket of jelly. The meat is therefore grey on its outer fringes and white, pink and dark in the inner core surrounded by a delicate, soft crust. Nevertheless, second outing or not, I'm not mad keen. I'm waiting for that Eureka moment but maybe personal preference gets the better of me. It's better cold than hot but I still feel that tackling the meat is like slashing through rough undergrowth with my teeth playing the role of a blunt machete.

138.

PURVEYOR: Mrs Kings Pork Pies
PREMISES: Nottinghamshire
PURCHASE: Melton Mowbray Pork Pie
PLACE: 7 **PASTRY:** 7.5 **PRESENTATION:** 7 **PACKAGE:** 6
PALATE: 7 **PRICE:** 7 **PORTION:** 8.5
OVERALL: 50/70 Original vote stands.

I can only compare it to when you walk in a kebab shop on foreign shores and see the skewers and wonder why the meat has so many different colours and textures to it. Why isn't it all smooth and brown like the ones we have in our country? Probably because it's not processed shite we devour from the "elephant's leg" on the spit of your local kebab house. I suspect I'm just a food luddite.

Tuesday 2nd October 2012

I've had a hellish few weeks at work so I am treating myself to a dinner date. Bessie Arderns of Warrington to be precise. A brief obituary in the Warrington Guardian heralds their demise but then announces their resurfacing phoenix-style at the hands of family offspring. There's a discernible nip in the air as we hit October and what better to warm the cockles than a steaming hot sloppy meat and potato pie?

I'm salivating like a badly under nourished Labrador as I take the shady slip road on to the M6 by Knutsford Services. Over the official North West launch pad that is the Thelwall viaduct where Winter Hill, Welsh mountains, the Beetham Tower and Runcorn bridge are all visible to the naked eye. Warrington stretches for millions of miles across, it's incomprehensible. It should be a huge city based on land coverage, but it's a town and a slightly odd one at that. I drive through Woolston past a tree stump with dozens of trainers nailed on to it Damian Hurst style: "The tree of lost souls". There's twenty pensioners in full on rambling gear including appropriate headwear, ambling past a Toyota garage on a Tuesday morning.

As I hit the town centre, my SatNav directs me down residential side streets full of infernal speed bumps. Left, left, left again until I see the "For Sale" sign. It's shut. Shut down. Bastard. I'm ferociously attacking my phone searching for Warrington forums to get answers. I go to ask the old woman next door but she displays a canny change of pace to bugger off up her garden path and into her house.

It's slap bang in the middle of a long street of terraced houses and sadly today's consumer doesn't behave that way, they'd sooner bugger off to a supermarket and get two loaves of Kingsmill for two quid. It's a hammer blow so I consider my Plan B. Currells/Corralls/Coralls exist somewhere around here. I shall find them. I cruise the mean streets of Warrington through Latchford and Padgate where every corner has a sunbed shop but the other kind of bake is in exodus.

The Warrington forum appears to recommend a great pie shop, until I scrawl further down and it's full of irate locals fuming at the fact they're building a Sikh temple next to it. There's clues here which will lead me to the answer: Sikh Temple, Latchford Methodist Church, Currells Bakery. I feel like Dora the Explorer but with less hair. Ah, it's CURRALLS, with an A!

I'm a happy man. I'm greeted by a feast of pastries, including the curious cheese and bean slice. I ask for meat and potato being in that territory and she pulls one out of the back. I also clock the Curralls "special" pie. Having been pissed about enough today I am obliged to ask what's so special about it. It's a beef pie but made with a hot water pastry and seasoned with pepper and at 97p each it's rude not to. DONE!

The thrill of the chase, that perilous wait to see if they have pies left and the sweet satisfaction of freshly baked produce stinking out my car with an unsurpassable lardy aroma. It doesn't get any better.

I'm at Lymm services. There are people just a few hundred yards away from me spending a tenner in Maccies or paying three quid for a steak bake in Greggs, whilst I'm sat in a decrepit old Golf eating some of the finest pies man has ever discovered. The fools!!

139.

PURVEYOR: Curralls
PREMISES: Warrington
PURCHASE: Potato and Meat Pie £1.05
PLACE: 8 For elaborating as to the contents of the special
PASTRY: 8 A crispy outside generating a distinctive click when I put the knife through the bottom; yet soft on the inner casing. The crust lid doesn't completely cover the pie, which possibly explains why the aroma is attacking my senses like a swarm of angry wasps
PRESENTATION: 9 Served straight out of the oven with an immaculate smell to it
PACKAGE: 8.5 Sloppier than the closing scenes of Sleepless in Seattle with rich potato and lots of runny mince and gravy
PALATE: 8.5 Lovely blend with a hint of pepper romping through the middle
PRICE: 8 Cheap at half the price
PORTION: 7.5 The meat and potato is full sized, the special more of a snack pie

OVERALL: 57.5/70 I will express my adulation for this pie in the manner of an eight year old: <3 <3 <3 <3 :-)

Friday 5th October 2012

There's one little enclave of Booths I've given the swerve so far: Posh pies! Charlie Bighams (not as I keep calling them Ivor Bigguns). I get two steak and ale pies for £7.49 and they're attractively packaged in cheesecloth and string (similar to a traditional jam jar) and served in ceramic ramekins. They do steak or chicken and mushroom and a range of "fake" pies including Shepherd's & Fish. Fish pie in particular is not in my name – unless I go visit Grimsby at some point where this deviation may be considered acceptable.

The box is full of mission statements, spiel and even cartoons. "Crack open a bottle and steal back some time" it implores – to be fair you can do that when buying a kebab. "Let Charlie prepare you a truly delicious meal while you sit back and enjoy each other's company" – bit discriminatory against single people that, let alone greedy pigs who eat two pies in one sitting.

They're not the biggest pies though and the ramekins have already been earmarked to be utilised as ashtrays post-consumption. Or a cereal bowl for a toddler.

Is the ramekin heavy or the pie? I am requested to brush the pastry with milk or whisked egg before putting into the oven. Hang on, Charlie I thought you were preparing me a delicious meal (and charging me £7.50?) and you want me to do all the work?!?! For all your spiel Chaz I'd say you're on the back foot here.

There is a large lattice puff pastry which covers the top of the pie and folds a good inch or so beyond the rim of the dish so I can't see what's lurking within before putting it in the oven. Thirty minutes later it gets worse; as predicted the puff pastry is so tightly hugging the ramekin it is impossible to detach nor can you get a spatula in it due to the dimensions of the dish. I've got all my work cut out dislodging it and bunging it on the plate and then scooping out the admittedly fantastic gravy and chunks of steak floating around beneath. It ends up more of a stew or casserole with pastry on top than a pie though.

140.
PURVEYOR: Charlie Bigham
PREMISES: London
PURCHASE: £7.49 for 2 Steak and Ale Pies
PLACE: 7.5 Superlative marketing

PASTRY: 5 Sorry, this isn't my puff pastry vendetta resurfacing but it's top crust only and half of it is still stuck to the ramekin eighteen months later. Unforgivable. Portability 0/10

PRESENTATION: 7.5 A luxurious smell coming out the oven

PACKAGE: 7 Oceanic volume of gravy with the steak playing the role of the meaty lifebuoys

PALATE: 8 Sweeter than a virginal bride with molasses, cocoa powder, sugar and Worcester sauce combining in the gravy. Can't taste any ale though. Or anchovies (thankfully)

PRICE: 6.5 Free crockery/ashtray almost compensates the £3.75 price tag

PORTION: 7 Looks huge and feels weighty due to its bulbous lid and dish. Isn't huge at all

OVERALL: 48.5/70 Talk about making something simple over-complicated

Saturday 13th October 2012

No more supermarket foraging, we're actually going down south for two whole weeks. Whilst Emma is packing for me, packing for herself, packing for the baby, thinking of everything, I am sat on my arse looking up the finest pastry purveyors all the way along the South Coast plus stop off points.

I decide upon the Mad about Pies pub also known as the Farmer's Boy Inn for our outward bound comfort stop. It's a little off the beaten track but Emma won't know that. In fact she'll *appreciate* me taking her on a detour and showing her the marvellous Cotswolds.

The website of the Farmer's Boy Inn contains many videos of its charismatic proprietor, Phil Kiernan – an amiable Irishman taking you on guided tours of his premises which includes a shop next door selling wine, cheeses, pies and cider. He looks like a bit of a normal sized Niall Quinn and his face is plastered all over the place. Clearly a man who is passionate about his pies. Who can blame him for a bit of shameless self-promotion. TELL YOUR MATES TO BUY THIS BOOK NOW! Sorry.

Down the M5 we go, with each passing town the accent getting a little less Brummie and a little more "oo-ar", onto the M50 and then down some undulating country roads with stunning views of the Cotswolds. We find the Farmers Boy Inn at Longhope, complete with Phil's face on billboards and "Book Now for Xmas 2014" sign outside.

It's a top venue, a homage to the humble pie with low hanging oak beams and vines growing inside the pub and tankards hanging from the ceiling. The bogs are well kept and wall to floor with wisdom ("My dad was the town drunk; most of the time that's not too bad but in New York

City....") it keeps a cracking pint of Greene King IPA. One day I will own a place like this, mark my words....

Mine host walks in and is every inch the bon viveur his YouTube videos portray, engaging me in conversation before his good lady turns up carrying the most gorgeous nine week old German shorthair pointer puppy.

I'm so all consumed in the ambience of this marvellous environment that I nearly forget I've got a pie to choose and narrow it down to Steak and Guinness, keen to see the Irish owners influence coming out over the blue cheese topped version. Emma goes for a "bird's pie" – brie, broccoli and cauliflower and in my over-excitement I completely forget to order Jess a kid's sausage and chips. There goes the father of the year award again.

The steak and Guinness pie is £12.95 but comes with all the trimmings: new potatoes, pureed carrot and turnip, red cabbage, peas and the obligatory jug of gravy.

141.

PURVEYOR: Farmer's Boy Inn
PREMISES: Gloucester
PURCHASE: Steak & Guinness Pie £12.95
PLACE: 9 And not just for saving the blushes of some dickhead who forgot to order his daughter's meal. The beers flow regularly and staff are happy to chat and check on our welfare
PASTRY: 8 Golden and shiny. The missus, a slave to heartburn, actually enjoys hers even more than I enjoy mine. It's not too stodgy and there's loads of it
PRESENTATION: 8 Time flies in good company and the piping hot pies arrive in no time
PACKAGE: 8 A very deep pie leads to a high volume of filling; in this case tender blocks of steak floating in rich, dark Guinness infused gravy
PALATE: 9 You can really taste the cooked stout and the meat is marinated in it and complimented by more mouth watering full flavoured gravy to soak the veg in
PRICE: 7 Not cheap but I won't be eating again for some time
PORTION: 9 Seriously big pies of high quality
OVERALL: 58/70 You've got one happy family on your hands here as Emma loves her broccoli and stilton pie and Jessica polishes her sausage and chips off, when it's eventually ordered. (Still yet to graduate to pies though she has dabbled in pasties, well thrown one at me).

So, an ace start to my quest of trying to eat as many pastry products as is humanly possible, I mean spending quality family time together. We drive past the majestic Gloucester cathedral and it looks as holy as you can get with the sun blaring on to it in between a gap in the clouds. So I say a little prayer of thanks to the pie gods for the fine meal they have just bestowed upon us.

We barely get back on the M5 for half an hour before we need to stop again with Emma full of pop and me needing to ahem, drop my shopping after that feed. I don't hang about though given some of the 'interesting' offers on the toilet walls in Michael Wood Services, complete with phone numbers and un-necessary holes in the cubicles.

The forecourt appears to be full of ten year olds wearing flat caps and Ginsters adverts everywhere. I'm still at the foetal stage of my pasty research but I know that Ginsters are the awful X Factor catch all of the pasty world compared to the homespun local indie band strumming their hearts out down the local for beer money.

We drive on through Pennsylvania (!?!) and then on to Bathhampton where I get directed over a bridge by a bloke in hi viz simply stood in the road taking an extortionate 60p off every car that passes; he could be anyone! Try that in Wigan pal, they'd just run you over.

Sometime early evening we land in our holiday park in Poole and hit the pub. I survey the scene and I spot a man with a basin hair cut, surrounded by his family, lips pursed in anticipation, fork in hand about to munch on his pie. He is contented; he is king of his kingdom and indulging in one of life's simple pleasures; cherishing every mouthful, savouring the moment. Lovely scenes. We are truly a nation of pie lovers!

Tuesday 16th October 2012

Bognor Regis, a place so sleepy it's twinned with the Land of Nod. It does possess Turners however, a specialist family run pie shop with a very smart exterior, if a little bit marooney in colour.

As soon as I get out the car that unmistakeable waft of pies comes heading my way, I'm like a geriatric Bisto-kid. The lad serving is a chirpy Cockney geezer bearing more than a passing resemblance to Charlatans front man Tim Burgess. All about the pies in here, chicken and steak of various dimensions, served on their own or you can chuck in peas, mash and gravy for a couple of extra quid.

142.
PURVEYOR: Turners
PREMISES: Bognor Regis

PURCHASE: Steak and ale pie £2.30
PLACE: 8 The hot pies and mash are pulled down from a serving hatch which is a nice touch
PASTRY: 8 A highly decorative crust, crisp in the mouth but uneven and artisan in its form suggesting handmade and crimped. Highly portable as well, not that I've seen many Sussex folk walking around eating pies with their hands
PRESENTATION: 9 Amazing aroma and piping hot
PACKAGE: 9 A dangerously overcrowded population of prime steak lies within
PALATE: 8 Mighty and meaty
PRICE: 7 Over £2 takeaway but this is no average pie
PORTION: 8 Deep and oblong shaped
OVERALL: 57/70 A splendidly well filled pie from a vendor dedicated to fine food.

I'm stuck behind a chimney sweep in Littlehampton, established 1977 his van says – he must have lungs of steel. Is there much call for chimney sweeps in glorious Sussex by the sea in 2012? I mean to actually sweep chimneys not do a Dick van Dyke type jig? He's also got an Arsenal sticker in his van, so the old soot tickling game must pay handsomely if he can afford the tickets at the Emirates.

On to Brighton through the rolling South Downs where we overtake a funeral cortege with a white hearse. Brighton is of course a city. If you didn't know this, you'd have no problem finding out as every signpost, bus, bus shelter and bin has "City of Brighton" proudly stamped all over it. It's like they're bragging to all the visitors from mediocre provincial towns as to their civic superiority. You don't get Newcastle, Manchester or Liverpool getting all uppity about their city-ness, I know this much.

It's a strange place, it has got the vibe of a compact, bustling town but all a little bit geeky and freaky with just the faintest of city edge to it. A typical city approach to parking however in that there is fucking none any-where, just an agitated sweaty Northerner driving around aimlessly. Urban clearways and controlled zones all over the shop as if to say "Leave your car at home next time you air polluting nobhead".

I eventually learn that if you drive up to the metal shutters on the NCP's they miraculously pop up to let you in for a mere three pounds per hour. We head for London Road, a studenty, cosmopolitan area with flats the size of shoe boxes and roads that wind around the hills like they do in

Monaco. Desperately searching for bogs.

At ground level, every third person has dreadlocks and they're all white. Middle aged women in pop socks with facial tattoos and stick on eyelashes. Every form of human life is here but walking around the streets sporting the "piss stained jeans" look might be pushing it a bit, even to the Scouse gentlemen walking towards me swigging a can of K Cider.

We dive in McDonalds and eat there. Whilst there I slip out to find Bangers who promise home made pies. They sell sausages as well but no used cars.

They've got a great selection of pies although not all are in stock. The list includes chicken curry, chilli beef, sausage and onion (isn't this just pork?) and a Beano pie, containing er beans basically. I fancy either of these seeing as they seem to be a regional delicacy but they've both sold out seeing as it's now nearly 2 o'clock, after it took us longer to park than it takes Pluto to orbit the sun. So I'm stuck with a steak. It is nevertheless highly pleasing to see that pies have a home in the Bohemian area of North Laine, Brighton.

143.

PURVEYOR: Bangers
PREMISES: Brighton
PURCHASE: Steak Pie £1.60
PLACE: 7.5 Another cheerful chappie
PASTRY: 8 Smooth, soft and adorned with a pastry heart on top
PRESENTATION: 8 Served very warm considering the time
PACKAGE: 7.5 Mahogany coloured gravy smothering luscious steak chunks
PALATE: 8 The gravy is so rich it's got its own offshore bank account
PRICE: 7 Benchmark
PORTION: 7.5 Not the biggest pie but it has a raised roof, like one of those mobile homes
OVERALL: 53.5/70 Bangers: Pies with a BOOM!!

I quickly abort my final attempt – Forfar's Sussex Bakery around the corner – upon discovering that the heathens don't serve any pies and therefore deserve to have their entrance blocked by a gaggle of drunks who have just stumbled out of Ladbrokes.

Sunday 21st October 2012

Booted out of our caravan park, we hit the Jurassic trail with its stunning coastline and undertake the long Sunday drive to the boot of Cornwall; to another caravan park; this one sans central heating just as the weather has turned. A three bar fire on a grotty trailer park with ropey electrics – I know how to treat my girls eh!

Things are about to get a bit dark right now because in Cornwall there are no pies, only PASTIES!!!

So I will inevitably end up breaking the rules in pastry country. I have however been tipped off as to some fabulous ones. My mate Andy from Dorset raves about Hampsons of Hayle and Philps and I hear the Pengenna Pasties are ridiculously oversized. Grumpies, apparently loved by Chris Evans, will provide a pie alternative and they are my four to watch in Cornwall even though I'll end up eating eight. Imagine the outrage when my top pie turns out to be a pasty!

The Cornish Pasty Association outline exactly what a pasty needs to be in order to claim them as authentic, and are geographically protected to this effect. Go ahead, Google them, it's serious shit! The PGI is an EU thing which means that other people can't simply go selling Cornish pasties and claim them as authentic even though I seem to have been in dozens of places who try and do exactly that. At least half of their 53 members seem to have set up camp close to where I'm based in St Ives harbour.

Monday 22nd October 2012

What's not to love about a place called Praze-an-Beeble. Go on, say it again in a Cornish accent. Hayle today. Lots of flat white houses and seagulls angrily flapping and shrieking above. I head down a sharp hill and the big stonewashed building of Philps pasty shop appears like an angelic vision on the corner, just as a big fat lad emerges from the door chomping straight into a big fat pasty.

I skip in front of a combine harvester gambolling like a spring lamb, oblivious to the fact it's about to mow me down and head into the low roofed shop. There's a queue for pasties and a queue for the deli (for the missus). They do not sell pies only pasties, shitloads of them lined up in trays on greaseproof paper: beef, chicken, cheese, vegetable, breakfast and steak flavour. The minced beef are sized: standard, medium and large with the standard alone being the size of a shoe box. I opt for a small one at £2.15 as I've a few to get through and Man versus Cornish Pasty could be a challenge which finishes me off before it's begun. It comes in a branded wrapper and is about eight or nine inches long by my reckoning, even though men have a habit of exaggerating such things.

We drive into Hayle with its superlative railway viaduct where I spy another Philps shop, this one as big as a motorway service station so God knows how many pasties they make there. I'm looking for another esteemed local purveyor by the name of Hampsons. I drive through the centre several times with its delightful river and quayside but see no pasty shop. I drive so far that I come to another Hayles of Hampson, a red shop advertising "pies, pasties, filled rolls and salad bowls". Ooh, shall I have a salad?

There's a wide range of steak and chicken pies along with meat patties (Are we in Jamaica?) and a ton of sweet jars in the window. Yet I succumb to local protocol and head to the far end where I am greeted with some dangerously large pasties. They look like genetically mutated freaks of nature: about a foot long. Small £1.20 (they're not small!), Medium £2.10, Large £3.10. I initially consider a small one, itself the size of half a dustbin lid but then up the ante and plump for a medium, craftily pegged at 5p cheaper than their competitor up the road.

A few doors down is Hayle kebab house. Surely a kebab is just a spicy pasty which hasn't had its ends crimped? What we need now is a beach for the nipper to run around on with a bucket and spade while I sit on a deck chair and consume my own body weight in pasties, and sure enough there's a sign for one. We pass Hayle recreation ground first though and as Emma has already indicated that she has no intention of sitting in the car while I sit there undergoing death by pasty, I pull over and we let Jess have a run on the playground whilst I sit furtively in the car park examining two items which appear to resemble Goliath's feet.

144.

PURVEYOR: Philps
PREMISES: Hayle
PURCHASE: Minced Beef Pasty £2.15
PLACE: 7.5 For explaining what the hell is going on
PASTRY: 8 Semi-flaky outer, soft and fluffy and finished with a hand crimp at the side
PRESENTATION: 8 Furiously almost volcanically hot
PACKAGE: 8.5 A carefully arranged affair with compartments of sausage style beef segregated from the diced potato
PALATE: 9 I detect a bit of jelly attached to the beef which gives a warm, juicy taste to every bite as it permeates through the pasty's content. Very well seasoned too with a bit of a kick
PRICE: 8 Good pence per inch no doubt
PORTION: 9 Proper hansum, as they say around these parts. Or it's bigger than my fucking head – as I said just then!
OVERALL: 58/70 Bloody hell I'm stuffed already.

145.

PURVEYOR: Hampsons
PREMISES: Hayle
PURCHASE: Minced Beef Pasty £2.10
PLACE: 8 Highly tolerant of my pissing about choosing a pasty size
PASTRY: 9 Thick, sublime shortcrust pastry hand crimped at the side
PRESENTATION: 7.5 Good temperature
PACKAGE: 8.5 Dark chunks of meat encased in layers of potato and onions soaked in brine interspersed with the odd bit of carrot and swede
PALATE: 8 Not overly moist but there's a lot going on in here
PRICE: 8 Cut it in half and you've still got a meal for a quid
PORTION: 9 I may have mentioned it's dimensions once or twice during this review
OVERALL: 58/70 A real humdinger of a pasty: if you threw it at someone's head you'd probably knock them clean out (Disclaimer: Life of Pies does not condone this act).

The whole time I'm sat there eating three fat crows are sat on my car bonnet giving me evil stares. They're probably going to peck my face off in a minute when I get out having scoffed the lot in front of their furious looking scavenging boat races. It's like a remake of The Omen set in a Cornish adventure playground.

I'd planned to head to St Ives to stock up with more but there seems no point as I doubt I'll be able to eat for a week now. So we visit Land's End instead via a village which has a sign saying "Beware of the deaf cat." Sure enough it's stood in the road and no amount of beeping will shift the poor blighter. I can however confirm that if you want the country's most southwesterly pastry product, you can buy a Simply Cornish pasty for £3.50 from the thinly veiled theme park that passes for Great Britain's most south westerly point these days.

Tuesday 23rd October 2012

The quest continues in St Ives where we park on a pay and display so steep it's almost vertical. Much vaunted for it's picturesqueness, as we descend (abseil) into St Ives we can see the sum total of bugger all as it is shrouded in fog thick enough to crash an X Wing fighter in. We can hear the constant throng of seagulls overhead but we can't see the sea, even when it's upon us, such is the density of this pea souper. It's fair to say the place isn't pram friendly and there's mass panic as the sheer gradient of the path nearly makes me lose control of the pushchair and I must admit it's like walking drunk with the hazy air and sharp descents. But anyway, where's the pasties?

Are Warrens the Greggs of Cornwall? I was perusing through a little magazine in "the van" (as we call it) upon which they had a full back page advert telling us how they've been making the original, perfect, authentic Cornish pasty since 1860. However, their crime has been to become big with a string of branches and a spin off retail brand called Simply Cornish. I get a medium steak pasty for £2.60 with small and large variants – as ever take the size descriptors with a pinch of salt as they are all absolutely huge down here. Plus they have the obligatory breakfast pasties, chicken and cheese and onion.

146.

PURVEYOR: Warrens
PREMISES: Penzance
PURCHASE: Steak pasty £2.60
PLACE: 7.5 Generic
PASTRY: 7.5 Side crimped therefore a big ring of pasty knotted around the periphery. How dry this is defines how good the pasty is in my book – there's nothing worse than having a bite of something without any filling in it. Apparently you're not meant to eat this bit anyway, it was only ever meant to be used as a handle for the miners to eat the pasty with. They would traditionally chuck the crimped bit away due to the high levels of the arsenic on their hands in the tin mines. See, educational this!
PRESENTATION: 7.5 Hotter than a lava filled Louis Vuitton handbag
PACKAGE: 8.5 Whopping chunks of chuck steak, huge slabs of potato with other veg and swedes – no not Abba, the shit turnip type
PALATE: 8.5 A surprisingly opulent quality to this considering some of the Cornish pasty purists are ranting on web forums that Warrens are dreadful and commercial
PRICE: 8 Big pasty
PORTION: 9 Huge in fact
OVERALL: 56.5/70 Mass produced or not, this is a revelation to me.

We meander through the narrow, winding pedestrianised streets, interjected with the odd road sadly blighted by white van men nearly mowing down young children and OAPs, until it opens out onto a postcard perfect harbour with a crisp aquamarine sea bed and a shallow beach. Some tourist tit is still trying to run us over though. Why they can't park half a mile away up a mountain like the rest of us I don't know.

There must be a dozen pasty shops on the front in addition to the Pengenna Pasty place, whose card I've already earmarked, so there is a decision to be made. I peruse the menus and my choice will be made based on what Emma wants on this occasion: they must have a broccoli and stilton option. I'm loathe to go for one with a corporate name even though most of them have one, either way I'm running around like an arse: The Cornish Pasty shop has sweetcorn in it so that's a non-starter "this one's got sweetcorn in it" I shout loud enough to make fishermen turn around in John O'Groats, but they do have an impressive range of about thirty pasties.

The St Ives pasty shop might have a geographically advantageous nomenclature however I am quick to spot that it's pasties are both smaller and more expensive, so that one's out. As ever, I am getting seriously on Emma's tits, who just wants to sit on a soggy bench overlooking the quaint harbour eating her dinner whilst seagulls terrorise our daughter. I should stop fannying about right now. Back to the Cornish Pasty Company/Shop/Bakehouse whatever it's called.

147.

PURVEYOR: The Cornish Pasty Shop
PREMISES: St Ives
PURCHASE: Steak & Stilton pasty £2.50
PLACE: 6 A lethargic, disinterested, callow teenage surf bum
PASTRY: 8 Side crimped and delicate. Standard
PRESENTATION: 7
PACKAGE: 7.5 Very impressive chunk size. Populated with mainly chuck steak in fact, one half of it appears to consist solely of one huge singular block of meat
PALATE: 7.5 The stilton injects some impetus but without it the meat tastes a little insipid
PRICE: 7 Tourist trap prices
PORTION: 8.5 As Jordan said to the tabloid reporters, it's big but I've had bigger
OVERALL: 51.5/70 My pasty goodwill is running thin here.

We head back through the streets perusing the gift shops on the gloomiest day in history and it's the Allotment Deli on the bustling, pedestrianised Fore Street where I'm headed – for a pie this time – yes a pie! Their signs entice me in on the promise of "Gurt big pork pies" and "Hansum home baked shot putt sized Scotch eggs". "We are very cheesy" they proclaim and finally "Popeye would love our olives!"

I wander in to this shrine to home grown food, past a pack of tied up dogs yapping manically and there's delectable fruit and veg on display along with some huge pasties that have more familiar soft, shortcrust casing. Me, I want a Grumpies steak and ale pie and a slice of carrot cake for the missus.

148.

PURVEYOR: Grumpies
PREMISES: Launceston
PURCHASE: Steak and Ale Pie £3.00
PLACE: 7 A lovely establishment but no bag for Emma's carrot cake so I'm left wandering in and out of shops holding it aloft in my palm like a deranged badly dressed butler
PASTRY: 7.5 Bit soggy underneath but redeems itself with a solid top featuring a pastry map of Cornwall. On the portability front, it flaps a bit and it's ingredients come tumbling out when I attempt a hand job (pardon!)
PRESENTATION: 7
PACKAGE: 6.5 A bit of airspace in evidence and it's also seriously padded out with onions and mushrooms. You know the rules lads: if something's got mushrooms in it, you need to advertise the fact for the benefit of fussy bastards like me
PALATE: 7 The meat is tough and doesn't scream quality at me upon tasting it but what do I know? This must be one of those pies that middle class people convince themselves are great because they've never been to a back street butcher in Workington
PRICE: 5 For three pound? THREE POUND. I'm sorry
PORTION: 7 Reasonable
OVERALL: 47/70 They will be grumpy when they read this! They sell these at Harrods! And I'd rather have a pasty from Warrens. Maybe it's me or maybe they're not all that. Either way, stick to pasties in this part of the world is my advice.

When I re-emerge from the deli, Emma is handing over her credit card in the uber-expensive toy shop next door as punishment for me dragging her around the most beautiful harbour in the country, while I've been running in and out of pie (pasty) shops. You could have a different pasty for every day of the month here though and I just can't kick my affliction.

I have one more target on my list, the mighty Pengenna Pasties. Situated on the High Street in St Ives with a big red fronted shop. A man in a butchers' apron is standing behind a serving hatch beyond which lie rack after rack of gigantic stacked pasties on greaseproof paper and trays. I initially mistake their pasties for loaves of bread, such are their dimensions, and then....OMG THEY'RE AT LEAST TWO FEET LONG. Priced accordingly mind you.

I'm not sure how it's top crust sits with the Cornish protection Nazis, erm I mean enthusiasts, but I don't care, it's a beast of a pasty worthy of its own episode of Man versus Food.

149.

PURVEYOR: Pengenna Pasties
PREMISES: Bude
PURCHASE: Cornish pasty £3.30
PLACE: 8 Authentic and quirky establishment with a genial host
PASTRY: 7.5 Crimped at the top and to my eternal shame I burn the folding seam of the top crust a bit in the unfamiliar caravan oven. It's a touch difficult to eat, being crimped at the top, and I decide it best to cut in half and eat kebab style to stop the contents spilling out
PRESENTATION: 7 Fine when you don't burn it
PACKAGE: 9 Millions if not trillions of diced up pearls of potato, onion, swede and steak
PALATE: 7.5 Excellent contrast with soft and plentiful contents although felt a little dry and under seasoned in parts
PRICE: 8 Not cheap but will feed a family of four for a week
PORTION: 9.5 At least eight inches long (honestly) and no mean height and depth either. If a Cornish miner had a pasty of this magnitude for his lunch I wouldn't expect him to emerge for the afternoon. He'd be sat on his arse with a newspaper over his head gently blowing it up and down with his snorey exhalations
OVERALL: 56.5/70 If they've anything about them they'll adopt the slogan "Pick up a Pengenna". You may need a fork lift truck to do so however.

My waistline is aching like a heavily harpooned sea creature. Did I mention I'm running a half marathon in ten days? I won't need a fancy dress costume at this rate, "oh look that man is running dressed as one huge, human sized Cornish pasty"

Thursday 25th October 2012

So begins the journey back north which feels like one constant uphill drive. I do however have a planned stop off, not specifically designed to irritate the wife but which will undoubtedly do so. We're stopping off in Pinhoe,

Exeter home of Martin's Pies. Pinhoe, Pinhoe it's off to eat pies we go.

Exeter apparently has a historic quayside, cathedral and museums but this Thursday afternoon it is snarled up like an agitated lion. This causes no end of umbrage to my wife and daughter but I stick manfully to my task driving past no end of wig shops and tattooists.

Martin's is perched on a large hill flanked by terraced houses leading for a mile or so down to the M5. They possess a wide array of pies and savouries from steak to breakfast pie to the hyper-politically named Devon Pasty. At least I know why they do it now – to stop the Cornish secret pasty police turning up. The steak and stilton has me salivating but I've overdone the steak recently so being an ever considerate husband and father in the midst of a six hour car journey I plump for a chicken curry pie. I'm seriously considering a bag of lobster flavoured Burts crisps to compliment it with as well.

150.

PURVEYOR: Martins
PREMISES: Exeter
PURCHASE: Chicken Curry Pie £2.40
PLACE: 8.5 The old dear with her wonderfully soft "alright moi lovely, have a noice day" Devon accent soon has me eating out of the palm of her wizened hand
PASTRY: 7.5 It's got a little star on top for that is what this little beauty is
PRESENTATION: 6.5 Warmed up in the microwave and still not that insulated, nor does it give off that fine aroma I'd expect off a curry pie
PACKAGE: 7 Corners not quite filled in but rampant chunks of chicken smothered in chip shop style curry sauce
PALATE: 8 Me + curry + hot food + pie = vote winner
PRICE: 6 Unreasonably expensive
PORTION: 7 Oval shaped and deceptively deeper than it looks but a mere midget compared to what I've been feasting on the past few days
OVERALL: 50.5/70 Martins only slightly curries favour with me. Awful pun, indeed aw-phaal pun. Sorry I'm just tikkaing the piss now.

1st November 2012

In a twist of "coals to Newcastle" proportion, I find myself wandering around Tesco back home and chance upon the much loathed Ginsters associated with a range of competitively priced pies. The off the shelf cost is a mere quid thereby worthy of a speculative punt to see if they are as good/bad as their notorious pasties. I've sacrificed a full tray of half price Hollands pies at 50p a go here, so no pressure Ginsters....

151.

PURVEYOR: Ginsters
PREMISES: Callington
PURCHASE: Steak Pie £1
PLACE: 7 Tesco self check out
PASTRY: 7 My beef (!) with puff pastry is that you only ever get to eat around 80% of it as it goes all over the shop, but it holds together well. The base is a bit flimsy mind you
PRESENTATION: 7.5 Good vibes coming from the oven
PACKAGE: 7.5 I try to eat with my hands but quit after burning my fingers as the sloppy filling dribbles all over them. Minimal carrot, tons of steak and gravy. A useful work out for the gnashers
PALATE: 7 No added ingredients it boasts. Therefore a bit watery in parts
PRICE: 8.5 A quid!
PORTION: 7.5 The casing tapers off a little towards the base
OVERALL: 52/70 Good honest food is the Ginsters strapline. Glad to hear it as I hate those lying, deceitful foodstuffs that go around shagging other pasties behind your back when they tell you they're working late.

Friday 10th November 2012

Booths again for booze. Needless to say one thing leads to another and I end up taking home a Toppings pork pie. Their dinky pork pie looks a little bit insufficient for my appetite and the large ones are so voluminous they look like they would bugger up my car's suspension on the commute back up the M6 so I go medium for £1.60. Scandalously rejecting the advances of the pork and chilli and pork and scrumpy varieties. I pop it in the fridge and consume it the following day: Pork pie, lump of mature cheddar and a bag of Beefy Seabrooks = heaven!

152.

PURVEYOR: Toppings
PREMISES: Doncaster
PURCHASE: Pork Pie £1.60
PLACE: 7 Wrapped in cellophane and given the Booths official stamp
PASTRY: 8 Darker than a late night French movie yet marshmellow soft
PRESENTATION: 7 Eaten chilled
PACKAGE: 8 Splendid! Smooth, delightfully soft sausage meat encased in lush jelly which remains intact throughout
PALATE: 8 I often have concerns when the jelly is not dissolved enough as the pork pie can feel a little dry but this is juicier than a bucket of Opal fruits and bursting with flavour. I don't feel a shred of guilt polishing it off

while my daughter sits there watching Peppa Pig
PRICE: 7.5 An all meat price
PORTION: 8 Having it large
OVERALL: 53.5/70 A prestige product with golden hot water pastry and jelly atop.

Wednesday 14th November 2012

I'm not giving up on Bessie Arderns, much loved in Warrington. I've subsequently discovered they had another shop in Warrington and this time I've used the tools at my disposal i.e. Google Earth and indeed it appears to be perfectly functioning from the grainy six month old screenshot. Incidentally, this is at the second time of asking. At the first time of asking I am zoomed in on Clifton Street Bakery in New York, which might be a stretch in my lunch hour – and I suspect they may not deliver to Wigan.

I find it with ease and note the big BA lettering above the door. A gentleman, who has just got out of a brand new Merc and is a ringer for ever popular Leeds United chairman Ken Bates, pushes in front of me. The twat. Ken Bates orders a steak and kidney, decides he doesn't like the look of it and changes his mind to meat and potato. I'm tempted to go for the hot pots as they're the size of breezeblocks but I stick with the pie. The next question though as this heavenly concoction wafts through my car is – has the original recipe been retained?

153.

PURVEYOR: Clifton Street Bakery
PREMISES: Warrington
PURCHASE: Meat and Potato Pie £1.10
PLACE: 7 A quintessentially Northern manner
PASTRY: 7 The sticky top crust appears to be independent from the rest of the pie but somehow holds together
PRESENTATION: 8 Hot enough to steam up Ken Bates' specs
PACKAGE: 7 Not the densest filling but lovely golden potatoes
PALATE: 7.5 Mild doses of pepper with lots of sloppy gravy soaking into the doughy crust interior
PRICE: 7 Small pie, small price
PORTION: 6.5 I should have had the hot pot!
OVERALL: 50/70 A tasty little teaser but I still went and got a butty when I got back to work.

Saturday 17th November 2012

My little girl's second birthday so I'm in the kitchen knocking up a spag bol to feed twelve, hang on there's an idea....maybe for when I get that shop of mine – Bolognese in a pie? I've been harpooned pie wise because of the party plus my wallet is thinner than Albanian bog roll right now so I can only squeeze in a trip to nearby Golborne or Gow-bun as it's pronounced locally. When I'd mentioned that Pimbletts of St Helens had shut down a couple of exiled Wiganers I know were devastated, however upon their return to the borough, they confirmed I was talking bollocks – as the Pimbletts in Golborne has no connection at all to the defunct bakers in St Helens.

I have to be careful which lay-by I park up to eat today off the East Lancs as one of the Mudhuts crew has warned me that one of them is popular with gentleman who enjoy leisure pursuits of an adult nature, earning it the nickname of "the gay-by". Could be embarrassing as I'm certainly not one for sharing my pie.

I park next to some playing fields which I believe once witnessed the rare spectacle of me scoring a goal in a Sunday League game. I've got that chippy smell permeating through my nostrils and then I spot it: Tootells Butchers – we sell pies!! Hang on, that's not what I was looking for. But it is now!

First, H Pimblett where I pick up a meat and potato for just £1.05.

Then to Tootells Butchers just a few doors down resembling a pub with a large sign outside pendulating in the breeze. Their wares are out on the counter and the menu is up on a blackboard behind it. Meat, meat and potato and steak, that's your lot. But what more does a gentleman need? They've got a load of tinned veg and condiments there as well to compliment the meat and I have to declare a conflict of interest at this stage as the huge signed Wigan Athletic shirt on the back wall gives me particular pleasure.

As if to amplify the not-so-great sporting divide in the town, Pimbletts have several Wigan Warriors stickers plastered all over its windows and a "Try a Wigan Kebab" with the rugby's crest on it and the more neutral "Keep Calm and eat more pies". There'll be dyed in the wool rugby men who buy this book and upon realising that "one of them Laticsmen has written it" will probably ask for a refund. I'm a bit long in the tooth for all the feuding nowadays but there's more chance of a Palestinian and an Israeli shaking hands than a football fan and a rugby fan in Wigan getting along, such is the animosity.

There's an old girl doing the serving in Tootells but soon enough out comes Alan Tootell himself from the back. A distinguished chap with scraped back greying hair sporting traditional striped butchers' apron who greets me like an old acquaintance "Hello sir, what are we having today then?"

Two pies bagged and I'm as giddy as the kids on the roundabout at the playground next to where I've parked my car.

Today's taste test takes place overlooking a vista that I will probably end up moving to permanently one day, yes it's Wigan Cemetery in Ince. For the time being, a brief visit to pie heaven will suffice.

154.

PURVEYOR: H Pimblett
PREMISES: Golborne
PURCHASE: Meat and Potato Pie £1.05
PLACE: 8 Upgraded from 6 as I stand there simmering with rage whilst two old birds serve and chat to the same customer, oblivious to my existence. A bonny younger girl comes through and flashes me a smile and all is forgiven. She's all beads and bubble jacket and looks like she's just walked in from an all night rave
PASTRY: 9 Close to perfection. Fine soft shortcrust with only the crunchy crust lip providing a bit of solitary resistance
PRESENTATION: 6 A touch lukewarm unfortunately, the absence of a foil tray not helping
PACKAGE: 8 Standard healthy, sloppy, potato based mash with morsels of mince coming at me with aplomb
PALATE: 8 A lovely wet sensation in the mouth
PRICE: 8 Cheap
PORTION: 7.5 Deceptively large and heavy
OVERALL: 54.5/70.

I am met with interruption before devouring the second pie as two women walk past smoking with prams and multiple children in tow. I put my camera away, conscious that my behaviour may seem a touch shifty and before you know it two of their offspring (estimated age 5 or 6) decide to have a huge fight in the road in front of me following a verbal disagreement regarding the ownership of a bag of Quavers.

They play cat and mouse around my car, trading kicks and punches and both end up on the bonnet, as I sit there cowering, wiping pie crumbs from my face. The boy is pulling the girl's hair while their parents scream:

"YOU TWO, FUCKING GET BACK HERE NOW"

They turn to run and look dolefully at me through the car window, at which point she also helpfully shouts :

"YOU COME BACK NOW, THERE'S BAD MEN OUT THERE, THE

BOGEYMEN WILL GET YOU"

I slip my kitchen knife discreetly back in its sheath.
Only in Wigan. Now, where was I?

155.
PURVEYOR: Tootells
PREMISES: Golborne
PURCHASE: Meat and Potato Pie £1.10
PLACE: 8.5 Warm greeting upon arrival and a fond farewell with warm
pies in my hand
PASTRY: 8 A bit wobbly but manageable without spillage even when a bit
of crust gets stuck to the tray
PRESENTATION: 8 Even allowing for a break due to the commotion
outside, the pie retains its heat perfectly with a glorious smell emanating
from it. I'm always a bit dubious when I've two pies in the car which one
is giving off the Hollywood whiff, but it's definitely this one following an
up close sniff for confirmation
PACKAGE: 8 Sloppy, lucid filling but higher meat content than its
neighbour three doors down
PALATE: 8 Pinkish mincemeat bursting with flavour and devoured
with gusto
PRICE: 8 Still cheap
PORTION: 7.5 Butcher sized portion
OVERALL: 56/70 Two great pies, as difficult to separate as a pair of
squabbling infants engaged in an impromptu boxing match on my
car bonnet.

Saturday 24th November 2012

"Gonna get a stand pie from Wilsons in Crossgates. You know anywhere
that does a better one?"

So begins an eight page thread on laddish Leeds website One Mick Jones
run by former Loaded guru James Brown. Gauntlet thrown down in no uncertain terms and when a gauntlet is thrown down in Yorkshire, there's lots
of moody stares and lifelong friendships broken. It's a ticking time bomb.

Defiant debate ensues and far be it for me as a lily livered Lancastrian
to interject into their provocative pork pie proceedings. Blood spilled over
stand pies. I love that turn of phrase, ostensibly that it is a pie which
"stands" on display after leaving the oven.

So to Leeds and Bradford and its environs armed with that thread and
some butchers from the Pork Pie Appreciation group. I also solicit advice
from Bradfordian Keith Wildman, who comes up with one who only serve

pies to locals in the run up to Christmas. This parochial behaviour appeals to me no end. Not that I understand the association of pork pies with Christmas, must be a Yorkshire thing but I'm not objecting.

By eck it's blustery with my car blowing all over the M62 and I leave my SatNav to do its stuff, as I don't know my Bingleys from my Batleys and Bramleys, while I traverse the Pennines to the sounds of Kool and the Gang. Despite the Roses rivalry, we've probably more in common than we like to admit in terms of lifestyle, outlook and the love of a good pastry product. They do like their pies differently round here though.

The meticulous plan is to do a peripheral loop of Leeds and Bradford loading as many pies as possible into my car, a kind of Supermarket Sweep with me playing Dale Winton and the boot of my car being the trolley. My first task is to convince the proprietor of Hopkins of Birkenshaw that I'm a local and failing that I'll beg if I have to.

If I was from Bradford I'd be pissed off as the place is barely acknowledged on road signs until you get within a few miles of it, it's all about Leeds around here. I come off at Dewsbury (with its silent UU) and Cleckheaton, which recently finished runner up to Heckmondwike in the 2012 "Most Yorkshire Place name" award.

I head for Birkenshaw full of trepidation as to whether I will be granted ingress to the premises let alone be permitted to buy a pie. I'm even contemplating whether to attempt a Yorkshire accent. I park up next to a posh deli with the crappiest name I have ever heard (The Moon on a Stick) and smile feebly at an old dear, desperately trying to curry favour with the locals. Hopkins has a big sign outside "Hot Pork Pies on sale here" and a load of awards in the window. I'm greeted by growlers of various dimensions, alongside the odd Cornish pasty and steak and kidney and most importantly, a jolly non-judgemental Yorkshireman. I order a pork pie and a meat and potato at £1.05 each. The pies are warm and come in a branded bag listing their many accolades.

I get out and pass an off licence called The Ginger Whale – what is it with shit shop names around here – then a sewing and alteration shop called Pressed for Time – even worse – and hotfoot it to Morrisons as I need a wee. Then I consume my booty acquired to date.

In an interesting role reversal, the meat and potato is cold and the pork pie is warm so that's the one I go for first, keen to utilise its heat. Slicing it in half is a tester but when I get there I'm hit with a stunningly fresh aroma of sausage meat, and a little bit of jelly wriggles out and makes good it's escape. The meat feels a little tough and coarse to begin with but it is tantalisingly rich and all consuming on the tastebuds, with the jelly almost in liquid form getting free reign to soak itself into the pork. Cap well and truly doffed.

156.

PURVEYOR: Hopkins
PREMISES: Birkenshaw
PURCHASE: Pork Pie £1.05
PLACE: 8 He served me!
PASTRY: 8 Crisp, solid, hot water crust pastry
PRESENTATION: 8 Straight out the oven
PACKAGE: 9 Populated with slightly tough, coarse meat offering up lots of chewy resistance and the inside resembles the red colour swatch in the paint aisle at B&Q. If that doesn't make you emotional, the molten jelly will have you in tears of joy
PALATE: 9 Might be getting carried away here as it's the first of the day and I'm salivating like an under nourished dog but I'm speechless. A perfectly crafted combination of crunchy crust, moist meat texture and sublime, free roaming hot jelly
PRICE: 8 A highly reasonable price
PORTION: 8 Just the right size for a growler
OVERALL: 58/70 A truly gastronomic sensation.

157.

PURVEYOR: Hopkins
PREMISES: Bradford
PURCHASE: Meat and Potato Pie £1.05
PLACE: 8 **PASTRY:** 7.5
PRESENTATION: 7.5 **PACKAGE:** 8
PALATE: 8.5 **PRICE:** 7.5 **PORTION:** 6.5
OVERALL: 53.5/70 Another splendid pie which although of small dimensions, has plenty shoehorned into it with consistent rings of mince and potato so fresh it's green, encased in a crisp, golden crust. Fresh and full flavoured, creamy and well lubricated throughout, it smells gorgeous in the oven and is blowing steam off when it emerges.

After that pork pie I have to scurry off to Morrisons in Heckmondwike to buy some baby wipes to control my drooling and go for a wee. Thankfully I'd had the pie first as the stench in the bogs is so bad it'd put most people off food for a week.

I cross the green open square, wet with Autumnal hue, in search of Maughans. There's a highly eggy whiff to the shop, maybe because it's full of students who can only afford egg butties but the deli counter and cake display looks superb. They've got a good range of pies and even offer to

6666666

cut a plate pie into quarters for me. I plump for a pork pie, conscious that bakers may not get much truck around here from the more serious butchers, and get an "ooh you can't beat our pork pies" off her. A glowing endorsement indeed, though I would hardly expect her to say their pies are shit.

158.

PURVEYOR: Maughans
PREMISES: Mirfield
PURCHASE: Pork Pie £1
PLACE: 8 **PASTRY:** 6 **PRESENTATION:** 7 **PACKAGE:** 7
PALATE: 7 **PRICE:** 7 **PORTION:** 7.5
OVERALL: 49.5/70 A bit dry with not too much jelly in evidence and when I pick it up the meat jumps out and deposits itself on the kitchen floor (of course I ate it) Well filled with a raised centre and good quantity of sausage meat however.

Right, welcome to Bradford, home of Bradford City, Bradford Northern, fabulous curries and Rita, Sue and Bob too. There's a ring road of sorts but it's single lane, flanked by terraced houses and Morrisons and littered with shady coppers pointing hand dryers at motorists. Bronte Country sounds interesting but it transpires Haworth is a trek too far. Shame really as it sounds exactly the sort of middle class haven that will possess a bevy of artisan bakers selling posh pastry products and bread that you need a mortgage to buy.

The constant flanks of browny grey terraced houses give it the feel of a large town rather than a city, but some districts definitely have that edge to them as I pass through the beating heart of the city. It's Shipley where I'm off next. As the terrain takes on a more Asian flavour, I'm chugging along in mid morning traffic neck craning at Halal butchers and Polish delis looking for, well you know. I pass a large demolished Grattan warehouse, a sign of more prosperous times but now it's just a shell. I spent much of my childhood thumbing through the Grattan catalogue telling my mum what I wanted for Xmas, and a few years later peering innocuously at the lingerie section. It's all obsolete now: a shopping medium only maintained by the very old.

On through Manningham and again, there's hundreds of little convenience stores and I'm half tempted to pull up and bob in, but then I'm out of it again and driving alongside the large and regal looking Lister Park, with its turreted entrance. A breezeblock Greggs appears to signal the end of an inner city melting pot and the start of public schoolboys doing cross country runs as bridal shops and bigger houses emerge. I park up outside a cheese and chutney shop and seek out Melvyn Davies' gaff with its large italicised font. Standard cakes and breads and sandwich counter but there at the end of this elongated shop next to pasties and sausage rolls are a brace of pies: cheese and onion or meat and potato, one of each – that's your lot. Served straightaway, the pie is oval shaped, furnace hot in my hands and smells terrific. Nice one Melv.

159.

PURVEYOR: Melvyn Davies
PREMISES: Bingley
PURCHASE: Meat and Potato Pie £1.25
PLACE: 7.5 **PASTRY:** 6.5 **PRESENTATION:** 8 **PACKAGE:** 8
PALATE: 7 **PRICE:** 7 **PORTION:** 7.5
OVERALL: 51.5/70 High meat to potato ratio with a dark mince and gravy interior, raised in the middle, hence not quite filled, and possessing one of the thickest top crusts I've had, arguably a bit too much. Still quite deep and a cute shape to it.

Shipley has the strangest looking shopping precinct dominated by a clock tower with floors missing, and a highly impressive Salvation army building which resembles a castle. I'm now moving on to the notorious Otley butchers. Not only recommended via the One Mick Jones website but I also find a cracking write up on "How not to do a food blog" which confirms that the residents of Otley are indeed motley.

As I move into a Leeds postcode I find myself loudly singing the strains of Marching Altogether, despite being flanked by stunning Yorkshire Dales and vibrant countryside which opens out for miles in front of me. I seem to have accidentally circumnavigated both cities. It's just the way it falls as city centres now are a procession of Greggs, Starbucks, Nandos and McDonalds as they're the only ones who can afford the rates. The descent into Otley is undulating but offers an amazing view of the town as we drop down with it's beautiful reservoirs, towers and er....Waitrose.

The two butchery big hitters around here are Weegmanns and George Middlemiss. I gather Middlemiss is more nationally recognised due to its stack of awards, whereas Weegmanns is the more locally acclaimed, as evidenced by the queue snaking out of the door. As I've discovered, winning awards is more about entering shitloads of competitions rather than having genuinely better pies than someone who doesn't but we'll see. Time to go and join the throng.

It's a smart market town but designed for walkers not shoppers so I park up outside a health nutrition shop down the road where the proprietor will shortly be disgusted with me as I return to the car with a procession of growlers. She appears to have brown hair dyed grey in the middle and spends the whole forty five minutes I'm in Otley stood in her shop doorway yapping to a woman on the street. I could do with some supplements if I'm honest but she's going to think I'm a right barmpot with vitamins in one hand and half a dead pig in the other.

I pass the Otley Conservative club, clearly the locals are a separate demographic to Heckwondwike with its Comrades Club, and amble down the cobbled streets. I pass Middlemiss' first which has full on carcasses strung up around the walls and also a veritable cornucopia of pies in its window: lamb, chicken, beef, meat and potato plus a load of pork pies, some of which would break a tape measure in terms of diameter. The growler is handed to me in a branded wrapper, still warm, and I can feel the grease seeping through to my fingers. This is a good thing!

160.

PURVEYOR: George Middlemiss
PREMISES: Otley
PURCHASE: Pork Pie £1.10
PLACE: 7.5 **PASTRY:** 7 **PRESENTATION:** 7 **PACKAGE:** 8
PALATE: 8 **PRICE:** 7 **PORTION:** 7
OVERALL: 51.5/70 A dark, crispy, heavily glazed pastry which is a little tough on the gnashers in parts but worth biting through to get to the fine, cured sausage meat and bountiful supply of jelly encased within. Lightly seasoned to give stronger focus on the pork flavour which is tender and delicious, but the jelly is the star of the show here.

As I head to Weegmanns I also pass Wilkinsons Butchers who have a wealth of meat on display – on another day I'd be like a rat up a drainpipe but today I'm sticking to plan. Poor buggers, their produce may be excellent but imagine being the third best butchers in such a small town? Especially when butchers are dying out, like all sole traders, getting devoured by multi-corporates. As if to evidence this, I walk around the Market Place which is currently being polluted by a Greggs being fitted in neutral slate grey, as opposed to garish turquoise, as is the wont of town planners in posh places. I take my place at the back of the throng queuing for Weegmanns.

Weegmanns is a veritable institution, established 1869 and there are dozens of people scattered about in a series of disorderly lines. From what I can tell the left hand side is all cuts of meat, in front is a carvery and to my right are such delicacies as beef dripping, black pudding, potted meats and polony along with an army of pies winking seductively at me.

There's some weighty looking (Yorkshire) pasties for a quid and big stand pies in the window but I again resist the temptation to order half a dozen different ones and opt for the traditional Weegmanns pork pie for a mere one hundred and five of your hard earned English pennies. Not with apple, nor stuffing, just pork. There's tray after tray of them and people are buying by the dozen.

161.

PURVEYOR: Weegmanns
PREMISES: Otley
PURCHASE: Pork Pie £1.05
PLACE: 7 The queuing system is a bit of a mess. There's a big queue for hot barms and only two or three waiting for pies but the crafty geriatric in front of me orders a pork pie and then "decides" he wants a hot beef barm as well. Sneaky old bastard

PASTRY: 8 Golden, shiny and sticky which flirts with the gums like a common limpet
PRESENTATION: 7.5 They've been standing a while so the jelly has semi-solidified but nevertheless pleasantly warm
PACKAGE: 9 When I cut it in half, I've never seen as much packed into such a tight area. It is the Tokyo rush hour of the pork content world. The beautiful pink pork meat is gasping for air but it is restrained by a casing of lush silvery green jelly holding it hostage both inside and out
PALATE: 8.5 The sausage meat is so rich it should be sailing around the Mediterranean in its own yacht. The kind of pork texture that when you bite into it your teeth bounce off the filling
PRICE: 7.5
PORTION: 7.5
OVERALL: 55/70 Sumptuously well crafted.

Finally to Wilsons in Crossgates, one of the best butchers in the country - they ALL say that! The top end of Leeds looks quite well to do, there's subtle indicators, like the fact the goalposts have nets in them when there's not even a match on. And I mean all of them not just the boys' prep schools.

The local news is awash with rumours that Leeds United are about to get taken over by wealthy Bahrainis who will pump billions into them to make them a global force again. Is this another false dawn for this famous old Yorkshire club?

On to Crossgates through Seacroft and the more familiar Leeds terrain of endless council flats and rum looking estates and I find Wilsons on the main shopping street just a short hop off the main ring road. As ever, parking is at a premium and liable to cause open warfare when you park in someone's garden or a permit holders only bit. Oops. My peripheral vision spots the gold and green of Wilsons quality butchers so I saunter over and needless to say there's a parking spot right outside. When I return to my car someone has parked right up to my bumper to all but block me in and left a snotty note saying "Where's your permit!!" Salt of the earth Yorkshire folk!!

Wilsons is expanding as they've bought the plot next door and are turning it into a bigger deli. Me, I'm distracted by the great smell coming from the Crossgates fish bar nearby; my hunger is on the John Wayne a bit after all today's consumption but that is truly marvellous.

The pies aren't exactly prominent in here but I do spot some steak pies, Cornish pasties and sausage rolls on a back shelf. The enticement of a golden, circular gift of a pork pie for just 98p easily wins me over. However, I decline the option of accompanying mushy peas and gravy for another quid, although they've got ready made tubs if you want to take the works home with you.

162.

PURVEYOR: Wilsons
PREMISES: Leeds
PURCHASE: Pork Pie 98p
PLACE: 7 The woman who eventually serves me is a touch surly but at least she does serve me unlike the rest of the staff who are deeply engaged in "demise of Leeds United" chat with some old boy
PASTRY: 7 Dark golden brown and shiny and crispy
PRESENTATION: 7 Served warm-ish
PACKAGE: 8 It detaches itself from the crust after the first bite but it's of generous capacity. I suspect putting it back in the oven causes the meat to slip away from the crust due to the jelly melting and leaving a gap. This probably generates years of debate around here
PALATE: 8 A messy job but the sausage meat is fine, juicy and tender and the jelly luscious
PRICE: 8 Under a quid is not to be sniffed at
PORTION: 7 High centred and heavy
OVERALL: 52/70 It's good but I was kind of expecting something superhuman given their reputation, whereas in reality it's only the 3rd best pork pie I've had today.

I spot another butcher when I have eventually airlifted my car out of the tightest spot in Yorkshire called Sedgefields and spot the familiar mound of growlers piled high in the windows. Shall I? Again, I feel a bit sorry for the bugger – it must be a proper pain in the arse being situated around the corner from a competitor who claims to be the best in Britain. The bloke's just trying to earn a crust. Did it really take me 60,000 words to get that shit pun in?

After a full day at it, I feel wholly pork pie accustomed now and completely get why they are so loved. Serve up a hot pork pie in many other parts of the country and people will generally think you're barmy. It's the Pavlov's dogs syndrome, just like any Cornishman worth his salt would turn his nose up at anything that's not eight inches long with a side crimp containing swedes. A country of culinary contrast.

I head back across the M62 perfectly timed to terrify me as the motorway is jam packed with VEHICULO LONGO's as the Hull ferry has obviously just come in while I concoct an excuse to explain to Emma why I've been out nearly all day. I just got carried away like usual....

Wednesday 28th November 2012

Back in work and there's a place in Runcorn claiming to serve the best pies in Cheshire, a bold claim indeed. The skyline of Runcorn is one to behold and I always end up transfixed by the sight of the Mersey Estuary opening out beyond the billowing chemical plants. As I get led up above the town where the Cheshire Bakehouse is situated, the view opening out is truly spectacular.

My main concern when I arrive is that it appears to be a tea room type establishment, popular with backpackers wandering up to that world renowned tourist attraction Runcorn Hill. I've spent too long in the Lakes and a pint of real ale and stodgy pie always beats a pot of tea and scones hands down.

I wander in and hear the familiar tinkle of a bell and I'm immediately in a café with loads of people seated and a few scally workmen types propped up on bar stools around the perimeter. She turns to wipe the counter and till clean before serving me. I order the obligatory meat and potato pie and she doesn't even understand me, she literally can't tell a word I'm saying. Runcorn's not that far away and I haven't exactly got the sort of Wigan accent last seen down a pit in Victorian times. I suppose the accent is noticeably different though if you've ever overheard Sporty Spice having a conversation with George Formby.

I leave her to it to bang it in the oven/microwave whilst I use the bog.

£1.30 changes hands and I set off back to work with this hot chunky pie burning the palm of my hand.

163.

PURVEYOR: Cheshire Bakehouse
PREMISES: Runcorn
PURCHASE: Meat and Potato Pie £1.30
PLACE: 8 Aloof at first as she does her cleaning routine but I get a free wee out of it
PASTRY: 7 Nicely glazed but crust lip a touch crumbly
PRESENTATION: 9 Still scorching 20 minutes later when I sink my teeth into it giving off a strong almost uniquely cheesy aroma enveloping my car while steam fumes out of it like a chemical chimney
PACKAGE: 9 The most intensely filled pie I've had in some time – absolutely out of this world. Big chunks of prime beef, packed with potato and plenty of moist juices flowing around
PALATE: 8 I actually came here first in January and found it a touch dry and tasteless. Today this is rectified. Whereas some meat and potato fillings turn to mush – and I've not got a problem with that, it is a cheap feed owned by the working classes never to be purloined by haughty aristocrats – where was I....this does buck the trend as there is half a cow in here but the amount of juices flowing around and succulent potato chunks keep it nice and liquid throughout
PRICE: 8.5 A really stunning pie for £1.30
PORTION: 9 Wide and deep with a raised top crust which generates a bit of airspace yet you will not feel cheated in any way
OVERALL: 58.5/70 I'm lost for words. A truly fantastic pie.

Saturday 1st December 2012

Lancaster or Liverpool today. My options are dwindling as Em's in bed with a migraine. I've had my eye on Satterthwaites of Crosby for a bit but sadly it seems they closed for good last month, causing an outpouring of grief not seen since Lady Di passed away. (NB They resurfaced late 2013)

When Emma does eventually surface she says "ooh Lancaster, I'd like to go there!". It's nearly twelve o'clock – fuming here! Liverpool it is in search of Scouse Pie.

I ask some Scouse mates who come up with very little and I find a Mitchells Bakery on the internet which is part of a social housing project. Interesting, although described as a "Hippy commune" by some Daily Mail reading eurosceptic on one article. I'm really struggling to find anywhere that cuts the mustard and sells Scouse pies. I'll head for a branch of the legendary Sayers then – they MUST do them?

Being a woollyback entering this fine city is always met with a sense of fear and trepidation. They call us that because anyone beyond their city borders clearly is a farmhand who walks around chewing a bit of straw and er "does things" to sheep.

I used to work in Maghull many moons ago, I was a chauffeur. Well I say a chauffeur, I used to take my dad's mate to work as he'd been done for drink driving. He worked at a Toyota garage however so just occasionally he'd let me take one of the fast cars out and we'd drive down the chronically quiet M58 motorway at the speed of light for a laugh: Toyota Supra, Nissan 200SX you name it. Probably the best car I had was a long forgotten MG Maestro EFI Turbo which was like shit off a shovel. Oh how I loved that petrol guzzling bastard!

Maghull is generally considered one of the more demure areas of Liverpool although the first thing you notice upon entering is the top security Ashworth Hospital, home to Ian Brady. We used to play football against the wardens, they were right horrible bastards. Most of it appears to have been built over though. My SatNav insists on saying Maghull like Maghowl which rhymes with Raul, the footballer. Unfortunately, I have an affliction that whenever I hear Raul's name I'm forced to howl "RAULLLLL, RAULLLLLL" in a werewolf type manner.

The Maghull Sayers is on a little low level precinct at the side of the road next to Maghull's Premier Fish Bar, fortuitously called Maghull's Premier Fish Bar. It contains a serious amount of savouries inside from chilli pasties to sausage rolls and an army of pie types with two meat and potato sizes – small (99p) and medium (£1.20) but NO SCOUSE PIES!! They look discernibly different to the Hampsons and Pound Bakery brands however.

It has a moist filling containing juicy morsels of mince and large slabs of potato, which are impeccably soft along with a gentle peppery kick to remind you who's boss inside a very robust crust.

164.

PURVEYOR: Sayers
PREMISES: Bolton
PURCHASE: Meat and Potato Pie £1.20
PLACE: 7 **PASTRY:** 7 **PRESENTATION:** 7 **PACKAGE:** 8
PALATE: 8 **PRICE:** 8 **PORTION:** 8
OVERALL: 53/70 There's massive chunks of potato with a high meat content too and maybe even a bit of onion in there giving it a surprising luxurious taste. The crust is dark brown and well glazed, if a little crumbly in parts, but the pie possesses an admirable depth to it. You see – Scousers do like pies after all!

Still no Scouse Pie though so I head deeper into Liverpool on pie safari. This is why I get in a mess, as my obsession continually gets me into trouble. I head through Switch Island – famous for the big hand painted graffiti which used to be on the bridge at the end of the motorway which said "PIES THIS IS YOUR TIME". I negotiate the seething mass of traffic and head for Bootle docks. It's not the most salubrious place but the cranes and wind turbines towering in the sky make a fascinating panorama. On my right, I speculatively spot a corner shop called the Oven Fresh Bakery sat beneath some flats – you know the drill by now as I veer sharply across three lanes of traffic.

Nothing like an on the hoof discovery and the Oven Fresh Bakery again has a very wide choice. She runs me through the range – she doesn't mention it and I'm afraid to ask for a Scouse Pie: I might have only driven two miles further in but her accent is ten times thicker than the one in Maghull and I have to have my wits about me to keep up with her.

165.

PURVEYOR: Oven Fresh Bakery
PREMISES: Liverpool
PURCHASE: Meat and Potato Pie £1.10
PLACE: 7 **PASTRY:** 7 **PRESENTATION:** 8.5 **PACKAGE:** 7.5
PALATE: 7 **PRICE:** 8 **PORTION:** 7.5
OVERALL: 52.5/70 This scorching hot number is lifted straight out of a steel oven and consists of creamy mash and little tints of mince with a glorious smell to it. The crust feels a little thick and dry and I can feel HMS Heartburn is about to anchor in the harbour of my stomach. Another very solid (and cheap) pie nevertheless.

I plug in the next Sayers' address, as the one I had been guided to is just a bus stop and head through an area called Orrell. I see a row of shops and I'm doing the neck craning thing and hang on – yes!! A butchers!! A big burgundy canopy: GH Farrer quality butcher. I wander in and there's meats in the window, fruit and veg at the back and tinned stuff on the walls. Amidst the plate steak and cheese and onion pies and Phil Manion branded sweet pies, there – at long last is a square tray containing a Scouse pie. Cinderella, you shall go to the ball!

The old Scouse girls waiting ask "have yer got much to get lad?" Me, no not at all – just a Scouse pie. So they part the waves like Moses parted the Dead Sea and wave me to the front . "Aw they're lovely they are" says the lady behind the counter. Glowing endorsement over, I procure said pie for 99p and they wrap it in a polythene bag. See, I told you they were lovely people in Liverpool!!

Sometimes you've just got to ignore the internet and get out in your car and look for things yourself. Google can't do that for you (yet), can it kids?

166.

PURVEYOR: GH Farrer
PREMISES: Liverpool
PURCHASE: Scouse Pie 99p
PLACE: 9 **PASTRY:** 7
PRESENTATION: 7 **PACKAGE:** 7.5
PALATE: 7 **PRICE:** 8.5 **PORTION:** 7.5
OVERALL: 53.5/70 After my courteous welcome I am greeted with a pie that has a high meat content – (possibly mutton) mixed in with potato and slithers of onion. Clearly it only has a crust lid however, which brings into question it's credentials as a pie but I knew this before proceeding and its inclusion is justified due to it being a geographical variation.

A pan of Scouse is also a popular dish in Liverpool, something which my mother in law makes a belter of, although it's basically a Lancashire hot pot under another name. As for the Scouse Pie, it's best to lift off the crust and whack it on a plate. It's just a shame they stopped selling them in the away end at Everton: surely every football ground in the country should serve a delicacy pie prevalent to its local culinary roots?

Saturday 8th December 2012

I was never likely to get far in December but I've had my pass sanctioned to travel (just) over the border. What I haven't told her is that half the roads up here are closed due to ice, thus my mission is a perilous one. So I head for the hills and cross the Lancs/Yorks border through glorious wintry countryside, the kind that makes me want to hum Greensleeves. The peaks are all around me, capped with snow, whilst on the lower level horses shiver their poor bollocks off perched atop of imperiously steep verges.

I don't know much about Hebden Bridge, even Wikipedia only propels forward the nugget that singer Haddaway filmed his 1995 video "Lover be Thy Name" here. My incentive for going is that I was watching the news a while back when there were heavy floods and as I surveyed the carnage of people lining up sandbags and sweeping up their sodden shop fronts, there amidst the scenes of destruction, I saw the vision of an establishment called "Drive by Pie" in the background, while a bloke in a canoe paddled up the road. Upon checking their website they appear to have a stunning range of pies available. Not sure how the "Drive By" concept is factored in (more like "Paddle By") but what makes it even more appealing is that there is another pie shop next door. Intriguing.

I pass through Todmorden and the town of Portsmouth (!) whilst singing The Verve's Lucky Man because my wife lets me go and eat pies for a hobby, even though she's commented on my weight gain recently.

Next stop Hebden Bridge along the main Burnley to Halifax road which weaves seamlessly alongside the River Calder. My first sight is a large estate of plush new build houses trying desperately to look old build so they can be flogged for a song whereas on the other side of the road they're offering idyllic river cruises. It's about minus fucking five outside!

I had considered Hebden Bridge a normal Yorkshire town and was unaware of its status as a "hippy commune" (© that Daily Mail commentator) Every shop has the word "organic" in its title. Sakers Bakery has ample quantities of delightful looking bread and cakes on offer but the one thing it doesn't have is meat! Yes it's a veggie bakery. They even sell Quorn (presumably) sausage rolls! And pasties and pies but only cheese and onion, Mediterranean veg and Mexican chilli and cheese – see that'll do for me. It's a flat dish pie and is served excessively warm as the foil tray scalds my hand.

167.

PURVEYOR: Sakers
PREMISES: Hebden Bridge
PURCHASE: Mexican cheese and chilli pie £1.30
PLACE: 7 Pleasant enough, they're not wearing a "Meat is Murder" apron
PASTRY: 8 The top crust predominantly consists of cheese but hey, I like cheese
PRESENTATION: 8 Phew, what a scorcher
PACKAGE: 8 Not the regular filling but a kaleidoscope of colour exists within from red to maroon to orange to green and it's densely packed to capacity
PALATE: 8 Enjoyable. Any concerns over lack of meat struggling to satisfy are quickly addressed as I'm pleasantly surprised to find it gastronomically endearing. The chilli introduction is moderate, a gradual sensation rather than a spicy mouth explosion, which makes for a very well rounded flavour
PRICE: 7
PORTION: 7.5 At least five inches in diameter if a little shallow
OVERALL: 53.5/70 I can't see that there will be a massive market amongst vegetarians for this book if I'm honest, but nevertheless it wins the veggie vote.

I whizz through Hebden to head for Mytholmroyd. I park on a hump backed bridge overlooking avant garde balcony clad swish apartments. Hang on was that place closed then? Drive By Pie is definitely open. Apparently Waites are notorious for being erratic but not being open on a Saturday lunchtime is criminal.

Shite, it's shut! Not permanently mind as I can see the Christmas decs are up and there's drinks in the fridge. Yet the ultimate insult appears in the form of a printed A4 sheet of paper on the wall: "WIGAN BUTTY: HOT MEAT AND POTATO PIE AND BUTTERED TEACAKE £1.85". Grrrrrrr!!!!

So to Drive By – and this one's shut as well! Well not strictly true, it's open however it's now a bloody newsagents. The impressive Drive By Pie signage is still intact above the shop but on the wall underneath the main window there is a bedsheet pinned on with "Brooks Newsagent – now open" badly hand painted on it. Not amused here.

I've had one pie and no meat this morning and this makes me as unstable as a North Korean dictator. Time to get the phone out and sort out a Plan B. There's another Waites in Hebden Bridge centre, amidst the myriad of arty book and gift shops, so maybe I'll just park up and wander around till I find something.

I dump the car on a pay and display so close to the river that my front wheels are hanging over it and find the shop. Also closed but at least they have the decency to put up a sign saying closed all day Saturday. There's lots of butchers here but that is all they seem to be, meat only gaffs: joints and sausages. This is getting on my tits a bit now – what's wrong with you people?

Where do you get a pie in Hebden Bridge on a Saturday?!?

If I wanted some expensive trinkets or baubles hand carved by Egyptian peasant boys I'd be laughing, but the lack of pastry products to sink your teeth into is highly irritating.

I chance upon the drearily named Country Stores and notice that aside from the signage championing their new vegan takeaway (FFS!!) they appear to have some award winning pies in the window alongside a slow roasting ox. Praise the lord!

They are AJ Pies & Pastries Ltd and they have meat and potato, pork, chunky chicken, steak and onion and steak and treacle stout pies – sounds good but sold out so I'm left with the "award winning" meat and potato. I ask for a hot one and she pulls one off the shelf which I only notice later is burnt to an absolute crisp. The top crust is blacker than three in the morning!

She's sold me a dummy here. The pies were behind her so I couldn't even employ the old etiquette of pointing to the one I wanted, like you do with fish in the chippy (or indeed lobsters in a restaurant). She deliberately chose this savagely char-grilled beast for me rather than other non-burnt pies.

168.

PURVEYOR: A&J Pies
PREMISES: Huddersfield
PURCHASE: Meat and Potato Pie £1.90
PLACE: 6 For looking at their stock and thinking "Let's give this dickhead the really burnt one"
PASTRY: 6 I like my burgers char-grilled but not my top crusts. Unforgivable
PRESENTATION: 6 Nope nothing here either, it's lukewarm at best

PACKAGE: 7 Not a lot of it but a very high meat content and a bit of jelly as well. Well ventilated with a large amount of airspace between top of filling and roof of pie
PALATE: 7 dry, unsurprisingly
PRICE: 6.5 If A&J is the same as A Jones Pies then they've added 60p mark up AND ruined it
PORTION: 6.5 I'm just being bitter now
OVERALL: 45/70 Poor show. I don't know who does these pie awards but they won't be getting one off me unless it's the "most burnt pie sold to a customer 2012" award. Put that on your fucking wall!

Hebden Bridge eh? I've had a 'mare.

So I head back through Todmorden which is also bereft of pie shops save for the ones which I've done before like Mannings and Oddies or the perennially shut Waites and then on to Bacup back in Lancashire. It's not got a good reputation this place, famed for the gang of kids who stabbed a Goth to death a few months back. I did go watching Bacup Borough once though who seemed almost human if a little late in the tackle.

It's a fact that you always have to serve penance when crossing from Yorkshire to Lancashire, a no man's land in the form of bloody big hills and I think that's the way folk on both sides like it. A swathe of undulating isolation to separate the two warring counties.

Today that road to Bacup is steep and dangerously icy and not for the faint hearted but there's cars coming the other way so it must be passable right? The upcoming hills are blanketed with snow; I've got a white van man up my arse and a nervous Nissan Micra in front which is skidding all over the road. I'm too young to die, why does he always take the good ones first? (And me) The things I do for my pie.

"Welcome to Lancashire, home to careful drivers". Tell me about it, the bloke in front of me is getting overtaken by slugs in hi viz vests. Six feet mounds of snow at the side of the road. When I arrive, Bacup's probably a little bit more serene than the world gives it credit for, its biggest blight on first inspection being the plethora of 'When red light signals please wait here' temporary traffic light road signs. I've had my phone out in the meantime and found J&G Bakers, it's anonymity and vagary somehow enticing me to its furry environs. It's 1pm now after a morning spent hopelessly fannying around, so will they even be open or have any pies left?

Last chance saloon: can't see anything as I crane my neck left and right so I park up and tackle the slippery footpaths of Bacup. I get an even icier stare off a local body builder and his petite velour tracksuited bird, a look so menacing that it burns a hole in my head. No, I'm not from around here – and the glare implies that they know it. I need to wear a hoodie barely concealing a selection of neck tattoos to properly fit in from the looks of things.

It's way below freezing outside and a middle aged fella is walking down the road wearing a Fat Willy Surf Shack tee shirt, jeans cut off at the knee and smoking a cigarillo with a crate of Carling under his arm. Just one of those places.

Eventually J&G Bakers materialises in front of me. It's a sparsely populated shop with one customer in: a huge, bespectacled ginger lad who appears to be paying for his dinner exclusively with two pence pieces. Jesus this is painful.

I survey the scene and it's good to see two trays of festive mince pies at the back and pies starting at just a quid: meat and onion, cheese and onion and meat and potato. The Lancs/Yorks pie theory crystallises as the pie is filled again with creamy mash and much smaller cuts of mince. By the time you get as far as Blackpool or Preston it's nearly all potato to the extent that they just call it a potato pie much to a Tyke's chagrin but it's horses for courses.

169.

PURVEYOR: J&G Bakers
PREMISES: Bacup
PURCHASE: Potato and Meat Pie £1.10
PLACE: 7 **PASTRY:** 7 **PRESENTATION:** 7.5 **PACKAGE:** 7
PALATE: 7.5 **PRICE:** 7.5 **PORTION:** 7.5
OVERALL: 51/70 Not the deepest or thickest pie but silvery glints of fresh potato are complimented by rounded chunks of ground mince, the sort you get atop of a mighty meaty pizza. The crust falls to bits somewhat

when I extract it from the tray but it's soft with a well crimped crust edge and certainly fills a hole, coming to the rescue after disappointing Hebden.

Monday 10th December 2012

The internet has a nasty habit of turning entrepreneurialism quickly into plagiarism the second you type something into Google and you get it confirmed that some other bugger thought of that great idea first. There's been a programme on ITV at 4pm called Britain's Best Bakery, which involves travelling the country seeing what regional bakers have to offer and it's making me nervous so I've Sky+ed every episode to play back.

Thankfully it seems to be a touch more on the artisan side, focussing on fastidiously prepared cakes and breads as opposed to my crude attempts to wolf down as many pies as possible with the tastebuds of an insensitive skunk.

I feel like this book is a race against time. There's blogs out there, a football lad's 92 Pies book, Great British Bake Off and the Hairy Bikers, loads of people, mainly chefs, writing about pies. What felt like a novel idea now feels like a saturated market. Regardless of this, me and Mrs T are addicted to BBB. I love the passion that all these independent craftsmen and women possess and the language the experts use, which piss all over my own cack handed attempts to describe what I am eating.

I know the North West pretty well but I make a note of many of the entrants from elsewhere. Then somewhere like Broughton Village Bakery come up and the couple tell us they've sold their house and car and put everything they own into it, it's heart warming and in a non-patronising manner I'm thinking – yes I need to go there! Yes I will give them my business!

Tuesday 11th December 2012

200 pies consumed this year. I don't have a lot of time during the working week but I've developed a craving for pork pies (subsequent to my recent Yorkshire jaunts) and I know there's a butcher called Ken Boon in Chelford, a couple of miles from where I work so I'm going to whizz over. His name isn't Ken Boon but it's definitely *something* Boon.

I'd previously given it short shrift as it looks so small from the front but the Cheshire Pie Society blog speaks of it in revered tones so I'll give it a bash. Turns out they've got a website and on there they humbly claim to make some of the finest pies in the North – yes another one!

A five minute hop down icy country lanes finds myself parked up at the back of Boons. I pull into the car park behind an Andrew Ridgeley scaffolding van.

I'm surrounded by stable type buildings – not the most confidence inspiring sight when you visit a butchers. There are two serious looking big boned young men chopping away in the abattoir at the rear and inside there are steaks and chickens hung up, plus a big cheese counter then hey presto – a section full of pies.

I ask for pork pies as none are on display. A nation needs pork pies at Christmas I now know! I'm flummoxed because they're in a foil tray. I buy a (hot) meat and potato and get a whiff and it's bewitchingly good, the pork pie can wait: time to get stuck into this red hot stunner.

I pull into a lay-by only for the ex-Wham front man to attempt to pull into the same space seconds later. I've stolen his favourite lunchtime scoffing haunt, that's if he was indeed coming here to eat. He's seriously pissed off with me.

170.

PURVEYOR: AJ Boons
PREMISES: Chelford
PURCHASE: Meat and Potato Pie £1.78
PLACE: 7.5 Highly jovial festive spirits
PASTRY: 7.5 Very rich and sticky glazed pastry, a touch flaky in parts but of high quality. Biting into it and tugging on the crust causes a tremor which makes the filling spill out but this is managed by sucking bits of the gravy out at regular intervals to ensure it doesn't land in your lap. Find the leak. Control the leak. Minimise spillage. I could be an oil rig safety officer me
PRESENTATION: 8 Boiling
PACKAGE: 8 It comes oozing out: delightful centimetre square chunks of potato with lashings of mince and gravy
PALATE: 8 Opulent and peppery with flavour that comes seeping out of the pie and hits you right between the chops
PRICE: 7 Just on the periphery even though butchers are usually a bit cheaper than bakers
PORTION: 7.5 Oval shaped and deep
OVERALL: 53.5/70 Top notch.

Needless to say I'm now staring lustfully and dribbling at the pork pie, like a Disco Dave at ten to two looking for a slow dance but my phone goes and I get summonsed back to work.

I take it home and stick in the oven. The pastry looks a bit more shortcrust than water based and curiously the crust lid doesn't quite cover the pie giving you a tantalising teaser of what lies beneath with meat and jelly poking through. The meat is coarse and very pink but there's a lot of it and has been squared off inside rather than opting for the ice cream scoop approach.

It's encased in a tasty jelly which partially dissolves in the oven. The meat is a bit chewy but highly savoury and augmented perfectly with runny jelly and spice, giving the tastebuds a great hit.

171.

PURVEYOR: AJ Boons
PREMISES: Chelford
PURCHASE: Pork Pie £1.38
PLACE: 7.5 **PASTRY:** 7.5 **PRESENTATION:** 7 **PACKAGE:** 8
PALATE: 7 **PRICE:** 7.5 **PORTION:** 7.5
OVERALL: 52/70.

Saturday 15th December 2012

Desperately seeking Reuben Marsden today, a 19th Century Jewish immigrant famed for his butter pies who settled in Lancashire. Clearly he's not still alive but his baking might be. Good old Harry Pearson's Top 10 Bakers list (in a Guardian article to promote his marvellous cricket book *Slipless in Seattle*) continues to unearth hidden gems but this one looks by all intents and purposes a goner.

With its long tree lined avenues, Chorley is a place I came to as a fifteen year old full of hopes and dreams of being a footballer for a then Conference team, only to have them dashed due to a total lack of ability.

Now I'm back to eat pies. I arrive at the first Marsden shop and find a Handleys butcher/bakers: it's changed name and hands but more importantly it is open. The sight of a smiling, stout looking fellow with a newly broken nose, carrying a bag of booty out is enough to entice me through it's big, blue fronted entrance complete with matching Christmas decorations.

There's a big huddle of people inside but when the old bird shouts "who's next" they stand aside especially for me and I get a potato and meat pie for £1.30. I spot the butter one just a little too late, too busy admiring the pork chops and black puddings.

The Handleys crust looks soft and contains a funnel of semi-solidified gravy poking out of the top, a promising start which reminds me of the Wigan pies of my youth. Upon cutting it in half it has a very dark interior and the gravy comes spilling out but it is a wide crimped crust edge and everything about it just feels good. The crust is not strong enough though as evidenced by filling escaping out; when I put my finger on the base it pokes the insides out causing them to slop all over my festive Christmas jumper.

172.

PURVEYOR: Handleys
PREMISES: Chorley
PURCHASE: Potato and Meat Pie £1.30
PLACE: 7 **PASTRY:** 7.5 **PRESENTATION:** 7 **PACKAGE:** 8
PALATE: 8 **PRICE:** 7 **PORTION:** 7.5
OVERALL: 52/70 A quintessential meat and potato with great potential consisting of large hearty slabs of potatoes and succulent mincemeat wrapped in lashings of sloppy gravy. However, the bottom is too unstable to eat with the hands and it perhaps lacks a little seasoning.

Car dumped on the edge of Chorley as I continue on foot, searching for Reuben Marsden's other shop. Past a host of pawnbrokers and the beery fumes of a Last Orders pub. Chorley's position at mid-point in the triangle of Wigan, Preston and Bolton suggests it's shopping area should be decimated but it's bearing up well. My Christmas spirits are lifted by the sight of a full brass band doing carols accompanied by school kids and a mini fair buzzing with life.

I spot a butchers and a Glovers bakers but head on through Chapel Street looking for Marsdens. Right to the top and I am greeted with nothing but a decaying sign in the window partially covered in rotting newspaper. Marsdens is no more, I suspected this in truth.

I go to Glovers for a butter pie and she asks if I want a hot one or a warm one. I get fleeced for 27p vat putting the price up to £1.62 from £1.35. It's not that hot as I tuck in to this wonderful smelling Lancashire delicacy and wolf it down in record time.

173.

PURVEYOR: Glovers
PREMISES: Preston
PURCHASE: Butter Pie £1.62
PLACE: 7 Served in a branded wrapper by a young girl who really is as nice as pie
PASTRY: 8 The top crust is scored several times making it look like a Chinese symbol but it is solid overall
PRESENTATION: 7.5 A wonderful clean, fresh smell about it
PACKAGE: 8 Upon cutting in half I'm greeted by a spectacular mound of potatoes accompanied by an almost sickly yellow buttery mixture binding

it together. The butter bit can sound a bit off putting but the constituent ingredients are potato and onion, the butter just adds some mouth-watering moistness to proceedings

PALATE: 8.5 Glorious swathes of lush, fresh potatoes in a delicate herby sauce

PRICE: 6.5 Fight the pasty tax, don't apply it!

PORTION: 8 A weighty size but then spuds are cheaper than meat generally!

OVERALL: 53.5/70.

Thursday 20th December 2012

I'm not sure whether this is weak or resilient but I've booked the morning off to go Christmas shopping and my first thought is to head to Hebden Bridge to complete some unfinished business. Waites have a Facebook page and are advertising their turkey and cranberry pies so it must bloody open at some point. Despite being on holiday I've got a work conference call at 8.30am till 9am so I'm sat in a lay-by the other side of Burnley getting ready to pounce.

It is yet again a foul and fierce day on the Lancs/York border as the road meanders through the hills and at least one lad gets a fearful soaking from an unsighted puddle at my car's hands. Merry Christmas pal!

Streams are gushing down from the hills at a frantic pace and flooding the roads under the stunning Todmorden viaduct. I never thought I'd find the need to go to Hebden Bridge once in my life let alone twice. The signs upon exiting cry out "That was so Hebden Bridge" Does that even make sense? Disused factories and antiquarian bookstores. Fair play to them for reinventing themselves, a cultural necessity no doubt welcomed given the harsh economic evolution faced by many Yorkshire towns, but it sounds a tad preposterous and I'm not sure it would work everywhere though. "That was so Stockton-on-Tees" sounds a bit shit doesn't it?

I spot the open door and green canopy of Waites as a furious yellow haze of light emanates from the window, where girls wearing green hats and aprons cheerfully shout "Morning" waving their obligatory wrist tattoos. Manna from heaven.

Pies galore, so many I have to ask what the range is. A lot of them look quite deep but pork pie sized whereas others are small and plate shaped – one of those must be the meat and potato but no – turns out it's a tall, deep affair instead and peering through the porthole I can see lashings of dark meat and gravy in situ. I forego the "pie barm" option to focus solely on the pie.

174.

PURVEYOR: Waites
PREMISES: Hebden Bridge
PURCHASE: Meat and Potato Pie £1.15
PLACE: 7 **PASTRY:** 7 **PRESENTATION:** 7 **PACKAGE:** 8
PALATE: 7.5 **PRICE:** 8 **PORTION:** 7
OVERALL: 51.5/70 I've Waited (!) a long time for this and upon inspection
the pastry appears to be hot water based like a pork pie containing very
distinct chunks of steak and potato drowning in lots of warm opulent
gravy. It's deep, thick and engaging but a little bit disappointing diameter
wise and I can't help feeling let down as I'd built it up in my head to be a
pie of supreme stature. It's not.

There's something about the town of Glossop which amuses me. I think
it's because when you take away the double S you're left with Gloop. Anyway, I've seen enough recommendations for JW Mettrick & Son, over the
Derbyshire border, to pay it a visit en route to work. So off to Gloop I go
to sample yet more award winning pies (according to their fancy website)
Apparently their steak and potato pie, served at Gloop North End home
games was the best football pie in 2010 no less.

The natives of the Glossop parish have complained for years in a vocif-
erous manner about needing a bypass as the drive off the M67 over to the
Sheffield part of Yorkshire is one of the most tortuous there is: a crawling,
sprawling, seething mess of traffic. Although classed as Derbyshire and on
the edge of the Peak District, I suspect Glossop is pretty much an outskirt
of Greater Manchester (although it also has a reputation for being a League
of Gentlemen type place as it was filmed around here) but it seems harm-
less enough if a little gridlocked.

The reference point is a tall, thin steel chimney which towers above the
town like an industrial Beetham Tower, a reminder of a more prosperous
era as towns like Glossop now desperately scurry round trying to reinvent
themselves as tourist towns for walkers to compensate the fact that their
industries have been decimated.

I've grown to love butchers like this. The separate queues for hot food
are always a bit disorientating to out of town morons like me trying to
mentally record the interior but I have to step outside as the pies are in
the window: Dinky meat and beef pies, huge pork pies and big plate ones
which resemble russet brown satellite dishes.

I go to the takeaway counter and order a pie expecting something hot
to take away. The girl behind the counter make me look a right plum as
she walks out, brushes past me, reaches onto a cooler shelf behind me and
takes a cold pie off it.

No hot ones then? Must be on Sheffield/Derbyshire protocol. What on earth do they do for lunch, take it home and warm it up in the microwave? Are they too tight to pay VAT and taking no chances? Strange pie etiquette.

It is of a good size with a dark velvety crust raised in the middle on a rigid base and is definitely Yorkshire steak and potato not Lancastrian meat and potato if the whopping great chunks of steak and dark gravy are anything to go by.

175.

PURVEYOR: JW Mettrick
PREMISES: Glossop
PURCHASE: Steak and Potato Pie £1.30
PLACE: 7 I'm sure she was just being helpful
PASTRY: 7.5 Thick, lofty and crisp, the interior pie roof resembles a big meaty cave
PRESENTATION: 8 Clearly I have to cook this myself but after twenty minutes in the oven the steam is chugging out of it giving off a sublime whiff
PACKAGE: 7.5 The first bite reveals a huge chunk of tough juicy braised steak and a singular large slab of potato with enough gravy to give it a liquid feel in the mouth
PALATE: 8 A rich, meaty flavour as you'd expect complimented by moist but not too runny gravy
PRICE: 7 Excludes cost of cooking it
PORTION: 7 The raised ridge of the crust is unfortunately a ventilation space rather than extra filling
OVERALL: 52/70 It's a lovely well defined pie that you want to give a hug but dabbling on dangerous ground by failing to insulate it's cavernous loft with meat.

Monday 24th December 2012

Off to my brother in laws in Yorkshire for Christmas. But not before I pick up one final festive pie on the way, this time from Golcar, home of Bolster Moor Farm Shop, voted 2nd best pork pie by the Pork Pie Club.

I love the farm shop couture around these parts. Head off the M62 and loop back over a bloody big hill up to Bolster Moor perched majestically between Golcar and Slaithwaite (pronounced Sle-wit) It's gloomy in Golcar as you'd expect when you're driving up a road called Scapegoat Hill. Cars parked at owner's risk. Yeah thanks for that I've only got about £500 worth of presents for the whole family, my laptop and an iPad in the boot but I'm only nipping in for a growler. It's noisy and chaotic inside:

jittery, well heeled couples searching for a turkey and nabbing sacks of spuds, while young men in white coats are hosing down and scrubbing the fish counter.

The back wall is festooned with awards and posters of their successes including the five times Pork Pie club winners. The Real Madrid of the Pork Pie Club awards. They're clearly very proud and passionate about what they do but I can't see what I'm here for. It's a bit of a shambles full of people walking around randomly until I see a large wire steel trolley full of pork pies with an impromptu queue forming. I try to gauge the etiquette from the woman in front of me but she offers no clues.

"What pies have you got mate?"

"Just these stand pies left – I've got one pound and two pound stand pies"

He means weight not price I think....

From the size of them I'd best take a one pound then. They're clearly designed to be served up as part of a Christmas platter but this one's about to be eaten whole by myself.

The pie has a delightful coffee coloured crust consistent throughout and upon cutting into it I get a fresh cured pork meat scent hitting me. It's size and weight is vast and even half of it will be a formidable eating challenge but I'll give it a go.

I park up in a side street in Huddersfield to munch my pie. Before long, an overly made up woman walks past wearing a very short skirt, who pauses to look through the window. Shit where am I at all? Sorry love, that simply isn't the kind of pork I'm interested in right now. Shortly after, the only other person to disturb me during my fifteen minute porkfest walks past: a seedy looking chap wearing a long mac and in possession of a limp. It looks like I've parked up in an erm uncontrolled zone completely unbeknown to myself (your honour) with factories and warehouses, all eerily quiet if you get the picture.

176.

PURVEYOR: Bolster Moor Farm Shop
PREMISES: Golcar
PURCHASE: 1lb Pork Pie £2.99
PLACE: 7 Like an Egyptian bazaar
PASTRY: 8 Good, solid and golden. The roof is delicate, a textbook colour and a little bit sticky in the mouth
PRESENTATION: 7.5 Uncomplicated Yorkshire appeal to it
PACKAGE: 8.5 Full to the brim. Succulent but not too seasoned allowing it to concentrate on delivering its core flavours with an ample layer of jelly between crust top and meat
PALATE: 8 The pork is cured but intense with soft jelly interspersed

between huge scoops of sausage meat
PRICE: 8 Serves four (non ravenous)
individuals
PORTION: 9 It weighs a ton! I need
a trolley to get it out of the shop. If you
can get your gums around this from top
to bottom then you've got a bigger gob
than me
OVERALL: 56/70 It's becoming more and
more evident that the lads at the Pork Pie
Club of Sowerby Bridge seriously know their shit piewise. A truly joyous
pie at a joyous time of year.

Saturday 29th December 2012

Off to Penkridge in Staffordshire, popular haunt for away trips on the way
to Aston Villa and of course there's a bakery on the square, Jaspers. It certainly beats paying the prices at Villa Park where it's £3.20 for a Pukka pie.
At those prices I'd expect a pie jacuzzi to dive into and swim around in
while munching on chunks of steak.

They're queuing out the door of Jaspers, where the windows have steamed
up due to the mass of bodies huddled inside. The pasties look the popular
choice, perfectly formed in shortcrust or puff pastry. My mate Moore has a
corn beef one whereas I opt for their two pie varieties: a steak and kidney
(£1.20) and a "child's pork pie" (as it's dubbed by the culinary experts on
Arky's Coach Tours) and carry out my review in a nearby phone box.

177.

PURVEYOR: Jaspers
PREMISES: Penkridge
PURCHASE: Steak and Kidney Pie £1.20
PLACE: 7 **PASTRY:** 7 **PRESENTATION:** 7 **PACKAGE:** 7
PALATE: 7 **PRICE:** 7 **PORTION:** 7
OVERALL: 49/70 A distinctly average pie with dark gravy and slightly
jellyish meat. Clearly a local treasure of a bakery but with the emphasis
on bread, cakes and pasties rather than the humble pie. The pork pie has
a lovely hand raised shape to it with a shiny crust but my attempts to
review it on the way back are somewhat incoherent amidst the backdrop
of fifty sweary, drunken blokes crooning their finest rendition of Billy
Joel's "Love Really Hurts Without You" whilst savouring a 3-0 away win.

Saturday 12th January 2013

New year, new resolutions and time to reflect on what possesses a grown man to spend his Saturday afternoon driving to Worksop.

I've got the girls with me which means I'm unlikely to hit my quota. On the plus side I get the enchanting company of the two special ladies in my life but the downside is I usually only end up getting half the pies I plan to as it takes too long for them to get ready, get out and get around whichever region I am headed. I also have to converse, amuse and entertain thus making it difficult to get in the 'pie zone' and give those golden packages my undivided attention.

A touch of déjà vu as I head over the Woodhead Pass and spot the familiar grunt of an Iceland HGV labouring up ahead as my petrol light fades to orange. This place I'm going is only open till 1 o'clock, you've got a lot to answer for here Katona. It's a beautiful wintry day alongside the choppy waters of Longdendale Reservoir and pretty soon we're past the 'Welcome to Barnsley' sign situated in the middle of nowhere following mile after mile of rolling desolate hills, before hitting the town of Penistone which always manages to appeal to my childish nature. As the road turns into a dual carriageway I get a conciliatory light flash off the Iceland lorry as if to say "thanks for putting up with me" making me feel like a right twat for slagging him off for the past twenty minutes.

Worksop appears to be situated in a SatNav black hole as I'm frantically waving my phone and Emma's phone in the air while steering with my knees as I get haplessly sent around their one way system for the eighteenth time.

So to Wrights of Carlton In Lindrick, a corner plot situated down a quiet back street with an open kitchen full of people beavering away. There are large plate pies on display and "open porkies" – basically unfolded sausage rolls – thus forcing me to ask where the pies are and incredulously this award winning pie maker only has frozen pies. She pulls a bag of steak and ale out of the freezer and charges me £1.59 for one. This does not scream award winning pie at me if I'm honest.

I can see some dark gravy escaping from the crust but the foil and base feel badly uneven, folded over in parts and it isn't the most visually appealing prospect. Once cut in half the pie struggles to maintain its volume as it's basically a thick layer of steak propping it up on both sides. Furthermore it appears to have mushrooms in it forcing me to walk in the lounge with it and exclaim to the nonplussed wife "it's got mushrooms in this!"

I know some people like mushrooms in pies but they should at least be advertised as such and could also be perceived as compromising on meat content. It's not a heinous crime and for some people it may add flavour but it's nice to be informed as I'm none too keen on eating them. I mean would you buy a mushroom pie on its own? There's your acid test right there.

178.
PURVEYOR: WM Wrights
PREMISES: Worksop
PURCHASE: Steak and Ale Pie £1.59
PLACE: 7 Hey they broke up a three pack for me!
PASTRY: 7 Thick, crumbly, heartburn inducing, wobbly pie casing. It's redeeming feature coming in the form of two sweet pastry hearts adorning the top crust
PRESENTATION: 6 Not so much cold as frozen
PACKAGE: 7 High meat quality, nice gravy but lacking in volume despite being padded out with mushrooms
PALATE: 7.5 The splendid gravy saves it's bacon
PRICE: 6.5 Expensive for a frozen pie
PORTION: 7 Rounded oblong shape but with little depth to it
OVERALL: 48/70 Not off to a flyer in 2013.

Lunch is taken in a swish restaurant at Arrowe Farm Shop nearby. Needless to say there is an ulterior motive at work as the shelves are full of goodness to feast my eyes on, including a full rack of pies from Meadowfresh carefully nestled below a range of cheeses and a whole partridge ready to eat, the poor scrawny little bugger.

The pies are predominantly steak based: with onion, stilton, potato, ale, mushroom, kidney or indeed just steak along with chicken and mushroom. I plump for the steak and potato for £1.29 on the pie front but I am also drawn irresistibly to the pasties as well which are creaking and growling angrily on the shelves, due to their sizeable presence. The largest is the Derbyshire Pasty (sigh!) and it's simply too huge to ignore. It's a controversial choice of name given I'm actually in North Nottinghamshire, part of the Midlands, in a shop with a South Yorkshire postcode buying a Derbyshire pasty. It's the size of three counties anyway and shaped like a golden half moon.

While munching on paninis I contemplate hopping into Chesterfield while the girls finish their lunch but upon establishing it's not a mere five minutes down the road like I just told them, I quickly realise a lynching will be in order on my return and the "day out klaxon" is about to be sounded. I save it for another day and we head to Eureka in Halifax before I seriously piss Emma off. The little 'un loves it.

179.

PURVEYOR: Meadowfresh
PREMISES: Chesterfield
PURCHASE: Steak and Potato Pie £1.29
PLACE: 7.5 Charming staff
PASTRY: 7.5 A rounded oblong shape with a robust top and softer base which all holds together well to keep the flavour and heat intact
PRESENTATION: 8 The crust does its job perfectly ensuring I am hit with a wall of intensity upon opening her up
PACKAGE: 7.5 Featuring cubes of potato, liberal quantities of braising steak mixed in with rich gravy. It says it may contain bone but thankfully doesn't
PALATE: 7.5 The potatoes are deliciously soft and melt in the mouth with loose gravy and luscious steak all flowing around it's casing
PRICE: 7.5 See, that's a reasonable price
PORTION: 7.5 Ample
OVERALL: 53/70 It's a 7.5 pie alright.

180.

PURVEYOR: Meadowfresh
PREMISES: Chesterfield
PURCHASE: Derbyshire Pasty £2.99
PLACE: 7.5 As above
PASTRY: 7.5 A tiger skin pastry, not too flaky and doesn't darken too much in the oven
PRESENTATION: 8 Quietly intimidating package
PACKAGE: 8.5 Piled high with stewing steak, large slabs of potato and the less familiar content of onion, swede, peas and carrot
PALATE: 8 Moist enough inside to keep the meat and vegetables juicy and married together to make a fine symphony of superb ingredients
PRICE: 8
PORTION: 9.5 – 8 inches by 4, probably the size of two normal pies pushed together
OVERALL: 57/70 An unfeasibly large and appetising meal.

My consolation prize is found in the form of a Beefsteak and London Porter's Ale pie as I mope around Sainsbury later that evening, a wise move to buy one in given the inclement weather forming outside.

181.

PURVEYOR: Sainsburys
PREMISES: London
PURCHASE: Beefsteak & Porter's Ale Pie £2.99

PLACE: 7 Genuinely surprised with how genteel Halifax is, I might get a different view if I walk around a Lidl mind you
PASTRY: 8 Hand crimped and folded into a shamrock shape. Novel
PRESENTATION: 7 Nice box and that
PACKAGE: 8 Not quite full up but plenty of sweet and sumptuous chunks of meat and rich sauce come slopping out
PALATE: 8.5 Eureka indeed – you can actually taste the Porter in there! See it's not that hard! Yet the shallots, carrots and sugar give it a delightful sweet edge too
PRICE: 6 Perhaps worthy of a premium price but aren't supermarkets meant to be cheap?
PORTION: 7.5 Sad dad meal for one
OVERALL: 52/70 Just about edible with the hands but I keep a tray underneath as the uncontrollable filling and gravy attacks at high speed.

Wednesday 15th January 2013

Rochdale, or at least Rochdale Football Club, are noted for their pie and peas. But sadly after a bit of searching I discover their pies are now supplied by Clayton Park; I'm sure it wasn't always thus.

I'll still go for a gander mind you. I end up searching on a Rochdale Online forum, one of those typical community sites full of nostalgia soaked old dodderers reminiscing about days of yore. They'll definitely tell you where you can get a brilliant pie from, the only drawback is that the shop closed in 1952.

Failing that, I tend to seek out local knowledge through my football and writing contacts but I don't have any in Rochdale. There was that young female blogger from Rochdale who was blonde and attractive but I unfollowed her as much of her premise appeared to be about her being blonde and attractive. Nice girl mind you.

I come off the M627, surely one of the shortest and most pointless motorways in the world and head towards Rochdale. My first port of call is Smiths Confectioners not in Rochdale but nearby Castleton, home to the once wonderfully monickered Castleton Gabriels Football Club, sadly now renamed as Rochdale Town probably to generate wider appeal. Where's the romance in that?

I pull up outside the big orange front of Smiths, next to a newsagents where the local newspaper headline is 'Arm cut off in horror DIY accident'.

I walk in and scrutinise the shelves and walls for a price list. Starting at 60p we have a dinky pie and at the top end you can procure a huge meat plate pie for £2.80. There's cakes and crisps and drinks and a happy lady in an apron comes over to serve me.

182.

PURVEYOR: Smiths
PREMISES: Rochdale
PURCHASE: Meat and Potato Pie £1.30 (£1.08 cold)
PLACE: 7 **PASTRY:** 7 **PRESENTATION:** 7 **PACKAGE:** 8
PALATE: 8 **PRICE:** 7 **PORTION:** 8
OVERALL: 52/70 A well seasoned peppery effort but charging 22p to
have it hot is a bit cheeky. In truth I'm that hungry that I wolf it down too
quick to take a picture.

I head past a big green pub called the Farewell (which ironically appears to be shut down) and on to Wardle on the other side of Rochdale. It's a picturesque walking village at the foot of the South Pennines with a well kept main square and a butchers called Bob Watmough's.

The Village Bakery (also known as Tattersalls) doubles up as an off licence and convenience store and as I step out of the car I get a wonderful smell of clean, fresh air. It's a busy general store with everything from tampons to toilet roll and beans to bleach bottles. There's pies on display at the front and a few trays behind them containing four types of pastries: meat, meat and potato pies, cheese and onion and Cornish pasties. The core bedrock of a pie menu. "They're warm not hot" she tells me. I need to know the temperature to avoid disappointment. Or having the roof scorched off my mouth.

183.

PURVEYOR: Tattersalls
PREMISES: Rochdale
PURCHASE: Meat and Potato Pie £1
PLACE: 7.5 **PASTRY:** 6.5 **PRESENTATION:** 6 **PACKAGE:** 6
PALATE: 7 **PRICE:** 7 **PORTION:** 5
OVERALL: 45/70 Oh dear, this is desperately disappointing. A very small
pie with considerable airspace inside and a very thick, tough crust like a
hardened pork pie, which I nearly bust my teeth on.

I need to get home now as I'm on a half day to look after Jess while Em and her sister go to watch Psychic Sally. I'm not sure I believe in all that nonsense but I do know my future will involve eating lots of pies. Preferably bigger and better than this one.

My tummy is feeling seriously unfulfilled – I'm that hungry I pile into the factory shop of a biscuit factory by the motorway to take up their offer of a bag of broken ones for a quid.

Saturday 26th January 2013

Macclesfield away in the FA Cup and I haven't seen a single pie shop all day so I decide to get one on the ground. Surely with Macc being a non league club their fodder will be a fine standard of home cooked fayre? What I find is a large sign advertising Brassingtons and I am charged £2.80 for a meat and potato pie. Whether the thieving swines have whacked the price up because several thousand Wiganers are in town remains to be seen. I attempt to negotiate a lower price but clearly these ladies are in no mood to engage, despite having their Saturday afternoon enlightened by the visit of hundreds of inebriated football fans with rapier like wit.

184.
PURVEYOR: Brassingtons
PREMISES: Macclesfield
PURCHASE: Meat and Potato Pie £2.80
PLACE: 7 **PASTRY:** 8 **PRESENTATION:** 7 **PACKAGE:** 7.5
PALATE: 7 **PRICE:** 5 **PORTION:** 7.5
OVERALL: 49/70 A velvety felt-like buttery crust adds a real touch of class to this pie. It is occupied by lovely round morsels of potato, a decent meat content and slightly ventilated at the top. That price though, ooh it makes me hopping mad!

Tuesday 29th January 2013

A few of the lads who've got wind of what I'm doing were keen to learn where the best pies were in Macc and the truth is I don't know. My googling keeps coming up with one name again and again and that name is Broadhurst Butchers. Well they can't be as expensive as the one I had on Saturday I know that much. A quick canter through towards the rough end of Macc and there it is perched half way up a hill.

A gaggle of pensioners are just departing, resplendent with tartan shopping trolleys full of baked goods. I am pleased to be greeted with a front window full of pies and a hand written price list on the wall offering up beef, beef and onion, meat and potato, pork, pork and apple, pork and black pudding, fidget pies on Saturday only and FREE PIES which have the words "sold out" scribbled next to them. Ho ho ho.

They also have a complimentary sauce basket on the counter which is a nice touch, only tempered with a stern "only one sachet per pie please" warning scribbled underneath. I can't decide between meat and potato and pork so I plump for one of each, paid for with coins I've craftily picked up when a pensioner dropped his money all over the shop a minute ago

which I pocketed during the commotion. Finders Keepers old boy!
As if I would!

185.

PURVEYOR: Broadhursts
PREMISES: Macclesfield
PURCHASE: Meat and Potato Pie £1.30
PLACE: 8 For the free sauce and shit jokes
PASTRY: 8 Delightfully tender crust with a tributary of dried gravy
escaping from the ventilation point on top
PRESENTATION: 7 Temperature just about right
PACKAGE: 8 Densely packed chunks of mince and potato
PALATE: 7.5 A mildly seasoned affair with both constituent parts bound
and harnessed together perfectly
PRICE: 7 Saved by free sauce
PORTION: 7 Not the biggest but a lot packed into it
OVERALL: 52.5/70 Just a really great traditional pie from a great
traditional butchers.

On to the pork pie and as we say in the trade "mo' jelly mo' problems" as
it is absolutely covered in it both on top and inside; so much so that it spills
out into my hands whilst eating it.

186.

PURVEYOR: Broadhursts
PREMISES: Macclesfield
PURCHASE: Pork Pie £1.30
PLACE: 8 **PASTRY:** 7.5
PRESENTATION: 7 **PACKAGE:** 8
PALATE: 7.5 **PRICE:** 7 **PORTION:** 7
OVERALL: 52/70 It's served and eaten
cold but that does not detract from the
taste. Lightly seasoned meat with a
hardened pool of salty jelly on top
complimenting the semi coarse textured meat perfectly. I suspect it's the
type of pie that's primed for the "Yorkshire method" given it's abundance
of jelly but then I've not exactly had great success heating them up. Plus
I'm too bloody greedy to take it home.

Wednesday 31st Jan 2013

Pie and chips for tea (Greenhalghs). A last supper as Emma puts her foot down. A holiday discussion summit in advance of my forthcoming 40th birthday. We go from East Anglia to Turkey to Center Parcs to Benidorm and eventually Blackpool. We are NOT going to Suffolk for your 40th birthday. You are spending it with your family not driving around East Anglia looking for pies for hours on end.

She's the boss. And remarkably tolerant. I'll get there. Just a bit slower than I anticipated.

Saturday 2nd February 2013

So where to today then? Well given the discussion/debate/argument of last week it will be a local jaunt. I follow my nose, or rather a comment below the Harry Pearson article which states that "Eddlestons in Great Harwood do the best potato pie you'll ever taste". As I Google the address I spot a link to a food hygiene piece which tells me it's rating is nil – urgent improvement necessary!! Food hygiene – pah, bunch of jobsworths!!

Surely it will now be the cleanest baker in East Lancashire following receipt of this none too illustrious accolade?

My Great Harwood (near Blackburn) story isn't mine to tell but here goes anyway. Sometime in the Sixties, Wigan Athletic (then a non league team) were drawn away at Great Harwood in the FA Cup. As a veritable giant back then in the amateur game, the hosts were expecting a big travelling support. However, the weather turned fearful (as they say in olden times) and there was concern the game may not go ahead. One Wigan supporter who relayed the tale many years later, had been working away close to the area and went straight there. He turned up at the magnificently named Showground and wandered into their Supporters Club before the game only to find it deathly quiet and devoid of life. The game had been postponed, the pitch six inches deep in snow following a pre-match blizzard.

He walked towards the bar but was distracted by a solitary figure sat in a dimly lit corner, openly weeping and spinning the barrel of a pistol. It was the chairman of Great Harwood FC. "Five hundred pies I'd ordered, five hundred pies"

A mere fifty years later on I find myself hurtling up the M65 crooning along to the sound of Odyssey's Native New Yorker. I've just overtaken a van which says Polish Village Bakery on the side. Hmm I wonder? Might be time to engage in a spot of Solidarność with our East European brethren? (Alas, Googled later = no pies)

For the above narrative amongst others, it seems Harwood invokes a great deal of Lancastrian romanticism which is further embellished by a horse and cart clopping away along the road when I pull off the motorway.

The dominant feature in Harwood is the grand old picture house now sadly boarded up. The place in general looks a bit, well....closed. I wander nervously down the main street I clock the faded blue and gold front of Eddlestons with paint peeling off the exterior walls and I almost walk past as I'm not certain it's actually open.

I find a spacious store with barms and rolls beneath the counter and racks of hot pies. The meat and potato is £1.50 but it's a large discus sized plate pie, nearly six inches wide, and I can barely wait to get stuck into it. I'm parked between the Great Harwood Gym and the Police station. If I don't piss the gymgoers off, then the local pie loving constabulary will get narked with me waving a knife about.

187.

PURVEYOR: Eddlestons
PREMISES: Great Harwood
PURCHASE: Meat and Potato Pie £1.50
PLACE: 8 Brisk and efficient, cheery and curvy staff passionate about pies
PASTRY: 8 Lovely melt in the mouth buttery pastry curiously topped with four square peaks like a pair of little devil's horns
PRESENTATION: 7 Clean! Have some of that Food Standards Agency!
PACKAGE: 8.5 A generous capacity for a plate pie, anyone from over the Pennines would be aghast at the low meat to potato ratio but it works for me
PALATE: 8 A highly potatoey affair with the merest fleck of meat content. Perhaps a touch dry due to the size and volume of potato slabs, supplemented by further potato in the mash with mince. Lightly seasoned with a bit of onion in there but overall a fabulous pie. Dare I suggest a bit of Lancashire sauce would put the cherry on top here?
PRICE: 8 Not cheap but great value
PORTION: 9 A daunting size which just about fits in the palm of my hand and possesses both the diameter and the depth to fill the heartiest of appetites
OVERALL: 56.5/70 Would kick the ass of many a Wigan pie this.

The last time I visited the Reebok Stadium I tweeted a picture of an advertising hoarding featuring Carrs Pasties, my intrigue getting the better of me as usual. A chain of events was set in sequence where someone passed me on to someone else who happened to be a member of the Carr family and not only offered me a platter full of pies and pasties but also a guided tour of the factory. We exchanged pleasantries, followed each other and then just last week he unfollowed me, obviously bored shitless with my inane football chatter. I was never keen on a nepotistic arrangement anyway, it compromises my impartiality.

I head south through Abbey Village and past Turton towers, resembling a rocket ready to launch on a beautiful day. Flanked either side by the brown scorched hills of the West Pennine Moors, I'm tailgated all the way to Bolton by some shades wearing nobhead in a Porsche, as the A675 weaves it's merry way through a series of reservoirs which serve the North West of England with clean, pure water. Apart from that time I had a wee in one of them aged ten.

I climb over Winter Hill, home of the TV mast and sheep, some of whom refuse to remove themselves from the road forcing me to slam on and even Bolton looks beautiful on such a clear, fine day. I aim for the hubbub of downtown Halliwell looking for the Carrs Pasty shop and also passing another bakers called Mandy's four doors down.

There only appears to be one pasty on the shelf – bit of a drawback with it being a pasty shop an' all. They do pies too but I stick to the agenda as the pie woman gestures me forward with her index finger.

188.

PURVEYOR: Carrs
PREMISES: Bolton
PURCHASE: Meat and Potato Pasty £1.30
PLACE: 8 Speedy and polite enough to warn me that it's hot
PASTRY: 8 A perfectly crafted delicate form to it with a splendidly crisp outer texture and fluffy interior
PRESENTATION: 8 Comes in trendy branded wrapper bag
PACKAGE: 7.5 Light fluffy mix of mash with mince ringlets and filled right to the corners unlike a lot of pasties where you often find a stubborn rump of pure pastry towards the edges
PALATE: 8 A tantalising, all encompassing, all singing and dancing traditional meat and potato mixture with the faintest glimmer of pepper adding a bit of oomph to proceedings
PRICE: 7 Not being funny but have you seen what Ye Olde Pasty Shoppe are charging? (When it's open)
PORTION: 7 Compact with good capacity
OVERALL: 53.5/70 Yeah they're good but feel a touch homogenous and for this reason would only ever come second in the Bolton Pasty Wars.

Still I'm not done yet. Oh Mandy's, you came and you gave without baking....it'd be rude not to. I leg it up the road to the shop with the distinctive medieval-type font on the front of it admiring the Viennese fingers in the window. There's very few savouries out and the pasties again look infinitely more attractive than anything else in the shop. I enquire about pies and she points at a sad looking circular vessel sat in the corner of a hotplate like the runt of the litter. The last pie.

I can spot a meat and potato a mile off but this one is sat in the corner and falling to bits: the last poor, bedraggled, neglected mongrel in a dog's home. What it needs is a good owner to take it home and look after it and erm….eat it quickly.

189.

PURVEYOR: Mandy's Bakery
PREMISES: Bolton
PURCHASE: Meat and Potato Pie £1.20
PLACE: 7.5 **PASTRY:** 7 **PRESENTATION:** 7.5 **PACKAGE:** 7.5
PALATE: 8 **PRICE:** 7 **PORTION:** 7
OVERALL: 51.5/70 The crust is crispy, almost oval shaped and rigid. Whereas this sturdiness makes it ideal to eat with the hands it isn't recommended for anyone with false teeth. It has a sweet reassuringly inexpensive flavour and texture to it with hints of pepper and ingredients gently stock soaked and bound together.

Saturday 9th February 2013

Horsemeat found in pies scream the papers, I'll never eat burgers again says one angry reader. I've never understood this snobbery over eating one animal but not another. Once you hop into the carnivore bed all moral high ground is lost I'm afraid. If it tastes good, who gives a shit? Just because one is cuddlier than another, doesn't mean it's any less righteous to pop it in the oven. Anyway, as the horsemeat scandal continues to rage, what better way to spend a Saturday than roaming the country eating my own body weight in processed meat.

I was going to head to Skipton but with Emma being an absolute diamond, she approves me permission to plot out a more ambitious day breaking the back out of East Yorkshire with a nice circular route I have mapped out.

The sun doesn't want to get out of bed today and neither do I. It's so glum that I can barely make out the "I wish my wife was as dirty as this" scrawled onto the rear of the white vans I'm overtaking. The sky is barely illuminated by snow capped hills as I aim for Denby Dale, supposedly the home of massive pies. Not that there is a specific point of purchase for these voluminous vessels unless you count the ones you find in freezer compartments in supermarkets.

As I'm flying solo today I've dug out a load of old CD's to accompany me encompassing everything from Bez's Madchester Anthems, Ash, Carole King (for when I get all maudlin later with a stuffed belly) and somewhat aptly, given my ultimate destination, the very best of the Housemartins.

I get directed through Huddersfield and the ring road takes me through an area which resembles downtown Govan, complete with teenagers wearing onesies on a frosty morning to go and purchase cigs from the newsagent.

I reach Denby where the sky is shrouded by its stunning viaduct as I descend the hills to weave my way ethereally into Denby Dale. I still don't know what I'm looking for but it will appear in front of me, of that I am certain, and as I pull up outside the Post Office, Gawthorpes Butchers appears.

I am served by (I presume) David Gawthorpe himself who repeatedly calls me "Lad" but is jolly and chatty which is no mean feat at 9am on a Saturday morning. The pies are wrapped to go and scored with a series of crosses and dashes on the top crust to signify it's content, like a pastry Morse code.

190.

PURVEYOR: David Gawthorpe
PREMISES: Denby Dale
PURCHASE: Steak & Ale Pie £1.29
PLACE: 8 **PASTRY:** 8
PRESENTATION: 7 **PACKAGE:** 8
PALATE: 8 **PRICE:** 8 **PORTION:** 7
OVERALL: 54/70 X marks the spot on this highly prized treasure as a dark dense and sticky crust with a mysterious X scored into the roof gives way to nothing more than thick full flavoured boulders of steak.

While I'm here I pop into the Dale Bakery further down the road after spying the "Hot pies and pastries sold here" sign. It's a slightly different customer experience here as the girl serving appears to be slumped on the counter with her head in her hands. Not an auspicious start but she chirps up when the doorbell tinkles. I'm disappointed by their limited pie selection however. Their meat and potato again looks familiar, suggesting the Wrights Pies van (Crewe not Worksop version) has paid a visit to this establishment.

It's a bit suspicious. It feels too Lancastrian after we've travelled through West Yorkshire and are almost in South Yorkshire. The meat is mince and there's a high lumpy, potato content. I suspect it's been shipped over Snake Pass earlier this morning. The wide crimped top crust looks vaguely familiar and there's not a lot of pies on show which implies they may not have been baked on the premises. Hark at Poirot here!

191.

PURVEYOR: Dale Bakery
PREMISES: Denby Dale
PURCHASE: Meat and Potato Pie £1.10
PLACE: 7 All three girls warmly chorus a "see you love" on my way out which more than makes up for their initial inertia
PASTRY: 6.5 Thick, heartburn inducing crust edge
PRESENTATION: 8 A lovely pastry smell coming from the oven upon reheating
PACKAGE: 7.5 Tasty dominant chunks of potatoes with token mince elements
PALATE: 7.5 Delightfully fresh slabs of potato with a slight peppery kick
PRICE: 8 No complaints here
PORTION: 7.5 If Denby Dale really is the home of the world's biggest pies this one would get a complex
OVERALL: 52/70 A good solid pie despite me challenging it's dubious origin.

A train passes overhead futuristically as I double back under the viaduct and plot my next course. Given my penchant for underestimating distances I am pleasantly surprised to find that the Rob Royd Farm Shop in Barnsley is a mere twenty minutes away. Past the big "WELCOME TO BARNSLEY" sign in its big bold font which has absolutely fuck all behind it. They don't do themselves many favours down at the Barnsley Tourist Office.

On through Penistone, who still haven't changed the I to a Y, and then Silkstone, which sounds a bit racey for Yorkshire and is full of power walking pensioners. I guess they got the better end of the deal there namewise.

After traversing over and under the M1 on any number of occasions, I finally land on the outskirts of Barnsley, which seem a bit urban for a farm shop. One minute I'm in the grid style sprawl of slotted white fronted council houses, then a quick left and I'm out in the country again at the Rob Royd Farm Shop with its cafe, florist (for some reason) and panoramic views of the M1.

It sounds a bit Scottish but it is a little gem in the heart of industrial

Yorkshire. I nervously eye up the bogs in the posh cafe before deciding against it, put it this way – I'm feeling a touch delicate. I eye up the shelves filled with luxurious jams and exquisite wines before bolting towards the pie counter at the end. I plump for the steak and ale (£1.79) and the pork (£1.10) although have pangs of regret for not opting for the chicken and leek which looks highly presentable.

I'm served by a delightful young lady who humours me even when I yet again make a heinous school boy error breaking farm shop protocol, by waving a tenner at her. Pay at the till you dickhead! There's two more highly sociable girls at the till and I just love the way they say "two" around these parts.

192.

PURVEYOR: Rob Royd Farm Shop
PREMISES: Barnsley
PURCHASE: Steak & Ale Pie £1.79
PLACE: 8.5 **PASTRY:** 6.5 **PRESENTATION:** 7 **PACKAGE:** 7.5
PALATE: 7.5 **PRICE:** 7 **PORTION:** 7.5
OVERALL: 51.5/70 The crust shows exterior promise but has an almost shortbread like feel to it which collapses after I bite into it. However it redeems itself with the filling consisting of dark brown blocks of braising steak which come tumbling out, complimented by a total tsunami of ale soaked gravy.

I take the growler home and pop it in the oven for 20 minutes and sure enough when I cut it in half there is runny jelly all over the shop.

193.

PURVEYOR: Rob Royd Farm Shop
PREMISES: Barnsley
PURCHASE: Pork Pie £1.10
PLACE: 8.5 **PASTRY:** 8.5 **PRESENTATION:** 7 **PACKAGE:** 8
PALATE: 8 **PRICE:** 7.5 **PORTION:** 7
OVERALL: 54.5/70 'Tis a little beauty, generously filled and laced with jelly, requiring me to use all my dexterity to manage it by hand. A hot water pastry with a splendid hand crimped outer rim to it which is crunchy and crispy on the outside. Inside contains slightly coarse pinky reddish meat which is chewy but full flavoured. My stomach growls in appreciation at this fine growler.

Motorway service stations are so extortionate that you may as well chuck your wallet in the bin by the entrance. Nevertheless, they are one of the few places left in the country where you can still legitimately have a dump for free (if you take under two hours) After sitting in a steel box for ten minutes my stomach feels a lot more settled so it's off to Chesterfield to Jacksons. I head over the border to Derbyshire and Bolsover – imagine your claim to fame being home to a beast? I bet old Dennis likes a pie mind you.

The famous crooked spire lies up ahead, always impressively bent in the flesh. My problem is that this place is smack bang in the centre of town as I go hurtling down a pedestrianised street sending shoppers into retreat mode. I succumb to a pay and display and get my skates on through the church yard, scattering pigeons as I go with my clonking feet. I am accosted by a can carrying chav who stands in my way and stares at me like I've got three heads. It's like a one man remake of Michael Jackson's Thriller video.

Can't find this place anywhere and I'm on a meter. I hate asking people for directions, it's a sign of weakness; the failure and breakdown of my natural instincts. My salvation comes in the form of a man dressed in pink, peddling a static bike in the middle of the lively open market square. For charity I assume. I give him a quid and ask him where Falcon Yard is. He breathlessly instructs me and I wish him well with his endeavours.

In a peripheral corner of the market stands Jacksons Bakers, with bundles of perfectly crafted loaves and cherry cakes in the window. On my right there is a multitude of cooked, cold pies: steak and potato, lamb and leek, pork. And on my left I'm confronted by the standard hot pork carvery which they're particularly fond of around these parts.

"Have you got any hot pies?".

"No, they're all cold".

Gah!

I get a (cold) steak and potato for £1.95 and then cast my eye reluctantly over the other savouries as I need to eat: There's a range of unusual and innovative products on offer including a hash brown slice, which appears to simply be a hash brown with cheese plonked on top. However, I am won over by the daft named Armadillo pasty. She explains it to me but I can't comprehend her accent. Turns out an armadillo is nothing more exotic than a pasty called thus because of its shape. Gah again! Even when I try to buy something exotic I get scuppered! Four minutes left on the meter to wolf it down.

194.

PURVEYOR: Jacksons
PREMISES: Chesterfield
PURCHASE: Armadillo Pasty £1.45
PLACE: 7 A myriad of counters to manage

PASTRY: 8 A shortcrust well formed shell
PRESENTATION: 8 The only hot thing in the shop
PACKAGE: 7 She says steak I think but it's very much minced steak with a liberal sprinkling of carrots
PALATE: 8 It has a certain spicy injection into it with the combination of meat and veg harnessing together well
PRICE: 7 Just about
PORTION: 7 Don't get me prattling on about Cornish pasties again!
OVERALL: 52/70 If you don't know what an armadillo looks like, it looks like a top crimped Cornish pasty from Chesterfield.

195.

PURVEYOR: Jacksons
PREMISES: Chesterfield
PURCHASE: Steak and Potato Pie £1.95
PLACE: 7 **PASTRY:** 8
PRESENTATION: 7.5 **PACKAGE:** 9
PALATE: 9 **PRICE:** 7 **PORTION:** 8.5
OVERALL: 56/70 Not cheap but a truly brilliant pie. Considerable depth (almost too large for me to get my big gob around) and amply packed full of steak. The gravy is the star of the show with an impressive saccharin sweetness to it, like that posh Charlie Bighams one I had last year meaning it absolutely delivers an impeccably taste.

Right I need:
  A. The toilet (again).
  B. Petrol.
  C. To hotfoot it to Grimsby.
Thankfully I pull out of the car park and am greeted by a large, flowing A road outwards.

Shit! Grimsby's an hour and a half away and the M62 is shut on the way back, Emma will lynch me. Mission aborted, sorry Mr Pettit, sorry Grimsby....but imagine the fish pies they must do....no must resist....I plot a new course to Scunthorpe.

From the M18, I head to the M180 and then to the M181. Can't believe Scunny has got its own motorway even though it's completely pointless, as by the time I've got up to full speed it's time to slow down again. I'm heading for the market, more aimless fumbling around to follow no doubt. I think deep down I wanted to go to Scunny anyway. Turns out Scunthorpe is in Lincolnshire while Grimsby is in Humberside. I think that's kind of where I'm aiming for anyway.

Scunny is smart if a little bit roundabout heavy with streets that look like they've been drawn out with a ruler and a skyline dominated by a large Tata chimney with smoke billowing out from it. The Americanised grid style roads lead me through an estate punctuated by garish lilac and green fronted tower blocks and into a car park right opposite Scunthorpe Food Hall, which is free. Hurrah! On a Saturday too!

I open the double doors and the smells permeate immediately: the hot chicken stall; the fish market, the butchers and there it is – the Pie Store just to the right of a meat stall where a bloke with a wonky eye is selling bacon bits. It's about time things went seamlessly for a change, although I do struggle to get out of the place under the sheer weight of pensioners on mobility scooters.

As for the Pie Store, what can I say: Lots of pies and very cheap. I march up and down the counter expressively stroking my chin and surveying it's produce. The first one which catches my eye being the most decorative turns out to be a goat's cheese and caramelised onion – nah move along. I revert to an attractive poppy seed topped shortcrust pastry pie, which it transpires is a steak and caramelised onion pie for a quid. I ask him to get one of the large steak and ale ones for me as well.

"You know they're two for a quid you know?" (Did he say you know twice then? Yes I think he did).

"Yes but how much is it for one?".

"A quid".

"OK then I'll have two".

Pound Bakery economics at play again!

196.

PURVEYOR: The Pie Store
PREMISES: Scunthorpe
PURCHASE: Steak & Ale Pie 50p (2 for a £1)
PLACE: 9 Customer service par excellence; refusing to rip the customer off even when he's a complete plank, with the added bonus of free parking outside
PASTRY: 7.5 A slight flaw in that some of the crust is retained in the tray when I pull it out, yet the dark, golden puff pastry lid evaporates in the mouth with all the soothing impact of a wind chime
PRESENTATION: 7 A fresh feel to it
PACKAGE: 8 Slightly tougher and (probably) cheaper meat but plenty of it unleashed with a ton of gravy
PALATE: 8 A key indicator when the price is so low but it's actually a bloody good pie

PRICE: 10 Try as I might to find a reason to mark it down, I can't. I've paid four quid for far worse pies
PORTION: 8 Yep it's even of a decent proportion
OVERALL: 57.5/70 Remarkable value for a remarkable shop. Scunny market is where it's at.

197.

PURVEYOR: The Pie Store
PREMISES: Scunthorpe
PURCHASE: Steak & Caramelised Onion Pie £1
PLACE: 9 **PASTRY:** 8
PRESENTATION: 8 **PACKAGE:** 8
PALATE: 8 **PRICE:** 9 **PORTION:** 8
OVERALL: 58/70 The delectable hand made shortcrust version, topped with aromatic poppy seeds nudges above it's cheaper rival. The filling is delightfully sweet, with a rich gravy married with tender cuts of steak and smothered in sweet red onions. I'm forced to eat it off a plate however, due to the quantity of steak aggressively spilling out like angry revellers departing a pub on a Saturday night.

See I ramble on about hidden gems and this is exactly what I'm talking about! A splendid find and a wonderful little emporium selling gourmet pies at market stall prices.

I exit the car park and the town centre immediately cedes ground to huge Tata and Rainham steelworks which stretch for miles. Five minutes later I'm out in the countryside again with the Humber Bridge looming up ahead like a giant spider's web.

I'm getting quite giddy about this. I don't think I've ever been over the Humber Bridge before and whereas it might be a bit of a stretch to compare Hull to San Francisco, on a glorious day it is truly one of our country's finest man made spectacles, traversing the wide expanse of the River Humber through to the city of Kingston Upon Hull. A glorious last port of call on a busy old morning.

It is quite an exhilarating ride crossing the bridge while marvelling at the outline of Hull, like a roller coaster albeit with the ultimate sting in the tail when you get to the toll booth at the end and you're asked to part with £1.50. My phone goes:

"Where are you? Are you on your way back yet? I've got a hangover and need to go back to bed right now".

"Yes just on my way" (to Hull that is, he whispers with an evil cackle)

Good job I didn't go to Grimsby really.

I descend into the urban sprawl of Hull through the suburb of Hessle singing: "do do do do do do do do do do – do the Hessle" forgive me I'm halucinogenically tired. The roads are remarkably direct and wide (as indeed they have to be to get to the docks) flanked by hot tub factories on my left and cold stores on my right. The inevitable creep of gentrification is going on with redevelopment of marinas and the sprouting up of shiny new apartment blocks.

I head for the Old Town charging down cobbled streets barely wide enough to get my car down, hopelessly disorientated and searching for somewhere free to park until I ultimately just bang it on a road where there are meters. TWO POUNDS NINETY they want. I don't have that much change and I don't have time to go through one of those shambolic automated pay by phone nightmares. So I dump the car and make a dash for it, eight or nine wonderfully rustic cobbled streets away. Run fatboy run, earn that pie!

I'm looking for Hull Pie and I spot the world renowned Bob Carver's chippy (some accolade around these parts I'd imagine) that my contact told me to look out for next to the Trinity Market. It seems eerily quiet, best not be closed. But I push on the door and step inside to be greeted by two lovely Yorkshire lasses and a chalked up menu adorning the walls. Definitely veering towards the gourmet end of the market here and geared more towards the weekday office workers. It's £2.75 for a pie in a box served with mash and gravy, and they also do soups, sandwiches, a carvery and salads.

I clock the succulent steak and red wine but I've possibly overdone the steak today so I opt for a meatball marinara pie. They do a range of innovative flavours including Moroccan vegetables and falafel and daily specials including barbecued pulled pork pie. The sausage rolls look amazing but I can't come this far east and return with a sausage roll no matter how good they look.

198.

PURVEYOR: Hull Pie
PREMISES: Hull
PURCHASE: Meatball Marinara Pie including mash and gravy £2.75
PLACE: 9 They let me use their toilet and possibly threw in mash for free due to some confusion
PASTRY: 8 Ornate and decorative pastry, soft but not soggy bottom and a thick slightly uneven top crust
PRESENTATION: 7.5 A very well presented outlet and finally a warm pie
PACKAGE: 7.5 Excellent meatballs in a pasta sauce
PALATE: 7.5 My problem is when I try something different I end up

thinking it doesn't quite taste right and wishing I'd had the standard. The meatballs are delicious and accompanied by gravy and a mound of mash underneath, which are all great constituent ingredients. It just feels a bit odd. Perhaps a side of garlic bread would go better with a pasta pie?

PRICE: 7 An expensive pie but a highly affordable meal in a box

PORTION: 7 A very filling package all in at least

OVERALL: 53.5/70 An enlightening change although I still can't get my head around eating a pie in a box.

No penalty notices attached to my car, although I wouldn't be surprised in today's ANPR big Brother world to get a letter through the post and a £50 fine. Time to slowly make my way back westwards to relieve my hungover wife whilst admiring the rum buggers of Hull including one bunch of particularly fierce looking lads congregating outside a reptile shop, manhandling a snake.

My last visit is Fields of Anlaby which is difficult to say without breaking into a chorus of that song Liverpool fans sing. It's a discerning deli and butchers on the outskirts of Hull and this time I get parked for free in a residential area off the genteel village green. There's three counters with queues forming all the way around the shop and it's painstakingly slow. Needless to say, the fella at the front is ordering one of everything but instead of saying "I'll have one of everything" he is methodically ordering each item one by one.

I've seen this before many a time: that old British ritual of waiting patiently in line for your meat on a Saturday afternoon. This bloke is something else though and as the clock ticks, I progressively harbour desires to throttle him, chop him up and place him in the window between the Moroccan lamb kebabs and the Cajun chicken.

This is a minor blip and gives me chance to survey this fine emporium, its walls painted with cooking tips and a plethora of brightly coloured bowls of enticing delicacies strategically placed all around its environs.

I've sussed the pies out in the front window, and I'm intrigued by the sausage and tomato variety but not enough to buy it (sounds a bit too breakfast-y). There's also a variety of steak and dinky pork pies with glistening, teasing, shiny top crusts winking away at me. The large oval steak and potato pies are family sized but a quite capable fat bastard like me could eat one on his own, so I plump for both. Hang on did he say £4.45 then? The printed receipt confirms. Shome mishtake shurely?

They'd better be good. And to be fair the pies look absolutely out of this world, as everything in there does from fine meats and minted lamb casseroles to shepherd's pies (THEY'RE NOT PIES!!) with plenty room for traditional stuff like tripe and dog bones. It's no wonder people keep lobbing stuff in their baskets as it's the ideal place to generate a fine meal to put on the table at the weekend. This is evidently one of the finest delicatessens in the North of England. So bring on the pies....

199.
PURVEYOR: Fields of Anlaby
PREMISES: Hull
PURCHASE: Pork Pie £1.35
PLACE: 7 Not their fault every bugger has descended on the place, evidently it's the customers that are slow not the staff
PASTRY: 8 A rich golden brown hot water pastry
PRESENTATION: 7 Served chilled
PACKAGE: 8 Lots of slippery jelly peeping out of the top, a little teaser combined with Lincolnshire sausage type meat perfectly pink and fine
PALATE: 8 A touch fancy given the sage and rosemary and green herbs inside with the coarser jelly and sausage meat complimenting it perfectly
PRICE: 7 Yes this one is priced appropriately
PORTION: 7.5 Round and rigid
OVERALL: 52.5/70 A perfectly portable pie which isn't always the case when you pop a growler in the oven for twenty minutes. The jelly runs wild for a bit but then quickly returns to base and solidifies seeping into the crust and pork meat. Smashing.

Right, part two and putting my "riddled with wallet-based resentment aside" (convinced I've been overcharged) I do have a vague recollection of this being advertised as a pie for 2-3 people and it is bloody huge to be fair. So let's give it a bash:

200.

PURVEYOR: Fields of Anlaby
PREMISES: Hull
PURCHASE: Steak & Potato Pie £4.45
PLACE: 7 As above, a customer pool slower than a phone call to Australia
PASTRY: 7 The edges are a touch harsh but overall it's golden glaze gives off an authoritative air and is easy to hold despite its mammoth size
PRESENTATION: 7 To get this beast warm I leave it in the oven longer than a Christmas dinner
PACKAGE: 8 Predominantly rich chunks of stewed steak encapsulated in thick gravy coupled with tasty slabs of melt in the mouth Maris

Piper mash

PALATE: 8.5 Rich and delicious, a perfect combination with delectable meat and veg harnessed together seamlessly

PRICE: 6 Here lies the conundrum: I want a big pie but I want it cheap too

PORTION: 10 Roughly the size (and weight!) of a house brick, it is about 7 inches across, 4 inches wide and deeper than Barry White's haemorrhoids. Sorry

OVERALL: 53.5/70 This is a pie with "don't mess with me" stamped all over it.

Eleven pies in one day. A brief interlude is in order methinks.

What's that, you want to know who's in front? Oh I couldn't possibly FURNESS you with that information....

PIE RAMBLING

Clarks in Cardiff

Philps Pasty Shop

In Melton Mowbray

Greens, Barrow
(Courtesy of www.squidbeak.co.uk)

Checking out the measurements on
this Melton Mowbray Stilton Blue

A rogue hand moves in for the kill during the pie party parade

Getting the pies in for the lads –
Peppered Steak from Yorkes of Dundee

I drove by....and found no pie

LIFE OF PIES: A FEW OF MY FAVOURITE PIES

The Crusty Cob Meat & Potato Pie

A hot Burchalls Pork Pie

Dawsons Meat & Potato Pie

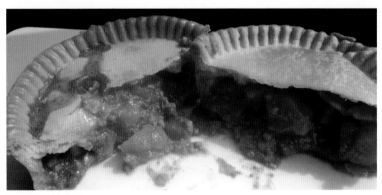

Bowens Meat & Potato Pie

Cheshire Bakehouse Meat & Potato

Clarks (Cardiff) Original Pie

A classic Meat & Potato Pie from Galloways

Greens of Barrow Meat & Potato Pie. The Hairy Bikers love them, and so do I!!

Greens of Barrow Meat & Potato Pie – A peek inside!!!

Cornwall's finest: a Philps Pasty

A pie from British Pie Award winners
The Pie Kitchen, Sufflok

Another pie from The Pie Kitchen, Sufflok

"The Stockport Pie" (Beef Stew) from Lord Of The Pies

"The Stockport Pie" (Beef Stew) from Lord Of
The Pies – the outside view

The Mad O'Rourkes Pies
"Beast" Of A Cow Pie

A Five Nations Pie from
Sweeney & Todds, Reading

Potts Pies of Morecambe – Meat & Potato Pie

Hopkins of Birkenshaw Pork Pie

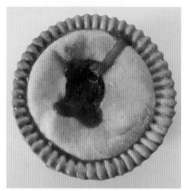

Another fine Wigan Meat & Potato Pie from Gents

Paul's Steak & Guinness Pie

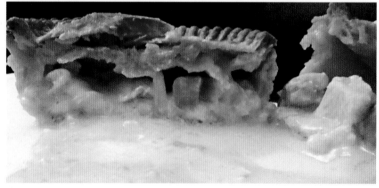

The Gourmet Chicken, Ham & Leek Pie from Morecambe Football Club

The crispy base

Part 3: 201-300

Aka: "Hello love, yes I'm just in Kilmarnock

THE CRISPY BASE. PART THREE: 201-300

Saturday 23rd February 2013

It is a meticulously planned mission although nothing quite prepares me for getting out of bed at half five after going to bed at two. Wigan Athletic are away at Reading, home of famous pie shop Sweeney & Todds; but I can't just go to Reading, oh no that would be way too easy. A plan has been hatched in my head to go west to Wales then through Bristol and on to Reading.

You see I've already been given the run-around by the internet this week when I tried to buy the URL for this (proposed) book title *Pie Eyed* only for some "entrepreneur" to come back demanding four figure sums. The Internet, being a right little shit, then advises me that Clarks of Bristol is not the same as Clarks of Cardiff, more a bastard offspring. And finally I've had no joy whatsoever trying to locate a Devizes Pie. Perhaps a small part of me is relieved about this last bit.

So I'll go to Cardiff as well. Then Bristol. And Swindon and Reading. It's a fair old bit of driving – or droiving as they say down here – but sometimes you've just got to put in the hours in this game.

The original Clarks Pies of Cardiff are fantastic by all accounts and have been a permanent fixture on my pie "Bucket List" since the book began. But my plan was to get one in Bristol then head to Wiltshire. Upon discovering that Clarks Pies of Cardiff and Bristol aren't the same establishment, merely a nepotistic arrangement – one of the Clarks family moved from Cardiff to Bristol in the early 1930s and set up his own shop – it only feels fair to try both.

The bakery's open from half five even if the shop doesn't open till 10 so I'll chance my arm. I've been ringing for days with no response until a charming Welsh lady answers and insists there will be someone there from quarter to nine, lovely. Then I'm getting nervous over the Bristol Clarks as there's no indication that they're going to be open on a Saturday either.

This time confirmation comes from a Scottish bloke: they're also open from 8am plus they'll have a mobile van situated outside Bristol City's ground from late morning. Splendid!

From there it's Wiltshire and then to Reading for my actual lunch with exiled Wiganer, Life of Pies marketing guru and all round good fella, Andy "Donuts" Brown, at the marvellous Sweeney and Todds.

The M50's closed. Over turned lorry. Probably the only time in the last few years I've ever needed to use such a non-descript motorway and it's fucking shut so I'm frantically searching an alternative with a fuzzy head. Meticulous plan gone tits up again, I'm going over the Severn Bridge twice, the only question is: Cardiff or Bristol first?

At 8.45am I meet my first *Welcome to Croeso!* sign as I head full on over the impressive concrete structure of the Severn Bridge which looms above the brown murky water like a giant transformer. I am glummer than the skyline however, when I find out that going westbound is free but eastbound costs £6.20. I've been shafted by some upended wagon driver.

I head through Newport and spot the stunning Celtic Manor resort perched imperiously on a large hill resembling a mini Niagara Falls. My SatNav doesn't start speaking Welsh as I head into Cardiff via the Americanised dual carriageway with its motels and garages lining the road (to cater for the event traffic which frequently gets snarled up on the way out). I'm guessing this place will be in quite a tough, inner city area capable of supporting a traditional pie shop for decades but thus far Cardiff is all rolling greens, domineering Victorian town houses and gothic churches masked in shrubbery.

The terrain gets a touch more urban with a medium sized stadium on my left and a big black bridge advertising Brains Bitter – *"The brains you want!"*

As I arrive in Grangetown I am met with the spectacle of a student walking an empty shopping trolley down the street, no doubt returning it to its rightful owner to get the quid back after carrying it home on his head last night. Then I spot several large Jamaican looking gentlemen huddled in a doorway smoking what appears to be a recreational form of medicine, before Clarks magically appears following a brief spell of rally driving down a rabbit warren of grid like terraced streets.

Wow! As I step out of the car I am genuinely blown away by the overpowering waft of freshly baked pies emanating from a place which looks every inch the local institution. If there's a better smell in the world than the aroma of baking pastry products then I'm yet to sample it. As advised, the shop is not open yet, but like a crafty butcher I find my way around the back to get my meat delivery.

There's a sign on the door saying "if shop shut ring bell". Unfortunately someone appears to have stolen the bell. I push on the door gently and it creaks open and I walk straight into the kitchen to be greeted by two big Welsh lads knocking out the produce.

I am struck dumb, stood in the doorway of their kitchen as they eye me suspiciously until one wanders over.

"Hi mate, can I have a pie?"

One English pound is handed over in Wales and I get a lovely warm pocket rocket in return, as fresh as you like. I enquire as to what it is and get the response "Beef and Potato".

They have other flavours on their website but I'm confident they've given me their hallmark, original large Clarks Pie here. What a result.

I'm one happy chappie as I drive back along the M4 with a steaming hot Clarks beef pie in the passenger seat. I just need to find a lay-by where this beauty is going to get it good style.

Life could only get better if a coach went past containing a hen party of chunky Welsh lasses who decide to collectively get their arses out in the window for me....and they do. They really do.

To the more demure offerings of the Clarks Pie however….

201.

PURVEYOR: Clarks
PREMISES: Cardiff
PURCHASE: Beef and Potato Pie £1
PLACE: 9 The personalised touch
PASTRY: 9 Impeccably dense crust throughout with a firm sturdy base yet delicate in the mouth, the sort of crust you find in an apple pie. A real triumph. Novel in origin, completely uneven and unique in form and hand stamped with CLARPIE to differentiate itself from its Bristol cousin and prove its authenticity (must be bad pie blood in this family). Not sure where the K has gone mind you
PRESENTATION: 9 You don't even need to eat it to imbibe in its goodness. The phenomenal, glorious aroma originating from a Clarks Pie is worth a quid on its own
PACKAGE: 8 Lots of dark meat and gravy, hints of potato and onion barely detectable but all harnessed in perfect symphony. It's not quite full to capacity but the contents still come tumbling out of the pie when I bite in and I find myself a more than willing recipient of a "Clark's Tache" as they call it around these parts

PALATE: 8 Rich and peppery mincemeat with onions and seasoning enhancing the flavour further
PRICE: 9 Brilliant value for a quid, even if this is wholesale price
PORTION: 8 I'll assume this is a large one
OVERALL: 60/70 I'd go as far as to say that this is the "Greens of the South". I may as well turn back now.

I go back over the Severn Bridge and down into Avonmouth where the M49 and M5 tower over the corrugated steel fronted council houses of Bristol. A fella walking down a cycle lane cheerfully nods to me. Bristol is a city built on hills and rivers and bridges and as I drive along the Avon basin, the grand Clifton Suspension Bridge gives an unsurpassable backdrop as the river meanders its way through the city. Soon I have sheer cliffs either side of me. They may have two crap football teams but Bristol more than makes up for it with its stunning architecture and landscape. There's signs ahead directing me to a football stadium, which strikes me as a bit dangerous given there are at least two teams in Bristol. Half the city appears to be out running above, below and alongside me this fine February morning.

I head for the busy shopping thoroughfare of North Street, Bedminster which is as welcoming as you like. This is in stark contrast to the last time I was here one Friday night getting chased by several angry Stone Island clad Bristolians shouting "cam on you facking Northern mankee" due to my football team having the audacity to beat their football team. I do a sneaky park up in Aldi and attempt to walk the last few hundred yards to Clarks number two without getting assaulted.

The shop front is almost wholly white PVC grill and the theme continues inside where the bloke serving through a tiny hatch is clad in a white apron and hat. He pops his little head through and cheerfully enquires as to my order. They do shortcrust and puff pastry options and the price is £1.50: yes a whole 50p dearer than their Welsh ancestors.

202.
PURVEYOR: Clarks
PREMISES: Bristol
PURCHASE: Meat and Vegetable Pie £1.50
PLACE: 8.5 He looks the part
PASTRY: 8 Wonderful thick shortcrust with a more defined, crimped outer ridge
PRESENTATION: 8 Hotter than an Aldi traffic warden
PACKAGE: 8 Lots of mince and gravy teamed up with small potato and onion chunks

PALATE: 9 Lovely. A very peppery kick which enhances the meaty flavour and is as Moorish as a bunch of 8th century Muslim invaders of the Iberian peninsula
PRICE: 7.5 Possibly an Achilles heel only as it is dearer than the product it was spawned from
PORTION: 8 Possesses the same elliptical shape as the other Clarks and similar delicate shortcrust

OVERALL: 57/70 Brightened my day and sent a ray of sunshine over the Aldi car park.

I emerge out of the other side of Bristol where picture postcard kaleido-scopic terraced houses sit precariously on cliff tops. Office blocks and council flats dominate the skyline as underpasses and flyovers weave their way through the urban sprawl.

I've been firing emails off to the Wiltshire tourist board all week to en-quire as to where I can procure a Devizes Pie but despite plenty of re-sponses I have no answers. It may just be a mythical pie only ever cooked in private within the confines of carnivorous lunatics' kitchens.

Given that the main ingredients are thin slices from boiled calf's head combined with brains and tongue, I'd be surprised if even folk in the West Country have that sort of kit knocking around in their fridge. Add in the more regulation slices of cold cooked bacon and lamb and rounds of hard-boiled eggs and you've got yourself a Devizes pie. Apparently it's good for treating irritable bowel syndrome as well, something I expect to arrive with a vengeance following completion of this book.

But can I get one? Can I fuck.

So I head for Malmesbury not Devizes because it's closer and I'm getting nowhere fast. Let's face it, I could spend all day looking for a Devizes Pie and indeed if I was *left to my own Devizes* I probably would.

Sorry.

There's a butchers in Malmesbury and a Hall Bakers too, which I tried and failed to seek out in Cirencester and of course I won't let it go; and did I mention I need to be in Reading in an hour to meet Donuts?

Anyway, Malmesbury: if you're under 12 you can enjoy the go karting, if you're over 12 just stand and marvel at the abbey and low arched bridges. I dump the car on the by now homogenised middle class middle England High Street and go hunting. Halls Bakery is very quaint and full of tradi-tional goodness with bloomers, granary loaves and cakes all attractively placed in the window alongside a full battalion of gingerbread men stood in rank file. Their pies are chicken, cheese and onion, steak and kidney (£1.75) plus some pasties but they don't seem like their priority. It's only upon alighting from the shop that I spot hungry patrons queuing out of the door of the Old Bakehouse and immediately the pangs of regret kick in as I conclude that it may have been the better option. Gah!

203.
PURVEYOR: Halls
PREMISES: Stroud
PURCHASE: Steak and Kidney Pie £1.75
PLACE: 7 **PASTRY:** 7 **PRESENTATION:** 7.5 **PACKAGE:** 7
PALATE: 7.5 **PRICE:** 6 **PORTION:** 6
OVERALL: 48/70 The darkest filling I have ever seen; it's almost black and full of subtle lumps of braising steak and kidney with gravy dripping on my chin, giving me a gravy beard to go with my Clarks 'tache. I got the same pie in Liverpool for eighty pence mind you.

I'm having a mare in Malmesbury and end up twatting my wing mirror driving down some road that is too narrow for anything bigger than a moped. I find the Triangle, which is not in fact a shopping centre but a triangular shaped road space. Some bitch jumps in a perfect parking space before me so I mount the car on the kerb, onto double yellows, directly outside. On a blind bend. No more Mr Nice Guy.

Whilst grinning manically amidst much swearing and shaking of fists off other road users, I bundle into Thomas's as flustered as a grounded flounder. I peruse what they have got which includes pork and a slice of gala pie, steak and stilton/ale/kidney (delete as appropriate).

They like their steak down here, therefore I plump for a weighty little steak and stilton number for £1.76 pence.

204.
PURVEYOR: Thomas Butchers
PREMISES: Malmesbury
PURCHASE: Steak & Stilton Pie £1.76
PLACE: 8 Very prompt when dealing with an agitated lunatic
PASTRY: 7 A golden brown puff pastry top containing several layers with a stronger base. This is best eaten upside down or using the crust as a handle as the flakes tend to stick to the fingers
PRESENTATION: 8 Extra mark for the pungent attack of stilton coming at me
PACKAGE: 7 A reasonable smattering of steak with gravy and cheesy sauce with borderline excessively chewy meat in parts – maybe they slip

a bit of calf's brain in there as is the Wiltshire way

PALATE: 8 The stilton infusion wins me over no end. It's not overdone to the point of being overpowering but it lets you know it's there

PRICE: 6.5 Hmm

PORTION: 7 Another in the traditional oblong shape and a reasonable individual size

OVERALL: 51.5/70 I'm one of *those* people whom if you put an actual block of stilton in front of me I'm repulsed but melt it and whack it in a pie and I'm on it like the proverbial tramp on a kipper.

As I hit the M4 trail once more I am treated to the sight of a low flying hang glider throwing what appears to be a live animal out onto the ground in some rum local tradition – a large town with all the trappings of a small city: namely a fucking appalling road layout and parking situation. I therefore have ample opportunity to circle Sweeney & Todds several times before I get the chance to actually step into the place.

I eventually dump the car on a multi storey on Donuts' advice and head for a pint. The place is situated on a peaceful side street connecting the main shopping area with a ring road and what a little gem it is. Butchers and pie purveyors at front of house, well stocked real ale bar upstairs and a compact dining area with low wooden beams downstairs. There's small rooms and cubby holes galore to stuff your face in which feel comfy and seedy in equal measure. Service is provided by a woman who must be 80 to a day and famously likes to get her weary bunions out (after she gets tired clambering up and down the stairs all day) and give them a rub while she's waiting to take your order.

They've got a huge range of pies at around £2.50 to take out. Although it has to be said the menu is only a guide and the available pies are rattled off from memory by said geriatric waitress. A magnificently quirky and unique establishment.

We're delighted to hear that the Five Nations is on the menu consisting of steak, Guinness, leeks, mustard and garlic so we both opt for that and a couple of pints of Wadsworth 6X. Certainly a pie and a half although there's also a vicar's pie which has every ingredient you can possibly think of in it.

205.

PURVEYOR: Sweeney & Todds
PREMISES: Reading
PURCHASE: Five Nations Pie (£6.50) with chips and gravy (£9.60 all in)
PLACE: 8 Another one reminiscent of Julie Walters "is it on the trolley" in Acorn Antiques but an impressive line in reeling off the menu and the wait for the food isn't long at all

PASTRY: 8.5 There's no outer crust rim but a very wide top crust completely encased with semi shortcrust/puff pastry lid with a dark colour and nicely decorated
PRESENTATION: 8 A place to cherish, like dining in someone's cellar. Absolutely oozing with character
PACKAGE: 9 The leeks are prominent with lots of thick gravy inside and rich chunks of meat which are succulently soft and complimented with the garlic and mustard coming through in every mouthful. It also comes with a boat of gravy as well and salad
PALATE: 9 The mix and innovation of flavours tastes like a meat based cocktail and the chips are blinders as well
PRICE: 8 Excellent value, take away or eat in, for really well crafted pies
PORTION: 8 A very wide and filling pie with considerable depth and around 5-6 inches in diameter. There's really no need for salad here
OVERALL: 58.5/70 Do we have to go the football match?

Bellies full of pie we wander across the road to the Allied Arms when Donuts says "Oh look the Home Secretary's over there out shopping!" And who should be walking in front of us but Theresa May and her husband closely followed by two smart but shifty looking gentlemen, dressed like Milk Tray men, desperately trying to look inconspicuous. She declines our offer of a pint.

Sunday 24th February 2013

Can I count this one? Why not, it's my book! You see I'm at a family gathering in Lancaster and we visit The Mill at Conder Green, where I order a suet pudding containing braised steak, bacon, Bowland ale, mashed potato and veg with chunky chips washed down with another pint of Bowlands ale. A posh Babbies Yed by all accounts!

206.

PURVEYOR: The Mill at Conder Green
PREMISES: Lancaster
PURCHASE: Suet Pudding £10.95
PLACE: 8 Highly attentive to detail, warm and engaging throughout and they manage to humour my two year old whilst she continually demands "WHERE'S MINE?"
PASTRY: 8 Sublimely soft, melt in the mouth suet dumpling-style and completely encased. Not exactly a crust mind you but

nevertheless a captivating feast

PRESENTATION: 7 A complicated arrangement to the plate

PACKAGE: 8 Meat overload with big chunks of steak, diced segments of bacon teamed up with onions, button mushrooms (urgh!) and gravy. Lots of it, and served with chips not veg!

PALATE: 7.5 Rich meaty flavours, hints of garlic, an exquisite parcel of joy

PRICE: 7 One must pay a premium for excellence

PORTION: 8.5 For several hours subsequent it feels like I'm carrying around a medicine ball in my tummy. It's big enough to block out the shadow of the Heysham Power Station looming in the distance

OVERALL: 54/70 This pastry based receptacle is a bit like Sport Billy's bag in that I just keep pulling more and more out of it but a great setting and a great big pudding.

Friday 9th March 2013

I have faithfully adhered to my wife's request to stay off the pies during my week long birthday crisis/celebration mini-break on the Fylde Coast. However, no sooner do we get booted out of our flat then all bets are back on again.

I tug on her heart strings by mentioning the wonderful bakery at Broughton Village and a day in the Lakes where we got married five years ago (missing a friendly away at Sheffield Wednesday in the process and I've still never been to Hillsborough!).

I've seen some sights over the past eighteen months but the shimmering waters of Windermere on a clear day as you drop down into Ambleside simply cannot be beaten. As we're out early, we alight the car mid morning and are hit with the overpowering stench of full English breakfasts being knocked out in the cluster of guest houses that encircle the centre.

We turn into Compston Road, opposite a church that implores you to "celebrate God's love" and the magnificent Wansfell Pike looms large. I once made Emma climb it during a romantic weekend away in pink shoes which I bought her after she conveniently forgot her walking boots. She half cut her feet open after walking eight miles because we got lost. Happy days!

Peggy's have rack upon rack of steaming hot pies and the meat and potato definitely looks the one to indulge in. A plate pie priced at £2.00 with a raised centre, it's twice the size of all the others and twice the price. They've got pork pies and chicken and mushroom, cheesy scones and a range of sumptuous cakes; and it looks every inch a classy, traditional bakery. The service is painful and slow considering the time of morning. But then they're never in a rush around these parts.

207.

PURVEYOR: Peggy's
PREMISES: Ambleside
PURCHASE: Meat and Potato Pie £2.00
PLACE: 6.5 **PASTRY:** 8 **PRESENTATION:** 8 **PACKAGE:** 7
PALATE: 7 **PRICE:** 7 **PORTION:** 8.5
OVERALL: 52/70 An innovative yet traditional centre as three or four layers of thinly sliced potatoes sit on top of ground mince in a layered style. All within a large round plate style crust with a raised centre and an unmistakably authentic aroma to it.

After a potter about we head west where the actual Lakes dry up, yet the fells remain uniquely spectacular and are so sheer that it's only really possible to climb up them one way unless you're a nutter with an ice pick. We're on the A593 heading past gorgeous Coniston although I've no idea how these things have the audacity to call themselves A roads. I can only assume it's because the scenery is so breathtaking nobody will mind the sheep and middle aged map readers dawdling in the road.

Situated across the way from the amusingly named Black Cock Inn, we head to Broughton Village Bakery which bewitched us both when we were watching Britain's Best Bakery and makes a delightful haunt for a spot of lunch. Broughton is sat within a valley and has its own perilously steep access road to enter the village and a town square which is eerily quiet. I walk into Barclays Bank and they won't give me any money because I'm not a customer nor do they have a cashpoint. So I walk to the Post Office where they have the oldest cashpoint you've ever seen.

We were enchanted by this place on telly due to the care and attention provided by its hosts and the fervour which they put into the magnificent food they bake. Easy to perform for the camera – yet from the second we walk in we feel at home and it becomes clear that this is a uniquely warm and idyllic place. Relaxed and ambient, we quickly settle in and the girl serving brings some chalk and crayons over for Jess. We order some mesmerisingly fine homemade lemonade that quenches the thirst like raindrops in the Sahara. WHO NEEDS ALE!!

Did I really say that? Seriously, with music from Carole King to Marvin Gaye we are as chilled as polar bears and could spend a week in here. Ah yes the food! I indulge in a hearty beef stew in a bowl the size of a bathroom sink while Emma has an equally large receptacle containing homemade broccoli and stilton soup, both accompanied by a hefty wedge of bread to dunk in. A proper walker's feast!

Nothing is too much trouble for the staff in that lovely accent they have which sounds like "posh Geordie" to my untrained ear. Before long mine hosts Sean & Chrissie pop along for a chat, looking considerably less stressed than they were on telly but every bit as attentive and personable. They've built a little treasure trove here and I can't fail to warm to people like that who put their heart and soul into everything that they do.

However, onwards to the shop and there's so many amazing cakes, breads and preserves that it's a food lovers paradise packed with no end of decadent sweet luxuries.

Time to load up the car as Emma invests in a "Rucksnack", which is a speciality bake submitted on the telly, containing gin, chocolate, Kendal mint cake and Damson berries in a flapjack casing while Jess gets a muffin and I get a traditional caramel shortbread.

Now have I forgotten something?

The minced beef pies are £1.60 to take out and they also do cheese and onion, huge sausage rolls and Cornish pasties made the traditional way.

I take the pie home and upon pulling it out of the oven later that evening, it is with delight that I peer through the air vent in the top and see a splendid moist pool of gravy and perfectly braised mince bubbling away excitedly from within.

208.

PURVEYOR: Broughton Village Bakery
PREMISES: Broughton-in-Furness
PURCHASE: Minced Beef Pie £1.60
PLACE: 9 Walk in here with the worst mood in the world and you'll still come out smiling
PASTRY: 8 The crust has a distinctly artisan feel to it throughout with classic double shortcrust and hand crimped wavy permed edges, plus a circular porthole in the middle. Best eaten with a fork mind you
PRESENTATION: 8 Steam comes billowing out of the porthole like it comes off Popeye after a double dose of spinach.
PACKAGE: 8 Fully flavoured mince, soft melt in the mouth onions with lots of free flowing rich gravy
PALATE: 8 I can't say I find minced beef the most exhilarating flavour but it certainly comes across as being of a high standard
PRICE: 7 Reasonable
PORTION: 7 I could eat another if I'm honest
OVERALL: 55/70 A supreme location to watch the world go by whilst scoffing a meaty pie.

Whoops, there appears to be a butchers next door. I'm not going to pass up that up am I?

Melville Tyson is the name, another compact little emporium of luxury foodstuffs. I'm pleased to see pies scattered about as the lady serving points to a load more behind her and then rattles off an implausibly long list whilst pointing ferociously at each one. I initially choose a Scotch pie but back down when I notice it's made in Scotland – does that mean all their pies are bought in? I revert to the meat and potato – as it's the biggest and has a delightful looking crust on it.

209.

PURVEYOR: Melville Tyson
PREMISES: Broughton-in-Furness
PURCHASE: Meat and Potato Pie £1.50
PLACE: 8 For going through the full repertoire in a highly prescriptive manner
PASTRY: 8 Soft centred and well glazed
PRESENTATION: 7 Purchased cold but doesn't completely overwhelm in the oven
PACKAGE: 8 A good depth to it and a healthy meat to potato ratio with diced cubes of both
PALATE: 8.5 Has a fine, fresh taste to it and packs a punch like its namesake Mike
PRICE: 7 Acceptable
PORTION: 8 A larger than average diameter and depth to it
OVERALL: 54.5/70 For an opportunistic purchase, this belter certainly cuts the mustard in our house.

We take the Cumbrian coastal road from Broughton to Barrow, which is mystifying and hypnotising as little pockets of blue, bright shoreline ebb and flow against beautiful fells on the other side. The Kirkby we pass through is very different to the Kirkby I know, until eventually sleepy, lazy bungalows recede to more earthy looking council houses and factories as we hit the edge of Barrow. I will return soon to explore your earthy pastry based jewels!

Tuesday 12th March 2013

[Sings] Don't much about Mobberley. Don't know much biology. I've got a fifty minute window at work to nip and get a pie so I've sussed out Goostreys Bakery, not in Goostrey which is where you can find amongst other things Jodrell Bank, but in the well heeled village of Mobberley situated between Wilmslow and Knutsford. I drive past it the first time whilst clocking a place called the Mobberley Bakery – wow has this place got TWO pie shops? Sadly as I drive out the other end of town I realise it has more likely undergone a rebranding exercise. I do a U turn in the driveway of some huge house with a gated driveway and park up to indulge in the now familiar tradition of piespotting. It's a working bakery with bread and cakes on display to my right, pies to the left and a sandwich counter. Hmm – the pies are either very small or a long, long way away. I need a magnifying glass to see them. This isn't going to end well.

210.
PURVEYOR: Mobberley Village Bakery
PREMISES: Mobberley
PURCHASE: £1.20 Meat and Potato Pie
PLACE: 7.5 **PASTRY:** 8 **PRESENTATION:** 7 **PACKAGE:** 7
PALATE: 7 **PRICE:** 6 **PORTION:** 5
OVERALL: 47.5/70 What is actually a half decent pie is sadly ruined by the fact it is miniscule. No wonder there is such high life expectancy in this affluent area if the pies aren't big enough to satisfy an anorexic hamster.

Saturday 16th March 2013

I've been trying to work out what the hell is going on in the Morecambe "Pie wars". Do a quick search and you end up finding Potts Pies, resplendent with Morecambe scarf on their website and awards on show. However, it turns out that the reason I can't find the award winning best pie in football and that the chicken, ham and leek isn't on their website is because they don't make it. They never did because they were relieved of their matchday duties several years ago and Morecambe took their catering back in house. I'll need to try both obviously.

I can't speak with too much authority of the rivalry between Lancaster and Morecambe, be it from a football or tribal sense but the pie rivalry must be alive and kicking given the perceived competitiveness of output around these parts.

The approach to Lancaster is flanked by the small village of Galgate with its 115 year old football team and the smart, sporty campus of Lancaster University. The dreamy spires and gothic architecture of Lancaster are as close as you'll get to an Inspector Morse type scenario up north (if you can ignore those scruffy tower blocks by the river). Even they are slowly getting crowded out by the continual and inevitable sprawl of gentrified plush new flats hugging the River Lune as it heads out to sea.

I park up around the corner from Potts, outside a house amidst twitching curtains, and I am hit with the mesmerising aroma of freshly baking pies. They've got decorative stained glass windows with their name over the front and a little van parked across the road emblazoned with Potts Pies. I'm imagining that this place is run by that squat opera singer who won Britain's got Talent for some reason. Paul Potts Pies. Or maybe Pol Pots Pies, with a range of Cambodian infused savouries hand baked by the infamous dictator.

They have some samples on the counter and I go for one with a bit of green in it which I believe to be broccoli, stilton and potato. It's cold and it's not for me. Beef and Garlic sounds a tad unappealing too, purely because they are advertising the garlic. If it was just a beef pie with garlic in it, (or with other things like the Five Nations Pie) then I wouldn't give a shit. I'm just odd though.

I get both the girls undivided attention once I find myself at the front of the queue and I am confronted with pies stacked high and lots more in the oven. There's a huge range and the pork and stuffing pies look aesthetically pleasing but I opt for the trusted meat and potato. It's £2.10 but an absolute beast. I'd planned to go straight onto Susans as my next port of call but I can't keep my hands off this. I'll just eat half. Nope, the whole thing is devoured in seconds. It wasn't me, it was my willpower.

Upon completion I feel slightly inebriated at the sheer volume of pastry I've wolfed down. It's a real big hitter, leagues ahead of the dross you get served up at some football grounds.

211.

PURVEYOR: Potts Pies
PREMISES: Lancaster
PURCHASE: Meat and Potato Pie £2.10
PLACE: 9 Attentive staff and free pie while you wait for your pie
PASTRY: 8.5 Sturdy where it needs to be; soft and velvety on top and plenty of it
PRESENTATION: 8 Directions: Come off the M6 at Junction 34 and follow the wonderful waft from Potts
PACKAGE: 8.5 A thorough filling of fresh potatoes interspersed with meaty mince chunks
PALATE: 9 The potatoes taste freshly picked, almost green, and there's a magical peppery kick which hits you by surprise; an unexpected throw back to the days when pies were laced with seasoning to disguise the fact that the ingredients were not the best (but these are)
PRICE: 7.5 Over £2 but three times the size of that horror I had midweek
PORTION: 9 It's a chunky effort and the weight, as much as the

dimensions, are impressive. It must be five inches wide and close to a couple of inches deep
OVERALL: 59.5/70 A handsome hunk of a pie, crafted with care, love and attention which packs the punch of a Mixed Martial Arts specialist. If this place was down the road I'd be twenty stone.

Situated at the bottom of the biggest hill in Lancaster if not the north of England I find my second target: Susan's Bakery – although it's now called the Old Mill Bakery aka Buttylicious and it appears to be for sale. Not to be deterred I step in and find this cafe has a seating capacity of four metal chairs and nobody serving despite a crafty bell ring upon opening the door.

212.

PURVEYOR: The Old Bakery
PREMISES: Lancaster
PURCHASE: Meat and Potato Pie £1.65
PLACE: 6 A man cannot wait for pie!
PASTRY: 6.5 Crumbly and heartburny
(I know heartburny is not a word as such, but if ever there was a time to introduce it into our vocabulary....)
PRESENTATION: 8 Certainly smells the part
PACKAGE: 8 A dark and moody interior with such contrast it feels like two pies in one with dark meat and gravy on top and subtly marinated potatoes gently resting underneath
PALATE: 8.5 Softly seasoned spud and generous delicate meat with gravy oozing out of it, a pie for many tastes
PRICE: 7 Just about
PORTION: 8 Good luck carrying it up that bloody big hill
OVERALL: 52/70 Not quite the Potts standard but a worthy pie.

Onwards past Lancaster Castle which towers majestically over the city and its sprawling, convoluted traffic system below. I'm not sure where Lancaster ends and Morecambe begins segued as they are with a stream of retail parks. I hit Morecambe's West End, I'd heard it was rough around here but it doesn't look that bad. Just low level suburbia, the sort of sleepy seaside retreat streets with an invisible coastline lurking behind. I wonder what the girls are like around here? Maybe I'll ask the Pet Shop Boys.

The above pies were merely the aperitif for the visit to the area however after my midweek attempts to get hold of Morecambe Football Club's actual pies. A mate off Twitter, who follows Morecambe, tells me to ring up. What? In this day and age? Pick up the phone and actually speak to another human being? What's wrong with email/texting/tweeting/Facebook page posting?

Anyway I watch those chef types on telly, they're noticeably highly strung and sweary aren't they?

"No he'll be sound, he'll love it" my mate says. And he does.

"Is Graham there?"

"You mean Chef?"

"If he is the chef then yes"

Nobody calls him Graham. Everyone calls him chef. Never THE chef. Just "Chef". Beautiful.

I tell him of my quest and of course I'll pay for the pies. He's happy to oblige. I just need to turn up before a home game. I don't even need to watch the match – not something I'd object to normally but I need to be in Yorkshire by 1pm. "Don't come after 12 because I'll be too busy". A good chef is always busy. And Chef is a very good chef. A proper award winning chef.

So there on the right hand side is the gleaming spectacle of the Globe Stadium, home of Morecambe Football Club. It's deserted at 11 in the morning and Graham's fears about me parking are unfounded as the place is eerily quiet, nay deserted, ahead of their crunch game versus top of the table Gillingham. I walk into the main reception and ask for Graham.

"I'm here to see Chef".

She gets on the phone.

"A man here to see Chef".

Still can't get my head around that.

The receptionist is lovely and helpful, not at all phased by some fool turning up in her office demanding pies several hours before kick off. She likes the chicken and leek but she's a meat and potato girl at heart, especially on a Saturday! Saturday's a pie day she says! A kindred spirit!

I'm impressed with how grand this place is considering Morecambe were a non league team for so many years. I love lower division football clubs, and they deserve love; so much more love than the gigantic behemoths gobbling up millions of fans everywhere from Kuala Lumpar to your local pub. They work so hard in their communities and have a special quirkiness to them which is worth miles more than a pile of trophies.

A youngish chap comes bouncing down the stairs and hands me what appear to be two huge circular bricks wrapped in tin foil. Graham I presume?

I get straight down to the business of thanking him profusely for taking time to let me sample his pies. We have a lovely chat and he explains how they sell the pies direct now as wholesale, but I take care not to occupy too much of his time and close by asking for a score prediction. 3-0 says Graham. Who to? Who knows as Gillingham are flying. Morecambe later earn a credible 1-1 draw.

With that he scampers back off up the stairs to feed the impending thousands. I've just got to feed myself as the two spherical objects I am carrying are clunking away and need defrosting. I have a chicken, ham and leek and a meat and potato in my mitts. Perfect!

213.

PURVEYOR: Morecambe Football Club
PREMISES: Morecambe
PURCHASE: Chicken, Ham & Leek Pie (£3 at matches)
PLACE: 9 Hand delivered by the creator!
PASTRY: 8 It's marked with one dot to help the staff signify it's flavour on match days I guess and the pastry is soft and appetising. I love the angular shape of the pie which goes beyond the perpendicular, giving it a semi plate pie style
PRESENTATION: 8 The sort of gourmet aroma you simply don't expect at a football match
PACKAGE: 9 I'm attacked by a creamy, cheesy sauce and hot chunks of hock style ham, tender chicken and fresh dark green slivers of leek. A good bite to it but nothing too tough. An outstanding formation!
PALATE: 9 The sauce is totally overwhelming and of a luxurious standard that most football fans simply aren't accustomed to getting at the match and it's no wonder Morecambe have a pile of accolades to their name
PRICE: 9 They charge £3 when purchased at the game with peas and gravy, but it's a high quality product. Needless to say Graham refused my money
PORTION: 8.5 Heavy and deep with a unique look and feel to it
OVERALL: 60.5/70 Like Morecambe's receptionist, I like my meat and potato and I'm sometimes a bit dubious about chicken in a pie, but this is simply breathtaking.

214.

PURVEYOR: Morecambe Football Club
PREMISES: Morecambe
PURCHASE: Meat and Potato Pie (£3 at the match)
PLACE: 9 They know their pies
PASTRY: 8 This one has four decorative dots on it and is a little bit rigid on the outside. Possibly because it was over cooked by someone who is

not and never will be a master chef i.e. me. It's still velvety soft in the centre and highly manageable with the hands

PRESENTATION: 8 Taking it home and reheating has its pitfalls but actually offers the opportunity to eat it fresh out of the oven

PACKAGE: 9 High meat content, lots of dark gravy and fresh sliced potato. Individual ingredients all moist and fresh lubricating the pie perfectly with every bite. A killer combination

PALATE: 9 Marinated and soaked in stock like a mini-casserole on the slow cooker. Like a fully encased hot pot – this is a good thing!

PRICE: 9 Ahem

PORTION: 8.5 Again it possesses the same angular shape with considerable depth and style

OVERALL: 60.5/70 Morecambe fans and visiting spectators should leave their butties at home when visiting the Globe Arena.

As for Graham Aimson, well what a fabulous chef. But more importantly a thoroughly nice chap. A chef who exhibits his exquisite talents for lower division football fans rather than posh folk who pay a hundred quid for something that resembles three pieces of Lego on a plate. North Lancashire once again proves a real hotbed of pastry products.

Monday 18th March 2013

I was only going to the bank. Then I spotted it. Despite having worked in Knutsford for ten years on and off, I'd never even noticed it. Woods Butchers are about to set me off on a chain of events: my very own British Pie week, a week after the official one. I've probably way over-represented the Cheshire area and the North West in general but as I've only got two weeks left here I'm exercising my right to use my lunch hour to get my batting average up.

I've no idea how I've missed this place as Woods Butchers looks the bollocks of a butchers (if you'll pardon the phrase) with burgers, sausages, rack of lambs and chicken skewers aplenty. There's a few folk fannying about so I'm left waiting a while whilst kind of being half acknowledged by a tall chap at the end. Seems I don't have to queue up to buy a pie although I have been stood there like a plum for five minutes. I shuffle past the fine meats to salivate and inspect them. "Are you just after a pie mate? You look hungry."

Seeing as I was chatting to my workmate John from Wolverhampton earlier (who insists he'll only eat a pie if it's dark inside), I swerve the meat and potato and opt for the steak and gravy. I've no idea what a chirpy, lofty Scouser is doing selling Scottish pies in the heart of affluent Cheshire, but it looks a competent effort.

215.

PURVEYOR: Woods
PREMISES: Knutsford
PURCHASE: Steak & Gravy Pie £1.19
PLACE: 8 **PASTRY:** 7.5 **PRESENTATION:** 7 **PACKAGE:** 7.5
PALATE: 7.5 **PRICE:** 7.5 **PORTION:** 7.5
OVERALL: 52.5/70 A slow start but like the pie it quickly warms up. The crust has a pinstripe, almost lattice, top and the pure steak and gravy tastes richer than the woman who I nearly knock over on the way out carrying a Chihuahua in her handbag.

Tuesday 19th March 2013

Thing is I've always had a list of places to visit near work but now I know I'm leaving it's turned into a last rites style bucket list. The one I've had listed for ages is "The Pie Life", a luxury establishment in Staffordshire. I'd noted it down from the start but it felt too far to get to in my dinner hour.

Upon further scrutiny of their list of stockists they can be procured from Godfrey Williams in Sandbach. Definitely doable so I hop in the car.

I park up in front of an imposing church and head into the cobbled main square. It's deathly quiet in Godfrey Williams as I amble down the aisles flanked by elegant foodstuffs whilst a middle aged woman appears to be pursuing my every step around the shop.

"Can I help you with anything?"

"Yeah pies – have you got any?"

They don't have The Pie Life pies for the Life of Pies. The best they have is some small oval pork pies right at the end of a counter which contains more cheese than an Eighties theme pub. Disconsolate, due to the absence of the large plate pies, I wolf down the growler without any thought of review and head through the market where the butcher also claims to sell great pies, though there are none on display.

I eventually find Brooks across the square. I knew there was another place – I've been here before on football stop offs for a hot pork barm and sure enough they're doing a roaring trade.

I fall prey to the "two queues" sucker punch: one for food and one for the butchery as some fat get pushes his kid forward, like a human shield, in front of me, followed by his own wobbly frame, while I stand there dawdling. He's ordering lamb baps, pork baps, turkey baps and just stops short of asking the lady serving to show him her baps. They do have an impressive array of pies in a multitude of flavours (all with decorative pastry lettering) which aren't likely to run out any time soon. The butchers section looks ace too with more sticky skewers than you can shake a sticky skewer at.

216.

PURVEYOR: Brooks
PREMISES: Sandbach
PURCHASE: Meat and Potato Pie £1.65
PLACE: 6.5 **PASTRY:** 8 **PRESENTATION:** 8 **PACKAGE:** 8
PALATE: 8 **PRICE:** 7 **PORTION:** 8
OVERALL: 53.5/70 The top crust is adorned with either a 2, S or Z and is
a touch flaky, resulting in a spot of bother as I cut through the Z-like
lettering but it adds volume and a certain crispness. An unusual oblong
shape for a meat and potato, once inside it resembles a savoury
hundreds and thousands, with finely chopped and diced mince, potato,
onion and gravy all jockeying for position and giving off a rich and
thorough meaty flavour combination.

A very proficient effort but as I return to work I'm still fuming about the Pie
Life omission when my Mr Magoo eyesight once again comes to the fore as
I pass through Holmes Chapel and I spot a huge Hovis sign painted all over
the walls. How can I have missed this? How on earth over all these years?
A bit of Googling back at the office reveals this is Mandevilles: not just any
old baker – no! A couple of years ago you could have walked in here and
bought a pie off none other than Harry Styles of One Direction!

Wednesday 20th March 2013

So today's a shoe in then – assuming I can get past the throng of screaming
teenage girls hanging around outside on the off chance they might get a
glimpse of a former local heartthrob who has just popped in for a pasty.

I remember when I used to do a five mile run at lunch, now I do a five
mile drive to the pie shop. May as well enjoy it while it lasts.

It's nearly 1pm and there's no sign of Harry. I manage to grasp the last
meat and potato pie in the shop (looking all dejected and forlorn on the
shelves) and cheer it up by demolishing it in seconds.

It's a lovely craft bakers with homemade jams, condiments and a serious
looking bread slicer on the counter, which looks like it could be lethal in
the wrong hands.

217.

PURVEYOR: Mandevilles
PREMISES: Holmes Chapel
PURCHASE: Meat and Potato Pie £1.42
PLACE: 7.5 The young lass behind the counter is of pleasant demeanour
considering she probably gets spat at by prepubescent schoolgirls as

she walks down the street because she's met Harry. Plus she gives me the last pie. I'd be hiding it under the counter

PASTRY: 8 A double crusted rim gives it a real crunchy bite

PRESENTATION: 8 Piping hot and flavoursome, reeks out the car and comes in a lovely golden wrapper

PACKAGE: 7.5 Fine, meaty and uneven

PALATE: 8 It has an earthy, natural, almost watery taste to it in stark contrast to some of the peppery monsters I've tried and carries it off beautifully

PRICE: 7 Not yet cashed in on their claim to fame

PORTION: 8 Highly satisfying

OVERALL: 54/70 A gem of a place which doesn't know it's beautifu....shit credibility slipping away fast here.

Thursday 21st March 2013

Time to bump another up the list. I must admit "a convenience store which sells its own pies" doesn't overly appeal so I'm once again relying on the recommendation of the Cheshire Pie Society that John Moors of Winsford will come up with the goods here.

Home made pies, off licence, post office and convenience store all rolled into one. Convenient indeed as I've a load of fanzines I need to post out.

Winsford is home to salt mines so I'm expecting an excessively seasoned effort, as I once again traverse the widest dual carriageway High Street in the country. This time I drive right up to the end past B&M Bargains, Aldi, the Job Centre (the biggest building which is always a worrying sign) and Foodcraft (the amazing pie shop cum chip shop). I bang a right past the tattooists until I see John Moors on my left down a quiet suburban street.

Inside there is a hot glass display shelf behind which sit meat, meat and potato, cheese and onion and steak pies. I opt for the meat and potato which is blisteringly hot and smells sublime, filtering through my car with a hypnotising aura about it. As promised they look uniquely homemade and there's tons of them. They also do a selection of wines, beers and spirits if you want a can of Special Brew to go with your pie. They really should throw in a bag of pickled onion Space Raiders and call it a "meal deal" if they're going to compete with today's modern multi-corporate convenience stores.

I'm a happy chappy despite the woman in the post office being a right surly cow. That is until disaster strikes as my car conks out whilst heading back up the A50 and I'm forced to drive the last few miles back to work with my exhaust clanging along the ground making an infernal racket. No way I'm stopping though: 20 miles an hour with the hazards on. First I'll eat the pie *then* I'll ring the AA Man. Priorities!

218.

PURVEYOR: John Moors
PREMISES: Winsford
PURCHASE: Meat and potato pie £1.40
PLACE: 7 Post Office grump aside, no issues
PASTRY: 9 A quirky unconventional shape and taste: homemade, uneven and raised in the middle to the extent that it resembles a mini-Krakatoa ready to erupt
PRESENTATION: 8 Emitting balmy levels of heat and smells more fragrant than a nun's armpit
PACKAGE: 8 A plentiful supply of content with gravy soaked dark mince on the top tier and sozzled, sweet tasting potato underneath which spills out from the first bite
PALATE: 8 Saccharin sweet in parts but a good wholesome meat and potato
PRICE: 7
PORTION: 7.5 Complete with loft conversion
OVERALL: 54.5/70 Every pie lover deserves a convenience store like this situated at the end of their street serving up lunchtime pocket rockets. Maybe you once did, like me.

Friday 22nd March 2013

In the meantime I've been exchanging more emails with the Pie Life people and they give me a list of alternative stockists including Alsager Farm Shop, so I decide to round "Pie Week" off by bombing three junctions down the M6 and back in my lunch hour. I possess an irrational hatred of Alsager. When my uni football team (Nottingham) played their lot it was always open warfare. They were a right bunch of dirty bastards but unfortunately (with them being a sports college) they were also better and fitter than us leaving us no option but to kick the buggers back. Mind you we took the same approach with Loughborough so it may have been us.

You'll find Alsager Hall Farm Shop down a quiet little lane next to a quaint village pub. The car park is heaving and it certainly is an authentic farm shop, in that there are animals running wild outside and I park up next to a dismantled tractor. Oh and it stinks. Yet inside it's a different story. Spick and span and I quickly go on the prowl in the food hall and return with a trio of appetising products.

I firstly manage to locate the elusive steak and potato plate pie from The Pie Life. I then survey the meat counter and if there isn't a little hand raised pork pie there going by the name of Winkle, which I find mildly amusing as that is what I used to call my ahem, little chap when I was a small boy. And to complete the hat trick I bag a locally made steak pudding from the freezer, after my discovery last month that I had criminally under-represented this delicacy.

I head off back towards the motorway and get scuppered by a rapidly descending level crossing barrier next to a big BAE Systems plant. Go on – one last time for old time's sake: "FUCK!! DON'T YOU BASTARDS KNOW I'M ON MY LUNCH HOUR??!!"

Controversy alert: Did I mention that these luxury handmade pies from the Goldhurst Farm Bakery are actually boasting about the fact that they only put a top crust on their pies? Their logic being that it leaves more room for its filling. Gee, I feel so stupid now!

Still, they do a range of steak pies (this one is a not inconsiderate 480 grammes) costing a mere £2.59 and served up by a posh gentleman with a monocle on the wrapper. In it there's beef, potato, celery and it takes a whopping 35 minutes in the oven but then it's a whopping pie.

219.

PURVEYOR: The Pie Life
PREMISES: Staffordshire
PURCHASE: Steak & Potato Pie £2.59
PLACE: 8 Their customer service to help me get my pie is spot on and the woman in the farm shop is competent, even managing to answer the phone whilst serving me and mouthing "Bloody PPI"
PASTRY: 7 Well it's audacious I'll give them that but it does make it a little less of a pie in my book. And to add insult to injury, a small part of the crust remains lodged on the tray
PRESENTATION: 7.5 Lovely pastry aroma but metal on metal when eating with a knife and fork doesn't go down well with me as I have more fillings than that Jaws bloke out of James Bond. Ouch!
PACKAGE: 8 Deep and meaty with lashings of gravy and insanely fresh tasting potatoes
PALATE: 7.5 Not too strongly seasoned and a rustic natural flavour to it. Only let down by a slightly metallic taste brought on by the lack of surrounding crust
PRICE: 7.5 A large appetite satisfying package
PORTION: 9 It's of such grand dimensions that I cut it into quarters and I'm sure non-fat bastards could eke this out into a hearty family meal

OVERALL: 54.5/70 Should really be called a hot pot as an oblong tray based effort but nevertheless a most satisfying scoff.

220.

PURVEYOR: Winkles
PREMISES: Wolverhampton
PURCHASE: Pork Pie 93p
PLACE: 7.5 **PASTRY:** 9
PRESENTATION: 7 **PACKAGE:** 8
PALATE: 7.5 **PRICE:** 8.5 **PORTION:** 7.5
OVERALL: 55/70 As for the amusingly named Winkles of Wolverhampton growler, it has a beautiful shape and splendidly soft texture. There's no crunchiness here (to the delight of denture wearers) and inside there is a large ball of finely chopped sausage meat, flanked by a quarter inch of jelly on either side. I remove it from the fridge ten minutes before eating it and every mouthful sends me to heaven and back.

Finally, I may have mentioned it in Lancaster but allow me to refresh the concept of a "Babbies Yed". Ostensibly this is an affectionate localised term for a steamed steak pudding, dubbed as such due to its cute resemblance to an infant's bonce. In the case of Brockley's it's a handmade pudding wrapped in a light crust pastry case cooked to a secret recipe from over 60 years ago, using the finest locally sourced beef.

Upon discovering this little beauty I was powerless to resist especially as it's steak and ale (thus evading my tentative kidney aversion). I've just got to cook it now. Steam it in a pan with the lid on in ¾ inch of water for 45 minutes: what could possibly go wrong? DO NOT ALLOW TO BOIL DRY it says in aggressive capitals. It's like those angry texts I get from the wife which say DO NOT HAVE ANOTHER PINT. COME HOME NOW. It usually means the opposite doesn't it? It means: STAY OUT! DRINK LOTS!!

Is that burning? You dickhead!

I'd been checking regularly listening eagerly to its furious whistling and bubbling noises with steam blowing off it like Billy-o, then the second my back is turned....

The steam nearly scalds my hand clean off as I remove the lid and the top looks decidedly soggy. I give birth to this beautiful baby by upending it onto the plate and I'm faced with a delightfully soft encased suet type pastry which only a mother could love. Alas, upon cutting it in half the pudding gives way and sinks flaccidly all over the plate.

Yet that is the end of the negatives as Batman and Robin come flying to the rescue in the form of sumptuous soft casing and intense meaty filling which draws out an irresistibly tasty meaty combination.

221.

PURVEYOR: Brockleys
PREMISES: Alsager
PURCHASE: Steak & Ale Pudding £1.50
PLACE: 7.5 **PASTRY:** 6.5 **PRESENTATION:** 7 **PACKAGE:** 7.5
PALATE: 7.5 **PRICE:** 7 **PORTION:** 7
OVERALL: 50/70 A meaty treat crammed full of steak and gravy despite almost drying up in the pan.

Saturday 23rd March 2013

The bloke in front of me in the pie shop has a Kestrel perched on his shoulder. And I don't mean a green can, I mean an actual bird of prey.

I'm in Conwy again for Emma's brother's birthday, with all the family decamped to a coastal castle like a scene out of The Prisoner. Except the beach like the rest of North Wales is six inches deep with snow.

As we potter about Conwy there's talk of going to the chippy as we sit in the pub plotting our restricted movements. It smells amazing to be fair, but while everyone deliberates I sneak out to the Popty Conwy to scoff a pie, eating it huddled in the doorway of a bingo hall.

Once the bird man of Alca Y Traf steps aside, I get my pie and am delighted to discover a range of complimentary sauces for a chilly day. I also treat myself to some Jones of Cymru "Hal Y Mon" Sea salt and vinegar crisps for good measure.

222.

PURVEYOR: Popty Conwy Bakery
PREMISES: Conwy
PURCHASE: Meat and potato pie £1.35
PLACE: 8 **PASTRY:** 8 **PRESENTATION:** 8 **PACKAGE:** 8
PALATE: 8 **PRICE:** 7.5 **PORTION:** 7.5
OVERALL: 55/70 A textbook effort. Lovely mash with generous slabs of fresh potato binding together the mince and gravy and that all important peppery kick. The perfect tonic on a wintry day.

Monday 25th March 2013

Wow! A commute with a difference: What a way to ignite your morning by travelling on the A55 towards England; with a backdrop of great big leopard skin hills on one side topped with melting snow, the Irish Sea on the other and the whole of the Wirral emerging up ahead. Simply breathtaking.

Of course my mood is further heightened by the fact I've just pulled a pair of crackers in the Penmaenmawr Spar (easy for you to say) at seven in the morning.

Not before the counter assistant leaves me standing there with two pies in my hand, making me look a right plum and forcing me to ask for a bag in Welsh – six pence!

223.

PURVEYOR: Treflach Farm
PREMISES: Shropshire
PURCHASE: Pork and apple topped pie £1.95
PLACE: 6.5 Not happy about "bag-gate"
PASTRY: 8.5 The top is in effect the apples but there does seem to be a thin crust of sorts lurking beneath
PRESENTATION: 7 Consumed straight from the fridge after a five mile run, the perfect refreshment. A proper farmer's delight with sweet crunchy apples blended with spicy sausage meat
PACKAGE: 8.5 Consistent, dark pork meat topped with Bramley apples (counting towards my five a day)
PALATE: 9 A different experience for the palate but it works and for once the jelly is not the star of the show but combines to form a holy taste trinity
PRICE: 7 A touch pricey
PORTION: 8 A generously sized growler
OVERALL: 54.5/70 Pork and apple go together like Ant & Dec. But tastier and with fewer shit puns.

224.

PURVEYOR: TJ Parry – Jones & Daughters
PREMISES: Trefriw, Conwy
PURCHASE: Meat and Potato Pie £1.85
PLACE: 6.5 **PASTRY:** 8 **PRESENTATION:** 8 **PACKAGE:** 9
PALATE: 8 **PRICE:** 7 **PORTION:** 8
OVERALL: 54.5/70 Much like the butcher who manufactured it, this little cracker is quite a mouthful. Deep, dense and dangerously over-capacity inside, encased in a perfectly crafted crust with a rich flavour in every bite.

Friday 29th March 2013

I've tried to get to Kent, I really have; via the world wide web at least. My main object of desire relates to an early Nineties trip to Gillingham when I was young and daft. I started drinking at 7am on the train and was still going at 3am the next day. The only thing I ate all day has gone into mythology as possibly the best pie I have ever had. It was a steak pie from Gillingham FC. It was the size of a manhole cover and cost £3.20, probably nearly as much as it cost to gain ingress to the terracing in this fallow period in Wigan Athletic's then un-illustrious history. Try as I might I can't find the vendor and it seems Gillingham have long since sold out to mass production caterers.

It's a long way to go without a definitive goal so you'll have to forgive me if I cheat when on a Friday night Booths' run I spy a "cook food" pie made in Sittingbourne, Kent, priced at the extortionate £4.75 in the freezer section. Steak and red wine: Tender topped rump beef cooked slowly with vegetables and Merlot wine and covered in shortcrust pastry with the chef's signature on the front.

I take it home, peel off its clothes and place it in the oven for 45 minutes. It's another top crust only I'm afraid, yellow from where it's been egg beaten and slightly raised at the edges. As it's frozen, it's hard to see what meaty delights lie underneath, save for a little vent hole in the middle where the contents will gently breath as it cooks.

Upon pulling it out of the oven the shortcrust pastry has softened and the gravy has splattered all over the plastic tray. I seek out a fish slice to sever the pie in half and perform a lift and drop on to a plate. You can't eat a top crust with hands alone unless you have a hand shaped like a spoon, impenetrable to 100 degree temperatures.

The crust lifts out with the meat and veg and I am left with a large pool of gravy swilling around in the bottom which I pour over; as a consequence what I end up with is more of a stew than a pie.

It looks and smells fabulous however so I'm tolerating this dining experience whilst compromising my principles. It's got beef, Merlot (5%), carrots, leeks, celery in it....oh it goes on forever ingredients wise.

As for the taste well BOOM it's a beauty which blows me away with a flavour so wealthy and powerful you could put a pinstripe suit on it and call it an investment banker. You can actually taste the wine in there – but it is just one of a number of exhilarating sensations encountered whilst eating this.

My only concern is that there's not an awful lot of it – especially given the price – and I supplement the feed with a couple of slices of buttered bread to mop up the residual Windermere-sized lake of gravy thrashing violently around the plate.

225.

PURVEYOR: Cook Food
PREMISES: Sittingbourne
PURCHASE: Steak and red wine "pie" £4.75
PLACE: 7 **PASTRY:** 7.5 **PRESENTATION:** 7 **PACKAGE:** 7
PALATE: 9.5 **PRICE:** 7 **PORTION:** 7.5
OVERALL: 52.5/70 The variety and quality of taste is out of this world. However, it is not a pie. It is a fraud. A charlatan, a bounder and a cad. Remove thyself from my kitchen at once, you filthy casserole with a singular crust!

Saturday 13th April 2013

A trip to Wembley to watch little Wigan Athletic play in the FA Cup semi final and I immediately succumb to my mate's party snack pack recommendation, consisting of a Galloways meat and potato pie, a small meat pie, a Wigan Athletic decorative cake and a citrus Oasis to "pre-tox". Everyone else on the coach is cracking open tinnies, we're drinking Lattes and reading the broadsheets. We've earned our Pathetic Casuals reputation over the years. I have however procured a bottle of potent looking 55% rum off my mother from Martinique mind you. It looks like out of date Gaviscon. Both pies devoured by 9.30am and the rum cracked open soon after.

To Gerrards Cross, a place devoid of pubs and lots of people simply bugger off to London. Any chance of a pie shop then? I've got that itch again. I skip a mid-morning pint at the only place that's open, a Chef & Brewer with fish mains at £15 a go and pound the streets of Posh Spice's home town searching for that elusive eatery amid the plethora of boutiques and brasseries.

Gotcha – Strattons! A handful of pies and pasties amidst the bread and cakes. "Are these pies hot or cold?" I enquire.

"We can only serve them cold but we can warm them up in the microwave".

Is this a local Buckinghamshire by law (pie-law?) or something? She flips the tray off and pings it in. I collect my haul and proceed around the back of the building to eat my pie by the bins. Inconspicuous is my middle name. It doesn't look the sort of place where folk walk around eating a pie in their hands if I'm honest.

226.

PURVEYOR: Stratton Bakery
PREMISES: Gerrards Cross
PURCHASE: Steak and Onion pie £1.95

PLACE: 7.5 **PASTRY:** 6 **PRESENTATION:** 7.5 **PACKAGE:** 7.5
PALATE: 7.5 **PRICE:** 6.5 **PORTION:** 7
OVERALL: 49.5/70 Hey I wasn't expecting miracles but this is very, very soggy; not helped by the removal of the foil tray as a stabiliser. Just about manageable in the palm of my hand with minor spillage. The content is actually surprisingly decent but the crust is too wrinkly for this to be seriously considered.

Saturday 20th April 2013

What starts as a brief sortie frequently turns into a pie endurance event: a marathon on the eve of the real London marathon. The other week, my mate Moore (who is a proper grafter not an office stooge like me) said there was a bloke at work who had been raving about a place called Philippes of Skipton. Details are a little cagey on the internet but I manage to seek it out. The trouble is once I start googling I am assaulted by a wave of recommendations from sites as diverse as Trip Advisor and Mumsnet.

I have a gander on One Mick Jones where they are raving about Stanforths and then Sutcliffes is thrown into the mix as well. BOTH Champion pork pie makers. Then I come across another one called Drake & Macefield supposedly better than the lot put together.

So to Skipton whilst overtaking dozens of coaches of moody looking Cardiff fans on their way to Turf Moor to celebrate their impending promotion to the Premier League. Something tells me the M65 was never meant to be built, given the way it scythes through hundreds of grid style terraced houses arranged like loaves of bread on a sloping hillside; it makes for quite the spectacle though.

Through Colne and past Boundary Mill (home of the tall but small pork and apple pie) and a surreal terraced street steeper than the Matterhorn, with a strip of village green in the middle. I head past Foulridge, which despite its unattractive name possesses several shimmering reservoirs which yachts flapping about on it. It's a tired, snarling road full of day trippers headed the same way as me and upon arrival in Skipton there's a deluge of tourists spilling out on to the road as I turn on the main square.

The first dominating feature you see when you arrive in Skipton is not it's imposing castle, but the towering Bradford and Bingley building. Where once we built castles to protect our assets, we then built financial services behemoths and now both are crumbling. Ooh bit of politics there.

The castle soon emerges behind it with the pub of the same name doing a roaring trade with outside drinkers on the first day of summer. Yet just before I turn the corner as I head over the Mill Bridge, I see it: "Stanforth's

Celebrated Pork Pie establishment" with a gaggle of pensioners peering into the window, tongues hanging out like undernourished Labradors.

The car park is seething with anger and impending road rage as people scrap for spaces. I bide my time and march back into Skipton carrying an empty Tesco bag to store my pie multiples. It's a little hot to be arsing about doing shuttle runs.

Stanforths have got Pork, Pork & Apple, Pork & Black Pudding, Steak & Potato, Steak and Kidney and some huge stand pies in the window for a fiver. I merely want a little tiddler and I walk in to be met with a cheery chap in an apron.

"Pork pie please".

"An 'ot one?".

"Aye go on then".

There's just the right amount of wet grease coming off and seeping through the branded Stanforths bag, which by the time I crack it open a few minutes later has to be peeled off. Schoolboy error number two occurs when I tilt it slightly as I lift it out the bag: Tributaries of hot fugitive molten jelly escaping all over the place including my shirt cuffs. Beautifully done!

227.

PURVEYOR: Stanforths
PREMISES: Skipton
PURCHASE: Pork Pie 99p
PLACE: 8 Pleasantries are exchanged with a man who looks like every butcher who walked the earth
PASTRY: 8 A feathery hot water crust with a tough well defined edge
PRESENTATION: 8.5 A veritable little fireball of a growler
PACKAGE: 8 Coarse texture but a reassuring quality and quantity about it with a brown grey pigment to the meat
PALATE: 8.5 The sausage meat is a little salty and tough but softened up by the surfeit of jelly invading every corner (plus my hands and chin). Truly the best way to eat a pork pie in Yorkshire, indeed anywhere
PRICE: 7.5 Fighting back three figures
PORTION: 7 Dinky but heavy duty growler
OVERALL: 55.5/70 Wear gloves if you don't like it rough.

I walk past three other places on my way to Stanforths, none of which were on my list, but I head back towards Otley Street through the main thoroughfare of Skipton, with its wide market square selling everything from clay ducks to flat caps to the more modern dodgy DVD's and phone covers. It's taking me a while to move through the sheer volume of people and I cut a forlorn frustrated figure of an irritated little man in a hurry to fill his bag full of pies.

I knew there were two pie shops on the part pedestrianised Otley Street but I am taken aback to find a third one sandwiched between the first two. If we assume that the sprinkling of tea shops are also capable of knocking up a pie then you could go on a pie all dayer around these parts – it's a little piece of pie heaven. I stick to the script and head into Sutcliffes with its big traditional red and white canopied front.

Sutcliffes (no relation to Peter as far as I am aware) do me a pork pie served cold and eaten cold despite me being almost sidetracked into buying a Steak and Copper Dragon Ale pie which sounds ace.

228.

PURVEYOR: Sutcliffes
PREMISES: Skipton
PURCHASE: Pork Pie 99p
PLACE: 7 **PASTRY:** 7 **PRESENTATION:** 7 **PACKAGE:** 7
PALATE: 7 **PRICE:** 7 **PORTION:** 7
OVERALL: 49/70 A dense scoop of sausage meat of the standard pork pie buffet fare, with a nice layer of jelly around the edges, encased in the traditional hot water pastry. A bit average really. Does heating it up really make that much of an impact?

I nip back to the car and short sleeved vultures are circling like kerb crawlers looking for parking space prostitutes "Are you going lad?" Me, I'm too busy pissing my sides at a large pheasant stuck in the radiator grill of a mobile home. I try to take a photo but at that point the owner (of the vehicle not the pheasant) turns up and takes umbrage at my admittedly quite odd behaviour, obviously thinking I work for the RSPCA.

I navigate once again through the narrow streets back out to Otley Street to the in betweener: Craven's Bakery. What hope for The Craven Bakery then – sandwiched – no pun intended – between two of the purported best butchers in North Yorkshire?

Well it's a gutsy effort and they have a good range of pies and pasties. However, there's no pork pie and I'm not surprised, given the competition, so I opt for the oval shaped steak and potato. It's a very potato heavy pie (always a bold move on t'other side of the Pennines) but very well filled with the raised crust in the middle containing a further annexe of filling.

229.

PURVEYOR: Craven Bakery
PREMISES: Skipton
PURCHASE: Meat and Potato Pie £1.20
PLACE: 8 **PASTRY:** 7.5 **PRESENTATION:** 7 **PACKAGE:** 7.5
PALATE: 7 **PRICE:** 7.5 **PORTION:** 7
OVERALL: 51.5/70 A predominantly potato based pie with a few cheeky little chunks of mince popping up intermittently, strong definition on the crimp and a teasing bit of gravy spillage poking out of the middle. Nice and fresh and I'm sure their sandwiches and breakfasts (not to mention the chocolate fountains) are lovely but I get the impression pies are not their forte, probably because if they muscle in on the butchers turf they'll end up getting chased down the street with meat cleavers.

So to Drake & Macefield and this time it's £1.10 for another hot pork pie. This gaff has more of a deli feel to it with everything from ox tongue, beef dripping and Cartmel sticky toffee pudding on show

The Drake & Macefield is an excellent pork pie yet very different to the two I've already consumed. The jelly is semi solidified and the sausage meat is pink and peppery. The crust is uneven and the lava like jelly comes bursting out of it. Yet again, I find myself peeling the pie from the wrapper partially drenched in grease while the jelly makes its presence felt like a drunken uncle at a wake.

230.

PURVEYOR: Drake & Macefield
PREMISES: Skipton
PURCHASE: Pork Pie £1.10
PLACE: 7.5 **PASTRY:** 8 **PRESENTATION:** 8 **PACKAGE:** 8
PALATE: 7.5 **PRICE:** 7.5 **PORTION:** 7
OVERALL: 53.5/70 A big peppery scoop of sausage encased in tons of jelly with a very bacon-like taste to it, all wrapped in a delicious moist classic hot water pastry.

I meander back down Otley Street to bid farewell and can only marvel at its wonder which includes the Craven Cross Shopping Centre: there's even a cafe in there selling pies! It's only when I turn around to admire the little mall that I see beyond; back on the main street directly opposite – you guessed it....A GREGGS!!

What on earth would possess anyone to visit a Greggs when you are blessed with all these great pastry purveyors on your doorstep?

I return to the car past the bewitching aromas of a chip shop and an ice cream stall. I drive out to Philippes where I end up going through some housing estate which gives me the most stunning view of the whole of Skipton, before dropping back down into flanks of grey slate terraced houses. It is at the end of one of those streets where I find the black fronted Philippes. I head there quickly before the shuffling curtains turn into a doorstep confrontation from a pyjama clad lady who appears to be mouthing "who the fuck's that" through the window. A big burly chap with music blaring from his car gets out and does the same. Don't take all the pies lad!

As I enter two old biddies are stockpiling bread and cakes without a care in the world and all I can spot are two pork pies out on a tray. The fella in front is asking a lot of questions about the pies. He plumps for a meat and potato – the last one! This isn't a problem though as it's not what I came here for. "What pies have you got left love?"

Pork and some sort of cheese roll type thing. "I'll see if they've any steak in the back" she adds. Bingo! I'm delighted as this is their hallmark pie, the one I've been told to acquire.

From the second I drop it in the car the aroma emitted from this pie is truly astounding and unlike anything I've ever had before or since. It's got a furiously appetising whiff and there's definitely something in this; a most worthy tip off. Yet from the second I take ownership I can tell it's going to be a Marmite pie. Not literally – but a pie that divides opinion. The meaty aroma is so rich and wealthy that it smells of gourmet cuisine and cat food all at the same time.

231.

PURVEYOR: Philippes
PREMISES: Skipton
PURCHASE: Steak and Onion Pie £1.55
PLACE: 8 She goes out the back to rummage for the pie I want rather than flog me the stuff that's been out on the counter all morning. Going the extra mile! Well the extra ten yards
PASTRY: 7 A highly controversial offering. The top crust has a sturdy quality to it with hand crimped edges and has a shiny, well glazed coating. It even gives a token nod to the traditional London pie with its oblong shape and thick overhanging crust lip. However, the bottom is a touch soggy making it hard to manage in the hands and ultimately falls apart somewhat
PRESENTATION: 9 For the phenomenal smell alone: this pie has the Lynx effect! Or should that be Stinks effect?
PACKAGE: 8 Rich peppery gravy comes roaring out like an angry lion

spitting dark fire all over my fingers, the wrapper, the tray, you name it.
Rich chunks of meat and a dominant, full blooded gravy
PALATE: 8.5 A distinctive, almost unique, taste for both meat and gravy, full
flavoured, aromatic and very, very peppery yet also quite sweet in parts
PRICE: 7 It's all steak (I think)
PORTION: 7.5
OVERALL: 55/70 The best pie in the country? Probably not but a bloody
good one and highly distinct. I can see why it's a pie that would evoke such
passion as it's definitely got something about it, in spite of that slight animal
feed whiff about it which I found amazing but also slightly unpleasant.

Skipton done and dusted, and I never even got to the "Famous" Skipton
Pie and Mash Shop. Skipton breezes comfortably into the Top Ten pie
hotspots league table with it's fine range of butchers and bakers and one
can only imagine how much jelly would be spilled should it ever get in the
ring with its fellow Yorkshire growler heavyweight up the road Otley.

Saturday 27th April 2013

I've walked past Burchalls in St Helens many a time and it barely seems
open. The internet seems to be saying they queue for hours out of the
doors for their famous pork pies but you'd be forgiven for missing it sometimes. There's no lights on and no sound but then through the window I
see a mass of motionless bodies beyond steamed up windows: it's the infamous pensioners with Tupperware boxes and Tartan trollies, queuing
all around the perimeter of the shop.

There's only one tray of pies and they're gone in seconds as the queue
hardly abates. So the second youngest bloke in there apart from me (must
be in his fifties) asks where the rest are. "It'll be ten minutes for pies" the
cheery response comes closely followed by weary sighs.

We all know old codgers love queuing but I'm getting impatient here. You
can tell the age of the clientele as I am the only one playing with me phone.
I bolt for the door as another body squeezes in and head for the market: the
Yates Greer stall in fact. A mate of mine raves about their sausages. 'Tis a
warm and sunny day in St Helens where the buskers and Big Issue sellers
secrete themselves at even markers either side of pound shops and pawnbrokers. The accordion player's rendition of Lady In Red gets battered hands
down by the Afro-Caribbean lady singing Rivers of Babylon mind you.

The market stalls have a little number clip on the corner of their establishment so finding them isn't a problem. There's the token market stalls
which the big supermarkets appear to have not yet monopolised: a wool
stall, a barbers and a serve your own pet food stand. I manage to swag the

last Pimmies M&P but my attention is also arrested by one of Yates Greer's home made pork pies. It has a layer of jelly on top of it deeper than Lake Ontario, it's smothered in it; a gleaming paste glistening and winking at me seductively and I can't divert my eyes from it.

Pimmies are legendary in St Helens. They went bust but now they've re-opened and sell them through stockists including this one in St Helens' market. I recall their pies being well ventilated with a large gap between filling and crust and a strong peppery taste to them which was right up my street, along with a supersoft casing reminiscent of Twiss bakery in Wigan – another RIP as it sadly burnt down a few years back. A pie factory burning down in Wigan, can you imagine the mourning?

232.

PURVEYOR: Pimmies
PREMISES: St Helens
PURCHASE: Meat and Potato Pie £1.30
PLACE: 8 **PASTRY:** 8 **PRESENTATION:** 7 **PACKAGE:** 7
PALATE: 8 **PRICE:** 7.5 **PORTION:** 7
OVERALL: 52.5/70 My memory may deceive me but the Pimmies seems a lot shallower than I recall albeit more compressed into the top crust. It's a fusion of taste – sweet and fruity in parts and peppery in others with a lovely smelling pastry. It seems there's lots of subtle changes here: full marks for keeping the flag waving but not necessarily for the better. I think if I was to have just one desert island pie from St Helens it'd be a Greenalls.

You know those "introduce yourself" type interrogation threads that appear on internet message boards? Well we used to have a thread on the Mudhuts website and one of the questions was "Do you eat the jelly off the top of a pork pie?". (The answer is: of course you do, you eat the lot). Yet in spite of this, the jelly is rarely found on the outside.

This is coated in it. I reckon it'd be better heated up but I also reckon I'd cock it up. There must be half an inch of jelly on top at its deepest point.

233.

PURVEYOR: Yates Greer
PREMISES: St Helens
PURCHASE: £1.20 Pork Pie
PLACE: 8 She aptly described products on request and I receive a bag for my combined £2.50 outlay
PASTRY: 8 Delightfully crisp with considerable give in the middle
PRESENTATION: 7 Market stall chic

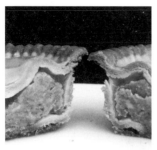

PACKAGE: 8 Liberal portions of both jelly and a double scoop of pinky-grey sausage meat inside
PALATE: 8 Low levels of seasoning detected allowing the earthly pork flavour to flow through in every mouthful
PRICE: 7.5 Bit pricey for a cold pie off a market stall in St Helens
PORTION: 7 A good half inch of jelly on top
OVERALL: 53.5/70 A handsome looking chap, kind of like Richard Greer.

As I return to Burchalls I pass an establishment called Tasty Chicks which is a part lapdancing bar/part barbecued chicken stall and in its window there is a mound of pasty products winking alluringly at me. I barge my way through the door past another convoy of tartan trolley wielding pensioners to investigate further. They've got steak and onion, meat and potato and pork in the shop alongside the obligatory large glass oven with chickens spinning around on a rotisserie under a sordid looking red light. More importantly they stock a range of condiments from HP Sauce to Biggafat peas and other pie-friendly accessories, all the accompaniments you could ever need. Do I want a spoon or fork with it they ask me? I scoff knowingly. Cutlery, pah!

They sell both Cottoms and Taylors pies and one of the Cottoms is about twice the size of the others. I assume it's a meat and potato but I make an about turn when she pulls a regular sized one off the shelf and point to tell her "I want that one" in an Andy from Little Britain-stylee.

A few minutes later as I am unravelling this pie by attempting to lift it out of the tray in a lay-by, I uncover a hideous realisation: it's top crust only. Well of course it is you knobhead, you've just bought a HOT POT!! If only they'd offered me a fork to eat it with....

234.
PURVEYOR: Cottoms
PREMISES: St Helens
PURCHASE: Hot Pot £1.30
PLACE: 7.5 **PASTRY:** 7 **PRESENTATION:** 8 **PACKAGE:** 8
PALATE: 8.5 **PRICE:** 7.5 **PORTION:** 8
OVERALL: 54.5/70 The frequently more spicy and longer soaked hot pot serves up an interesting contrast with definitive flavour coming through in generous slabs of potatoes, mince and carrots. A real hearty treat despite its solitary top crust.

Finally back to Burchalls and you can smell the pork from around the corner punctuating the air along with the waft of cigarette smoke from the ropey looking boozers on Westfield Street. One of them is called Dreams but looks more of a nightmare given some of the monsters hanging out of it at 11am on a Saturday morning. Once inside there's a gaggle of female assistants cutting up the meat and a bloke with glasses and an ear-ring who brings the pies out of the back. The guvnor I presume?

They only sell one type of pie, it's called a pie and it's ingredients are posted on the glass counter: Pork and jelly appear to be the main constituents. They're £1.12 a chuck, served invigoratingly warm off the oven fresh trays and don't have a cat in hell's chance of cooling down given the number of vulture-like patrons descending on this establishment.

235.
PURVEYOR: Burchalls
PREMISES: St Helens
PURCHASE: Pork Pie £1.12
PLACE: 7.5 At Burchalls the pie is the personality. On a practical note they are served double wrapped to give some insulation from the heat and the grease doesn't filter straight through to your hands
PASTRY: 8.5 Highly uneven and very acute almost Scotch pie style crust edge which rears up above the delicate middle. No tray so I recommend a plate to catch the juices so that you can turn the pie on its side to mop up the jelly
PRESENTATION: 9 The perfect temperature more or less straight out of the oven
PACKAGE: 8.5 A double scoop of spicy sausage meat and abundant levels of juices flowing through
PALATE: 9 From the second I break into it, piping hot peppery pie juice spurts all over the place. A messy, fiery full bodied affair. Phenomenal!
PRICE: 8 Pensioners know value!
PORTION: 7.5 Above average on the growler scale
OVERALL: 58/70 A sensational discovery. There might be some long lost rugby league link here but this is definitely a pie which has adopted the Yorkshire style methodology in the heart of West Lancashire (or Merseyside as some would have it).

Saturday 4th May 2013

To the West part of Bromwich today where crucial relegation points are at stake but I'm more nervous that I've left adequate time to tick all the Black Country butchers off my list pre-match.

I've got esteemed Wiganer Tony Topping in the car who will gorge on cowpie with me and also proof read this tome several months down the line. I explain my routine: addresses are noted down, timings are put in place but if I see something else I fancy on route, I reserve the right to deviate off course.

We exit the M6 at junction 12 to be hit with a glorious expanse of water either side. Hang on isn't this the place where Collymore used to go dogging? Wolverhampton has more roundabouts than Skelmersdale and we head for the Mander Centre, home of Walter Smith butchers. Tony and his lad head for the retro comic book stores and the pub while I leave my car on a meter and go pie hunting.

They might be playing "Sunshine After the Rain" in The Mander Centre but in truth it's a bit drab with empty units aplenty, no doubt a casualty of the jazzed up Bull Ring down the road. Walter's gaff is an oasis of vibrant meat heaven nevertheless, with St George's flags fluttering in the throng of activity. The all important "queue of pensioners" is evident but I can't see any pies, just loads of joints of meat and kebabs and a hot carvery buffet kiosk at the front.

I spot a cheese and potato pie which looks a bit cottage pie-ish to me, indeed no different from an actual cottage pie next to it. Two pork pies for a fiver; family sized! Supremely dark in colour and very, very large. Plus they've got a fine array of meat pies to suit all appetites. After getting my nosh, my eyes are diverted to the tray of freebies on top of the counter and I sample a wedge of Moroccan lamb and some bread pudding.

The pork pie is dark and double wrapped in shiny checked cloth style paper. It's glazed, hand pressed and populated with a dark, coarse meat. Meant for 2-3 people I inevitably set about scoffing it singlehandedly.

236.

PURVEYOR: Walter Smiths
PREMISES: Birmingham
PURCHASE: Pork Pie £2.99
PLACE: 8 I haven't got a clue what she's saying but free food usually works for me
PASTRY: 8 A dark, decorative and durable top crust which holds together with perfect portability
PRESENTATION: 8 Delightfully presented and double wrapped
PACKAGE: 8 I'll concede I'm not the biggest fan of the tough, rough filling but there is certainly plenty to gnaw at as it's topped to the brim with meat and jelly

PALATE: 7.5 Raw, genuine meaty flavours prevail in every bite; a pie made the natural way
PRICE: 8 A chunky price but an overwhelming size
PORTION: 9 It's a beast of a pie, best eaten by turning it on its side as you won't be able to get your gob around it otherwise. I start to get lockjaw 15 minutes in and I've still only eaten half of it
OVERALL: 56.5/70 Walter doesn't falter with a belter.

237.
PURVEYOR: Walter Smith
PREMISES: Birmingham
PURCHASE: Minced beef and onion pie £1.69
PLACE: 8 Unlike the lady serving, I don't have to repeat myself
PASTRY: 8 A dark, flaky top crust and the crimper must have long fingernails but it gives it a personalised feel along with the sticky semi-welded underside. Tough, crunchy crust edges and having seen some of the clientele of this place I'd be concerned about their dentures
PRESENTATION: 8 An amazing waft emanates from the oven while it cooks, perhaps getting me a tad over-enthusiastic for what is actually inside
PACKAGE: 7 A touch underwhelming perhaps, a little bit like the traditional Cockney pies with only a thin layer of meat presented
PALATE: 7 Adequate but no killer punch for me
PRICE: 6.5 A bit pricey for what it is
PORTION: 7.5 A shrinker
OVERALL: 52/70 Pork takes the honours.

I walk deeper into the Mander centre amidst the cheerful strains of "You can call me Al" searching via GPS for my next destination and Wolverhampton comes to life as the precinct opens out into a large pedestrianised shopping area, where a shouty evangelist is bawling out an impromptu sermon whilst retreating gingerly from the local constabulary.

Michael Kirk's is down a side street, another spit and sawdust butchers full of middle aged staff enjoying Wolves based banter with the customers; well it's more of a post mortem seeing as they've just been relegated. It's always good to see goose fat and beef dripping being openly handled in front of you on a Saturday morning and there's a real authentic feel about the place with sawdust on the floor plus that unmistakeable butcher's smell. There's meats galore: joints and kebabs and faggots and a not inconsiderable number of pies on the back shelf. Being confronted with a large plate of wobbly liver is a bit much for 11am on a Saturday morning mind you after I polished off a quarter bottle of single malt last night.

Both shop and website *(www.porkiepie.co.uk)* are championing their award winning porkers so that seems to be the option to go for. They're the national pork pie champion 2005. Eight years is a long time to be bragging about it mind you.

238.

PURVEYOR: Kirks
PREMISES: Wolverhampton
PURCHASE: Pork Pie £1.05
PLACE: 7.5 A cheerful ambience despite the demise of their beloved Wolves
PASTRY: 8 A splendid russet coloured, oval shaped, hot water based pastry. A little soft in parts but sits perfectly in the hands
PRESENTATION: 7 It looks warm on a greaseproof sheet but it's served and eaten cold
PACKAGE: 8 Coarse, choppy, dark meat with jelly piped in throughout yet remarkably delicate to the bite once you get past the crunchy crust
PALATE: 8 A fusion of different pork flavours with every bite
PRICE: 7.5
PORTION: 7.5 Deceptive, deep and satisfying
OVERALL: 53.5/70 Like the Walter Smith one before it, the Black Country definitely gives a token nod to the Melton Mowbray style of pie and I think I'm starting to like them.

To Mad O'Rourkes in Tipton or is it Dudley? I don't know. It's in a fairly non descript residential area but comes with an illuminating reputation. On approach it appears heavily scaffolded: shit it'd best not be closed! There does appear to be a door slightly ajar as we head around the back to park up. It's fine, just giving the old bird a bit of a facelift, as evidenced by the blue emulsion on my hands due to completely missing the "WET PAINT" signs plastered everywhere. "You are now entering the world famous Mad O'Rourkes Pie Factory" – bold statement; I like my pies yet I'd never heard of it till I started researching this book but it promises Bostin' Value Food whatever that means. It all augurs well for this afternoon's nosebag. It is a big dominating corner plot which once operated as an entertainment venue where a young Frank Skinner first plied his trade.

The interior is heavily decorated with pig's heads on the walls, fancy slogans and traditional cooking utensils including huge steak pans. Everything you see is a homage to pies and their ingredients, although I suspect they are taking the piss with their "Hamster pie" range above the bar. And the bar – if them making their own pies isn't enough to tempt you in, they also have a range of select real ales from the nearby Enville brewery. I devour a pint of Lump Hammer Gold, served in a traditional handheld glass, way too quickly for somebody who is driving.

The decor is minimal with benches and chairs with sawdust scattered on the wooden floor. It appears to have a good mix of clientele from students to families and the centrepiece on the wall is a huge oven. Onto the pies and there is a wide selection on the menu, each with its own quaint nickname ranging from Posh & Becks (Steak and Stilton), a Nigella (Posh Bird) Chicken pie and the slightly less than politically correct Barrymore Pie (Faggots). Not that they exclusively serve pies as they also do a range of grills and burgers and a "Pierates" children's menu. There's probably a vegetarian option or two in there if you're not completely repulsed by the ceramic pigs' heads peering down at you from the ceiling.

I opt for their signature Cow Pie dish at just under a tenner; meat and veg all self contained in a huge dish with a puff pastry lid and shortcrust pie horns poking out of it in true Desperate Dan style. I pay at the counter and see a large West Indian lady toiling away in the kitchen, pots and pans crashing everywhere. I do like to see a busy kitchen. I get a spoon with a number on it for my troubles and a wait of no more than twenty minutes.

The pie when it arrives isn't that intimidating on first glance and my initial reaction is "where's the chips" as my co-diners have received theirs as an accompaniment to their "Posh & Becks" – served up in one of those fancy little wire chip pan baskets. This is mere bravado however as there's way too much food in this pie for one person to eat: carrots, potatoes, button mushrooms, a bit of kidney yet enough meat alone to amply feed a family of four. Gargantuan slabs of intricately flavoured steak swimming in dark, wholesome gravy. The puff pastry alone is six inches tall. It's top crust only mind you.

I break off the cow horn and use the sturdier pastry to mop some of it up, although the fresh tasting carrot and potatoes also serve as an excellent complement to the masses of beef contained within.

I get halfway through and pause to catch my breath and mop my brow, like a marathon runner starting to waver although he hasn't even passed the ten mile mark. I dive back in, like a boxer springing back off the ropes. This is insanity, I deliberately skipped breakfast but this is a struggle, as the lads polish off their sides of chips and minted peas. IT'S JUST A PIE MAN – SOLDIER ON YOU SOFT GET!!! This is not for the faint hearted – it doesn't actually look that demanding when they deliver it to the reinforced table but it's a beast of a pie.

I can feel a little white flag poking out of my bulging stomach. The lid is detached and with a quarter of this monster left I know it has me beaten. I'm doing no more than move the food around like a hyperactive child trying to make the plate look more empty so I can leave the table and go back on my Nintendo DS. I feel less of a man but this is a remarkable pie and I finally down tools feeling suitably full but not to the point of making myself ill for the sake of it.

As the lunchtime trade dies off, we skulk off quietly with my head bowed in shame. I didn't realise that you get a certificate for finishing it – or a red one for failing to do so. We carefully negotiate the doors trying not to plant our fingers in paint again and hit the road still marvelling at the justified reputation of Mad O'Rourkes.

239.

PURVEYOR: Mad O'Rourkes
PREMISES: Tipton
PURCHASE: Cow Pie for £9.99
PLACE: 8 Worth chucking a few quid tip in their old tin bath for its stodgy ambience
PASTRY: 8 Only puff pastry top crust but nice touch with the pastry horns ideal for mopping up surplus
PRESENTATION: 9 Steaming hot inside
PACKAGE: 9 Ridiculous variety but high quality as well
PALATE: 8.5 Style with substance in this case
PRICE: 8 Bostin' value as it says on the door
PORTION: 10 I've bitten off more than I can chew here. Insane portion sizes
OVERALL: 60.5/70 If you're serious about pies you need to come here once in your life.

A semi-beaten man is then finished off by traffic carnage as the M5 round-about near West Brom's ground resembles downtown Napoli. My two co-travellers bolt for the door and hop out whilst it takes me till twenty past three to navigate the gridlocked traffic and pay a fiver to park. Even after the mammoth feast I still have one more objective for the day. I've been hoping to get hold of a chicken balti pie for ages made by the original man-ufacturers, but with little success.

After numerous email exchanges it seems they don't sell them at many football grounds any more or to retail trade. God bless Kevin of Shire Foods who offers me a box of them if I can just get to Leamington but I can't. A whole box! Whatever would I do with them? The wife would go mad about them clogging up the freezer and they'd defrost anyway by the time I got home with them. They seem to have lost the football market in recent times so I'm forced to shove a Pukka down me as it only feels right to have a curry pie in the West Midlands.

240.

PURVEYOR: Pukka Pies
PREMISES: Leicester
PURCHASE: Chicken Balti Pie £2.90
PLACE: 7 Only because I went ten minutes before half time
PASTRY: 7 Puff pastry
PRESENTATION: 8 It's all about the smell
PACKAGE: 8 Chunky chicken, hot curry sauce and hints of chilli and onion, as compact as a fart in a doll's house
PALATE: 9 One for the heat lovers with a decent smattering of meat included and green and red chillies floating around menacingly waiting to assault the tastebuds
PRICE: 6 Football ground prices
PORTION: 7.5 Of circular form and reasonable depth
OVERALL: 52.5/70 I happily missed the rare occasion of a Wigan Athletic goal to stuff with my face with this beauty.

Saturday 11th May 2013

I was otherwise occupied on this particular date.

Saturday 18th May 2013

I made a conscious decision not to start promoting this book on the internet until it was at least three quarters finished, just in case it never came to fruition. I guess if you're holding this in your hands then you now know the answer. The other drawback is that now I've got a web presence and demand interaction then all manner of people and companies start coming at me with recommendations. Plenty I have done, plenty I'm yet to discover.

So I nip to the Fylde coast on a gloomy morning after me and Emma had been up till 3am watching Boardwalk Empire and drinking Prosecco. Loch Lomond feels a bit far but the Wyre estuary seems do-able. I'd heard of this bakery before but binned it off my list. Then a mischievous tweeter by the name of @UnscaryMonster contacted me telling me I'd not lived till I'd had a meat and tater from Beans of Cleveleys. Described as more of a hot pot than a pie with huge layered slabs of potato and luscious gravy the gauntlet has not just been thrown down but drilled into the floor with a steam hammer.

I've bought a cooler bag to keep the pies fresh and chilled but there is absolutely no need for it as it is freezing and pissing down. It's not just raining, it's gushing like a tap but at least I should be able to gain access to

259

the seaside with relative ease. The road to Fleetwood is spectacularly grim given the adverse weather conditions.

I know little about Thornton Cleveleys except it's so special it's got two names rather than one. I eventually hit the sights of the Wyre Valley and a huge pub which takes the name of the river. I once tried to write a TV series about Blackpool drug overlords, which I was going to call The Wyre.

So Beans Confectioners. Confectioners I like that. Maybe I should just have a cake? It's smack bang in the centre with nowhere to park. At one point I actually find myself driving straight into Cleveleys station headlong towards an oncoming tram. As you do.

Bollocks to you Tesco pay and display! By the time I've run over, queued, bought a ticket, stuck it in my car and got soaked, I could leg it to the pie shop and back. So begins the first ever human sized game of Temple Run through Thornton Cleveleys shopping precinct. They'll not come out in this weather.

Wrong! Traffic wardens everywhere! They've got hats and aren't arsed about a bit of rain and I'm completely disorientated after almost getting run over by a fat chap in a motorised wheelchair wearing a Man City shirt. I'll let you have that one for free after Wembley last Saturday are kid!

Clearly I'm in a rush and fail to take in much apart from a fine array of lush bread and appetising cakes of all creed and colours. Currant buns ahoy! Then I spot the hot glass display cabinet stacked full of pies. It is a mere one hundred pennies for the recommended meat and potato but they also do the traditional butter pie, oval pork pie and somewhat relevantly: a bean and potato pie. A noble effort but I'm not convinced about that combination.

241.

PURVEYOR: Beans
PREMISES: Thornton Cleveleys
PURCHASE: Meat and Potato Pie £1
PLACE: 7 The old dears dally a bit but then they've bean (sorry) baking since 1933 so I'll let them off
PASTRY: 8 An early hiccup as some of the crust remains hiding in the bag and the lid continues to detach itself, but it is a Premier League pastry with a raised centre
PRESENTATION: 8.5 I ask for a hot one and get a hot one and even though it gets drenched along with myself it still stinks the car out good and proper
PACKAGE: 8.5 As promised it's a layered pie full of dense, juicy potatoes and light coloured meat with a cute hole in the top to intoxicate you into the flavour which comes oozing out when you bite in

PALATE: 8.5 Orgasmically sweet potato and mince, rich and invigorating
that hollers out it's homemade quality
PRICE: 8 With free parking (not)
PORTION: 8 It's not huge but it's a good weight
OVERALL: 56.5/70 A classic Lancastrian meat and tater, probably not the
best I've ever had but still a fantastic effort and I maybe have gotten a bit
fussy over the past eighteen months.

Time to head to the sanctuary of home, away from the torrents and there
appears to be a country and western festival going down in Garstang.
Yippee aye oh you poor buggers you're going to get fucking soaked!

Friday 24th May 2013

Tesco in Wigan is gridlocked but the weekend starts early! I'm here because I was looking up Melton Mowbray pork pies in advance of my pilgrimage and I discovered Walkers Pork pies. They're opening a shop in
Leicester soon to sell their wares but it might not be open in time so just
as well they sell them in every Tesco superstore in the land.

I'm also after a bottle of red wine for later but the shelf is devoid of
Chateauneuf du Pape as there's a £1 discount on it. I'm not having anyone
in Wigan had even heard of Chateauneuf du Pape a year ago.

So the story goes that [puts on Uncle Albert voice] during the war when
food was in short supply, Walkers, a traditional butchers started to use the
meat dripping to make crisps. Seventy years later they decided to pay Gary
Lineker a small fortune to advertise them.

I scan the by now familiar contents of the deli counter including the
obligatory part consumed Gala pie, the size of a breezeblock with an egg
inside it. It must be a funny shaped chicken gives birth to those eggs. It is
very much an "applaud the incoming batsman while sat on the outfield
scoffing a pork pie while swigging a pint" type of summery pie.

I have the feeling this pie won't be a perfect pink given its origins. It's
contents are pork and bonestock jelly encased in a hot water pastry and
the fluted edges are clearly a trademark more akin to sweet cakes than
savoury pies, with their jagged cake tray style shape.

242.
PURVEYOR: Walkers
PREMISES: Leicester
PURCHASE: Fluted Pork Pie £2.75
PLACE: 6.5 A touch tardy in Tesco. Plus she also asks me if I just want
one. HAVE YOU SEEN THE FUCKING SIZE OF IT LOVE?

PASTRY: 8 I've touched upon it's flutiness but the bottom is rigid and just a little bit greasy – which I like as I often worry a pork pie eaten in isolation can be a tad dry
PRESENTATION: 7 Served chilled
PACKAGE: 8 Coarse and plentiful as you'd expect with lots of grey, white and pink chunks of uncured pork and blobs of jelly deposited throughout its interior
PALATE: 7 A light dusting of spice to give flavour to the meat and the jelly nestles nicely in the mouth. The acid test comes when I go to put the second half of it back in the bag for later, as planned, and end up just carrying on scoffing. Or maybe that's the acid test which confirms I'm a fat get
PRICE: 7.5
PORTION: 9 Jacamo sized
OVERALL: 53/70 A useful livener ahead of next week's trip to….Melton Mowbray.

Friday 31st May 2013

Friday evening and Emma is sending me on an ale run, so seeing as I'm the one doing it I'm going to visit an old friend in a new location: the two turreted Booths in Chorley in fact, perched next to the Sir Henry Tate Wetherspoons in the town centre. Is he the Tate Modern geezer or the bloke who invented sugar? Either way I had no idea he was from Chorley. File him alongside Reg Holdsworth and Phil Cool. I know exactly what I'm looking for tonight but still need to conduct the by now time honoured quarumvirate quest of the four pie depositories: snacks, chilled, deli, freezer.

I'm a little disorientated if truth be known as although this place seems to stock the same things as my regular Booths, everything is in a different place plus it's posh enough to warrant a smoothie bar and an olive counter. So it takes me a while to find my bearings and the pies of Cloughbane Farm Shop.

Yes they're Irish! When Irish pies are smiling!

They're not thick Booths – they know that there are clowns like me who leap giddily at the chance to eat something new from somewhere different. By that I probably mean the same type of food or ale we usually eat or drink but with a flavour twist or a new brand; for clarity I don't mean something completely outlandish such as a cat ciabatta or a heron casserole.

The chicken, ham and leek gets the thumbs down from me purely because it has sweetcorn in it and I'm left with the choice of steak, onion and mushroom or mince and onion pie to be washed down with 7.2% Peroni Riserva and a couple of barrel shaped bottles of Efes.

243.

PURVEYOR: Cloughbane Farm Shop
PREMISES: Cookstown, Northern Ireland
PURCHASE: Savoury mince beef and onion pie £3.99
PLACE: 6.5 Pleasant enough but seems determined to flog me a Booths card just because the old ditherer in front was using one. If I took out a store card from every bloody shop who offered me one, my wallet would resemble a third trouser leg. Why do people who you are already buying stuff off always try and sell you more? Oh Booths, you've done it this time, you're better than this!
PASTRY: 7.5 Oh yes – the pie. Puff pastry, a bit flimsy underneath
PRESENTATION: 7.5 Cooking instructions followed to a tee and it's piping hot inside with a great aroma emanating from the oven
PACKAGE: 8 Lean and tasty minced beef complimented by a healthy portion of veg with onions, carrots and peas all present and correct. The large carrots in particular are devastatingly soft, forming a flawless double act with the meat
PALATE: 8 Even though I prefer my peas on the outside, they don't detract from the wonderfully juicy meaty overtones of tender gristle-free mince
PRICE: 7.5 I froze this and ate it later. My notes (unaware of the price) said "if it's under three quid it's an 8". It wasn't
PORTION: 9 At 650 grammes this really is a pie that should be shared but needless to say I didn't
OVERALL: 54/70 As I doubt I'll be able to saunter over to Belfast, this pie will have to be the Irish flag bearer and I will remain ignorant of the Ulster pie scene. If this is to be the barometer then they certainly like to mix up their veg in their pies.

As I exit Booths, the sun gives me a gleaming wink and the beer garden of the Sir Henry Tate draws me in like a tractor beam and I indulge in one of life's simplest pleasures: that cheeky, solo Friday pint after work. Cheers!

Saturday 1st June 2013

My need to visit Southport is twofold. First, there's a bakers called Graysons which I drive past every time I go to the sister-in-laws but as we usually go on a Sunday it's always shut. Yet the missus once bought me a caramel slice back and it was stunning. There's also a place called Mellors which I remember from my youth during trips to Southport, a traditional old bakers based on Lord Street. It seems Mellors are now owned by Martins, the Mancunian bakers. They'd been going since 1842 and went bust. As Churchill remarks on a Southport forum (presumably no relation to either the former prime minister or the dog) "This is so sad, I have eaten their cakes all my life!".

One of the finest sights in the North West is descending Parbold Hill on a clear day with Blackpool, Southport and North Wales all in full view. As I've not got the wife and little one in tow it enables me to indulge in a bout of audacious overtaking like a big kid and the route to the seaside (as you'd expect) contains more than its fair share of docile old codgers chugging along.

Soon I'm near to Ainsdale and you can always tell when you're by the coast because people have tatty dinghys in their front garden instead of fire bombed couches. Apparently Steven Gerrard has been known to saunter around here, surely the last person you'd expect to saunter round scoffing a pie with gravy dribbling down his chin.

The traffic grinds to a halt as bunting appears with market stalls, bouncy castles and merry go rounds lining the streets – ah the Ainsdale show, I forgot. I park right outside and find Graysons to be a charming establishment with fake wooden beams and panels sat beneath a red canopy and masses of cakes in the window. A pleasant young girl serves me and I order a meat and potato pie (£1.48 hot) with a smell that sends my tastebuds incandescent with glee. Oh yes – and a caramel slice.

244.

PURVEYOR: Graysons
PREMISES: Southport
PURCHASE: Meat and Potato Pie £1.48
PLACE: 8 They work the bill out with a biro on a paper bag which leaves a high margin for error but is nevertheless endearing
PASTRY: 8 It's got that fantastic, homemade wobbly shape about it ready to explode at any time
PRESENTATION: 9 A glorious aroma
PACKAGE: 8 Intensely packed with big slabs of potato and slightly peppered mince
PALATE: 9 I can't put my finger on why but it's definitely got the X factor, or the M&P factor if you prefer; it's borderline perfection
PRICE: 7 Mersey Riviera uplift duly noted
PORTION: 8 Certainly filled a hole
OVERALL: 57/70 Yes the pie is brilliant but what of the caramel slice? Well it's sweeter than a fairy princess and if you've only got £1.50 on you,

I'd seriously consider buying two of these instead. The Graysons millionaire shortbread will make you feel like a millionaire, or at least like you have paid off a credit card bill or two.

Never under estimate the value of a good caramel slice...!

I head through the millionaires row opposite Birkdale golf course past striking houses occupied by the 1987 Liverpool double winning team; Dalglish, Hansen, Lawrenson et al whilst across the road there is the faintest glimmer of sand dunes. Birkdale is all boutiques, beautiques and beauty salons (Are these three separate things?) to cater for the local WAGs, although there's something for the discerning gentleman as well in the form of Polanski's barber and toupee fitting centre across the road.

Beneath their identikit canopies the shops all look alike but I park up beside the post office and clock CH Lathams behind me: home of the proper Wigan pie it states. But first the butchers! They've got Aphrodite lamb, Teriyaki chicken, pork medallions and more kebabs than you can shake a shitty skewer at, all being paraded around by a cheeky Cockney host. So I am left with just one question of Broughs: WHERE ARE YOUR PIES AS ADVERTISED ON YOUR WEBSITE?

Nothing. Nada. Zip. Bugger all. The Londoner gets on the blower to ring their Ainsdale shop, bless him, but the damage is done.

I cross over back to Lathams who are keen to promote the fact that the owner is a Wigan born lad, to give it that further seal of authenticity and with butter pies on the menu amongst dozens of others it looks a blinder. It's situated on the corner of the cutest cobbled cul-de-sac you'll ever see, full of terraced cottages flanked by flower beds. The infamous butter pies have gone but the young lady serving with a pierced tongue will do me a hot meat and potato for £1.44 (I smell price fixing!) There's a large deli counter and an upright freezer full of plate and individual pies plus a hot pot which resembles an upside down crash helmet.

245.

PURVEYOR: Lathams
PREMISES: Southport
PURCHASE: Meat and Potato Pie £1.44
PLACE: 7 **PASTRY:** 7 **PRESENTATION:** 7.5 **PACKAGE:** 7
PALATE: 7 **PRICE:** 7 **PORTION:** 7
OVERALL: 49.5/70 It's a runny, sloppy juice-laden affair liable to cause a messy stain on your pants, with a natural meaty flavour prevailing inside soaking into the potatoes. Shame about the butter pie as this hearty hand burner was adequate but not mind blowing.

I decide to run for the hills with my paltry two pie booty and head home but not before a drive down Lord Street to see whether a favourite bakery of my youth still exists. Southport's tree lined shopping mile has lost a bit of its sheen over the years with Mecca Bingo and B&M Bargains moving in and there is an embarrassingly generic look to it: all Costas, Greggs, Wetherspoons and right opposite the five star Vincent hotel is a POUND BAKERY!!

There's probably other pie shops around here but judging by the smell emanating from the back seat I've already found the best. Then I spot The Old Bakehouse. Well there's a dead giveaway! On the double yellows and out the car, I peer inside and it's full of workmen sat stuffing their faces. Sadly, it may have been a bakehouse once but now it's just a caff. Still they've got some meat and potato (definitely Hollands) and chicken and veg so I take one of the latter off the hands of the rotund Scouse fella serving, who offers to warm it for me which I decline, suspecting this involves microwaves.

246.

PURVEYOR: The Old Bakehouse
PREMISES: Southport
PURCHASE: Chicken and Veg Pie £1
PLACE: 7 **PASTRY:** 7 **PRESENTATION:** 7 **PACKAGE:** 6.5
PALATE: 7 **PRICE:** 7 **PORTION:** 6
OVERALL: 47.5/70 So what does constitute a chicken and veg pie these days? Lots of gravy, fragments of chicken, one piece of carrot and half a dozen peas it seems. It's woefully small as well.

This isn't exactly a good advocate for my chicken pie aversion (Morecambe excepted) but what can I say? Pies are like women; they come in all shapes and sizes, some of them are attractive, some get left on the shelf but all of them deserved to be loved, even if some get loved a little less than others. And if you are female and reading that last paragraph, just cross out the "WO" bit so that I don't look like a massive sexist. Thanks in advance!

Saturday 8th June 2013

Hoorah! The day has finally come!

I bounce upstairs at 9am to find Emma still in bed "Come on, come on we need to hit the road"

She knows. She can physically see my arse twitching right now. I'm terrible and totally incapable of hiding it.

This doesn't quite stretch to her jumping out of bed and getting ready in double quick time mind you.

I've not helped matters really. We were unpacking the shopping last night and while Emma's loading the fridge, I'm putting cans in the cupboard, one of which slips from my fingers and cracks her on the head. It's not like she's had twelve lots of brain surgery, bacterial meningitis and suffers from terrible migraines as it is though? Whoops!

Soon we're headed down the A50 which slices through the country like a zip on a cardigan and it's a double pilgrimage today. First, we are off to the obscure county of Rutland to visit Britain's official best bakery called Hambletons. It's situated in a former nuclear bunker and produces goods such as a pippin – a pork pie in apple shaped pastry. Of course, ten minutes up the road is Melton Mowbray where I will procure the most authentic pies they can supply and then to Nottingham shopping or something to keep the wife happy.

Rutland resembles one massive Center Parcs populated by identikit families wearing identikit fluorescent helmets, plodding around on shiny new mountain bikes and circling the vast Rutland Water. The smallest county in the UK and 80% of it appears to be one lake.

Hambleton Bakery HQ really is in the middle of bloody nowhere, down some country lane, which is down some other country lane, which you have to go down a couple of country lanes to get to. I don't know what my current tally is for "car ending up in farmers field" but strike one more up.

Still, if you're going to open a shop in the middle of nowhere then it's safe to say you're backing yourself. The tiny little shop is doing brisk business and full of goodness such as billionaire tarts (no thanks I've got one at home – arf) a range of their famous sourdoughs, plus rack upon rack of fresh baked bread.

The girl serving explains that they only really sell the Rutland Pippin here, with few other savoury offerings, so that evidently will be my poison. As an alternative, she directs me to the Ploughman's' Parcel: a savoury focaccia dough filled with celery, apple, a cheese I can't even pronounce and chutney, topped with seeds – it looks glorious! The nuances of the place explained, I also opt for a large sourdough loaf wrapped in a splendid bag which will be the ideal accompaniment to the missus' soup diet she's on all next week (which I may indulge in myself to humour her). Fresh bread smeared in Lurpak and dipped in soup: food of kings.

To quote the website: *"The Rutland Pippin baked in the shape of an apple is filled with ham hock, stilton cheese and apple and pureed quince"* – A quince is a pear, not an ageing American paramedic detective with a penchant for solving moiders. The snack is a cross between a pastry and a dough, and yes I know it's not a pie.

247.

PURVEYOR: Hambleton Bakery
PREMISES: Oxton, Rutland
PURCHASE: Rutland Pippin £1.85
PLACE: 8 Charming service in the shop
PASTRY: 9 The innovative pastry shape blows me away like a discarded packet of crisps in a hurricane but the tenderness of the bite is exceptionally soft, all topped off with a perfect pastry stalk (which falls off)
PRESENTATION: 8 Presentation is paramount as the Pippin is wrapped like a toffee apple and ornately decorated in red tape with a twizzle
PACKAGE: 9 Great variety and quality within
PALATE: 9 A kaleidoscope of taste sensations with something different in every mouthful
PRICE: 7 Just about saves the day due to its niche appeal and innovation
PORTION: 7 Erm apple sized? Golden delicious not Bramleys mind you
OVERALL: 57/70 A beautiful accompaniment to a lunchbox or served chilled from the fridge. The arguments may rage as to whether this is a fruit or a pie. It is however completely encased and a cracking handheld snack.

We're in and out of Rutland and into huntsman country before you can say "Tally Ho" and despite attempts to call upon some farm shop for food and sustenance, we find it somewhat decrepit so bolt it back to Melton. Ah yes Melton Mowbray. Melton Tony Mowbray to give it it's full name, although the locals seem to just prefer Melton.

Melton Mowbray is the rural capital of food so I'm not sure being stuck behind a horsebox is a positive sign.

We get on a pay and display by the Melton Mowbray Toy Soldiers band headquarters and eschew our farm shop pretensions in favour of the Wetherspoons across the road. Sorry but I can't feed my wife and baby un-cooked pork in pastry. There's also a department store next door called Boyes Boyes Boyes, as advertised on Central television by busty Italian Sabrina. If not it should be.

An indicator as to what Melton is about can be found on the town signs which point to the bus station and public bogs and poke out a pinkie in the direction of "Ye Olde Pork Pie Shop" thus enabling me to find it easily. I have my doubts as to whether many stand there to marvel at it, given that the Asian fella flogging carpets across the road gives me a funny look as I take shady photos of the shop whilst narrating into my phone in a clandestine manner.

I wander in to be greeted by hundreds of ready wrapped Dickinson & Morris pork pies of various flavours and dimensions. You can get them topped with anything from gooseberry to chutney to stilton but I opt to go "vanilla" and just buy a humble pork pie. There's nothing worse than when an iconic brand gets all cocky, looking at you here Heinz with your "chilli beans" and similar shit.

I pick up a leaflet, they've been going since 1851. Other local offerings they serve up include gooseberry chutney and Melton hunt cake. Not sure I approve of that kind of stuff but if you do it involves sultanas and currants soaked in Caribbean rum (no doubt manufactured and imported over by West Indian slaves) and of course the stilton is never far away. Their hampers look fantastic and without getting involved with the politics, they know how to bloody live well around here….the aristocracy eh? Whiskey marmalade and fine wines! Hampers ranging from £59 to £180! Not that I heard too many tally-ho's in the Wetherspoons earlier.

Back on topic and they are knocking out some other oval pies for half price: steak and ale and creamy chicken going for a quid. I'd be a fool not to. A whole £2.20 spent in total and back to the shops to drag the missus out of The Works.

The Melton Mowbray pie describes itself as being "coarsely chopped with a special blend of salt and pepper seasoning and no preservatives ….traditionally baked without a supporting tin which is gives it it's classic bow shaped sides". This whole Melton Mowbray business is serious shit and has a dedicated protection website (www.mmppa.co.uk) to keep out pie infidels.

Natural bone stock jelly is added to the meat to give it its succulent texture. Yes I concur! Enough! It is attractively packaged in its distinct crimson and blue along with the geographically protected stamp. They also won a Gold award in the 2011 British Pie Awards, which is intriguing as I'm pretty sure they organise it.

248.

PURVEYOR: Dickinson & Morris
PREMISES: Melton Mowbray
PURCHASE: Pork Pie £1.15
PLACE: 8 Knowledgeable as expected and adjoining to an indulgent looking sausage shop
PASTRY: 8 Featuring the unique, often imitated, design and a naturally formed uneven shape to it, it resembles a bow tie when viewed from the side apparently. Bit of a stretch but I see what they're getting at
PRESENTATION: 8 Iconic packaging
PACKAGE: 8 Considerably deeper than you'd think for an individual pork pie, benefitting by the raised crust in the centre. Packed to the brim with meat plus an amply sufficient layer of jelly

PALATE: 8 There's a definite added degree of authenticity about it which takes a bite or two to register, but the opulent sausage meat infusion comes bouncing through soon enough and the jelly augments it perfectly

PRICE: 8 I will buy one of those hampers one day!

PORTION: 8 A tad unfair this bit as I could have bought an 800g one. But even this entry price little tiddler alone is no mean size and I have to crank my jaw open a considerable way to get my gob around it

OVERALL: 56/70 Everything about it oozes quality and authenticity, it's got that aura about it like Kellogg's Cornflakes or Lurpak Butter that rivals constantly aspire to.

I also procure a creamy chicken pie from the same establishment which I had for me tea and recall it being terrific. I'd love to tell you what special ingredients were in it but by the time we get back from Leicestershire, unpack the car and put the little one to bed, it's half ten, I'm half cut and therefore I haven't a clue what the lovely little green herbs in it are.

249.

PURVEYOR: Dickinson & Morris
PREMISES: Melton Mowbray
PURCHASE: Creamy Chicken Pie £1.00
PLACE: 8 **PASTRY:** 7.5 **PRESENTATION:** 8 **PACKAGE:** 8
PALATE: 8 **PRICE:** 8.5 **PORTION:** 7.5
OVERALL: 55.5/70 The crust is very dark even before I put it in the oven for twenty minutes and it holds together terribly after cutting into it. But salvation comes in the form of its intricate plaited crimp and amazing tender white chicken breast, enveloped in a herby luscious creamy sauce. John from work might not approve but I do.

Melton is also home to Stilton cheese, which I didn't know, I thought it was from Wiltshire. Swindon/Stilton easy mistake to make. I perambulate through the pedestrianised town centre, with its surfeit of covered market stalls, expecting a pie shop on every corner but it seems they are more preoccupied with sweet things around here. The road opens out into a square where the hollering voices reach fever pitch and I spot a market stall knocking out pork pies which would knock you out if someone fired one at you from a catapult. They look like semi deflated tractor wheels.

I spot a decent butcher around the back but it's gone three o'clock by now and he has very little left of note. I'm in Melton Mowbray for fuck's sake, they should be queuing out of the door! As it stands, the biggest queue I've seen all day is for the barbers, as the local gents wait patiently in line for their Saturday night shag cut.

So I revert back to the Blue Stilton stall on the market for my third slice of MM love. They've got pasties and wraps and standard pork pies but I opt for the family sized monster "keeps fresh for seven days" it says on the wrapper, which is roughly about how long it will take me to eat it. The pork and stilton option enables me to combine both their famous exports in one pastry capsule. They also possess an ace range of cheeses with curry, chilli and apricot infused slabs, if cheese is your bag.

250.
PURVEYOR: Blue Stilton Market Stall
PREMISES: Melton Mowbray
PURCHASE: Pork & Stilton Pie £4.00
PLACE: 7 Considering he was bawling his head at me the first time I walked past, I could have shoplifted an entire tray without him even noticing second time around
PASTRY: 8 Thick and decorative with a sleek leopard skin look to it, one pastry spot presumably denoting the pork and stilton flavour
PRESENTATION: 7 I'd be dubious about the freshness claims
PACKAGE: 8 Hollow at the sides but a large expanse of meat encased by another half inch of jelly
PALATE: 6 I'm not a huge fan of stilton but I know what it should taste like and there's hardly any at all here. The meat is slightly less coarse than the Mowbray standard, appetising in parts, which could work in its favour but again I suspect points to cheapness
PRICE: 7 Monstrous pie but priced accordingly
PORTION: 9 I don't know about looking like a bow tie, you could put a bow tie on this lummox and stand it up in a doorway outside an East Midlands nightclub and make it ask drunken revellers for ID it's so bulky
OVERALL: 52/70 I think they sold me a pup here.

With Melton exhausted we retire to it's fine country park for a duck feeding ramble. With me proving to be the ultimately father figure by shitting myself in no uncertain terms from a wildly hissing goose when my daughter is looking for a bit of protection. I drop my bread.

"You wouldn't drop your pie" goads Emma.

"That is correct darling, because I wouldn't feed it to the ducks in the first place!".

Saturday 22nd June 2013

I've had this circular four county adventure tour of the (Northern) Home Counties planned in my head for a while. It's 5.45am and the early bird catches the worm or indeed the pie. I've had five hours alcohol induced sleep and feel like shite. Yesterday was the longest day and it seems surreal as it looks like mid-afternoon yet the roads are deserted, save for a Shearings' coach and a Greenhalghs pie van.

The Four Counties excursion may seem an impressive one but it is also a touch lazy on my part, a residual attempt to get around as many other parts of the country as quickly as possible before bringing my mission to a conclusion.

I saunter through the Potteries to the early morning lullaby of Classic FM before the Arctic Monkeys kicks in to send me stomping through the toll road. By the time I hit Northampton, it's still only 8am. Is this place open? Do they have pies? It's a butchers, of course they will!

Now it appears that there's a village fete on in the picturesque village of Kislingbury. They're NOT going to get the weather however, as it appears primed to heavily but briefly piss down whilst locals stand there frantically erecting gazebos.

Entry to the village is via a single lane road over a quaint hump backed bridge and as it's a tiny place I'm a little concerned that this establishment might not be here. I locate it hidden down a side street and there are two butcher-looking types inside keen to engage me in idle chit chat about the shit weather.

I order myself a grand pork pie which, in stark contrast to their website, is all they actually sell and it's very Melton Mowbray-esque in stature. I've never quite worked out where Northampton sits but I suspect we are still technically in the Midlands.

251.

PURVEYOR: Elliotts Butchers (yes, like Fred!)
PREMISES: Northampton
PURCHASE: Family sized pork pie £4.05
PLACE: 8 Bloody nice chaps
PASTRY: 8 Delightfully decorated, folded in at the top and well glazed with a rigid bottom
PRESENTATION: 7.5 For a cold pie it actually has a bit of scent to it
PACKAGE: 8 Intensely coarse and tough with diverse colour pigments in there, reflecting the different parts of the pig I'm chomping. All encased by a good half inch of jelly with enough depth for me to just about get my gob around

PALATE: 8 It has a splendidly spicy kick to it and a delicate peppery aftertaste
PRICE: 7 Family sized I suppose
PORTION: 9 I have to take a breather half way through until I see the rest looking at me dolefully saying "Come on! Finish me off you big daft lump!"
OVERALL: 55.5/70 A big bruiser of beguiling beauty.

Time for the dubious pie panel to get out their foldable chairs and warm their hands on a brazier I'm afraid, as I can't help seek out a notable regional pastry product.

The town of Sandy is the home of the Bedfordshire Clanger and no book on pies/pastry products would be complete without a clanger or two.

I exit the M1 at junction 13 and head for Ampthill (home of cartoon gangsters the Ampthill mob) and pass the Amazon warehouse, who could save a fortune on petrol simply by moving around the corner from our house, seeing as the missus appears to have her own personal lorry load coming to our house every day.

I end up on a nice, shiny new road headed for East Anglia and ponder how a place called Sandy can exist so far inland? Maybe it's just named after the singer in Grease? I get a tad disorientated when I see a sign saying Cambridge THE NORTH and there's a road shut at a marvellously named place called Moggerhanger. Time for a challenging detour as I head over the River Ouse – Ouse your daddy! Through the village of Everton – yes honestly – and on I go, yawning like Chewbacca until the sight of a sex shop at the side of a road, where you'd normally find a Little Chef or rejuvenated curry house, wakes me up somewhat.

At last! And far from being a sleepy seaside town, Sandy is quite industrial at first glance. As I enter this fair hamlet at 9.10am, I spot my first pack of chavs of the day, one of whom is wearing a fetching pink shirt unbuttoned to the waist and a Fusey style haircut. Lovely!

I bung the car in the market square and get parked right outside Gunns Master Bakers – I said Master Bakers!! Since 1928 in fact. The café is quiet but hopefully they will be only too keen to drop a clanger into my lap. It is situated fortuitously next to a dentist, in case you chip a tooth on a top crust. I order a gammon and apple clanger, they also have a vegetarian one, a Christmas one (IN JUNE??), a breakfast one and a range of slices and sausage rolls all served up in a personalised Gunns wrapper.

I find myself a lay-by and get my clanger out. Oo er missus! The aroma is difficult to place but upon breaking into it, it cranks up a notch as it's a surreal experience actually trying to work out what it is you're eating half the time.

A clanger is nothing more than a sausage roll made out of suet folded at the ends, served as a snack that the good ladies of Bedfordshire would give their husbands as a mid-day energy booster during a hard day's agriculture. The ingenuity comes from there being meat and veg at one end (main course) and sweet apples at the other (dessert).

252.

PURVEYOR: Gunns
PREMISES: Sandy
PURCHASE: Bedfordshire Clanger £2.20
PLACE: 8 Brisk and cheerful not as described on THE INTERNET as "surly, slow and miserable"
PASTRY: 8 Perfectly encased in gentle suety pastry. The only trouble is to my untrained eye I can see no discernible difference between either end and inevitably make the schoolboy error of biting into the dessert bit (containing apples) first. All over Bedfordshire right now, ruddy cheeked farmers are roaring with laughter at this dozy Northern idiot!!!
PRESENTATION: 8 Like a golden light sabre in the hands
PACKAGE: 8 Part gammon, part apple but plenty in it
PALATE: 8 The gammon offers up chewy resistance and the potato and onion is fluffy and well seasoned, I just can't get my head around the other end which resembles a McDonalds apple pie
PRICE: 7
PORTION: 7.5 I was expecting bigger but it feels quite heavy. Larger than a sausage roll, smaller than a pasty
OVERALL: 54.5/70 Hey it's different!

Time to reverse back through Clophill and Ampthill. There's a notable lack of farm shops around here which is a shame as, just for once I'm ahead of schedule and scanning the road side eagerly goading perfection to randomly hit me straight in the face.

I only noted down Westoning as a back up option but what the hell I'm driving past anyway. What has this quaint little hamlet got to offer me, apart from lunatic mobile home drivers attempting to bundle me off the road? I immediately spot the canopy of a bustling butchers and ignorantly park up on double yellows in the posh cul de sac behind.

The service is abominably slow but they have an impressive range of pies, of which I opt for a steak and ale and a game pie for £1.75 each. There's not been enough game in this tome as it stands. They've got huge plate pies, steak, venison, sausage rolls and pasties, along with some savage looking desktop growlers and a load of sausages and black puddings. They're also literally chopping up animals out the back.

The service is painfully slow which could be forgiven seeing as they are

274

chopping and slicing as they go but this is exacerbated by some Cockney wanker, opportunistically pushing in front of me and demanding half the shop when I momentarily turn my head to eye up a growler. Twat.

253.

PURVEYOR: Deacons
PREMISES: Westoning
PURCHASE: Steak and ale pie £1.75
PLACE: 5 **PASTRY:** 7.5
PRESENTATION: 7 **PACKAGE:** 8
PALATE: 7.5 **PRICE:** 7 **PORTION:** 7.5
OVERALL: 49.5/70 I have concerns as there is a thick double layered top crust which often means the bottom, by default, ends up a little soggy. But this is well contained with some fairly substantial chunks of steak swimming in rich authentic gravy.

I don't know the first thing about game. What is game anyway? Why is it called game? You don't go around calling fish "match" or fowl "competition" do you? The world doesn't make sense sometimes. I've not a clue what could be in here, possibly a bit of bunny rabbit or pheasant, which makes it a bit awkward with my two year old sat playing in front of me but I plough on regardless.

254.

PURVEYOR: Deacons
PREMISES: Westoning
PURCHASE: Game Pie £1.75
PLACE: 5 **PASTRY:** 7.5 **PRESENTATION:** 7 **PACKAGE:** 7.5
PALATE: 7 **PRICE:** 7 **PORTION:** 7.5
OVERALL: 48.5/70 The phrase "I'm game if you are" is maybe not appropriate here. By all intents it's the same as the steak pie but with different texture and colour pigments in the meat. There could be duck, pheasant, rabbit, who knows in here and I've no idea what the lighter coloured meat is. But in conclusion I'm just a boring get.

Back over the M1 and last night's late one is catching up with me as I veer from shaking like a shitting dog with cold to an almost feverish delusional temperature. Fight my way through it: never underestimate the healing power of pies. Toddington is a notorious football fans stopping off point and once had eight pubs surrounding it's village green, many of which are now no more. I've no idea where I came up with Childs Bakery from but they've been on my list forever, I've got them down as some historic craft bakers from the back of my mind. Well, guess what....they aren't!

There's a blackboard outside advertising their wares: fresh bread, take-away snacks – SNACKS!!!! JUST SNACKS??? You see it's more of a village store than a bakers with fruit and veg, drinks and provisions aplenty and the obligatory lost cat appeal poster in the window. What they don't have is any pies. I ask and she says they have none left. It's not even 10.30am on a Saturday morning for God's sake!!

Not willing to leave empty handed I'm left to choose a "slice", these being: mozzarella and tomato, cheese and onion, chicken and potato or a sausage roll. I choose the unusual combination of chicken and potato which is £1.20 or £1.44 served hot, so ping in the microwave it goes as I bang my head on the counter repeatedly in dismay.

255.

PURVEYOR: Childs
PREMISES: Toddington
PURCHASE: Chicken and potato pasty £1.44
PLACE: 7 **PASTRY:** 6.5 **PRESENTATION:** 7.5 **PACKAGE:** 6
PALATE: 6 **PRICE:** 6.5 **PORTION:** 6
OVERALL: 45.5/70 Oh dear! Fluffy puff pastry, hardly any filling and a bland, greasy offering.

You know what though? Things are about to get infinitely better as I ne-gotiate one final trek cross country to Oxford to a butchers to try and get one of Pauls Pies. I discovered another pie blog via Twitter a few weeks ago, run by a bunch of chaps called the PieRateers. This lot have eaten nearly as many pies as me, 200 at the last count (which increased to 400 as at August 2014). They wax lyrically about Paul's and meticulously rate it as top of their pops.

It's only 40 miles away but it's 40 miles of those meandering sluggish A roads I've come to hate over the past couple of years. Past Aylesbury whose most famous son must now surely be Emmerson Boyce (Chief lifter upper of the FA Cup just over a month ago). Welcome to Buckinghamshire, birthplace of the Paralympics. I pass through the town of Wing (home to Wing's Chinese chippy), and on through another eight picturesque Cotswold-esque thatched villages, all ultimately getting out-quainted by Quainton itself. I head towards Bicester, the place where gravy was in-vented, or at least where the Bicester kids come from, subsequently known as the Bisto kids. Sorry, forgive me – I'm tired.

I wonder which side of Oxford I will pass through today anyway, the dreamy spires bit or the shitty council estates? Yep it's the posh (congested!) bit!!

Looks a bit small this place, and they seem to be advertising it as a grocers/fishmongers rather than a butcher. Fruit & veg outside, fish inside, a bit of meat and I can't find any pies. Am I doing something wrong around here? Finding a pie is like finding an honest banker, practically impossible: they are an endangered species.

"Got any more pies mate?".

"No, he's coming again Thursday!".

There's one chicken and mushroom Paul's Pies left and no steak and Guinness, which is the one I'm looking for. So I'm left to disconsolately power my way back up north veering over cycle lanes. I buy the chicken one but diplomatically decide not to eat it just yet.

Tuesday 25th June 2013

I'm craving a meat and potato after that somewhat disappointing foray down south at the weekend. So to complete a promise I made in Bradford last November: To Morrisons of Chorley! It's got a big chimney so it must have hot baked goods on offer. Indeed, you can get a meat and potato pie for the princely sum of 85p. And you know it's a meat and potato because it says it is, the flavour ingeniously etched into the lip of the pastry crust. A superb touch (probably mass manufactured mind) Morrisons Chorley, you are the real deal!

It's handed to me perfectly sealed in a brown paper bag with a foil inner. Just as well seeing as the pensioner behind me while I'm queuing at the kiosk is coughing so violently she is hacking up green phlegm all over my basket. Serves me right for paying at the ciggie counter I suppose.

256.

PURVEYOR: Morrisons
PREMISES: Bradford
PURCHASE: Meat and Potato Pie 85p
PLACE: 7 Tardy at the lottery counter which offsets the fact that the girl on the deli counter goes out of her way to locate a nice hot one for me
PASTRY: 8 It has the potential to score very, very highly with its unique embroidered, (oh alright then STAMPED) crust rim but I feel it's a touch crumbly and hard to manage and it nearly falls to pieces in my hands. The insurance of a foil tray underneath is a necessary pre-requisite I'm afraid, as bits are prone to come randomly slopping out
PRESENTATION: 7 A good all rounder
PACKAGE: 8 Squared off cubes of potato, rich flavour intense mince, all

in a creamy gravy which in its desire to find some space jumps out of the pie and into my hands

PALATE: 8 Succulent and well balanced throughout with a melt in the mouth texture about it

PRICE: 9 No complaints about 85p (2 for £1.60)

PORTION: 8 A generous size with a wide base

OVERALL: 55/70 Morrisons zoom to the top of the supermarket pie charts following this assured effort.

Saturday 20th July 2013

It's the hottest day of the year and I'm going to Barrow to get pies. It's 7am and I've already got a sweat on. There's nobody about this morning, apart from impeccably dressed pensioners carrying their newly purchased morning papers back from the shop.

The things is, once I'd visited Greens last summer and had another sniff around local websites many locals furiously claim that they don't even make the best pies in Barrow any more, let alone anywhere else. Pies seem to generally play a big part in the life of Barrow folk.

I must be nearly there as I head down a rabbit warren of terraced streets and a sports ground appears. They say in London you're never more than ten feet away from a rat, well in Barrow you're never more than ten feet away from a football stadium, you just drive around and around and more appear all looking exactly the same. It seems so against the modern sport ethos to have two such similar grounds, with their big blue corrugated iron stands poking out from beyond terraced streets, and sadly one of them will surely get eaten up by the rampant retail park mob before long.

McLey's sits on the corner of a quiet terraced street like Greens and there appears to be a queue forming so I take my place at the back behind a heavily tattooed lad wearing a Chelsea shirt – you're a long way from London mate!

Their wares are advertised as fresh bread and pies daily and there's a minimal selection but it all looks fabulous including some scrummy looking shortbread biscuits. The pies are small but ferociously hot with no tray and there are notable similarities but also discernible differences, between the Greens pies of Barrow: the potato is diced here not layered, yet the gravy juice is similar in that it comes gushing out. The sort of filling you just want to suck out of the pie burning your mouth in the process.

257.

PURVEYOR: McLeys

PREMISES: Barrow-in-Furness

PURCHASE: Meat and Potato Pie £1.20

PLACE: 8.5 The most talkative woman in Barrow
PASTRY: 8.5 Delicately soft with a crisp crunchy casing underneath
PRESENTATION: 8 Smoulders like hot lava in my hands and smells divine
PACKAGE: 8 A very lucid mix of hot meat and veg which has me drooling
PALATE: 9 Fresh crunchy potatoes with hints of pepper
PRICE: 8
PORTION: 7 Small but compactly filled
OVERALL: 57/70 A valiant rival to that other place around the corner which I can't get out of my head.

I head further into Barrow and end up flanked between the mammoth BAE buildings and retail parks. My senses are blown away by the chirp of seagulls and the smell of freshly baked pies, as I head for Barrow Island in search of Frys. I've no idea if this is actually an island, I know they used to have an exceptionally violent amateur rugby team but that's it. I know Walney Island is a proper one but there's fuck all there except a grim caravan park. I tried to visit Piel Island as well once as there's a pub on it but the missus refused to get in the little rowing boat that takes you across.

Barrow Island is a mesmerising place. Literally like nothing I've ever seen before. I drive around several times, mainly because I'm lost, and I'm totally bewitched by the dazzling Victorian tenement block architecture. The whole area is surreally quiet and tranquil like a ghost town, with not a sound on the streets apart from the low drone of The Eagles "Hotel California" emanating from a pub juke box. Why is it deserted? Where are all the people? Where's the bloody pie shop?

I can't deduce whether the four storey tenement blocks are rough flats or glammed up new build apartments. I suspect the truth is somewhere between the two. I don't pretend to know bugger all about architecture but the look of buildings holds a certain fascination and they simply blow me away. Even if they have had a rebuild they are immaculately true to their roots. Built in the 1900's to house the influx of migrant ship builders and dockyard workers into the area, these russet coloured buildings leave me aghast with awe; a real architectural find – all perpendicular angles and sandstone.

It falls into place now: Fry's is shut. Of course it's shut. Even before the ship building industry was decimated, there probably wasn't much of a need for them to ever open on a Saturday to serve the workers and why change that habit now?

Dejected, I make for the town centre where I park on Fell Street pay and display with no warden in sight, unless he's cunningly disguised as a tramp sat on a bench drinking cider, I chance it and sprint to Thomas' Bakery.

I pick up a meat and potato for £1.40 although this place does have alternatives, including a slightly obscure cheese, potato and bacon. They've got a plaque on the wall commemorating them winning bronze in the 2013 Best football pie awards, which I assume is at Barrow FC.

258.

PURVEYOR: Thomas's Bakery
PREMISES: Ulverston
PURCHASE: Meat and Potato Pie £1.40
PLACE: 8 The Cumbrian friendliness again shines through as the young lass serving displays textbook courteousness, despite having the life mithered out of her by some old dear elsewhere in the shop
PASTRY: 8.5 It's got a little porthole in the middle which has cracked a bit like an egg waiting to hatch, but it's sumptuously soft and perfectly portable
PRESENTATION: 8 Delightful aroma enough to get me excited as it reheats
PACKAGE: 9 An exceptionally packed to capacity pie displaying the traditional layered sliced potato "Barrow style", absolutely heaving with hearty goodness
PALATE: 9 It's an absolute winner in my book given all its constituent ingredients, dominated by succulent potatoes interspersed with peppery mince
PRICE: 7 On the cusp considering its local competition
PORTION: 8 Deceptively deep
OVERALL: 57.5/70 The Barrovian bakers just keep racking up record scores and deservedly so. I have no vested interest here except to say, like Wigan, it's pure meat and potato country. It may be a Cumbrian outpost but many hundreds of years ago, I'm told it bent right round to touch Lancashire like a contortioned Pilates class member and the influence is still shared.

I'm still owed a pie from Frys and thus in my peripheral vision, I discover Diggles and dive straight in. I manage not to get vexed by the multiple counters for breakfast bars and delis and order another meat and potato to round things off. It turns out they're from Lancaster and are putting on a very bold front if they're hoping to muscle in on this turf....

259.

PURVEYOR: Diggles
PREMISES: Lancaster
PURCHASE: Meat and Potato Pie £1.60
PLACE: 7.5 Organised and functional
PASTRY: 7 A solid golden casing with
a crisp and crunchy crust lid
PRESENTATION: 8 Steaming hot and
smells stunning
PACKAGE: 8 A low meat to potato ratio
(as is often the way around these parts)
but golden potatoes interjected with small flecks of mince meat are
plentiful and ripe
PALATE: 9 A rich, stock-soaked potato flavour prevails giving an almost
casserole/hot pot type richness which seduces me rotten
PRICE: 7
PORTION: 8
OVERALL: 54.5/70 Diggles: a pie to make you wiggle.

Saturday 27th July 2013

Another piece of the jigsaw comes to fruition as we head to East Anglia
for the weekend. Emma's a star but sensibly puts her foot down and demands a three night stay due to the distance, thus forcing me to miss
Wigan's prestige friendly at home to Dundee United.

My revenge is to scout a pie stop in Lincolnshire in lieu of a conventional pub lunch. My good mate Ives, who upped sticks from Wigan to
move to rural Lincolnshire, raves about a producer called Wilcox's but
they are proving a little elusive to track down, save for a garden centre
in Sleaford. Coincidentally, it's also about halfway to Norwich. That's my
target but with two borderline incontinent girls in the car it always proves
a challenge.

It's a couple of hours of bombing down the A1, which is hairier than
Brian Blessed's nether regions, with every lunatic in the country cutting
me up; hen dos, drunken Dundee United fans hanging out of coach roofs
all merging together on a chaotic Saturday afternoon. I find myself at the
Four Seasons Garden Centre, Sleaford. I can't find Wilcoxs but there is an
in house butcher here. A butcher in a garden centre, obviously!

Emma goes to change Jess while I peruse the deli – no pies – but the
butcher does them, hot and cold, and with it being around 25 degrees outside, I opt for a cold pork and stilton pie for £1.80 which is handed to me
nicely chilled.

On to the restaurant within, where I may also have a pie! However – THE LAST PIE HAS GONE!! None left I am informed by a teenage female shop counter assistant with a wrist tattoo, which makes me nervous when I've got a two years old's little wrist in my hand. Get with the times Jimmy!!

I'm not overly devastated as what remains looks like school dinners: top crust only and served from a big oblong tray. The service is shit, drinks are warm and we are besieged by flies whilst tucking into some flimsy paninis. I'll have my pork pie later no doubt, wistfully overlooking the lake at the hotel where saddle backed pigs will be grazing.

260.

PURVEYOR: G. Simpson
PREMISES: Sleaford
PURCHASE: Pork and Stilton Pie £1.80
PLACE: 7 **PASTRY:** 7.5 **PRESENTATION:** 7 **PACKAGE:** 7.5
PALATE: 7 **PRICE:** 7 **PORTION:** 7
OVERALL: 50/70 A supremely squared off growler with pockets of Stilton, jelly and bountiful coarse quantities of sausage meat within its dark mysterious crust.

Several hours later we make it to the Elm Farm Country House Hotel in Horsham St Faith, near Norwich Airport where it appears that the exceptional Groupon deal I've forked out for (only the best for my girls etc etc) also covers dinner so I get my pie after all.

The place is surreally quiet for a Saturday night and I find myself asking the bar staff why. Turns out they had a wedding booked in but the bride got itchy feet two weeks ago and cancelled the whole lot. The silly mare has cost them thousands, hence they have a raft of rooms to fill at short notice, in a desperate tale of woe.

It's a big old country house which could really be somewhere special but just seems a little drab and under-invested right now, not helped by jilting fiancés leaving them out of pocket. Whether it's lack of money or lack of impetus, I can't help thinking someone with a bit of drive could really transform it into a beautiful country house as it has splendid grounds. The pigs slope around in their shed but the black swans are truly beautiful specimens with necks like question marks and cherry red beaks. Unfortunately, you only have to stand in the dog shit on the lawns once to form a negative opinion. My trainers still stink to this day.

As for the pie, well it's menu price is about £7 and it's fair to say it's rescued by fantastic chips. The pie is served in a Betty's hot pot style dish topped with puff pastry, which seems more the norm in pubs, with a fully encased crust scandalously overlooked. It is served up by the same lad who checked us in, showed us our room, served us at the bar, took our order, brought us the food and probably bloody cooked it too, God bless him.

261.

PURVEYOR: Elm Farm Country House
PREMISES: Norwich
PURCHASE: Steak & Ale Pie £6.95
PLACE: 8 **PASTRY:** 7 **PRESENTATION:** 7 **PACKAGE:** 7
PALATE: 7 **PRICE:** 7 **PORTION:** 7
OVERALL: 50/70 Presented with a good three inch of bouffant puff pastry; from a side angle it looks like Beavis (or is it Butthead) therefore flatters to deceive somewhat and underneath is not exactly spilling out. There is a dollop of medium grade braised steak inside and I can definitely taste the ale; or something distinctive anyway. The chips on the side are superb along with mushy peas so luminously green they could pass for a gang of miniature aliens.

Monday 29th July 2013

It's 7am when my alarm goes off but this is not just any morning, it's the day I go pie hunting in East Anglia. It is officially the quietest I have ever managed to get up in my life as I know that if I wake either Emma or Jess then I'm in scuppered. As it stands, it is the sound of neighbours having showers, shaves and yes – highly audible shits in the adjoining rooms, which present the biggest threat to the tranquillity.

I have a plan but I'm not sure whether it will come off. I've also got to blag the hotel receptionist to let me use their fridge to stow whatever pies I get overnight to preserve their condition. Yesterday we spent family time at a theme park in Lowestoft which my two year old loved. So yesterday I was happy and today I am happy. I have earned myself one whole morning and a bit of lunch to conquer East Anglia, an area of considerable geographical expanse and not necessarily the most efficient roads. I will get my pies. WOE BETIDE IF I DON'T!

Whenever I visit a place, I have this geeky tendency to take heed of where the signposts out lead to, and it appears that the only place people ever want to go when leaving Norwich is Ipswich. It's a sluggish route out too seeing as Norwich's ring road appears to be a series of single lane suburban streets bolted onto one another in a vaguely circular fashion, lined with an ever forthcoming stream of sleepy bungalows.

I may be in Norwich but I am acutely aware that I may have neglected Essex somewhat. That bad experience with Percy Ingles may have put me off a tad but I have a chance to rectify it today after finding something of merit. Pyes Farms aka Essex Larders not only serve pies (the clue is in their name) but something which goes by the name of a Dunmow Flitch, a localised pasty made with bacon: not a pie admittedly but the sort of quaint regional delicacy which needs tracking down. They don't actually have a shop but I reckon I can be in the sleepy textiles enclave of Long Melford within the hour, near the Suffolk/Essex border, where the 150 year old Ruse & Sons butchers can be found who stock their produce. Then I'll work my way back up.

From there I intend to head for Bury St Edmunds to visit two ladies who won top prize at the 2013 British Pie Awards. I've been mithering the life out of Carol and Sally via email and it transpires that I will literally have to visit their kitchen, where they make the pies for The Pie Kitchen. Yes it seems their chicken, chantenay carrot and bacon pie is so homemade I have to raid their fridge to get my hands on one. The Pie Kitchen is literally a kitchen where they make pies. The ladies are in demand and I'm a mithering pest. On the eve of my visit it appears to have all gone quiet on me, even now when I am due to be there in a couple of hours. Let's drive!

Much like the South West, in East Anglia it takes forever to get anywhere due to the complete absence of motorways and general shiteness of A roads, but I eventually find myself on the spacious A11 with London a mere 106 miles away.

The landscape is so flat I find myself humming along to the theme tune to Van der Valk until I hit Thetford, where lush forests pop up to colour in the barren landscape. I get an early morning tour of the place which is full of ponds and lush rivers, bridges and ornithological shit and still no email. I decide to look for a back up in Bury St Edmunds and hit upon Barwells Butchers, whom according to some crappy website I keep landing on called QYPE serve "a great range of pies".

If you ever wonder where all the sugar in the world comes from, you've probably never been to Bury St Edmunds and it's sugar refinery, it is fucking huge! It dwarves the entire town. It's like being in Detroit. It looks like something out of Star Wars, like the grand palace of Alderaan, except it's more likely populated by hairy arsed fork lift truck drivers not Princess Leia lookalikes with their hair in bunches.

There's only me could get stuck behind a road sweeper chugging along a single lane traffic road at 9am in the middle of nowhere. I love that the local paper is called the Bury Free Press, it may as well have a strapline underneath saying "Communists not welcome".

I restart my phone, still no email.

The prize for the best place name today goes to the serene hamlet of Bradfield Combust on the main Bury to Sudbury road, which sounds like something you'd find in a specialist hardware store.

Phew! Carol's replied "can you wait until midday". I need to be back in Norwich for midday, I'll have to call her. No more emails!

Anyway, I'm finally in Long Melford after miles of rolling countryside flanked by luminous yellow corn fields. It's a million miles from downtown Wigan with its stately homes, large village green and wide uncluttered High Street – and there is Ruse and Sons, and it's open!

They've got a big stack of pies, though I'm not sure they're Pye's pies and some impressive looking pasties. Dunmow Flitch perhaps? I ask him what he's got here. The gent behind the counter rattles off his wares in an impenetrably thick yet homely Suffolk accent and I get a tad lost in it. Steak and kidney? Chicken & Leek? Steak? He's trying to distract me into buying his ace looking sausage rolls as well and I've got to admit they look the pick of the bunch. I'll take steak.

I'm not having they sell these at Harrods: they're completely concave in the middle, very light in the hands and not exactly oozing quality.

262.

PURVEYOR: Ruse & Sons
PREMISES: Long Melford
PURCHASE: Steak pie £1.80
PLACE: 7 Accent 9.5, Additional attempt to flog sausage rolls 4.5
PASTRY: 6 A dreadfully droopy disappointment with a very soggy bottom despite the presence of a foil tray. Even allowing for the puff pastry I doubt this is more than half an inch thick and I have to hold the pie up with my thumb in the middle to stop it sagging
PRESENTATION: 7 Flimsy
PACKAGE: 6 A woefully short supply
PALATE: 8 Yet what steak and gravy there is seems of very high quality
PRICE: 6 Probably a standard price given North/South divide but a very poor offering
PORTION: 6 Gone in two minutes and I'm no speed eater
OVERALL: 46/70 I think my enquiries must have got muddled somewhere along the way as I do not envisage this pie being served up at Harrods. I should have got a pasty. Or a sausage roll. However, number 1 they're not pies and number 2 nobody ever got excited over a sausage roll.

The same street sweeper clogs the road up on the way back, the inconsiderate get, but I've finally got a date with Sally, or is it Carol? It's Carol. I'm sat in a Sainsbury car park waiting for her to ring back. Bugger this, there must be a pie shop in Bury town centre (Barwells!)

Not a chance. As I pound the pedestrianised streets, so compact that the bottom of the window cleaners' ladders are in the middle of the road,

I find little of note to feed the sugar shifting natives. There's one of those Greggs that looks nothing like a Greggs and a West Cornwall Pasty company but Barwells is nowhere to be seen. It's now a patisserie/coffee shop. Back to Carol.

I plug her address in the SatNav and get there early, so I drive past to the top of her estate where I have to turn around in someone's drive. At which point the angry resident comes flying out of his garden, aggressively waving his hedge trimmers and yelling "go to the end of the road if you need to fucking turn around". Good morning to you as well sir!

Thankfully, as rude as this irate gentleman is, Carol is polite as she invites me into her home along with her charming daughter Evie. We chat about my project and her fledging business for a good twenty minutes and then she hands me a raft of pies – if that is the indeed collective term, as I insist she takes a tenner for them. A large Chicken and Tarragon, a large Chicken and Leek and an individual steak and ale pie. The pastry based contents of her fridge before baking starts again in earnest after having more or less sold out at the weekend, given the massive interest since winning the awards. "Always put them on a baking tray to avoid soggy bottoms!!" I knew that! Well, unwittingly I did.

Surveying my haul, I have two plate pies which retail at £6.50 but will easily feed a family of four and an individual steak and ale thrown into the bargain. Sadly, she has no chicken, chantenay carrot and bacon in stock, nor the chicken and chorizo which sounds right up my street or steak and stilton, which is another number in their range which Carol is rightly proud of.

The three of us share the two family pies between us when we get home and they are marked together for posterity. And from the second it goes into the oven I can tell it's going to be a blinder....

263.

PURVEYOR: The Pie Kitchen
PREMISES: Bury St Edmunds
PURCHASE: Chicken & Tarragon Pie/Chicken, Ham & Leek Pie
£10 the pair (£6.50 each)
PLACE: 10 To invite me, a slightly unhinged stranger, into the kitchen where Britain's best pies are made is an honour indeed
PASTRY: 8 Thick and sturdy with an individualised decorative pastry chicken on top
PRESENTATION: 8 The aroma rampages throughout the house, leaving no corner untouched, with a beautiful pastry vibe and unseen creamy aura about it
PACKAGE: 8.5 A deep hearty filling in both pies with large fresh chunks

of chicken throughout. Pie number one is delightfully seasoned with tarragon, the second possesses the addition of ham and creamy leeks. Both are encapsulated in a rich, luscious sauce. Bursting at the seams
PALATE: 9 Given I had to share these out, the missus proclaims it to be "lovely" whereas Jess wolfs hers down and gives it the ultimate seal of approval, by squirting apple juice all over her empty Disney plate
PRICE: 7.5 Not cheap but massive and of course bona fide award winners. Buy in bulk is my tip!!
PORTION: 9 Anybody can knock up a plate pie but they are often shallow; this one has remarkable depth with close to an inch and a half of filling, and a foil tray that sits at a right angle meaning that the contents do not taper off. Approaching dustbin lid proportions but definitely no rubbish inside here
OVERALL: 60/70 We simply can't decide which is best and at first veer towards the tarragon before concluding that the chicken, ham and leek takes the honours. My crude, primitive side decrees that two types of meat inside seals the deal but in truth both are truly special pies.

264.
PURVEYOR: The Pie Kitchen
PREMISES: Bury St Edmunds
PURCHASE: Steak & Ale Pie
PLACE: 10 **PASTRY:** 8 **PRESENTATION:** 8 **PACKAGE:** 8.5
PALATE: 9 **PRICE:** 9 **PORTION:** 7.5
OVERALL: 60/70 A double layer of thick chunky steak surrounded by rich tasty gravy lapping away at it like waves against a shoreline. The pie has the signature pastry cow on top with an A on it, but it is a very thorough multilayered, slightly flaky pastry and the cow cuts in half easily: often these novelty pastry bits refuse to cut and make a mess of the pie, not today! It's brimming with flavour and a full blooded steak taste punctuated with the faintest hint of ale and gravy thick almost to the point of becoming jelly.

From Bury I get to within 12 miles of Ipswich before veering northwards again towards the town of Diss, a splendid place name. How their local council haven't implemented a marketing campaign entitled "Don't Diss Diss" I don't know. I'm seeking the Tudor Bakehouse (A Britain's Best Bakery contestant) of this parish and I'm starving after handling pies for four hours and eating the sum total of none. I may have to succumb to sausage rolls if that's all they sell hot around here. I'm also an emotional wreck after the hedge trimmer incident.

I determine that this small chain also has premises in the even more surreally named Eye, which as a smaller town may be easier to get in and out of. I bang my hands excitedly on the steering wheel and shout to no-body in particular "YES!! I'm off to buy a pie in Eye!" Indeed their mar-keting slogan could be "Say Yes to Eye".

The main square is rustic and languidly paced, you could even describe it as a lazy Eye. I spot the Tudor Bakehouse and am delighted to find hot pies and slices on display, yet on closer inspection they look a little generic for an artisan bakery. I plump for the steak and kidney as at least if they've been bought in, it's a flavour I've not had before. He reaches for the steak bake at first "WOOOAAAH!! Hang on a minute lad – PIE. I want a pie!!"

I get to within ten miles of Norwich and pull over to polish off this fiery little hand grenade.

265.

PURVEYOR: Tudor Bakehouse
PREMISES: Harleston
PURCHASE: Steak and Kidney pie £2.00
PLACE: 7.5 A polite efficient chap who resembles the milky bar kid. Except he doesn't shout "the steak pies are on me"
PASTRY: 7 Rigid and crunchy and just about edible with the hands
PRESENTATION: 7 It comes in groovy packaging and is served nice and hot in a red foil tray
PACKAGE: 5 Speechless. Apart from one large piece of kidney and some (admittedly tasty) gravy there is nothing but a void; a vacuum; a sea of nothingness inside this pie where there should be meat. Five is being generous, unlike the bakers of this comestible
PALATE: 7 The paltry steak portion is reasonable with palatable kidney and sublime gravy
PRICE: 6 At least 50p too much considering the skimp factor
PORTION: 7 A big enough frame just not much inside it
OVERALL: 46.5/70 This isn't some bigoted North/South bias coming through I promise – see The Pie Kitchen for evidence to the contrary. It's just that some of these pies just aren't very good. I suspect in bakers at least, they may be a bit of an afterthought rather than their primary reason for trading.

I head back to Norwich and with three miles to go it's still nothing but greenery, until the inevitable Tesco Superstore emerges over the horizon like an evil military base. Ideally the huge "Welcome to Norwich" signs would feature a grinning Partridge with outstretched arms but they instead opt for a more moderate, understated slogan of "Welcome to Norwich: A fine city".

I endure a pretty tortuous drive through suburban streets until Earlham Shopping Centre appears, where I'm looking for the greengrocers. An organic one – the obvious place to buy a pork pie.

My twitter feed frequently features the cheerful outlook of Norfolk's self styled "Pork Pie queen", a lady called Sarah Pettigrew who runs a business called Brays' Cottage, who make fantastic pork pies.

They actually have organic pies in here as well with an intriguing looking pastry and such wild and wacky flavours as cheese and potato, Moroccan lamb and chickpea, Mexican chilli. But alongside the quiches, there's some homemade sausage rolls and Brays Pork Pies, medium sized in the chiller and priced at £2.59. I pop one in a brown paper bag and take it to the counter.

266.

PURVEYOR: Brays Cottage
PREMISES: Holt
PURCHASE: Pork Pie £2.59
PLACE: 7 The kookiest, chicest, hippiest pie girl I've ever met. Goes with the territory I suppose
PASTRY: 8 A very sticky, comforting glaze almost like a normal shortcrust pastry rather than hot water based, which is deliciously melt in the mouth
PRESENTATION: 7.5 Chilled is the only way here
PACKAGE: 8 It's not massively overly substantial but there is a dark alluring quality to it throughout. They'd go mad in Yorkshire mind you as there's NO JELLY IN IT AT ALL
PALATE: 9 I've never tasted a pork pie like this before: spicy yet fruity with meat that is consistently dark and tender. But a real experience and a novel concept possessing a myriad of secret ingredients
PRICE: 7.5 It's bigger than a single but not quite a huge one
PORTION: 8 Held within a large shiny crust, it's a reasonable size
OVERALL: 55/70 Dubbed 'The Perfect Pork Pie' these are indeed a unique work of art and have a re-assuring quality and ingenuity to them.

Finally to Metfield Bakery in the centre of Norwich (another finalist in Britain's Best Bakery), as I face the daunting challenge of trying to park in Norwich city centre, where spaces are as scarce as water in the desert, forcing me to plonk the car on double yellows over an alleyway.

It seems it's not Metfield Bakery, it's called Louis' Deli and upon entering I am faced with a large steaming tray of sausage and bean pasta, another

tray of Lasagne, a load of freshly made potato salad and some rather enticing sausage rolls. They're hot at least, so I order a sausage roll and a
cheese and tomato roll for the wife. Then I'm forced to ask the inevitable
question.

"Yeah we've got some in the fridge there".

Not their own mind you but that's their choice. I actually remember
watching their charismatic, if a touch eccentric, owner on Britain's Best
Bakery telling the nation "everybody loves a good pork pie" before making
one for a baking challenge. So where are yours then?

267.

PURVEYOR: Metfield Bakery
PREMISES: Norwich
PURCHASE: Pork Pie £2.50
PLACE: 7 **PASTRY:** 8 **PRESENTATION:** 7 **PACKAGE:** 7
PALATE: 7 **PRICE:** 6 **PORTION:** 7
OVERALL: 49/70 Clearly the place has an artisan feel about it but I still
feel a little bit let down. The pie has a large scoop of sausage meat
surrounded by a layer of jelly within a soft, sticky crust. It's moribund.
However, I can confirm that the sausage roll is spectacularly good, as I
wrestle half of it away from my two year old to munch upon.

Tuesday 30th July 2013

We're booted out of the hotel and Emma wants to go for a wander around
Norwich to visit old haunts as she spent a year here doing a PGCE. I'm
happy to comply so long as my demands to go to the Lovejoy-esque town
of Holt in North Norfolk for lunch (to indulge in its fine department store
food halls) are also met.

Needless to say, as soon as we arrive in the city centre, I slope off to the
outdoor covered market on a mission, foraging through its colourful
canopied rabbit warren grid of stalls in search of something meaty to
munch upon.

The market is alive with buzzing chatter emanating from little cafes.
There is a butchers but upon inspection their offering appears to consist
of nothing other than a pig chopped up on a large table, where customers
are invited to point at the bit they want. I eventually come across Pickering's sausage shop with its range of over 30 bangers from around the world,
from the Caribbean to North Africa and the Highlands of Scotland, all-
bookended with a few pork pies and pasties....

268.
PURVEYOR: Pickerings
PREMISES: Norwich
PURCHASE: Pork Pie £1.50
PLACE: 7 **PASTRY:** 8 **PRESENTATION:** 7 **PACKAGE:** 7.5
PALATE: 7 **PRICE:** 7 **PORTION:** 7.5
OVERALL: 51/70 A hand raised yet well defined crust containing a slightly coarse but generous helping of decent sausage meat.

Another average effort albeit if you're having a barbie it looks the place to go. Nevertheless, I find Norwich highly agreeable and unlike any city I've been to before, with a centre brimming with history and architecture. It has the preserve and pride of a small market town but a hell of a lot bigger. Emma finds the Next, Jess finds "the Mister Shop" (aka the Mr Men shop i.e. Waterstones/The Works) and I go for a nose at BBC Norfolk and saunter about the greasy spoons. Jess is fascinated by the rainbow coloured porcelain gorillas, which for some inexplicable reason crouch alongside the public benches.

Finally to Holt, home to antique dealers and diamond merchants, situated right near the top of the balloon of Norfolk. It's not named after former Norwich City legend and subsequent Wigan Athletic and Aston Villa flop Grant Holt. I'm seeking out a Mr Kew's speciality pie at the spacious Larne & Bakers food hall and plump for the chicken, leek and rarebreed bacon pie for £4.85 rather than the cheaper mince pies from another baker. I attempt to leap in front of a posh woman loitering around the counter area but she gives me a smug look and nabs the last cheap one. In your face! That wasn't what I was after anyway snooty chops!

269.
PURVEYOR: Mr Kews
PREMISES: North Walsham
PURCHASE: Chicken, leek and rarebreed smoked bacon pie £4.85
PLACE: 8 People are just so....nice around here
PASTRY: 8 Featuring a decorative pastry chicken on top as the sweet, smelling pastry rises beautifully in the oven
PRESENTATION: 7 I follow the cooking instructions to a tee but it could have probably done with a few more minutes
PACKAGE: 8.5 Upon opening her up I am assaulted by a leek; there are bountiful chunks of chicken too but the bacon is the real star of the show, all wrapped in a fine white sauce
PALATE: 8 It's impeccably creamy with real full flavoured bacon

complimenting the chicken and softened up by the almost sickly sweet sauce

PRICE: 6 Dear!!

PORTION: 8 A big size but still only an individual pie and the price arguably does not reflect that

OVERALL: 53.5/70 Saucier than a Carry On film with appetising bacon prevalent throughout.

We finally head for home but not before stocking up on provisions and I finally get chance to visit a Budgens, a proper "Booths of the South" establishment as I get sent for lunch while the missus stays in the car. I think we all know how this is going to go by now.

There's no decent cold sandwiches so I go to the deli counter to get some paninis heated and I encounter stacks of Newitts Pies, plus a few of the more established Higgidys. And to my great delight it turns out to be a real gem of a pie. It's the ones I uncover by accident that often provide the greatest satisfaction.

270.

PURVEYOR: M. Newitt & Sons

PREMISES: Thame

PURCHASE: Steak Pie £1.99

PLACE: 6 It's not their fault but 12 minutes to warm up a panini has me fuming inside

PASTRY: 8 Flaky lattice puff pastry on top with a softer underneath but retains its shape throughout

PRESENTATION: 8 I'm hit with an explosion when cutting in to it. It smells so good my patience gets the better of me as I continually burn the roof of my mouth, like a frustrated school child, due to my unwillingness to wait for it to cool

PACKAGE: 8.5 Plenty of volume as lashings of steak chunks come bouncing out of it like mini boulders, coupled with gravy so rich it's got its own beachside house on Sandbanks

PALATE: 9 The steak is intensely meaty and teamed up with a fruity overpowering gravy

PRICE: 7 Bit expensive at supermarket prices

PORTION: 8 A familiar and traditional oblong steak pie size but with remarkable depth and considerable incision beyond the pastry

OVERALL: 54.5/70 As "just happened to be passing" speculative efforts go, this must go down as one of the better efforts.

Saturday 10th August 2013

I'm in Wetherspoons. They used to do pies when I started this book, made by Dunkleys of Northampton. Award winners apparently. I'd tried ringing Dunkleys direct prior to going to Northampton last month but they were a little rude to me on the phone. I'd still like to try them but all 'Spoons offer on their menu to this very day is a steak pudding.

It eats away at me so much that I log on to the internet later that evening and fill in a 'contact us' type web form. Several weeks later I get a letter from JD Wetherspoons through the post expressing regret that there were no pies on the menu and that it will not be possible to change it until the next menu cycle, but thank you for your feedback. I also get another letter behind it addressed to Mrs H Jones of Barry, expressing regret that she had a "bad experience" in the Sir Samuel Romilly in Pontypridd.

Wednesday 14th August 2013

Shit just got real. Handing over suspicious packages through car windows on pub car parks. The car park is that of The Crown Inn at Worthington (itself a fine creator of home baked pies), and the car belongs to Mudhutter scribe Orrible Ives, formerly of Norley Hall in Wigan. The council estates in Wigan are all called halls. I always have visions of portly Americans turning up with £2,000 cameras around their necks, expecting to be shown around the stately home and invited to tea by the lord of the manor; whereas they're more likely to be invited for a glug of cider by the gentlemen who congregate by the bins outside the shopping precinct. Anyway, Ives – whose accent I am amused to find has gone a bit more "oo-ar" – moved to rural Lincolnshire with his good lady a couple of years ago and has brought me back a large plate steak and ale pie from one of his local haunts along with a large block of Haslet. Whatever that is. It looks like drugs and knowing Ives it probably is.

Apparently haslet is pork meatloaf and this greasy, sweaty little bundle is going to get carved up and slapped straight on my butties in the morning. It is served cold, as indeed most things appear to be in that neck of the woods, presumably because they don't have microwaves in farmers fields.

271.

PURVEYOR: Grasmere Farm
PREMISES: Lincolnshire
PURCHASE: Steak & Ale Pie £4.00
PLACE: 9 Hand delivered so I can't complain here

PASTRY: 8 Very flaky yet sturdy underneath and an ornate top crust
PRESENTATION: 7.5 At least six inches in diameter so I leave it in the oven for an eternity before diving in
PACKAGE: 8.5 Topped to the brim with what tastes like braising steak but not too dry
PALATE: 8 An unusual experience to say the least, as the meat flavours are so raw and distinct that at one point I suspect Ives has pulled a fast one on me and sent me a game pie instead. Very much his idea of a prank to tell me it's steak when in fact it's donkey meat or something. It's an intense experience which veers from dry to wet; the juices coming to the rescue when the meat gets too thick and dry, although noticeably some gravy has escaped and dried out on the tray. The meat is unfamiliar with a slightly reddish colour to it which I consider might be a little undercooked, but Ives later informs me that it's specialist Lincolnshire red beef particular to only a few Lincolnshire farms. Told you he's a good lad!
PRICE: 7.5 Huge pie with copious amounts of highly prized meat
PORTION: 9 A bin lid full of beef
OVERALL: 57.5/70 Ives comes up trumps with a great family pie probably best sliced and served up with mash, peas and a jug of gravy.

Friday 24th August 2013

I will be going to Scotland sometime soon but I don't fancy my chances of getting up to Aberdeen, Dundee or Inverness, even though my current employer has depots there and has suggested I go and see a few people. When I work I work and have little time for gallivanting around anywhere which can't be reached in a lunch hour. To get there and back in a day seems improbable so I will be heavily reliant on THE INTERNET to magic the pies to my doorstep.

After a period of intense frustration dealing with their website, I pick the phone up. On the other end is Frank Yorke of Yorkes Butchers of Dundee, who, judging by his name, might be in a position of authority within this company. He expresses considerable apologies once he has quelled his anger at their shoddy e-commerce attempts, copying me in for good measure as he sends an email bollocking his web hoster. From that moment on, everything about my venture into online retailing goes seamlessly.

The Steak and peppercorn from Yorkes are sold at both Dundee clubs, St Johnstone and in corporate areas at Old Trafford, but most importantly they can be delivered to my door in a matter of days. I hit upon the idea of feeding our dedicated fanzine sellers and hangers on, with a box of pies while they stand there flogging the magazine on a matchday. The lads who sell are worth their weight in gold, they do it for free (as do I!) and never let me get the ale in at Christmas or end of season and stand there selling in all weather. Well, until there's a spot of rain. I decide to reward their loyalty with a free pie out of the generosity of my heart.

But for now, bollocks to them: I need to eat MY pie.

The Scotch pies are nearly always circular tin shaped with very rigid, acute crust edges and a thin, sturdy base. It's a double crust lid, slightly offset from centre and a splendid little porthole in the middle from which dried gravy comes spilling out. I bung it in the oven for twenty minutes and it comes out as hot as a rocket.

272.

PURVEYOR: Yorkes
PREMISES: Dundee
PURCHASE: Steak & Peppercorn Pie £1.62 (£19.50 for a box of 12)
PLACE: 9 Arriving in an ice compressed box, the pies are impeccably fresh and delivered straight to the door from an owner who seems genuinely delighted in my interest
PASTRY: 8 A little flaky on top but sturdy and sublimely soft pastry
PRESENTATION: 8 There's only one thing better than the smell of a pie baking in the oven and that's the smell of TWELVE pies baking in the oven
PACKAGE: 8 Not the deepest but what lies inside is the finest quality steak wrapped in a sumptuous peppercorn sauce
PALATE: 9 We all love peppercorns don't we? They explode in my mouth but it's pure flavour not fieriness ensuring that the steak itself can be assessed and savoured. It has an affluent reassuring quality to it
PRICE: 8 Now only £1.39 on the website....but with £100 minimum order for delivery. Bah!!
PORTION: 7.5 A satisfying feed but you'll still want another
OVERALL: 57.5/70 Chief sellers Migs, Finton and Lee collectively decree this to be the best pie they have ever had, although they admittedly haven't scoffed as many as me the past two years.

Sunday 9th September 2013

A very different Saturday night was spent wandering around Tesco: small bottle of red wine, creamy pasta (no chilli), box of safety pins, head patches for the missus....hang on what's this – a microwaveable Chicken Balti pie for £1.50, suppose I'd better give it a go. If it's made by Shire Foods that would be all the better.

Wigan 10k completed in a respectable 49.32 minutes. Fuelled by approximately 340 pies. Surprised myself there. And celebrated with a couple of pints and a Galloways meat and potato.

Back to business and I can't see this ending well, it resembles a cross between an elaborate bag of crisps and one of those awful Rustler things. I pull it out of the sub-style wrapper and it at least smells of pastry. No foil tray. Probably just as well as it's microwaveable cooking time is a mere 115 seconds. It claims to be diced chicken in a fruity curry sauce, in shortcrust pastry topped with puff pastry. It's also laced with red peppers and I hate them.

273.

PURVEYOR: Tesco
PREMISES: Hertfordshire
PURCHASE: Chicken (microwaveable) balti pie £1.50
PLACE: 7 Procured straight off the shelf
PASTRY: 6 Damp and soggy
PRESENTATION: 7.5 It at least smells authentic
PACKAGE: 6.5 Upon severing the beast in half, I am hit with slithers of pepper (which I swiftly jettison off to a corner of the plate) whilst grabbing a magnifying glass to inspect for prized meat content
PALATE: 8 Because it's still a curry pie
PRICE: 6.5 Extortionate given its supermarket prices
PORTION: 6 As shallow as a glamour model
OVERALL: 47.5/70 I don't think the world is ready for a microwave pie yet.

Tuesday 17th September 2013

I'm "between jobs" as they say. Needless to say me and Emma have diametrically opposed views on my newly found freedom during the daytime hours. My view is that I now have time to accelerate and complete my mission. Her view is that with no future income forthcoming, going out and spending money on pies and incurring petrol costs is somewhat frivolous.

I've been speaking to a lad from Barnsley a bit who is setting up a fanzine and he raves about the growlers produced by a chap called Percy. Today I'm heading to Manchester to find work/get her birthday presents but I will break up the day by nipping over Snake Pass to get a growler or two. I need lunch right?

So it is I find myself heading over the Pennines again, hopeless and job-

THE CRISPY BASE. PART THREE: 201-300

less, in search of Percy and his legendary pork pies. It's based in the village of Jump, a place so loved by the Pointer Sisters they wrote a hit song about it in 1983.

After a productive meeting with a man who will hopefully find me work, I head east where the shiny tower blocks give way to the sprawl of Openshaw and Gorton. I spot a Dawsons Bakery in Denton but unfortunately it's on the other side of the dual carriageway as I head on to the M67. I'm definitely getting cravings here.

They escalate as I hit the lavish sounding Mottram in Longdendale as a geriatric hitchhiker with a sign saying "Immingham" blocks my way. Bit precise there mate – it could liven my journey up I suppose but the old ones are usually the worst. I'd have to drop him at the butchers anyway.

Up ahead I see the mother of all HGV's; I can't cope with this tortuous journey again, I'm too hungry. It's right then that I spot the Hollingworth Bakery, which I'd been oblivious to on every other previous journey. I roll the car onto the kerb, run in and get a meat and potato pie. I'm so distracted by this beauty I've not noticed a HGV pull right up my arse to within six inches of my bumper, most unnerving, like a huge monster waiting to swallow me whole.

I decide to drive on until I find a lay-by which has a green container in it, that someone has spray painted with a telephone number for NUDE HANDY CAM MODELS. Lovely.

274.

PURVEYOR: Hollingworth Bakery
PREMISES: Hyde
PURCHASE: Meat and Potato Pie £1.40
PLACE: 7 **PASTRY:** 8 **PRESENTATION:** 8 **PACKAGE:** 8
PALATE: 9 **PRICE:** 7 **PORTION:** 8
OVERALL: 55/70 The smell emanating from this little cracker is overwhelming and it has that almost perfect cheesy, buttery taste to it, with a strong well textured crust encasing generously stock-soaked potatoes.

Not that this place has a reputation but as I happen to tweet that I'm on my way to Barnsley, at least three people tweet back telling me "you must go to Percys". Therefore I will!

Jump has an impressive array of red brick council houses nestled around it like angry wasps, yet it is peaceful and full of warmth if a little quiet. The land that time forgot. Well the land the Tories forgot if we're being precise. The type of village that broadsheets send Southern journalists Oop Norf to write patronising articles about. It's deathly quiet as I park up opposite a John Smiths' pub and a closed down bookies. On the next street corner proudly stands Percy Turners, between a chippy and a hairdressers, with racks of eggs in the window.

There's a singular steak pie and a sausage roll in the window but behind that a tray loaded with growlers. The fella in front of me is ordering a dozen.

"What's yours love" asks the serving lass, full of earthy Yorkshire charm and it's tied and sealed in a polythene bag and dispatched in seconds. It's 65p. Or [SIXTY FIVE PENCE] in computer video printer speak. Unbelievable Jeff.

275.

PURVEYOR: Percys
PREMISES: Barnsley
PURCHASE: Pork Pie 65p
PLACE: 8 An excellent sleight of hand
PASTRY: 8 Slightly unusual in that it seems a little bit more shortcrust rather than hot water pastry, yet it is tender, crisp and perfectly formed
PRESENTATION: 8 Served cooling from the oven
PACKAGE: 9 A deep clump of pinky reddish sausage meat wrapped in a good half inch of the most luscious molten jelly which slops out everywhere initiating an impromptu game of cat and mouse
PALATE: 8.5 A certain spicy element to the meat coupled with salty jelly combines to make a stunning fiery affair
PRICE: 9.5 sixtyfivefuckingpence. She even hands me a free piece of dried blood with my change!
PORTION: 7 Bearing in mind the price it's still a good couple of inches deep
OVERALL: 58/70 This place hasn't changed in forty years, indeed neither has the price and this is no bad thing. A simply amazing melt in the mouth pie at a stunning price.

I turn back on the Manchester to Sheffield road to Parkside Farm Shop, which has an acute turn off down what appears to be a private driveway to someone's house. It's got serene, ornate gardens and it feels like I've walked into a wedding venue but the farm shop is crammed full of goodness. They make their own sauces and chutneys and there's meat all over the shop. The service is slow but mainly because they're doing the meat cleaving as they go and the woman in front of me seems to be ordering one of everything in the fucking shop. One by one.

It gives me time to survey the selection though and my eyes are first drawn to the rabbit and red onion pie, they also do minted lamb and hotpot and of course pork pies. They've also got big plate steak and kidney and chicken and mushroom pies and a huge pork pie topped with cheese and pickle which must be twelve inches across. I go through the card several times in my head whilst I wait for this daft mare to order eighteen different types of Barnsley chop.

I end up buying three due to my wait and the fella serving is perfectly courteous, helpfully advising me that "the rabbit pie is the one with the two bunny ears on the top". That figures.

276.

PURVEYOR: Parkside Farm Shop
PREMISES: Barnsley
PURCHASE: Pork pie £1
PLACE: 7.5 Sound when he eventually gets to me
PASTRY: 8 Firm texture and again slightly shortcrust, scored twice across the top. Hint of unevenness but not enough to make it fall to pieces
PRESENTATION: 8 Eaten hot out of the oven on recommendation
PACKAGE: 8 Filled to the brim and squared off – no ice cream scoop used here
PALATE: 8 A robust sausage flavour, not too peppery and smothered in jelly
PRICE: 8 Great value for a quid
PORTION: 8 An above average growler size
OVERALL: 55.5/70 I think I've finally settled the old hot/cold debate: hot wins every time, even if it does mean the meat can slip out of its casing and wriggle around the kitchen floor. Another belter.

277.

PURVEYOR: Parkside Farm Shop
PREMISES: Barnsley
PURCHASE: Minted lamb hot pot pie 1.85
PLACE: 7.5 See above
PASTRY: 9 After 25 minutes in the oven it's supremely crisp but not too hard and has a very uneven, homemade shape to it
PRESENTATION: 7.5 No discernible smell but upon cutting it in half, smoke comes billowing out of the pie like a steam engine
PACKAGE: 8 It's not minced lamb it's minted lamb as evidenced by huge swathes of stringy braised lamb meat in there
PALATE: 8 I can't deny that I was more enticed by the hot pot element than the minted lamb as I like my food spicy but this nevertheless hits the mark without being overly minty
PRICE: 7.5
PORTION: 8

OVERALL: 55.5/70 An interesting effort which is almost wholly meat with a handful of peas and a tiny bit of potato spilling out.

278.

PURVEYOR: Parkside Farm Shop
PREMISES: Barnsley
PURCHASE: Rabbit & Red Onion Pie £1.85
PLACE: 7.5
PASTRY: 7.5 It's solid but cracks up a little when I cut into it. Nice touch with the cute bunny ears on the top crust. Elmer Fudd wholeheartedly approves
PRESENTATION: 7
PACKAGE: 7 Plentiful slices of chicken-like meat and slithers of onion come spilling out, a promising effort which is ample and moist throughout
PALATE: 6 Sorry. I tried. It might be subliminal guilt but what I expected was maybe something like lamb or pheasant, what I got was chicken breast with a slightly pungent odour coming off it
PRICE: 7
PORTION: 8
OVERALL: 50/70 What's up Doc? I'm an uncultured bastard, that's what's up.

I decide on one last jaunt into Stockport to visit the self-styled Lord of the Pies, hopping off the M60 and negotiating the rabbit warren of tight knit undulating town centre streets. I can never fathom out Stockport; I never know which way is North. It always seems so big and disorientating, almost more sprawling than Manchester, with horrendous traffic jams and tower blocks and office buildings plonked everywhere.

I search around the compact, hilly, narrow streets heading around the back of the Robinsons Unicorn brewery and the hat factory, before parking up around the corner outside a nightclub.

Lord of the Pies is another late entrant as they've been regularly popping up on my twitter feed and I hear their pies are worth writing about. I opt for their hallmark bake, the Stockport pie for £2.75, which is effectively a fully encased beef stew. There's others with mushrooms in; chicken, ham and leek and some cheesy ones but they all look very aesthetically appealing and well crafted. There's a smashing little cafe and clearly a lot to be proud of here but hey, the proof of the pie is in the eating so let's crack on.

It's of above average diameter and reasonable depth with perfect cooking instructions on the wrapper. It's known as a Stockport pie, consisting of ground beef stew and British potatoes, basically an upmarket meat and potato costing £2.75. Upon pulling it out of the greaseproof wrapper I am delighted to see a sprinkling of herbs on top of the attractive top crust. I have only one thing to say and that is that this pie is magnificent. Into the oven you go my beauty.

279.

PURVEYOR: Lord of the Pies
PREMISES: Stockport
PURCHASE: Stockport Pie £2.75
PLACE: 8 I'm a touch flustered as I'm on a meter which I've (again) forgot to pay for but the gentleman serving is amiable throughout, explaining his range with clarity and putting me at ease by calling me chief, captain or some other military title
PASTRY: 9 Simply fabulous, wonderful shape to it and topped with crispy herbs
PRESENTATION: 8 Upon unwrapping I am overwhelmed by the smell of sweet pastry. It's like a siren playing sweet music through my ears while my nose is continually punctured with a rod of heavenly smells every time I revisit the oven whilst it's cooking it. Just gets better and better
PACKAGE: 8 A circular layer of mincemeat, golden slabs of potato and rampant slithers of onion operating in a free role throughout. There is no sloppy gravy here but the combination of the three constituent ingredients makes it delightfully moist and a real treasure on the tongue
PALATE: 9 Fantastic contrast in flavour with all items contributing: ground mince at the top, potatoes at the bottom with onions adding a real sharpness and juicy edge to the content. It's like every meat and potato pie I've ever had but with a bit of added oomph to it
PRICE: 8 Some may baulk at the £2.75 price but this is a pie and a half. When you consider that it justifies it's tag as a gourmet pie then suddenly it becomes remarkably cheap
PORTION: 9 Just the right dimensions for one hearty appetite
OVERALL: 59/70 A late addition to the party but the magnificent Stockport pie has gatecrashed in every sense. This is a pie beyond parallel to satisfy even the most demanding of appetites.

Monday 7th October 2013

5am on a Monday morning and I am electing to get up of my own accord. Emma has come good on a promise to let me go up to Scotland on a pie hunt before I start my new job. I've had it mapped for months but not had the chance to execute. So it is that I find myself careering up the M6 in the pitch black crooning along to "I wanna know what love is…" with 18 pound coins jangling away in my pocket. I'm taking no chances in getting lumbered with any of those infernal Scottish notes in my change.

The black of the night gives way to grey as I arrive in the Caledonian country after traversing through treacherous fog thicker than a whale omelette. The sun lifts it's weary head and I am greeted with hundreds of miles of rolling hills with wind turbines in the distance piercing the skyline like huge metal triffids.

Of course the question as to how to do Scotland in a day is indeed a thorny one, given I could probably justify spending a month here due to the reputed quality and diversity of pastry products on offer. My logic is to go for the notable or recommended choices I've had put my way and plot a route around them starting at the top and working my way down. There's no way I'm going to Inverness until such a time as somebody offers to pay me to do so, therefore my top marker will be Loch Lomond and the Trossachs.

The Mhor Bakery in Callander has been recommended to me by a Cleveland Pieman off Twitter. After nearly 200 miles of brutal motorway slog, the last twenty or so bathe my sore eyes: tree lined roads with forests, fisheries and whisky distilleries and snow-capped peaks peering out from the distance. Let's face it, there's not too many words in the British language which get most men (and some women) as excited as "whisky tours" with the possible exception of "beer festival".

Set at the foot of wooded hills shrouded in mist, Callander is stunningly beautiful. The pay and display is set by a lake so peaceful that I don't even begrudge paying £1.80 for the privilege. I've already clocked the Main Street Bakery further down so after my mammoth journey up here, there's little doubt I'll be doubling up. It doesn't take me long to go into gluttony mode. To paraphrase John Virgo "the aim of the game is to pot as many pies as you can".

The stores appear to have recurring and heart-warming themes: Fishing, golf, whisky, chunky knitwear and pies. Ace isn't it? The Mhor Bakery has breads to die for with spectacular round sourdoughs tumbling into the window display and they are advertising Advocaat, blue cheese and sour dough toasties. Advocaat or Avocado? I forget it's been an early start.

I order the steak and black pudding pie but I can't resist a Bridie: it's distinct shape, pastry and of course name seducing me even though it is basically a pasty. I'd ideally make a pilgrimage to Forfar but if you're wondering why I haven't, then check where it is on the map, it'd take a week to get there! Bridies are called thus because it's what the bride used to serve up on her wedding day in this part of the world for good luck, hence the horseshoe shape.

I'd planned to go to a supermarket and grab a load of Forfar Bridies in the hope of picking up one with some Forfar authenticity but my impatience gets the better of me. This one's cheap at £1.30 and almost replicates the traditional horseshoe shape.

I don't quite understand why black pudding is a Scottish thing, I always thought they were made in Bury. But never mind here goes….Black pudding is undoubtedly a love/hate food and I must concede I am one of those food luddites who is mildly repulsed at the sight of a big black thing on my breakfast plate. However, I am expecting it to be much more palatable when chopped up into small chunks and placed in a pastry. After twenty minutes in the oven, there's juices dripping all over the tray and the crust is a wonderfully dark colour, slightly puff pastry-ish compared to your standard Scottish pie with dried gravy spilling out of the top crust.

280.

PURVEYOR: Mhor Bakery
PREMISES: Callander
PURCHASE: Steak and black pudding pie £1.80
PLACE: 8 At 9.45 in the morning a load of Japanese tourists are clogging the place up by asking for full descriptions of everything on the menu. The lassie serving, with marvellous guile, senses my agitation, side steps them gently and asks "Can I just serve this gentleman first?" Professionalism that – right there
PASTRY: 8 A bit dark but highly sturdy and well crafted
PRESENTATION: 8 A proper lip burner
PACKAGE: 8 Consisting wholly of dark meat and black pudding it's aggressively good
PALATE: 8 Ban kidney from all pies and replace with black pudding, I'm converted!
PRICE: 7 Bit touristy around here, perhaps bumping the price up
PORTION: 7 Standard Scotch pie size
OVERALL: 54/70 The soft texture of the black pudding compliments the tougher steak perfectly wrapped up in a thick juicy gravy leaving you in no doubt who's the boss here. A very Mhor'ish pie if you will.

281.

PURVEYOR: Mhor Bakery
PREMISES: Callander
PURCHASE: Minced Steak Bridie £1.30
PLACE: 8 **PASTRY:** 7 **PRESENTATION:** 8 **PACKAGE:** 7

PALATE: 7.5 PRICE: 7.5 PORTION: 8
OVERALL: 53/70 The filling doesn't extend all the way across but what there is possesses a higher meat content than your average English pasty with much fewer random root vegetables. The mincemeat is full flavoured, if a little on the salty side, and the exterior is robust despite multiple layers of flaky pastry threatening to spill all over the show.

I leg it down to Main Street Bakery which I'd clocked previously. This time I plump for a Scotch pie, keeping it real brother. The lady serving has a delightfully soft accent to warm the cockles of my heart but no, they don't have any toilets in the café, there's public conveniences across the road.

282.

PURVEYOR: Main Street Bakery
PREMISES: Callander
PURCHASE: Scotch pie £1.10
PLACE: 8 PASTRY: 8 PRESENTATION: 7.5 PACKAGE: 7.5
PALATE: 8 PRICE: 8 PORTION: 7.5
OVERALL: 54.5/70 It's already a bit dark before it goes in the oven and the egg glaze permeates through whilst it's warming. The crunch of the crust marries perfectly with the delicate, fluffy, light brown mince possessing a slight spicy peppery kick, which causes both me and the rich juices to dribble onto the sleeve of my jumper.

"Dunblane, Dunblane" as Tattoo off Fantasy Island might shout. Yes I'm off to Dunblane next, famous for Andy Murray and that maniac with a gun. The only rationale I have for going there is someone once tweeted a picture of a butchers there and they had a rampant selection of pies in the window. Isn't that reason enough? It's only twenty minutes back down from Callander where my dalliance was brief but I'm mightily impressed.

Back on the road as I go roaring towards the Central Belt – is this actually what Scottish people call the connecting areas from Edinburgh to Glasgow or is it a patronising thing English sales managers have dreamt up, in much the same way Americans talk about "the EMEA region" in a derogatory manner? It's the REST OF THE WORLD YOU NOBHEADS!!

For my sins, I've sub consciously avoided the urban conurbations of Glasgow and Edinburgh, simply because they didn't feature in the top five to visit, plus I did nae fancy my chances of getting in and out of there alive.

I take a shortcut through the village of Doom* trying to spot rare red kites swirling through the sky as I go. (*Doune – artistic licence).

Oooh the CITY of Dunblane – get you – I had no idea! Was this before or after Murray won Wimbledon? I imagine it's a city in the sense that

Brechin famously is a city (if you follow Scottish football results) as it appears to be merely a moderately sized village with a Barratt estate bolted onto it. I've also unwittingly fulfilled a lifetime's ambition to drive on all of the first ten motorways, after trundling down the Motorways M7, M8 and M9 today already.

Over the river and I get parked up on Dunblane's cobbled High Street, my front wheels creeping nervously over a disabled spot. It has a surreal calm about it with tweed jackets, and flat caps aplenty, as I potter down to Bennetts tucked at the end. I am immediately taken aback by the two pound steak pie staring back at me – weight not price – it's the size of a rail freight carriage. Beyond that I can see very little as the windows are all steamed up although I can confirm it's steak with everything round these parts: haggis, back pudding, ale, peppercorn and so on, and on this occasion I plump for a peppered steak.

Clearly an excellent choice as it stinks the car out with sweet, lardy pastry and peppery overtones which filter through my knackered aircon. A stunning choice of pies and no mean supply of meats either. I then spot another butchers across the road. MUST RESIST COMPULSION TO CONTINUALLY VISIT BUTCHERS!

283.

PURVEYOR: Bennetts
PREMISES: Dunblane
PURCHASE: Steak & Pepper Pie £1.70
PLACE: 7.5 A marginal language barrier but a pleasant enough chap
PASTRY: 8 An ever so slightly soft, lardy pastry with a bit of give on the sides moulded in the traditional Scottish tin shape
PRESENTATION: 8 Windows steamier than a Turkish bath
PACKAGE: 8 Chockful of stringy braised steak which thankfully isn't as chewy as it looks with reasonable depth to it
PALATE: 9 Well paint me orange and call me a life ring, the peppercorn sauce doesn't just rescue this pie, it earns it a knighthood for services to flavour. The steak meat is dominant but it is undoubtedly the peppered sauce which resuscitates this effort high into the pie echelons
PRICE: 7 It is quality steak I suppose
PORTION: 8
OVERALL: 55.5/70 Warming up nicely now. I mean the pie trip not my fire-fumed internal organs.

I still need a piss after spending five hours in the car already today and it's getting so painful that I find myself singing an Aria "Where are the services, I really need a piss" to distract myself from an untidy accident.

As I'm scooting down the M9 I mercifully find that there are some services and my patchwork tour of the Caledonian land leads me to Stirling Services for a brief interlude.

Refreshed, I make for the Boghall Butchers of Bathgate, a triple award winner recommended by the Scottish Master Craft Butchers. Will it be steak and haggis? Or their award winning Scotch pies?

I thought Bathgate would be a little bit rough but I am greeted with lush roadside forestry in what is clearly a grandiose Edinburgh commuter belt. Complete with Stepford Wives in evidence out power walking and a train station which goes on for miles confirming my initial commuter belt assertion.

I'm not there yet though as Boghall Butchers is a further two miles on but I'm pleased to see it's not in the centre so there's no infernal shopping centre to navigate. There's a sting in the tail as I pull off the main road onto one of the biggest council estates I've ever seen, which winds around forever as I drive over seriously rigid speed bumps. There's no sign of anything other than box-like, white stone houses on Boghall Drive which go on for fucking miles and creep up into the hills. It's a proper rum estate full of low level tenement blocks which look mildly terrifying to a Englishman a long way from home. Calm down lad, it's just full of life, I say to myself as I get a curious look from a housewife in her dressing gown playing with her daughter on their front lawn. I hit a school with a chippy next to it and drive around the back onto another residential area. There is no way there's anything other than a crack den down here but then it weaves around again and there I spot it poking out around the side of a wee shopping row: the Boghall Butchers "SAY AYE TO A PIE" is their cunning strapline.

Hmm what if I say yes rather than aye? Do I receive a pork chop instead? Shall I put the accent on or not? Get outed as a wee Sassenach from the off and deal with the mirth or attempt a shit Scottish accent?

Enough deliberation: THIS IS THE LARGEST SELECTION OF PIES I'VE SEEN IN THE NORTHERN HEMISPHERE IN ONE PLACE.

You name it, they've got it, plus a shitload you haven't heard of and wouldn't think to make up. Some of the more inventive ones include Chicken Balmoral pie, Steak and bean pie, Lasagne pie, Chicken carbonara pie (!), Haggis and gravy pie, a load of curry pies with a range of bridies, sausage rolls and a million and one type of steak pie variants.

The only problem is that I can't get bloody served. Whereas this gradually ratchets up my intolerance levels, I can see they're run off their feet so I am trying to hide my frustration. And after all I'm hardly likely to drive all this way and bugger off in a huff without buying something. They don't know this mind you as I meekly request a singular award winning Scotch pie.

If anything I've been lucky as two minutes later approximately thirty West Lothian refuse collectors descend on the place like a swarm of neon green wasps to clean up the stock.

284.

PURVEYOR: Boghall Butchers
PREMISES: Bathgate
PURCHASE: Scotch Pie 95p
PLACE: 9.5 Not to put too fine a point on it she says "you've waited that long you can have it for free" which is very good/stupid of her considering there's sadly little chance of repeat custom. Little does she know that this idiot has travelled over 200 miles just to sample this pie. Or maybe she's a bit more savvy, hears my English accent and gives me a freebie to curry favour?
PASTRY: 8.5 The crust has a sensational crispness to it which reverberates around my earlobes without presenting my teeth with too much trouble. The meat juices are pooled in a little indentation in the traditional Scottish top crust
PRESENTATION: 7.5 It's bubbling away on top and covered in salt
PACKAGE: 8 Compact and almost exclusively light brown mincemeat; the cheaper alternative to steak but no less fulfilling an experience
PALATE: 8.5 A very genuine, natural flavour just sat the right side of not being too greasy – just the way they like it around here
PRICE: 9 Not just because I got it for free
PORTION: 7
OVERALL: 58/70 It gets a big AYE from me! I wonder whether when I go to Newcastle I will be asked to say WHY AYE to a pie?

I've no time to hang around and admire this place however as no pie excursion to Scotland would be complete without sampling a Killie pie.

I'm thirteen miles off Glasgow and already I see signs of impressive urban structures up ahead. I feel a touch reticent as the M8 takes me through its centre that I should have infiltrated its deep underbelly, maybe had a wee canter around the Gorbals. I assume that is the Gorbals over to my right consisting as it does of thirty storey tower blocks. Nobody does tenement blocks quite like Glasgow.

The M8 scythes through central Glasgow seamlessly, giving a voyeuristic panoramic view as to what an absolute growler of a city it is, leaving me full of pangs of regret. I'm soon out the other end and headed for Killie though as the terrain gradually gets flatter and greener once more.

Kilmarnock (strapline: *the creative place*) follows a similar flight path to Boghall in that it looks highly salubrious on initial inspection, but before long I'm careering around some depressed estate similar to the one made famous on The Scheme. I get on the Burns Precinct multi storey and I've already spotted another butchers as I hang over the railings to see what lies below.

I descend the steps and the door opens directly onto a Brownings the Bakers, manufacturers of the Killie pie – how's that for convenient? "Say Aye to a Killie Pie" – there it is again! Don't mind if I do!

The shop is full of schoolkids; it's just that time of day. In fact there's some sat on my car when I return with my first haul – which is a Killie Pie and a Steak and Haggis pie purchased on an enticing two for £2.60 deal (£1.70 each). They've got an impressive variable range including a chicken curry pie and macaroni pie and the obligatory bridies but I can't come to Scotland and not eat haggis right? They also have a separate price list up titled the 'healthy menu'. I seriously hope they're not suggesting that pies aren't healthy?

The pies are taken cold and boxed and it's a good 48 hours when I sample them. I'm starting to feel a touch lethargic due to the volume of Scottish steak I've consumed in the past two days. However, the prospect of eating such a momentous pie is enough to perk me up a bit.

285.

PURVEYOR: Brownings
PREMISES: Kilmarnock
PURCHASE: Killie Pie £1.30
PLACE: 8 A bonnie blonde lassie shouts "What can I get fir ye?" three times. It's not her, it's me. I've got some kind of ear infection and am deaf as a post today. An extra mark for persistence
PASTRY: 8 The whole package is very light even when in the box, but the crust is remarkably thorough given its weight and follows the traditional round Scottish shape
PRESENTATION: 8 It's scorching hot after a mere 15 minutes in the oven, giving off enough heat to warm a Highlands village in winter
PACKAGE: 8 Not the deepest but packed full of quality braised steak and swimming, nay drowning in gravy
PALATE: 9 As it comes in a box I am able to check the ingredients but there's nothing special in there, just a simple combination to create a classic steak pie which I wolf down. If the first half sees the Killie pie

race into a devastating two goal lead, courtesy of its prime beef and sumptuous gravy, the second half sees a further devastating two goal salvo as I bite into a huge chunk of steak and wave after wave of gravy keeps coming in flavour filled attacks, in a tremendous gastronomic treat
PRICE: 7.5 Not necessarily cheap but a fine product
PORTION: 7.5
OVERALL: 56/70 Only the fourth best football pie in Europe? I'd like to see the first three!

After tackling rabbit in recent weeks, now I'm on the lamb hearts and lungs, beef kidney and liver. Oh and oatmeal. Still, it's all about the taste. I may be sick if I think too hard about it after just watching Whitechapel on telly with its' scenes of cannibalism.

If the Killie pie gets off to a flyer, the opposite can be said for the steak and haggis, as upon pulling it out of the oven and cutting into the pie, a bit of kidney pops out and sticks to the knife so I lick it off. I'm not a fan as you're probably aware by now and as if to continue this inauspicious start at the same time my daughter is filling up her potty.

However, it's steaming hot and full of dark and dangerous meaty treats and gradually improves as I tuck in. It's called a traditional short eating pie – as opposed to what, a pie that you drink? I assume that refers to it being wolfed down rapidly.

286.
PURVEYOR: Brownings
PREMISES: Kilmarnock
PURCHASE: Steak and Haggis Pie £1.30
PLACE: 8 **PASTRY:** 7.5 **PRESENTATION:** 8 **PACKAGE:** 7
PALATE: 7.5 **PRICE:** 7 **PORTION:** 7
OVERALL: 52/70 As with the Killie pie the second half ramps it up a bit but admittedly this isn't perfect to old fussykecks tastes being a wee Sassenach and I'd probably be happier with just steak in it. Furthermore, it's the only pie I have in Scotland which comes in a foil tray and there are gaps in the tray plus airspace in the pie.

I crash back down the steps, where the acrid smell of bleach and disinfectant is just about fighting off the pungent piss, to find Aulds and check out that butchers. The precinct is over-run with schoolkids eating chips and slightly older gentlemen in trackies loitering outside Poundland, one hand on a can, the other down their kecks. Yet the booming noise of lively chatter inside the shopping precinct is highly invigorating. I picked Aulds out as it is a mid-sized Scottish chain which would have a nice rounded selection in there and I'm visiting the Kilmarnock branch purely because I'm here anyway.

I find it just by the entrance and on first inspection the only pies they have on display are savoury rhubarb flavour, until I spy a couple of the end amongst a raft of pasties.

So I'm forced to ask the question. Twice, as she doesn't understand me first time.

"What pies have you got?".

"Steak and haggis and plain".

Did she say plain then or plate? And what is a plain pie? I don't want a plain pie, I want a brilliant pie!

Therefore my decision is made for me as I reluctantly order another steak and haggis leaving nothing to chance. It's a somewhat pricey £1.79 for not the biggest pie and the service is hardly with a smile.

287.

PURVEYOR: Aulds

PREMISES: Greenock

PURCHASE: Steak and Haggis pie £1.79

PLACE: 6 She appears to be walking around with a big grey cloud hovering over her head and I do very little to prevent dampening her day even further

PASTRY: 6.5 Very much in the Scotch pie shape but the top crust is flakier than a politician's promise. Having been out of work for a few weeks now, I am sporting a particularly fetching beard which serves as a fertile nesting area for the millions of flakes falling off the pie. Not keen

PRESENTATION: 7 The bag it comes in is probably the best part

PACKAGE: 7.5 Consisting of brown and occasionally pink steak meat along with some black haggis

PALATE: 6 I don't personally find the haggis offensive or exhilarating, it adds an extra component to the flavour but this pie is let down in general due to it being dryer than a sunburnt prune

PRICE: 6

PORTION: 7

OVERALL: 46/70 Maybe the locals are right to join the queue for Greggs after all....

Up and down the steps again; this time it's smelling a bit stale farty – hardly surprising given the calorific intake of the locals (yes I know about pots and kettles) as I weave through the chip eating masses. The only locals who aren't eating chips are munching on a Greggs pasty, shocking scenes although there's also a dangerously middle class couple sat outside a coffee house. I wonder if Greggs sell Scotch pies up here? There must be forty people queuing inside and out, I can only think the price is the attraction. I go for a yomp down a pedestrianised street and find little else of note so head back to Pollok Williamson, with its eight foot statute of a grinning butcher outside. Bloody hell, even the ice cream parlour next door seems to have pies on a rack in the window.

Upon entering I notice the huge vats of curries and stir fries which you can dish up a portion for your lunch. However, 'tis the pies I have eyes for and again there is an impressive range of plate options including a steak and link pie (links = sausages I later discovered) plus minced and braising steak pies. I ask about the little ones at the back: Scotch pie, steak and onion, steak and this one is a plain steak but with a Scotch pie type shell, she tells me precisely. I choose a 92p Scotch pie.

288.

PURVEYOR: Pollok Williamson
PREMISES: Ayr
PURCHASE: Scotch Pie 92p
PLACE: 8 **PASTRY:** 8 **PRESENTATION:** 7
PACKAGE: 8 **PALATE:** 8.5
PRICE: 8.5 **PORTION:** 7.5
OVERALL: 55.5/70 It's laced with more salt than a Siberian outpost but the meat simply melts in my mouth with a hit so sharp it's like receiving a hefty kick to the plums. The filling is generously packed in with the familiar fluffy mince and juice causing yet more spillage on my chin, whereas the crust has a marvellous uneven shape to it and an authentic crunch.

Time to hit the road before the English nutter constantly running through the car park carrying pies gets rumbled. I think some of the dippy locals think I'm dafter than they are.

I can't resist stopping at Happendon Services on the way back down, which seems to be a Tebay Farm Shop type affair. Yet I'm appalled to find out that the only pastry products they have are Ginsters. I cause some disgust of my own by accidentally walking into the ladies toilets because the signs are all in Gaelic (your honour).

Saturday 2nd November 2013

It's raining. Hard. Consequently I am flapping like a rattlesnake in a tumble dryer. From blue skies to torrential rain in ten minutes puts a £600 print bill in jeopardy as it's fanzine day.

Yesterday my long suffering wife stayed in to await delivery of not only four boxes of fanzines but a box of pies from Inverurie in Aberdeenshire. 5 Steak, 5 Kiwi pies and an extra bridie for myself, to push the order over the £20 mark. I decide I'm having one of each so I compensate the fanzine sellers quota by pulling a couple from Greenhalghs and Scunny market out of the freezer. I desperately need it to stay dry otherwise I'll be left with soggy fanzines nobody will buy and soggy pies nobody will want to eat. These things are sent to try us; well soak us.

I will firstly soothe my fears by having a pie, a Kiwi pie. That doesn't mean there's a Kiwi in it; I think it means it originates from New Zealand. It's got a succulent steak and mature cheese filling.

289.

PURVEYOR: Davidsons
PREMISES: Inverurie
PURCHASE: Kiwi Pie £1.80
PLACE: 8 I like to poke fun at THE INTERNET but I am once again left to marvel at the fact you can order a box of pies from the Highlands and get them delivered straight to your door in immaculate condition within days, without even having to speak to a human being
PASTRY: 8 The now familiar circular tin form with a generous blob of dried cheese of top as a prelude to what lurks inside
PRESENTATION: 7 I don't get the anticipated cheesy whiff
PACKAGE: 7.5 Not the deepest but plenty of robust luscious chunks of steak
PALATE: 8 The steak tastes thorough and competent and each chunk I suck out slips down with ease but I perhaps expected a bit more from the cheese. Sometimes the truth is in the burps and nevertheless mine are exceptionally meaty for several hours afterwards
PRICE: 7
PORTION: 7.5
OVERALL: 53/70 Beefier than a convention of Ian Botham lookalikes.

290.

PURVEYOR: Davidsons
PREMISES: Inverurie
PURCHASE: Steak Pie £1.65
PLACE: 8 **PASTRY:** 7 **PRESENTATION:** 7 **PACKAGE:** 7
PALATE: 7.5 **PRICE:** 7 **PORTION:** 7
OVERALL: 50.5/70 There's no doubting the authenticity or quantity of the succulent steak meat but for me it's lacking a bit of gravy as it's a touch on the dry side. The fanzine lads declare that "Yorkes was better".

291.

PURVEYOR: Davidsons
PREMISES: Inverurie
PURCHASE: Minced Beef Bridie £1.59
PLACE: 8
PASTRY: 8 It's a little flaky yet it pulls it off as the base is splendidly dark and tasty in that sweet semi-burnt kind of way
PRESENTATION: 8 The pastry seduces me whilst it's heating in the oven
PACKAGE: 8 It looks exactly like it does on the website and again there is no veg in it, no potato or carrot just a barely detectable hint of onion and the integral ingredient of beef
PALATE: 8 Plump and moist selection of minced beef
PRICE: 8 Excludes delivery charge
PORTION: 8 This gift to the bride is around six inches long
OVERALL: 56/70 If you're going to get married, do it in Scotland.

Saturday 9th November 2013

Just received a text from Emma "Our Fridge is full of bloody pies"

And it is! The amazingly considerate and tolerant Mrs Tarbuck has cleared the fridge and stocked it with no less than 24 pies from Paul's Pies of Oxford, NZ Gourmet Pies of Newcastle and Legges of Bromyard. One lot were left down the side of the house as requested, another lot she was in to collect and the third were delivered to a neighbour, who upon discovering they were pies expressed understandable regret at handing the box over. I'd have done the same.

For tomorrow I will have a pie party! Despite being 40 years of age I have never hosted a dinner party in my life. So I've no idea how this will go but I'm inviting three mates around to sample some fine produce in a piefest to end them all.

I've stocked up with mash, gravy, mushy peas, pickled onions and red cabbage, condiments and sauces galore and a barrel full of booze to numb the noise of seven kids running riot in our house. Rob's bringing some homemade red wine, Lee's missus Carolyn has baked a pair of sweet pies for afters and Neil's brought twelve bottles of Orval, a repulsive 12% strength ale we developed a masochistic liking of during our recent trip to Bruges. We've scattered some little white pills across the table to really get the party going later – that's right GAVISCON!

The three suppliers are all on my list and all have a bit of contrast about them. The New Zealand gourmet company have the most innovative flavours, Legges look to be the biggest and Paul's have the reputation and artisan flair about them. If there's a bakery in heaven it will smell like my fridge does right now.

All three pies come in polystyrene temperature controlled boxes and the Legges one in particular is true to its Herefordshire roots, presented as it is in a box of straw, which Emma was kind of hoping contained some expensive jewellery. Only a gem of a pie in here sorry love!

Legges prove the most popular with the guests, in particular the steak and stilton and their chicken and bacon pie quickly becomes known as "the beast" after Rob has craftily ordered a second pie for the kids – who are happy just eating pizza and the chips I have accidentally grilled for them. Whoops!

Emma and Jo go for the Homity Pie from Paul's, which gives me pie envy when I spot it, that I haven't ordered one, while Neil orders a bagful for midweek sustenance.

There's controversy as I carry out the pie procession and someone notices that the Christmas Pie I'd laid out is going back in the freezer until....erm Christmas. The lads are not impressed.

All the pies are received favourably and wolfed down with aplomb including a Paul's Steak & Guinness Pie for myself, before we retire to the lounge and revert to "sad dads" mode indulging in a Gangnam style dancing competition which the dads arguably enjoy more than the kids.

Of course the upshot of this rare outing of my cackhanded hosting skills is that I end up with a load of surplus pies to try out in the subsequent few days. I decide to go for the NZ Gourmet Pies first who have the pick of the flavour range including spinach and goats cheese, minted lamb, Mike's chilli beef, Thai green curry, peppered steak and of course the Kiwi Pie.

292.

PURVEYOR: NZ Gourmet Pies
PREMISES: Newcastle
PURCHASE: Steak and Cheese Pie £3.00
PLACE: 8 Well packaged, delivered on time, very helpful and great comms. Christ I sound like I'm on eBay
PASTRY: 7.5 Ever so slightly flaky but it's a crust which really grows on me and hangs together well
PRESENTATION: 8 Smells sumptuously cheesy in the oven as you'd expect
PACKAGE: 8 Whopping chunks of steak. It means the cheese isn't prevalent throughout as the meat barges it out of the way, but there is a decent sized layer on top with the odd carrot thrown in for good measure

PALATE: 7.5 The steak is very thoroughly cooked and succulent with the cheese adding a delightful interjection
PRICE: 7
PORTION: 7.5
OVERALL: 53.5/70 It's good to know that if I was ever to emigrate I could still get my gums around a nice portable pastry product, even though New Zealanders taking pies to Newcastle does feel a little bit like well, taking coals to Newcastle....

293.
PURVEYOR: NZ Gourmet Pies
PREMISES: Newcastle
PURCHASE: Mike's Chilli Beef Pie £3.25
PLACE: 8
PASTRY: 8 Again it's a bit flaky but somehow this perfectly complements the fiery contents inside, the top crust comes perilously close to detaching itself mind you
PRESENTATION: 8 Just one singular hit as I remove it from the oven sends me doolally
PACKAGE: 8 Packed with chilli beef and butter beans rather than the more conventional chilli beans
PALATE: 9 If you don't like an angry, aggressive explosive filling in your pie, then this one's probably not for you, fortunately I do. A perfect and ingenious way of combining two meals in one
PRICE: 7.5 It definitely feels more gourmet than the steak and cheese due to the flavour and originality
PORTION: 8 A deceptive amount of depth to it
OVERALL: 56.5/70 Who is Mike and does he only make this pie?

Paul makes pies too, this time in a slaughterhouse in Oxfordshire and I have been lusting over their Steak and Guinness for too long now. This being exacerbated further when I risked life and limb driving to Oxford only to find their stockist had none left.

294.
PURVEYOR: Pauls Pies
PREMISES: Oxfordshire
PURCHASE: Steak & Guinness Pie £3.50
PLACE: 9 Great communication throughout, excellent delivery and a genuine interest in my project
PASTRY: 10 It's perfect. Indeed, the combination of shortcrust and suet pastry is beyond perfect. The top crust resembles a crown and this is

certainly a pie fit for a king. The craftsmanship exhibited in creating this crust belongs in a pie museum. It's unlike anything I've had before and long after the pie is gone I can still taste it

PRESENTATION: 8 A pastry combination is always going to have a positive impact in the kitchen

PACKAGE: 8 The contents come tumbling out of the pie which has considerable depth to it. My own fears are confirmed when I find it contains large swathes of mushrooms however this is more than offset by the presence of delightful slithers of bacon, onion and top quality chunks of beef

PALATE: 8 Setting aside my mushroom phobia it still has plenty of fizz to it; lovely soft gravy and a delectably moist combination of its constituent ingredients

PRICE: 7 I literally have to buy a baker's dozen to meet the minimum delivery

PORTION: 9 A very ample singular portion

OVERALL: 59/70 Pastry par excellence and clearly this is a pie made by a master craftsman. I'm only gutted I didn't get a homity one – it may have yielded an even better score from this mushroomphobe.

So to Legges of Bromyard in Herefordshire, another fine pie producer I picked up off Twitter and I'm bloody glad I did. Due to my guests wanting five and them coming in boxes of six, I have to juggle a bit and can only have one of their pies and after much deliberation I opt for the Steak & Stilton.

295.

PURVEYOR: Legges of Bromyard
PREMISES: Herefordshire
PURCHASE: The Publican (Steak & Stilton pie) £5.50
PLACE: 8 All sorted online and over the phone, miraculously easy as usual
PASTRY: 8 It looks moodily dark even before it goes into the oven and I'm getting heartburn just looking at it, yet the crust is surprisingly light and holds its shape remarkably well

PRESENTATION: 8 From the second it goes in the oven it's like a swarm of invisible cheesy wasps are chasing me around the kitchen

PACKAGE: 8 Delightful slithers of succulent beef and a big layer of cooked jelly at the top; lots of saucy flavour throughout teamed up with Wye Valley Butty Bach ale

PALATE: 8.5 There's a wonderfully full blooded flavour about it; meat that is cooked to perfection and enhanced by the presence of Stilton, which I can't actually see yet I can taste in every mouthful

PRICE: 7

PORTION: 9 "Man versus Pie" as dubbed by Rob – a couple of inches deep and a good four or five inches across

OVERALL: 56.5/70 This pie will intimidate you then invigorate you!

Anyone for a picnic? Maybe not in November but I've still got a box of Paul's Pies to get through so I decide to indulge in a picnic pie (served cold) next.

296.

PURVEYOR: Pauls Pies
PREMISES: Oxfordshire
PURCHASE: Picnic Pie £4.50
PLACE: 9
PASTRY: 8 The P for picnic has depressed into the lid a touch but the now familiar magnificent crown shape of the top crust marks this out as a prestige pie
PRESENTATION: 8 Of course the beauty of this is that I don't have to wait till it's cooked. Getting it out of the foil tray is no mean feat as it is tightly compressed in there but after removal what I find is another work of art
PACKAGE: 8 A beautifully layered pie arranged as pork then chicken with bacon and onion in a free role throughout. The meat infuses into one and I can only describe it as a gourmet sausage roll even though it's much deeper and grander
PALATE: 8 Mildly spiced but an excellent combination
PRICE: 7.5
PORTION: 8 Big enough to share at your notional picnic but needless to say I don't
OVERALL: 56.5/70 See, I actually want a picnic now....

Saturday 30th November 2013

"Let's go to Ikea and Gemini retail park" I suggest. Wife sufficiently hood-winked again. What she doesn't know is that I've been emailing the Great North Pie Company for a number of weeks (after someone recommended them) and have eventually located Kenyon Hall Farm Shop on the out-skirts of Warrington.

LIFE OF PIES

You can't beat a farm shop at Christmas can you? And I've got to have my fun before I spend hours wandering around M&S. I wander in and make a beeline for the pork pies on the shelf. They're not Great North's, they're Burbushs of Penrith, famously sold at the fantastic Tebay Services on the M6.

I plump for the pork and gooseberry option as – hey it's nearly Christmas. Plus I've been used to playing the gooseberry many times over the years.

I briefly panic over the Great North Pie Co but there's no need as they're on sale at the cafe counter to take away. The flavour choices are somewhat unique, if not spectacular, and change every quarter. There's venison and black pudding and a bean, beetroot and barley pie. I'm torn between the Lancashire Cheese and Onion and the Boxing Day turkey curry pie. I've possibly neglected cheese and onion pies a bit and quite like them but with the festive season approaching the turkey curry pie gets the nod (£3.69). There's chestnuts and peas in it with turkey mince in a spicy curry sauce. Gutted that the beef shin pie isn't available, let alone the steak and oyster pie with nettles and bramble jelly. You really have to check their website to appreciate the flavours which change regularly.

297.

PURVEYOR: Great North Pie Co
PREMISES: Stockport
PURCHASE: Boxing Day Turkey Pie £3.69
PLACE: 8.5 A rapid flurry of emails followed by an invite to their premises where they offer to make me my very own pie! (If you're reading, consider this a nudge....)
PASTRY: 8 drizzled with sesame seeds and a circular Scotch pie form to it with acute angles
PRESENTATION: 8 I nuzzle up to it before putting it in the oven and it has a reassuringly authentic curry scent to it
PACKAGE: 8 Generous portion of turkey mince interjected with peas and a whole host of other ingredients
PALATE: 9 Soft, generous turkey mince infused within rich homemade curry flavouring. The taste upgrades with every mouthful as it just keeps giving me more, until I'm begging for less as the gradual curry kick just veers the right side of overwhelming
PRICE: 7 Evidently gourmet
PORTION: 8 Sharp sides but of good diameter
OVERALL: 56.5/70 Amazing piemakers with amazing flavours!

The Burbushs pork and caramelised gooseberry pie is double wrapped and sealed in polythene to retain freshness. You'll have to forgive me as if I

318

have had gooseberries before I can't remember, so I haven't got the foggiest what they taste like. My guess is a cross between a grape and a blackberry.

298.

PURVEYOR: Burbushs
PREMISES: Penrith
PURCHASE: Pork and Caramelised Gooseberry Pie £4.40
PLACE: 8 A bit tardy in the farm shop but highly apologetic when I eventually get served
PASTRY: 7.5 A highly rigid effort albeit with no top crust which is kind of expected with a fruit topped pie. The prospect of the semi-pureed fruity topping sinking into the meat compensates it not being fully encased
PRESENTATION: 7.5 I give it a good old whiff: nothing offensive about it although it feels a little greasy
PACKAGE: 8.5 A good couple of inches of fine pork meat topped with a good half inch layer of gooseberry. There's also a decent casing of golden jelly which only starts half way down the pie, presumably to keep it segregated as gooseberry and gelatine bone stock may not be a preferred combination
PALATE: 8.5 A touch tart but it contrasts well with the lightly spiced sausage meat which is superb
PRICE: 7
PORTION: 9 They make them big up in Cumbria and you need a pretty big mouth to bite into it from top to bottom
OVERALL: 56/70 At 450g it's a hefty portion but as I've been running around a five-a-side pitch for an hour, it's polished off with deadly instinct. Unlike my five-a-side prowess.

Saturday 7th December 2013

I'd nearly forgot the Christmas Pie from Pauls. You see, like the big stiff I am I thought I'd freeze it till December (yes lads: instead of sharing it with you)

Described as "the perfect addition to your cold Christmas platter" it is similar to the picnic pie with turkey instead of chicken and the all important addition of double cream and chestnut stuffing with a cranberry topping.

299.

PURVEYOR: Pauls Pies
PREMISES: Oxfordshire

PURCHASE: Christmas Pie £4.99
PLACE: 9 **PASTRY:** 8
PRESENTATION: 7 **PACKAGE:** 8
PALATE: 8 **PRICE:** 7 **PORTION:** 8
OVERALL: 55/70 It's another open topped affair but the layering is truly spectacular on the eye: cranberry topping followed by stuffing, which dominates proceedings and tastes as rich as pate, then turkey meat, sausage, bacon and onion. The perfect accompaniment to putting the decorations up!

Friday 20th December 2013

Unlike Mariah Carey, all I want for Christmas is to go to Newcastle. It is my last port of call before shutting down the book. I have it all planned out with military precision, exactly where I need to go and what I will have at what time. Alas, I've been unable to find a day to do it in so I'm forced to console myself with a clandestine beer or two in the German Christmas markets, after queuing at Pandora for half an hour to get Emma's Christmas pressie. Then I see the pie stall....

It's the Crusty Pie Company from Halifax and as well as the usual suspects they have chilli firecracker pork pies, the obligatory turkey and stuffing pies; festive beef with horse radish sauce – is there only me who finds the name, let alone the taste, of horse radish a tad disturbing – a six pound (price not weight) Boar pie – a growler which probably really does growl at you and a chunky Steak and Yorkshire real ale pie. The chilli pork scratchings also catch my eye and they have a selection of Indian food on top of the display counters too.

The Steak & Ale pie isn't cheap at £3.50 and it's difficult to ascertain how much of the price is inherent and how much is down to the general mentality of ripping off Chrimbo punters at the Manchester Markets. As everyone knows, those £4.00 pints of German lager are really just a can of Aldi's own brand Stella "Saint Etienne" poured into a pint glass while the barmaid makes a "schwooshing" noise.

Pie procured and the train home is carnage, as indeed it has been all week: an uneasy mix of Christmas shoppers and drunk bastards bawling and brawling their way down the aisle. The stopper from Manchester Victoria to Wigan (via Hag Fold International) is scary at the best of times. I'm only surprised Michael Portillo hasn't travelled this route on his Great Continental train journeys of the world series to be honest.

I'm wedged in a middle seat with my manbag clenched between my legs within which are two further shopping bags. One contains a £120 Pandora bracelet, the other contains a £3.50 pie. If anyone damages my pie there will be serious bother!!

I soon find myself wedged into the window seat as one passenger departs at Atherton, to be replaced by a huge West Indian lady who makes it evident that she would like more room by continually grinding her not inconsiderably sized butt cheeks into my thighs so hard that I'm nearly on the tracks.

Back to the pie and it is a fair weight with a solid crimp. However, on turning it underneath there appears to be what looks suspiciously like mould. Now I'm not going to get carried away before it goes into the oven as very often pork pie jelly can seep through and take on a greyish appearance on the crust contour, so I may have got it wrong. Either way, at £3.50 a pop there's no way it's going in the bin so I bang it in the oven for twenty minutes at gas mark five. It's giving off that slightly lardy pastry whiff but the meat and gravy remains a guarded secret tucked within its pastry casing.

Upon exiting the oven and burning my hand (as per usual), the crust sides have sagged a touch, a sure fire sign that's there's plenty inside. I lift it up to check and yes the little black dots are still there, but all is forgiven upon opening up this beast and finding that it is darker than a French arthouse movie; densely packed with sumptuous looking large chunks of meat and dark gravy.

300.

PURVEYOR: The Crusty Pie Company
PREMISES: Halifax
PURCHASE: Chunky Steak and Yorkshire Ale Pie £3.50
PLACE: 6 German and disinterested
PASTRY: 8 A crisp if not crusty crust enabling perfect portability with the hands
PRESENTATION: 7 The smell isn't evident, save for the pastry glaze but after cutting it open steam flies off in all directions like a Pearl & Dean advert
PACKAGE: 8 Absolutely heaving with stewing steak with an above average chunk size which is perfectly complimented with rich gravy and savoury spicy jelly
PALATE: 8 Possesses a remarkable kick (traced down to the jelly and gravy) which attacks my tastebuds with considerable aggression putting earlier concerns firmly to bed

PRICE: 6 At half this price it would be an absolute steal for a lunchtime feed, but despite being priced in the gourmet range it does have more of a "Terry takes a break from plastering the walls to read the Mirror, have a mug of tea and chomp on a steak pie" feel to it

PORTION: 8 A good inch and half deep

OVERALL: 51/70 Despite some early concerns about pricing and freshness, the Crusty Pie Company Steak and ale pie is exceptionally filling and leaves my appetite feeling decidedly battle weary.

The last few crumbs

The final filling: 300-314

And it's good pie from him....

Friday 27th December 2013

I really am finished up now. Really am. Just nipping to Aldi for some affordable Friday night grog and a focaccia. That's a type of bread, or if you live in Wigan it's the act of going around to someone's house to get hold of them before they go out.

The Aldi has a certain charm situated as it is slap bang in the Arndale, a multilingual babble of voices and tongues, filling their baskets with shit crisps. All human life exists here but I kind of like it, or rather the cheap ale they put out.

Still you know the rest....the potato and meat pie is 75p and the steak and ale puff pastry pie is a mere 99p. It's branded as Crestwood and upon pulling the meat and potato out of the wrapper, the dimples on the outer casing make it look vaguely familiar, almost as if some of the unscrupulous vendors I've been to in the past have been passing this one off as their own but not at the same knock down price.

301.

PURVEYOR: Aldi
PREMISES: Atherstone
PURCHASE: Potato and Meat Pie 75p
PLACE: 7 **PASTRY:** 8 **PRESENTATION:** 7 **PACKAGE:** 7.5
PALATE: 7 **PRICE:** 9 **PORTION:** 7.5
OVERALL: 53/70 From the one queue for all tills to the precision on the cooking instructions, it all points to a high standard of Teutonic efficiency. The creamy mash is of a good standard with hints of onion adding discernible flavour; a touch watery in parts but all things considered I've paid a hell of a lot more for a lot less over the past two years.

302.

PURVEYOR: Aldi
PREMISES: Atherstone
PURCHASE: Steak Pie 99p
PLACE: 7 **PASTRY:** 7.5 **PRESENTATION:** 8 **PACKAGE:** 8
PALATE: 7.5 **PRICE:** 8 **PORTION:** 8
OVERALL: 54/70 So to the puff pastry topped steak pie costing just 99p for 200g of goodness. I'm greeted with a calm dark interior of soothingly soft steak chunks aplenty and proceed to burn my tongue due to diving in a little too quickly.

Saturday 4th January 2014

Let's go through this charade one last time then shall we? It starts on the Thursday night:

"What's going on this Saturday?"

"Well – this Saturday is the day you said it would be OK if I went up to Newcastle to finish the book and then I'm getting back for three to go the football."

"Hang on, so you're getting up at the crack of dawn to go to Newcastle, then going straight on to the football without coming home?" *(Yep she's got it, he thinks silently).*

"WE might want to do something. WE might want to spend some time with you!"

"But but but you know I've got to finish this book and you agreed that as soon as we got Christmas out of the way I could do it!"

After a full two minutes of me sulking she comes clean:

"Me and Jess are going to a panto this Saturday anyway"

At this point I should call her bluff and tell her I want to go to the panto with her but she'll see straight through me and probably order an extra ticket. She's made her point and guess what:

IT'S GAME ON!!

I've got rampant paranoia about this jaunt already, purely because it's the last piece of the jigsaw. Upon leaving the house at some ungodly hour, I notice that my mirror light in my car has been on all night. I can't bear to look as I gently turn the key: I open my eyes to find it gently purring away and before you know it I'm bombing up the M6 one last time to Kirkby Stephen whilst listening to the dulcet tones of the Bee Gees.

To Durham, Sunderland and Newcastle today with a full itinerary and a couple of beers in the Toon with some sound Geordies I know. There's a great article online featuring the best 20 pies in Newcastle – unfortunately it's only useful if you happen to be visiting Newcastle in Sydney.

I find myself questioning my sanity one last time as I head across to the North East in the pitch black, swaying and singing along to Elton John's 'Don't Let the Sun Go down on me' with Smooth FM being the only station I can pick up. I could be waving a lighter out of the sun roof for all anyone would know. The sun rises as I traverse the desolate, beautiful moors towards Scotch Corner: flood warnings, ice warnings yet all is calm. It's the perfect day for one last hurrah.

My first stop is Dicksons – a famous North East purveyor who have been going 60 odd years. I'm heading to the historic town of Houghton le Springs. I really wanted to go to Hetton Le Hole as I've been saying it like a Frenchmon all the way up: 'Etton le 'Orle. However there's no pie shop there.

There's a bit of a new town vibe about the place with the huge box shaped Wetherspoons and the signposted estate Houghtonside looming up on the hillside. Down an alley and onto the main street: Greggs, Ladbrokes, and tanning stores. Dicksons: right on the main drag directly opposite Greggs, staring it out like a jaded but resolute boxer. The 3 pies for £3 deal looks a cracker arranged in trios next to a rather intimidating looking black pudding.

I get a minced beef and a steak and even though there are hot ones on offer the "cold" ones are still warm i.e. freshly baked: nice one!

303.

PURVEYOR: Dicksons
PREMISES: South Shields
PURCHASE: Steak Pie £1.54
PLACE: 7 A very happy chap who is quite content to let me stand there ogling his pies this fine morning
PASTRY: 8 Nothing exceptional but a solid performance. Great texture and a double crimp which is sturdy enough to withstand the rigours of a hand eaten chomp. I finish off by holding the rim and sucking luscious gravy out of it
PRESENTATION: 8 As soon as I put it in the oven the delightful buttery pastry starts to waft through the house in truly heavenly fashion
PACKAGE: 7.5 Bit of air space at the top but an excellent average chunk size plus it's swimming in gravy
PALATE: 8 The steak is full blooded and the gravy has a splendid peppery kick to it
PRICE: 7.5 Buying in bulk your best bet
PORTION: 8 Oblong shaped and heavy
OVERALL: 54/70 This is simply a pie with 60 years of craft behind it permeating through every mouthful.

304.

PURVEYOR: Dicksons
PREMISES: South Shields
PURCHASE: Minced Beef and
Onion Pie £1.18
PLACE: 7 **PASTRY:** 8
PRESENTATION: 7.5 **PACKAGE:** 7
PALATE: 7.5 **PRICE:** 8 **PORTION:** 7.5
OVERALL: 52.5/70 The minced beef and
onion is of similar stock. The raised roof in
the centre leaves a bit of headroom but
there is nevertheless a considerable layer of mince within. I was perhaps
expecting the tender meat to be a bit lighter in a transitional nod to the
Scotch pie, but it is most definitely dark and encapsulated in the same
rich gravy as the steak version.

I retreat to the car and I'm forced to turn my headlights back on as there
is no Sun in Sunderland today; just a seething mass of tower blocks in the
sky and the odd decent butcher on ground level.

Eventually I drive onto a multi-storey right in the middle of said tower
blocks but it does the trick as I manage to spot the shiny facade of Deben-
hams and a view of the entire city of Sunderland, engulfed in hundreds of
braying seagulls.

I wander around the disorientating pedestrianised streets in something
of a daze, which some may say is the best way to be. I couldn't possibly
comment. The lack of parking situation has pissed me off and now I'm on
foot things aren't improving as the shoddy GPS on my phone sends me
walkabout.

If the posh bird was in the mood for opening her mouth she'd
probably say "YOU HAVE JUST WALKED AROUND IN A FUCKING
CIRCLE" as is quite evident. I just want two pies, a quick piss and I'll be
on my way.

I eventually hit the precinct that I'm looking for but first I spot a Cooplands; they don't sell pies do they? Oh hang on what's this, they DO sell
pies. My mood improves greatly as I realise a bonus pie is in the offing.
First the Famous Swiss Muller Bakery up the road. There's no savoury pies
on display so I am forced to ask and she returns with two different types
on a small tray. Steak and Mince and onion are the default choices in here
so I opt for the latter.

It's an individual plate pie and despite being slightly raised in the middle, it's dimpled on the underside and it's unequivocally the shallowest pie
I've had in my life.

305.

PURVEYOR: Muller Swiss Bakery
PREMISES: Sunderland
PURCHASE: Mince and onion pie £1.25
PLACE: 7.5 For the tray demonstration
PASTRY: 8.5 In this pie of extremes the crust is baked to perfection with a snappy crispness and some real baking expertise in evidence
PRESENTATION: 8 The golden disc gives off the most amazing pastry aroma whilst baking in the oven
PACKAGE: 5.5 Paper thin and not even that thick paper; tracing paper thin. Barely a centimetre deep. Paltry paper. Like this page you're reading right now – yeah that's how thick it is!
PALATE: 8 What does exist is a remarkably mouth watering decadent layer of mince meat I've rarely experienced elsewhere. It's stunning but there's just not enough of it
PRICE: 7 For diameter not depth
PORTION: 6 Dimensions = 5 inches wide x 0.5 inches deep
OVERALL: 50.5/70 A dangerous dearth of delight in this dinky dude.

My morbid fear of offending people by walking into their shop with other pies has resurfaced, so now I know I'm getting three, I nip to the Pound Shop across the road and buy a six pack of Lucozade to improvise stashing the pies in an upright manner. The Pound Shop barometer hones in on warm North East accents, people full of hope and cheer; plus the obligatory teenage scallywag getting dragged out by his collar by security, whilst a multipack of Boost bars trickle out of his trackie bottoms.

It turns out Cooplands are not from Donny but have branches all over the North and they present an aesthetically pleasing pie and a top crust which is perfectly formed and has a small horizontal score mark. The underneath is a bit softer and I can see the semi transparent dark gravy which lies inside. It's an easy pie to handle with the minimum of dexterity and upon pulling it from the foil tray, I notice they've doubled up on trays. Whether that's the standard, specifically for my benefit, or a pure accident I have no idea but it dramatically reduces burnage.

306.

PURVEYOR: Cooplands
PREMISES: Scarborough
PURCHASE: Steak Pie £1.12

PLACE: 7 **PASTRY:** 8 **PRESENTATION:** 7 **PACKAGE:** 8
PALATE: 7 **PRICE:** 7.5 **PORTION:** 7.5
OVERALL: 52/70 It's a little belter with some unique charms, despite probably being mass produced. There's little spare room for manoeuvre inside as it's maxed out with steak and gravy and has a pastry that is fresh and crisp. Perhaps just a touch under seasoned.

I head for Olive Street where the squawk of seagulls and burglar alarms subsides and I'm delighted to find that the pie shop of the same name is open for business, with steak and chicken pies adorning the window along with a range of pasties. I am just beaten to the door by a Chubby Brown lookalike which feels highly appropriate around these parts.

This is a proper little find and no mistake: intrinsically traditional and welcoming with pies that look to die for. The huge overhanging top crusts ticks all the home made boxes for me and look highly intriguing.

307.

PURVEYOR: Olive Street Pie shop
PREMISES: Sunderland
PURCHASE: Steak Pie 99p
PLACE: 8 A delightful old dear who must be all of four feet tall with a wrist tattoo (old school) yet is remarkably fleet footed and affable to the core
PASTRY: 8.5 A fascinating homemade pastry with a towering bouffant top crust, giving the pie the appearance of a giant mushroom (perish the thought). Lots of dense shortcrust overhanging a slightly tapered underneath which is almost too deep in parts, but it's still pastry from the gods
PRESENTATION: 8 A cheeky and irresistible aroma
PACKAGE: 8 Considering the price it's positively loaded with thick, chunky, authentic cuts of beef augmented by lashings of gravy and jelly lurking within
PALATE: 8 A highly natural earthy appeal to this pie with not too much spice or seasoning, just a whole hearted natural flavour
PRICE: 9 The steaks (pies) are not high here, they're ridiculously cheap
PORTION: 8 Although the crust dominates proceedings it's still a fair old size
OVERALL: 57.5/70 Guess what, the sun is shining again now.

One last desperate frenzied half an hour, as I frantically try to get out of the shopping centre, out of the car park and out of Sunderland. My mate Reuven isn't answering his phone; I'm sweating; my head's killing me and I haven't a clue which of the three ways to get to Newcastle I need to take. Stressful business this pie eating lark. I give a fleeting but inspired glance at the Alexander Bridge and the gigantic Stadium of Light perched ominously on the river and head further north.

The lads are in town already so I don't need to plunge through the Tyne Tunnel, I suffice myself with another two bit motorway – the A194 (M) which heads to Durham. This glorified A road, along with the one which carves through the centre of Newcastle – the A167 (M) – can now be added to an impressive list of shit motorways I've traversed on my escapades, such as the A601(M), the M627 and the utterly pointless M181.

Still I need to concentrate on the road; I'm as flustered as a snared halibut here and pretty soon I find myself passing the Gateshead athletics stadium. My biggest athletic feat of the day will be getting to the Toon before wetting myself.

I glide into Newcastle and I soon espy the imposing Tyne Bridge, the "wobbly bubbly type building that I don't know what the fuck it's called" and in the background St James Park – if indeed I'm allowed to call it that in today's commercial age.

I snap out of my daze in the NCP off the Quayside. Do not leave valuables on display says the sign, so I pay heed and endeavour to move the pies procured thus far into the boot before locking up. Help yourself to whatever you like but leave me my pies. There's a pleasant wintry nip in the air as I head up Grey Street in the surprisingly compact yet hilly city centre.

I meet Reuven and Adam at the top of Grey Street and they guide me through the streets in my bewildered state to the French Oven. Set within the grandeur of the impeccable Grainger Market, home to butchers, bakers and maybe even a candlestick maker. Its stunning, decorative architecture reflects the feel of Newcastle city centre and its beautiful buildings with marvellous brown stone as you head down to the quayside, which are light years away from the marauding mobs of stag and hen parties at ground level.

There's a healthy queue and an impressive range of pies on show not to mention artisan breads and wonderful cakes. Their best seller is a Scotch Pie. Yes you heard correctly: a Scotch pie in England in a French bakery. Other faves include the pork and apple with lattice top crust, lots of beef and steak pies and a range of curried pasties. I decide to go different and plump for a Pan Haggerty Pie and a Minced beef and mushy peas pie. Yep: the mushy peas are IN the pie.

Pan Haggerty is a North East delicacy which yields a marginally open topped cheese pie with red onion and potato mash. I whack it in the oven for 20 minutes which only succeeds in turning the red onions black. Oops.

308.

PURVEYOR: French Oven
PREMISES: Newcastle Upon Tyne
PURCHASE: Pan Haggerty Pie £2.05
PLACE: 8 Top class Geordie lasses serving hot treats in a branded bag. Everything they sell looks hand crafted and there's great diversity in everything they do
PASTRY: 7 Clearly the top crust is just cheese but the rest is a bit crumbly and nearly falls apart in the oven
PRESENTATION: 8 Emits a splendid aroma which ultimately vindicates my decision to reheat it
PACKAGE: 8 Orange and fluffy texture (like eating a Sesame Street character) and dominant cheesy overtones with more maturity than a tax inspector
PALATE: 8 Think cheese on toast in a pie and you're getting there
PRICE: 7 Over two quid
PORTION: 7
OVERALL: 53/70 A very quiche-like pie but enough of a pastry shell to appeal to those offended by quiches. A different and appealing product from a real artisan baker.

309.

PURVEYOR: French Oven
PREMISES: Newcastle
PURCHASE: Minced beef and mushy peas pie £1.65
PLACE: 8 **PASTRY:** 7.5
PRESENTATION: 7 **PACKAGE:** 8
PALATE: 8 **PRICE:** 7 **PORTION:** 7.5
OVERALL: 53/70 I'm initially seduced by its appearance, as the large pastry pea on top resembles a nipple. The nipple effect you could call it. Unfortunately, when I cut in the crust gives way and collapses, meaning I have to transfer it onto a plate. The pie is generously packed with intense mincemeat, drenched in gravy with a layer of mushy peas stowed on top. The faint green, almost grey, colouring is obviously

due to dilution by the brown meat filling, so they're not quite luminous chippy colour peas but it does little to deter me from tucking in.

From there we wander down the hill to the Red House by the Quayside. Oh hello, the door appears to be pushed to? We wander in and hear a female voice "we're not open yet". Not an auspicious start. My schedule clearly said open from 11 and it's at least quarter past.

We bugger off to a caff around the corner going by the marvellous nomenclature of "Quay Ingredients" for a cappuccino. The word cappuccino sounds marvellous in a Geordie accent, second only to Sergio Tacchini.

Back to the Red House and this time a gentleman shouts from the back: "We've no food for at least half an hour".

At this point while I'm quietly sighing, Reuven forcefully jumps in and blows my cover:

"Hang on mate – this gentleman has come all the way from Wigan to sample your pies. He's gutted man!"

He's only got steak or mince but he'll see what he can do.

Thank you!

The mince sounds intriguing, cooked with onion and stout, but as the other two order steak, I jump on their bandwagon.

The lads explain the origins of a plate pie in the North East to me as it was when they grew up. They literally get a plate and cover it with pastry, add the filling then a top crust – bung it in the oven and serve it up an hour later with veg and gravy to make a great family meal.

I get a steak pie, mature cheddar mash, mushy peas and gravy not liquor (we're a long way from London!) There's loads of other flavours on their website and I get a pint of McConnell's stout from the Jarrow Brewery to wash it down with, from the fantastic selection of real ales and continental lagers.

The food comes served with a carton of mushy peas, plonked directly onto the plate in a shallow bath of gravy. It looks great presentation-wise but it causes us considerable consternation so we ask for a separate plate to dump our empty cartons once we've slopped the peas out. These are mere irksome trivialities and just for once, it's a pleasure to enjoy a pie in good company as opposed to my usual clandestine service station car park approach.

310.
PURVEYOR: Red House
PREMISES: Newcastle
PURCHASE: Steak Pie with mash, peas and gravy £7.95
PLACE: 8 I think we probably badgered them into providing us with good

service but they come up trumps after a bit of collective arm twisting, serving up hot grub within fifteen minutes of arrival

PASTRY: 9 It has a fabulously shaped outer rim and texture which is delightfully crisp and golden. A real winner of a crust. The bottom is a bit soggy but I put that down to it being plonked on a bed of mashed potato

PRESENTATION: 7 Plate arrangement causes some distress

PACKAGE: 8 Lots of lush cuts of meat in gravy. A beautiful combination

PALATE: 8 On its own the steak is a joy to behold but when incorporated with a mouthful of cheesy mash it really hits the mark

PRICE: 7 For a sit down meal that's about right

PORTION: 7 Although deeper than on first inspection, I could perhaps demand a bit more for that price

OVERALL: 54/70 The Red House has a spectacular location, almost directly underneath the Tyne Bridge, and manages to produce a fairly spectacular pie (with a bit of gentle persuasion).

We burn off the calories consumed by walking down the quayside to the Malmaison looking for Vincent Tan, as we've heard he was on the piss around here last night. We spot Cardiff manager Ole Gunnar Solskjaer, who responds to a member of his backroom staff requesting a cup of tea from the bar by saying "Go and get your own from the room, it's free"

With that I leave my Geordie mates to spend the day seeing if they can inflict any more psychological damage upon Cardiff City officials, as they get OGS to pose with a BSFC calling card. This is the British Sock Fetish Council of which I am a member: Socks, football, real ale and pies, what more could a man want?

Me, I want more pies!!

The roads north out of the Toon are slick and free moving – that'll be those shit motorways I was referring to earlier! I'm due back in Wigan in three hours but I can't help stop at Brocksbushes farm shop in Northumbria so Corbridge here I come. Or rather some farmers' field near Stocksfield as my SatNav sends me awry one last time. All I can see are miles and miles of greenery from my elevated view in the middle of nowhere.

The farm shop is rustic and low level, interconnected by a series of wooden huts. Needless to say my first task is to wander into the cafe, pull the old "I'm looking for somebody" routine moving head from side to side before disappearing into the bogs. I discover massive plate pies in the caff and a whole load more on the deli counter including Burbushs of Penrith. I get my mate Moore a Penrith Porker, to apologise in anticipation for turning up half an hour late for the Wigan v MK Dons game this afternoon.

Me, I'm spoilt for choice. There's ham and egg pie; corned beef pies; chicken and leek but they're all a bit too big and scary for me. I decide to get a steak and team it up with a curious sounding chicken, leek and asparagus in a white wine sauce for Emma.

Yet again, I've lost count of pies. Time to wrap things up. And when you get to this penultimate stage there's a real sense that something exciting is going to happen. No pressure on you then Brocksbushes!

311.

PURVEYOR: Brocksbushes Farm
PREMISES: Corbridge
PURCHASE: Steak Pie £1.40
PLACE: 7 Very posh in this most northern county
PASTRY: 7 A crust of two halves. The top is as sleek as a cheetah but the bottom is disappointingly soggy. It has a wonderful tiger skin top and a marvellous crispness but underneath it's distinctly uneven, right through the foil tray, which some of the crust and contents refuse to dislodge from
PRESENTATION: 8 Sat in the bath nursing my glass ankles after a game of five-a-side, it's invisible allure wafts its merry scent all the way upstairs
PACKAGE: 7 It's not the deepest in what seems like more of a discus sized pastry than an actual pie but the squared off cuts of steak are of prime quality
PALATE: 8 Authentic, meaty and chewy
PRICE: 7 For the quality not the quantity
PORTION: 6.5 Not big but its form makes it a perfect "pie barm" candidate
OVERALL: 50.5/70 I have an urge to sing Brocksbushes city limits....

312.

PURVEYOR: Brocksbushes
PREMISES: Corbridge
PURCHASE: Chicken, Leek and Asparagus Pie £1.40
PLACE: 7
PASTRY: 8 Holds together well and has a delicious crispness to it
PRESENTATION: 7
PACKAGE: 7.5 Pieces of chicken, slithers of leek and if there is asparagus in here, it's well hidden and not of the offensive, squeaky

stalked variety, all encapsulated in a lush white sauce
PALATE: 8 A reassuringly expensive quality to it, to the extent I'm dribbling away here
PRICE: 8 As above the quality prevails over the slight lack of quantity
PORTION: 7 A 3-4 inch wide disc
OVERALL: 52.5/70 If my wife is reading and you've been looking in the freezer for that chicken pie I got you. Well I ate it. Sorry.

Saturday 11th January 2014

"Have you had a Macaroni Pie? Aw man, you can't write a book on pies without having a Macaroni pie!"

It's alright for Reuven – a lad from Aberdeen who watches Newcastle brings them down for him. Fortunately it's fanzine day today so I've used this as an opportunity to order a box full from a place that a couple of Aberdonians recommended.

I turn my nose up at the chicken curry, the bridies, the chicken and ham and the steak, the award winning Scotch pie, even a clootie dumpling whatever on earth that is and simply order a box of the buggers: 12 Macaroni and cheese pies for £17.76 plus delivery.

Highly popular north of the border, they look a little flimsy as essentially this is cheese and pasta in a shell, but I've got to say that the smell emanating from the oven is cheesier than a kipper tie. Upon pulling them out I am greeted with a feast of fromage and the advantage I have over my co-sellers is that I am in a position to eat mine straightaway. There's a hard outer shell of pastry beyond the cheese topping. One of the criticisms of the macaroni pie is that it does dry up a bit but no such problems here as I wolf it straight down. The doughy texture of the pasta only serves to compliment the cheese and makes it feel like you're really biting into something, giving it more volume.

313.

PURVEYOR: Murdochs Butchers
PREMISES: Moray
PURCHASE: Macaroni Pie £1.48
PLACE: 8 The lovely Natalie sounds dead nice and replies to my panicky email straightaway assuring me they'll be here for Saturday
PASTRY: 8 OK no top crust but the cheese substitute is an innovative and fulfilling experience

PRESENTATION: 8 Sensational smell coming from the oven
PACKAGE: 8 For the ingenuity and diversity of it
PALATE: 8 You like cheese – you like this pie! It has a distinctive advantage over a cheese and onion pie in that the pasta gives you something more substantial to bite into, with the cheese filtering through the gaps
PRICE: 7
PORTION: 7
OVERALL: 54/70 The lads on the bridge aren't impressed; My drying up theory has crystallised it would seem. It does make you wonder why nobody makes them south of the border though, like a pie lasagne without meat. Pie lasagne eh, now there's an idea?

Thursday 16th January 2014

I tried to come here before Christmas. I walked down Tib Street, where sex shops sit next to chip shops, and promptly bottled it as it was packed full of people on Christmas dinners. I ended up in the chippy and had a cracking chip barm complete with obligatory curly black hair in it.

The Pie & Ale House in Manchester's Northern Quarter is much quieter in January, indeed as I step in I walk right into the open kitchen and see them filling pastry casings right in front of me. I wander around to the bar area and the girl serving seems a little sluggish and I have to make all the running. She eventually serves me with a pint and tells me to take a table and she'll be over in a second. More like ten minutes but as she's a budding Mel Sykes lookalike I'm inclined to let her off.

I've perused the menu extensively before entering and I'm torn between the "play it safe" Three Cheese and caramelised onion or the slightly more exotic Mouflon, cherry and port pie. If I was being totally conventional, I'd probably be plumping for the Steak and Yippee Ale Pie but I am scared off by the mention of Portobello mushrooms. I've bravely learnt how to conquer my mushroom phobia during my adventures but I'm not quite ready for those huge big flappy ones yet.

"We've got two specials: zebra and horse".

Gulp.

Well if you're going to go out with a bang....

Horse. Zebra. Horse. Zebra. Horse. Zebra. HORSE. ZEBRA.

I've quite possibly had horsemeat in my youth when I spent time in Europe. Indeed, possibly the strangest thing I recall is once stopping for a pizza after a day's sunbathing at Venice Lido whilst on honeymoon and inquisitively asking what the "Cavallo" topping was on their equivalent of a mighty meaty. The man from Del Wigan, he says neigh.

Zebra is even rarer than horse but I suspect it essentially tastes the same, if a little stripier. In some senses it doesn't possess the shock factor of horsemeat, and is more of a novelty.

So I opt for the horse pie on the basis that it's shocking enough. And a pint of their own Yippee Pie Ale to go with it. There's a quiet ambience, only disturbed by the chatter of students on the next table talking loudly about the merits of various sex dating websites.

When the pie arrives it's of considerable diameter and no mean depth, drenched in fruity sweet gravy with a huge dollop of mash on top and a little pastry horse as its piece de resistance. There must be a whole horse in here.

At this point the battle of the senses is launched. A brutal blow by blow slugfest between brain and tastebuds. Half the fight when eating horsemeat is that you know it's horsemeat and consequently it can make it a little bit difficult to enjoy, especially when you're a food luddite like me. I persevere despite mild queasiness.

The taste is good, it's different, almost unique and I can really taste the red wine in the gravy. I'm not the biggest black pudding fan either but it provides a bit of respite from the testing horsemeat. When I do isolate the horse it doesn't taste too dissimilar to steak, if a little sweeter and not at all pungent. I know this is a quality feed but somewhere inside my brain there is a little man with a mallet banging away saying "YOU'RE EATING A HORSE HERE YOU DISGUSTING HUMAN BEING!"

Don't get me wrong, the plate is more or less clean at the end but I'm perhaps a little too eager to get a fork full of mash and dip it in the gravy, thus giving the horse meat the swerve in the initial stages (despite me repeating the mantra: "IT'S BEEF! IT'S BEEF").

314.

off one of Shergar's mates

PURVEYOR: Pie & Ale
PREMISES: Manchester
PURCHASE: Horse Pie £9.95
PLACE: 8 She needs a bit of coaxing initially but a real delight once she's warmed up. As for the place, well it's worth a visit for its range of ales and whiskies alone. A good place to take the missus; not that she'd be impressed with me today as I sit here polishing

PASTRY: 8 A superbly formed crust with lovely ridges, topped with poppy seeds and a pastry horse. I even detect a bit of suet in there. It does fall to bits a little after I've cut into it, meaning it's not one you can eat with

338

your hands

PRESENTATION: 8 There's a reassuringly rich smell of pastry prevalent throughout this fine little establishment

PACKAGE: 8 The inclusion of carrots and onion could be perceived as a bulking agent and marked down in other circumstances, but in this case it's necessary. Regardless of what it tastes like, there's no denying there's plenty of it

PALATE: 7 I can't make (horse's) head nor tail of it; it's unlike anything I've ever eaten before – one minute it's sweet the next it's tarty. How much of this is down to My Little Pony I simply don't know. A very odd, at times sickly, taste and strange aroma but also wonderfully rich

PRICE: 7.5 A highly substantial meal for a tenner

PORTION: 9 The size of a horse as it were

OVERALL: 55.5/70 It's not cricket to penalise a place due to my own culinary inhibitions so I can only conclude that this is a truly amazing pie, a smashing venue and I am enthusiastic enough to want to come back and try a different flavour (and sample some of their rare whiskies).

With that it's time to go. I walk back to Piccadilly station with a full, slightly queasy belly and incoming chronic heartburn, contemplating how to bring matters to a conclusion.

In some ways I've come full circle tonight from those early days of steadfastly refusing to deviate from a meat and potato. Even so I probably wasn't the man for this job. I was only ever playing at being a food critic, I'm way too conventional.

But I had my fun. And hey it was fun. Indeed, *neigh* it was fun! And I did it pieeeee-way!!

Golden pie awards

And other things....

Do you disagree with these scores?

Have you found a better pie somewhere else?

Would you like to feed me again and prove me wrong?

Why not visit the Life Of Pies website and tell us all about it

Together we can become a nation of better pie eaters

There's also plenty of blogs and extras relating to the book so visit www.lifeofpies.co.uk

Because life's too short to eat bad pies!

THE GOLDEN PIE AWARDS

Best overall pie: Greens Of Barrow

The Wigan Laureate Meat 'n' Tater Garter: Winner: Greens of Barrow
Runners Up: Morecambe FC, Clarks (Cardiff), Bowens (Adlington)

The Steak Pies are High Award: Winner: The Pie Kitchen
Runners Up: Pauls Pies, The Pie Store (Scunthorpe)

The Great Growler Goblet: Winner(s): These three were inseparable –
Percys of Barnsley, Hopkins of Birkenshaw, Burchalls of St Helens

The Not Paltry Poultry Prize: Winner: Morecambe Football Club
Runners Up: The Pie Kitchen, Pauls Pies (Picnic Pie)

The "Make Mincemeat of the Competition" Award:
Winner: Boghall Butchers
Runners Up: NZ Gourmet (Chilli Beef Pie), Pollok Williamson

It's not a pie but we kind of like them Best Pasty Trophy:
Winner: Philps of Hayle
Runners Up: Hampsons of Hayle, Meadowfresh (Derbyshire Pasty)

The "There are other meats out there you know" Diversity Certificate:
Winner: Great North Pie Co (Turkey Curry Pie)
Runners Up: Park Side (Minted Lamb Hot Pot); Pie & Ale (Horse Pie)

The Meatless Marvels Medal: Winner: Greenhalghs Butter Pie
Runners Up: Murdochs Macaroni Pie, Sakers Mexican Chilli & Cheese Pie

The Perfect Pub Pie Plaque: Winner: Mad Pies
Runners Up: Sweeney & Todd's, Farmer's Boy Inn

100 PIES YOU MUST TRY!!!
The "Life Of Pies" top 100 is unveiled

Position	Ref	Purveyor	Location	Region	Product	Score
1	118	Greens	Barrow	North	Meat and Potato Pie	61.0
2	213	Morecambe FC	Morecambe	North West	Chicken, Ham & Leek Pie	60.5
	214	Morecambe FC	Morecambe	North West	Meat and Potato Pie	60.5
	239	Mad O'Rourkes	Tipton	Midlands	Cow Pie	60.5
5	263	The Pie Kitchen	Bury St Edmunds	South East	Chicken, Ham & Leek Pie	60.0
	264	The Pie Kitchen	Bury St Edmunds	South East	Steak & Ale Pie	60.0
	201	Clarks	Cardiff	Wales	Beef & Potato Pie	60.0
8	116	Bowens	Adlington	North West	Meat and Potato Pie	59.5
	211	Potts	Lancaster	North West	Meat and Potato Pie	59.5
10	279	Lord of the Pies	Stockport	North West	Stockport Pie	59.0
	294	Pauls Pies	Oxfordshire	South East	Steak & Guinness Pie	59.0
12	6	Crusty Cob	Manchester	North West	Meat and Potato Pie	58.5
	205	Sweeney & Todds	Reading	South East	Five Nations Pie	58.5
	122	Gents	Wigan	North West	Meat and Potato Pie	58.5
	163	Cheshire Bakehouse	Runcorn	North West	Meat and Potato Pie	58.5
16	107	Galloways	Wigan	North West	Meat and Potato Pie	58.0
	83	Dawsons	Tyldesley	North West	Meat and Potato Pie	58.0
	156	Hopkins	Bradford	Yorkshire	Pork Pie	58.0
	235	Burchalls	St Helens	North West	Pork Pie	58.0
	144	Philps	Hayle	South West	Minced Beef Pasty	58.0
	141	Farmer's Boy Inn	Gloucester	South West	Steak & Guinness Pie	58.0
	275	Percys	Barnsley	Yorkshire	Pork Pie	58.0
	284	Boghall Butchers	Bathgate	Scotland	Scotch Pie	58.0
	25	Greenalls	St Helens	North West	Meat and Potato Pie	58.0
	145	Hampsons	Hayle	South West	Minced Beef Pasty	58.0
	197	The Pie Store	Scunthorpe	Yorkshire	Steak & Onion Pie	58.0
27	258	Thomas	Barrow	North	Meat and Potato Pie	57.5
	29	Foodcraft	Winsford	North West	Meat and Potato Pie	57.5
	272	Yorkes	Dundee	Scotland	Steak & Peppercorn Pie	57.5
	139	Curralls	Warrington	North West	Meat and Potato Pie	57.5
	271	Grasmere Farm	Lincolnshire	Midlands	Steak & Ale Pie	57.5
	307	Olive Street Pie Shop	Sunderland	North	Steak Pie	57.5
	196	The Pie Store	Scunthorpe	Yorkshire	Steak & Ale Pie	57.5
34	247	Hambleton Bakery	Rutland	Midlands	Rutland Pippin	57.0
	94	Giglis	Lytham St Annes	North West	Pork & Apple Pie	57.0
	257	McLeys	Barrow	North	Meat and Potato Pie	57.0
	202	Clarks	Bristol	South West	Beef & Vegetable Pie	57.0
	244	Graysons	Southport	North West	Meat and Potato Pie	57.0
	123	Gents	Wigan	North West	Hot Pot	57.0
	142	Turners	Bognor Regis	South East	Steak & Ale Pie	57.0
	180	Meadowfresh	Chesterfield	Midlands	Derbyshire Pasty	57.0
42	48	Sharlands	Huddersfield	Yorkshire	Meat and Potato Pie	56.5
	120	Pieminster	Bristol	South West	Shamrock Pie	56.5
	293	NZ Gourmet Pies	Newcastle	North	Chilli Beef Pie	56.5
	297	Great North Pie Co	Stockport	North West	Boxing Day Turkey Pie	56.5
	75	Burnden Park Pie Shop	Bolton	North West	Meat and Potato Pie	56.5
	241	Beans	Thornton Cleveleys	North West	Meat And Potato Pie	56.5
	146	Warrens	Penzance	South West	Steak Pasty	56.5
	295	Legges of Bromyard	Herefordshire	Midlands	Steak & Stilton Pie	56.5
	187	Eddlestons	Great Harwood	North West	Meat and Potato Pie	56.5

	98	Ye Olde Pastie Shoppe	Bolton	North West	Meat and Potato Pastie	56.5
	296	Pauls Pies	Oxfordshire	South East	Picnic Pie	56.5
	149	Pengenna Pasties	Bude	South West	Steak Pasty	56.5
	236	Walter Smith	Birmingham	Midlands	Pork Pie	56.5
55	195	Jacksons Bakers	Chesterfield	Midlands	Steak & Potato Pie	56.0
	64	Crown & Tuns	Banbury	South East	Steak & Ale Pie	56.0
	39	Rounds	Preston	North West	Meat and Potato Pie	56.0
	285	Brownings	Kilmarnock	Scotland	Killie Pie	56.0
	55	Haffners	Burnley	North West	Meat and Potato Pie	56.0
	298	Burbushs	Penrith	North	Pork & Gooseberry Pie	56.0
	40	Gornalls	Preston	North West	Meat and Potato Pie	56.0
	110	Lilys	Sheffield	Yorkshire	Steak and Potato Pie	56.0
	50	Hinchliffes Farm Shop	Huddersfield	Yorkshire	Pork Pie	56.0
	21	A Ryan & Sons	Much Wenlock	Midlands	Beef and Red Wine Pie	56.0
	176	Bolster Moor Farm Shop	Golcar	Yorkshire	Pork Pie	56.0
	84	Whittakers	Tyldesley	North West	Meat and Potato Pie	56.0
	248	Dickinson & Morris	Melton Mowbray	Midlands	Pork Pie	56.0
	291	Davidsons	Inverurie	Scotland	Minced Beef Bridie	56.0
	155	Tootells	Golborne	North West	Meat and Potato Pie	56.0
	105	Chilly Billys	Birmingham	Midlands	Pork Pie	56.0
71	27	Bradleys	Ashton-Under-Lyne	North West	Pork Pie	55.5
	283	Bennetts	Dunblane	Scotland	Steak & Peppercorn Pie	55.5
	288	Pollok Williamson	Ayr	Scotland	Scotch Pie	55.5
	227	Stanforths	Skipton	Yorkshire	Pork Pie	55.5
	43	DT Law	Rossendale	North West	Meat and Potato Pie	55.5
	277	Park Side	Barnsley	Yorkshire	Minted Lamb Hotpot Pie	55.5
	251	Elliotts	Northampton	Midlands	Pork Pie	55.5
	276	Park Side	Barnsley	Yorkshire	Pork Pie	55.5
	249	Dickinson & Morris	Melton Mowbray	Midlands	Chicken Pie	55.5
	314	Pie & Ale	Manchester	North West	Horse Pie	55.5
	7	Westwells	Manchester	North West	Meat and Potato Pie	55.5
82	38	Wienholts	Alderley Edge	North West	Steak Pie	55.0
	266	Brays Cottage	Holt	South East	Pork Pie	55.0
	274	Hollingworth Bakery	Hyde	North West	Meat and Potato Pie	55.0
	161	Weegmanns	Otley	Yorkshire	Pork Pie	55.0
	10	Philip Baker	Exeter	South West	Pork Pie	55.0
	61	Finigans	Crewe	North West	Meat and Potato Pie	55.0
	231	Philippes	Skipton	Yorkshire	Steak & Onion Pie	55.0
	14	Marshall Spearing	Macclesfield	North West	Meat and Potato Pie	55.0
	2	Muffin Man	Wigan	North West	Meat and Potato Pie	55.0
	28	Bradleys	Ashton-Under-Lyne	North West	Meat and Potato Pie	55.0
	36	Edwards	Conwy	Wales	Welsh Lamb Oggy	55.0
	91	Kevin Barry Quality Pies	Lytham St Annes	North West	Meat and Potato Pie	55.0
	256	Morrisons	Bradford	Yorkshire	Meat and Potato Pie	55.0
	299	Pauls Pies	Oxfordshire	South East	Christmas Pie	55.0
	222	Popty Conwy Bakery	Conwy	Wales	Meat and Potato Pie	55.0
	208	Broughton Village Bakery	Broughton	North	Minced Beef Pie	55.0
	82	Georges	Weaverham	North West	Meat and Potato Pie	55.0
	220	Winkles	Wolverhampton	Midlands	Pork Pie	55.0
	16	Pork Farms	Nottingham	Midlands	Pork Pie	55.0

TEN TOP TENS

Top 10 Steak Pies

1. The Pie Kitchen
2. Pauls Pies
3. The Pie Store
4. Yorkes
5. Grasmere Farm
6. Olive Street Pie Shop
7. Turners
8. Pieminster
9. Legges of Bromyard
10. Brownings

Top 10 Pork Pies

1. Hopkins
2. Burchalls
3. Percys
4. Giglis
5. Walter Smith
6. Burbushs
7. Hinchliffes Farm Shop
8. Bolster Moor Farm Shop
9. Dickinson & Morris
10. Chilly Billys

Top 10 Chicken Pies

1. Morecambe Football Club
2. The Pie Kitchen
3. Pauls Pies
4. Dickinson & Morris
5. Higgidy
6. Greenhalghs
7. Mr Kews
8. Pound Bakery
9. Leonardo's Deli
10. Tesco

Top 10 Mince Meat Pies

1. Boghall Butchers
2. NZ Gourmet Pies
3. Pollok Williamson
4. Broughton Village Bakery
5. Main Street Bakery
6. Cloughbane Farm Shop
7. French Oven
8. Dicksons
9. G.Kelly
10. Walter Smith

Top 20 Meat & Potato Pies

1. Greens
2. Morecambe Football Club
3. Clarks (Cardiff)
4. Bowens
5. Potts
6. Lord of the Pies
7. Crusty Cob
8. Gents
9. Cheshire Bakehouse
10. Galloways
11. Dawsons
12. Greenalls
13. Thomas (Barrow)
14. Foodcraft
15. Curralls
16. McLeys
17. Clarks (Bristol)
18. Graysons
19. Sharlands
20. Burnden Park Pie Shop

Top 10 Pasties

1. Philps
2. Hampsons
3. Meadowfresh
4. Warrens
5. Ye Olde Pastie Shoppe
6. Pengenna Pasties
7. Davidsons
8. Edwards
9. Island Delight
10. Gunns

Top 10 Gourmet Pies

1. Mad O'Rourkes
2. Lord of the Pies
3. Sweeney & Todds
4. Farmer's Boy Inn
5. Crown & Tuns
6. Pie & Ale
7. Broughton Village Bakery
8. The Windmill
9. The Mill at Conder Green
10. Red House

Top 10 Other Pies

1. Great North Pie Co (Turkey Curry)
2. Park Side (Minted Lamb Hot Pot)
3. Pie & Ale (Horse)
4. Pauls Pies (Christmas)
5. Michael Hart & Son (Venison)
6. Greenhalghs (Butter)
7. Murdochs (Macaroni)
8. Glovers (Butter)
9. Bakewell Tart Shop (Lamb)
10. Sakers (Veggie Chilli)

Top 10 Pie Towns

1. Barrow
2. Skipton
3. Melton Mowbray
4. Morecambe/Lancaster
5. Otley
6. Huddersfield
7. Sheffield (Hillsbrough)
8. Weymouth
9. Bolton
10. Oh and of course WIGAN

Top 10 Bargain Pies

1. Pound Bakery
2. Percys
3. Bothams
4. Manions
5. Morrisons
6. Hulsons
7. Ye Olde Pastie Shoppe
8. Pollok Williamson
9. Winkles
10. Blackburns

CREDITS (IN CHRONOLOGICAL ORDER)

Maurice Twomowers; FC United; Cheshire Pie Society
www.iateallthepies.co.uk; Foodcraft; Ken Barlow; @Cruyff_Des;
www.porkpieclub.com; www.wiganworld.co.uk; @john_neptune;
@philipmcginley; Ste Clandon; @NeilTague; @onedayinwatford;
Molineux Blue; www.squidbeak.com; @tonyhalp; Rob Power;
www.onemickjones.com; Dave Kaye; @KeithWildman;
http://www.hownottodoafoodblog.com/2010/06/long-goodbye-otleys-
butchers.html; Britain's Best Bakery;
Harry Pearson (http://www.theguardian.com/travel/2010/aug/12/top-
bakers-north-england); Good Pie Guide (defunct);
East of the M60: http://mancunian1001.wordpress.com/2011/03/15/yes-
we-ate-all-the-pies-the-not-so-perfect-ten/; @OliverCocker;
@davelee1968; Graham Aimson; Morecambe FC;
@NaplesofleNorth; The Guv'nor; @unscarymonster;
@Orrible_Ives; Elm Farm Country House;
Carol & Sally @ The Pie Kitchen; @WestStandBogs; Chris Griffin;
@ClevelandPieman; @twitkerr; Jack Broussine @ QMS;
@pierateers www.pierate.co.uk; @cognoscentinovo; #BSFC;
@aberdeenmag; @ScottyMacLennan; Tat; Manchester Central Library.

And finally a special thanks to the talented people behind the Mudhutter whose quality output has continued to amuse, inspire and somehow keep me at it all these years.

ADVANCE SUBSCRIBERS

In order to help fund the cost of printing Life Of Pies over 100 people generously ordered a copy in advance.

I am indebted to the "First 100" who invested and trusted in me. Their names and messages are listed below....

Tony Topping in Retroland

@MmmD0nuts – profanity, rumness & rum

Oliver Hodge: the ultimate pie eater, after Jimmy!

To my favourite Wigan based United fan, Paul

Ian Such (@iansuch) Good Luck with the book

To Chris, Love A, J, C & M

Tony Welsby – pie killing Latics fan….

Nick Farnworth

Grant Crowe Antipiedean

moonay – see eccy pie shop boys on youtube

Forza FCUM – Steven Wood

Alan Moore www.thisnorthernsoul.co.uk

Kathryn Richards

Liam Dyson – you reds

To Adam, grew up in a pie house

Craig Toft NE28 Politburo BSFC OKAY

To @jamesswyer, all the best

@Guinnessta When's the follow up "The Heartburn Years"?

Daniel Schofield

Emma Thompson

Old Wolf : I look forward to the freebie pies

@ChezCon69 & @BL4WN6 – Wigan pie, Bolton pudding!

Foodcraft: Fish, Chips AND Pies under one roof!

Catherine Brimelow: The pie's the limit

Neil Tague

Philip John Parry-Williams (spelt right this time)

Paul 'Coupey' Coupe

To John @unscarymonster Lomas with thanks

Anthony McDonagh aka @shinpad11

David Vernazza

Mick Griffiths

Cliff Griffiths

Bernard Long & Carol Dean

Andrew McDonald

Carly Blinston

Phil Moss

Joseph Kendrick – www.josephsgoal.org

Lynn Hopkins

Hope the waistline doesn't take a battering – Manny Flores & Family

Ken Barlow

Richard Sumner, Higher Heath/Worcester Park

The Pathetic Casuals: Neil M, Rob H, Lee W, Tony M, Dave P, Gorey & Stu D

Following the Latics from Blackpool to Bruges, Macclesfield to Maribor

Sponsored by Latte's, Broadsheets, Tapas, Leffe and Anusol.

Café Vlissinghe – where dreams come true.

John "Statto" Bullough

Marjorie Holt

Mike Barnes

Should folk with quiffs be allowed to eat Pies? Signed Big Ange

@mrjohncoyne

Stephen Dawson

To Bill: 'it must have started in Wigan….'

LIFE OF PIES

Jason Dearden: 'brought up on Pimbletts'

Chris Naylor

Honolulu or Siam….

Tony Howard/Alan Robertson

Paul Atkinson. Manchester. MUFC. FCUM

For Angela: Of The Popular Front Against
Soggy Bottoms – Martin

Ian "shaggy" Graham – for Dad, Ne Oublie 15-08-49

Colin Vickery

Philip McGinley

Sean Livesey (@livesey99) I don't even like pies

Stephen & Mary, Stafford Rangers 29.12.73

James Baker

Ian Trencher

David Trencher

Peter Trencher

David Davies

Colin Roberts

Andrew MacDonald – Springfield Park Town Ender

Pete Houghton

Bowen Pies @Bowenpies www.bowenpies.co.uk

Orrible Ives & Mrs Ives "Any shaggin' in it?"

@SockCouncil, RF, www.sockcouncil.com

For Martin, keeping true to the life of pies down under

For Jamo, Pies over pasta always

Please can we get some quality pies at the Lane!
@kentspurs

Darren Norton @knockernorton1

Anne and Steve, Twickenham Pie Eaters

Anne and Steve, Twickenham Pie Eaters

David Jones

Mark Hawkins BSFC#460

@bluejontown – #BSFC127

Gareth Brennan @theweebigman #Pie&Mash #QPR

Rich. Get out, enjoy some fine pies and ale

Debbie Sharman – Barnsley lass & pie lover

The grail of the modern world. Ed Halliday

@Kev_Cockney

Vaughanie

Stewart Gray Leicestershire Loyal BSFC104

@pauldurnin (Shed)

Bridport Latics

Gary Hall

Bruce Gorrie #BSFC65

Mark Smith @Smagpi

Pete Collins @pete_collins – thanks to the BSFC

G Wienholt traditional quality pies www.gwienholt.co.uk

Pierateer SJL of pierate.co.uk

Pierateer RAS of pierate.co.uk

INDEX OF PURVEYORS

NORTH WEST

No.	Purveyor	Location	Details
1.	Hampsons Bakers	Bolton	www.sayersthebakers.co.uk
2.	Muffin Man	Wigan	www.muffinman.co
3.	Wrights	Crewe	www.wrightspies.co.uk
5.	Slatterys	Manchester	www.slattery.co.uk
6.	The Crusty Cob	Manchester	63 Beswick St, Manchester M4 7HR
7.	Westwells	Droylsden	www.westwellsbakery.co.uk
8.	Martins	Manchester	martinsbakery.co.uk
9.	Sextons	Warrington	www.sextonsbakery.co.uk
11. & 12.	Pound Bakery	Bolton	www.poundbakery.co.uk
14.	Marshall Spearing	Macclesfield	12 Park Green, Macclesfield SK11 7NA
15.	Treacle Town Pie Co	Macclesfield	www.thetreacletownpiecompany.co.uk
17.	Reids [1]	Middlewich	47 Wheelock St, Middlewich CW10 9AB
18.	Pooles [2]	Wigan	www.poolespies.co.uk
23.	Allisons	Wythenshawe	177 Hollyhedge Rd, Manchester M22 8UE
24.	Rolling Pin Bakery	Wigan	129-131 Ormskirk Rd, Wigan WN5 9EA
25.	Greenalls	St Helens	100 Duke Street, St Helens WA10 2JN
26.	Blackburns	St Helens	96 Cambridge Rd, St Helens, WA10 4HA
27. & 28.	Bradleys	Ashton-Under-Lyne	www.bestporkpie.co.uk
29.	Foodcraft	Winsford	www.foodcraftfishandchips.co.uk
30.	Grimshaws	Wigan	270 Wigan Rd, Ashton-in-Makerfield, WN4 0AR
38.	Wienholts	Alderley Edge	www.gwienholt.com
39.	Rounds	Preston	249, Ribbleton Lane, Preston, PR1 5EA
40.	Gornalls	Preston	24 New Hall La, Preston PR1 4DU
41.	Cissy Greens	Rossendale	30 Deardengate, Haslingden, Rossendale, Lancashire, BB4 5QJ
42.	Mannings	Rossendale	33 Deardengate, Haslingden, Rossendale, Lancashire BB4 5QN
43.	DT Law	Rossendale	www.dtlawbutcher.co.uk
44.	Bread & Basil	Congleton	5 Bridge St, Congleton, Cheshire CW12 1AY
45.	Archers	Stockport	11 Hollins Lane, Marple, Stockport SK6 6AW
52.	Waterfields	Leigh	www.waterfields-bakers.co.uk
54.	Oddies	Nelson	129 Scotland Road, Nelson, Lancs BB9 7XR
55.	Haffners	Burnley	www.haffners.co.uk
56.	Boundary Mill	Colne	www.boundarymill.co.uk
58.	Arthur Chatwins	Nantwich	www.chatwins.co.uk
59.	Webbs	Northwich	56-58 Witton St, Northwich CW9 5AE
60.	Clayton Park	Accrington	www.pietastic.com
61.	Finigans	Crewe	2 Laura St, Crewe, Cheshire, CW2 6HA
62.	Phil Manion	Liverpool	www.philipmanionbakers.co.uk
63.	Hursts	Birkenhead	www.hurstsbakery.co.uk
74.	T&M Mayohs	Bolton	258 Plodder Lane, Farnworth, Bolton BL4 0BS
75.	Burnden Park Pie Shop	Bolton	294 Manchester Rd, Bolton BL3 2QS
79.	Co-op	Manchester	www.co-operativefood.co.uk
80.	Hollands	Accrington	www.hollandspies.co.uk
81.	Devonshires	Frodsham	www.devonshire-bakery.co.uk
82.	Georges	Weaverham	33 Northwich Rd, Northwich CW8 3EU
83.	Dawsons	Tyldesley	1 Shuttle St, Tyldesley, Manchester M29 8AW
84.	Whittakers	Tyldesley	31 Castle St, Tyldesley, Manchester M29 8FP
85.	Peter Herds	Wilmslow	www.peterherdcakes.co.uk
87.	Hunters	Bolton	www.huntersthebakers.co.uk
90.	Lainés	Blackpool	www.lainesbakery.co.uk

No.	Purveyor	Location	Details
91.	Kevin Barrys	Lytham St Annes	www.quality-pies.co.uk
92.	Uppercrust Bakery	Lytham St Annes	8 Station Road, Lytham St Annes, FY8 5DH
93. & 94.	Giglis	Lytham St Annes	www.giglis.co.uk
95.	Cowards	Frodsham	www.hecoward.co.uk
96. 97. & 108.	Greenhalghs	Bolton	www.greenhalghs.com
98.	Ye Olde Pastie Shoppe	Bolton	31 Churchgate, Bolton BL1 1HU
107.	Galloways	Wigan	www.gallowaysbakers.co.uk
109.	Bellfields	Bollington	80 Palmerston Street, Bollington SK10 5PW
116.	Bowens	Adlington	www.bowenpies.co.uk
117.	Halls	Chorley	www.hallsbakery.co.uk
122. & 123.	Gents	Wigan	2 Pepper Ln, Standish, Wigan, Lancashire WN6 0PX
131. & 132.	Marks & Spencers	Chester	www.marksandspencer.com
139.	Curralls	Warrington	6 Thelwall Ln, Warrington, Cheshire WA4 1LH
153.	Clifton Street Bakery	Warrington	51 Clifton Street, Warrington WA4 1BE
154.	H.Pimbletts	Golborne	28 Heath St, Golborne, Warrington WA3 3AD
155.	Tootells	Golborne	38 Heath St, Golborne, Warrington WA3 3DL
163.	Cheshire Bakehouse	Runcorn	www.cheshirebakehouse.co.uk
164.	Sayers	Bolton	www.sayersthebakers.co.uk
165.	Oven Fresh Bakery	Liverpool	2 Kirkstone Rd N, Liverpool, L21 7NS
166.	GH Farrer	Liverpool	93 Moss Ln, Liverpool, Merseyside L9 8AQ
169.	J&G Bakers	Bacup	216 Newchurch Rd, Bacup OL13 0TS
170. & 171.	AJ Boons	Chelford	www.ajboonbutchers.co.uk
172.	Handleys	Chorley	210 Pall Mall, Chorley PR7 2LH
173.	Glovers	Preston	www.gloversbakery.co.uk
182.	Smiths	Rochdale	www.smithsbakers.co.uk
183.	Tattersalls	Rochdale	www.tattersallsbakery.co.uk
184.	Brassingtons	Macclesfield	www.brassingtonsbakery.co.uk
185. & 186.	Broadhursts	Macclesfield	160 Hurdsfield Rd, Macclesfield SK10 2PY
187.	Eddlestons	Great Harwood	15-17 Blackburn Road, Great Harwood, Blackburn BB6 7DF
188.	Carrs Pasties	Bolton	www.carrspasties.co.uk
189.	Mandys Bakery	Bolton	455 Halliwell Road BL1 8DE
206.	The Mill at Conder Green	Lancaster	www.themillatcondergreen.co.uk
210.	Mobberley Village Bakery	Cheshire	103 Town Ln, Mobberley, Knutsford WA16 7EU
211.	Potts Pies	Lancaster	www.pottspies.co.uk
212.	Old Mill Bakery	Lancaster	47 Moorgate, Lancaster, Lancashire LA1 3PY
213. & 214.	Morecambe Football Club	Morecambe	www.morecambefc.com
215.	Woods	Knutsford	www.woodsbutchersknutsford.co.uk
216.	Brooks	Sandbach	25 High St, Sandbach CW11 1AH
217.	Mandevilles	Holmes Chapel	2 Macclesfield Rd, Holmes Chapel, CW4 7NE
218.	John Moors [3]	Winsford	101 Delamere St, Winsford, Cheshire CW7 2LX
232.	Pimmies	St Helens	www.pimmiespies.co.uk
233.	Yates Greer	St Helens	7 Tontine Market, Lagrange Arcade, St Helens WA10 1BL
234.	Cottoms	St Helens	Lock St, St Helens, Merseyside WA9 1HS
235.	Burchalls	St Helens	24 Westfield St, St Helens WA10 1QF
241.	Beans	Thornton Cleveleys	100 Victoria Rd W, Thornton-Cleveleys FY5 1AG
244.	Graysons	Southport	106 Station Rd, Southport, Merseyside PR8 3HL
245.	Lathams	Southport	www.lathamsthebakers.co.uk
246.	The Old Bakehouse	Southport	70 Manchester Rd, Southport, Merseyside PR9 9BA
259.	Diggles	Lancaster	www.diggles.co.uk
274.	Hollingworth Bakery	Hyde	56b, Market St, Hollingworth, Hyde, Cheshire, SK14 8HR

279.	Lord of the Pies	Stockport	42 St. Petersgate, Stockport, Cheshire SK1 1HL
297.	Great North Pie Company	Stockport	www.greatnorthpie.co
314.	Pie & Ale	Manchester	www.bakerie.co.uk

1 Change in ownership August 2012

2 Bought by Countrystyle Foods August 2013

3 After further research I suspect these to be Buglawtons of Leek

NORTH

118.	Greens	Barrow-in-Furness	24 Jarrow St, Barrow-in-Furness LA13 9SZ
119.	Cranstons	Penrith	www.cranstons.net
125.	Nortons	Stockton-on-Tees	www.blackwells-butchers.co.uk
126.	Ellisons	Redcar	1 West Dyke Rd, Redcar TS10 3EA
128.	Lunesdale Bakery	Kirkby Lonsdale	50 Main St, Kirkby Lonsdale, Cumbria LA6 2AJ
129.	Dales Butchers	Kirkby Lonsdale	www.dalesbutchers.co.uk
136.	Greggs	Newcastle	www.greggs.co.uk
207.	Peggys	Ambleside	Compston Rd, Ambleside, Cumbria LA22 9DJ
208.	Broughton Village Bakery	Broughton-in-Furness	www.broughtonvillagebakery.co.uk
209.	Melville Tyson	Broughton-in-Furness	www.melvilletyson.co.uk
257.	McLeys	Barrow-in-Furness	90 Sutherland St, Barrow-in-Furness LA14 2BJ
258.	Thomas Bakery	Barrow-in-Furness	www.thomasbakery.co.uk
292. & 293.	NZ Gourmet Pies	Newcastle	www.gourmetpie.co.uk
298.	Burbushs	Penrith	www.burbushs.co.uk
303. & 304.	Dicksons	South Shields	www.midickson.com
305.	Muller Swiss Bakery	Sunderland	www.mullerswissbakers.co.uk
307.	Olive Street Pie Shop	Sunderland	21 Olive St, Sunderland, Tyne & Wear SR1 3PE
308. & 309.	French Oven	Newcastle Upon Tyne	www.frenchoven.webs.com
310.	The Red House	Newcastle Upon Tyne	www.theredhousencl.com
311. & 312.	Brocksbushes Farm	Corbridge	www.brocksbushes.co.uk

SCOTLAND

76.	Bells	Lanarkshire	www.bellsfoodgroup.co.uk
272.	Yorkes	Dundee	www.yorkesofdundee.co.uk
280. & 281.	Mhor Bakery	Callander	www.mhor.net
282.	Main Street Bakery	Callander	56 Main St, Callander, Stirling FK17 8BD
283.	Bennetts	Dunblane	www.bennettsthebutcher.co.uk
284.	Boghall Butchers	Bathgate	www.boghallbutchers.co.uk
285. & 286.	Brownings	Kilmarnock	www.browningsbakers.co.uk
287.	Aulds	Greenock	www.aulds.co.uk
288.	Pollok Williamson	Ayr	www.pollokwilliamson.co.uk
289. & 290. & 291.	Davidsons	Inverurie	www.johndavidsons.com
313.	Murdoch Brothers	Moray	www.murdochbutchers.co.uk

NORTHERN IRELAND

| 243. | Cloughbane Farm Shop | Cookstown | www.cloughbanefarm.com |

YORKSHIRE

46.	Hadfields	Huddersfield	344 Blackmoorfoot Rd, Huddersfield, HD4 5NH
47.	AR Jones [4]	Huddersfield	3 New Hey Rd, Huddersfield, HD3 4AQ
48.	Sharlands	Huddersfield	www.sharlands.co.uk
49.	Parfitts [5]	Huddersfield	27 Westgate, Honley, Holmfirth HD9 6AA
50. & 51.	Hinchliffes	Huddersfield	www.hinchliffes.com
110.	Lilys	Sheffield	907 Penistone Rd, Sheffield, S6 2DD
111.	Beres	Sheffield	www.beresporkshop.co.uk

No.	Purveyor	Location	Details
112.	Helens	Sheffield	www.helensbakery.co.uk
113.	Staniforths	Rotherham	www.staniforths-rawmarsh.co.uk
114.	Seans	Sheffield	932 Ecclesall Road, Sheffield S11 8TR
127.	Bothams	Whitby	www.botham.co.uk
152.	Toppings	Doncaster	www.toppingspies.co.uk
156. & 157.	Hopkins	Birkenshaw	732 Bradford Rd, Birkenshaw, West Yorkshire BD11 2AE
158.	Maughans	Mirfield	59 The Knowl, Mirfield , WF14 9RW
159.	Melvyn Davies	Bingley	Littlelands, Bingley, West Yorkshire, BD16 1RR
160.	George Middlemiss	Otley	www.dalesnet.co.uk
161.	Weegmanns	Otley	4-6 Market Pl, Otley, West Yorks LS21 3AQ
162.	Wilsons	Leeds	www.wilsonspies.co.uk
167.	Sakers	Hebden Bridge	www.sakerwholefoods.co.uk
168.	A&J Pies [6]	Huddersfield	www.andrewjonespies.co.uk
174.	Waites	Hebden Bridge	9 Burnley Rd, Mytholmroyd, Hebden Bridge HX7 5LH
176.	Bolster Moor Farm Shop	Golcar	www.bolstermoorfarmshop.co.uk
190.	David Gawthorpes	Denby Dale	343 Wakefield Road, Denby Dale, HD8 8RT
191.	Dale Bakery	Denby Dale	369 Wakefield Rd, Denby Dale, HD8 8RP
192. & 193.	Rob Royd Farm Shop	Barnsley	www.robroydfarmshop.co.uk
196. & 197.	The Pie Store	Scunthorpe	Scunthorpe Market, High Street, Scunthorpe, DN15 6SY
198.	Hull Pie	Hull	19 Trinity House Ln, Hull HU1 2JA
199. & 200.	Fields of Anlaby	Hull	www.fieldsofanlaby.co.uk
227.	Stanforths	Skipton	www.stanforthbutchers.co.uk
228.	Sutcliffes	Skipton	5 Otley St, Skipton BD23 1DY
229.	Craven Bakery	Skipton	www.cravenbakery.co.uk
230.	Drake & Macefield	Skipton	www.drakeandmacefield.co.uk
231.	Philippes Bakery	Skipton	1 Russell St, Skipton, Nth Yorkshire BD23 2DX
256.	Morrisons	Bradford	www.morrisons.com
275.	Percys	Barnsley	16 Church Street, Jump, Barnsley S74 0HZ
276. & 277. & 278.	Parkside Farm Shop	Barnsley	Parkside Cottage, Sheffield Rd, Hoyland, Barnsley, South Yorkshire, S74 0EA
300.	The Crusty Pie Company	Halifax	www.crustypie.co.uk
306.	Cooplands	Scarborough	www.cooplands-bakery.co.uk

4 *Now Dukinfields*

5 *Ceased trading Feb 2013*

6 *Possibly same as 47. above but this pie was so awful it should be remain a separate review and be never spoken of again*

WALES

No.	Purveyor	Location	Details
31.	Harvies	Mold	Waen Farm, Nercwys, Mold, Clwyd, CH7 4EW
32.	Hulsons	Mold	37 Wrexham St, Mold, Clwyd CH7 1ET
33.	Leonardo's Deli	Ruthin	4 Well St, Ruthin, Denbighshire LL15 1AE
34.	Village Bakery	Wrexham	www.villagebakery.co.uk
35.	Ham Bone Delicatessen	Llandudno	www.hambone.co.uk
36.	Edwards	Conwy	www.edwardsofconwy.co.uk
37.	Tan Lan Bakery	Conwy	www.tanlanbakery.co.uk
137.	Peters Pies	Caerphilly	www.petersfood.co.uk
201.	Clarks	Cardiff	www.clarkspies.co.uk
222.	Popty Conwy Bakery	Conwy	4 Castle Street Conwy, LL32 8AY
224.	TJ Parry Jones & Daughters	Trefriw	Kendal, Trefriw, Gwynedd, LL27 0JJ

MIDLANDS

16.	Pork Farms	Nottingham	www.pork-farms.co.uk
19.	Lynn's Bakery	Telford	11 The Parade, Donnington, Telford, TF2 8EB
20.	Catherine's Bakery	Shropshire	20 Barrow St, Much Wenlock, TF13 6EN
21.	A Ryan & Sons	Shropshire	60 High St, Much Wenlock TF13 6AE
22.	Ludlow Food Centre	Ludlow	www.ludlowfoodcentre.co.uk
57.	Fray Bentos	Leicestershire	www.baxters.com
86. & 133. & 240.	Pukka Pies	Leicester	www.pukkapies.co.uk
89.	New Cooks	Biddulph	69A High St, Biddulph, Stoke-on-Trent ST8 6AA
101.	John Taylor & Son	Coventry	www.johntaylor-meats.co.uk
102.	Stoke Bakery	Coventry	www.stokebakery.co.uk
103. 236. & 237.	Walter Smith	Birmingham	www.waltersmith.co.uk
104.	Urban Pie	Birmingham	www.urbanpie.co.uk
105.	Chilly Billys	Birmingham	Edgbaston Street, St Martin's Market, Birmingham, B5 4RB
106.	Island Delight	Birmingham	www.island-delight.co.uk
115.	Bakewell Tart Shop [7]	Bakewell	www.bakewelltartshop.co.uk
130. & 138.	Mrs Kings Pork Pies	Nottinghamshire	www.mrskingsporkpies.co.uk
175.	Mettricks	Glossop	www.mettricksbutchers.co.uk
177.	Jaspers	Penkridge	Crown Bridge, Penkridge, Stafford ST19 5AA
178.	Wrights	Worksop	www.wrightscaterers.co.uk
179. & 180.	Meadowfresh	Chesterfield	www.meadowfresh.co.uk
194. & 195.	Jacksons Bakers	Chesterfield	www.jacksonsthebakers.co.uk
219.	The Pie Life	Staffordshire	www.thepielife.co.uk
220.	Winkles	Wolverhampton	46 Retreat Street, Wolverhampton WV3 0JF
221.	Brockleys	Alsager	Radway Green Business Park, Alsager
223.	Treflach Farm	Shropshire	www.treflachfarm.co.uk
238.	Michael Kirks	Wolverhampton	www.porkiepies.com
239.	Mad O'Rourkes	Tipton	www.madorourkes.com
242.	Walkers	Leicester	www.walkerspies.co.uk
247.	Hambleton Bakery	Rutland	www.hambletonbakery.co.uk
248. & 249.	Dickinson & Morris	Melton Mowbray	www.porkpie.co.uk
250.	Blue Stilton	Melton Mowbray	Melton Mowbray Market
251.	Elliotts	Northampton	www.elliottsbutchers.co.uk
260.	G.Simpson	Sleaford	www.gsimpsonbutchers.co.uk
271.	Grasmere Farm	Lincolnshire	www.grasmere-farm.co.uk
295.	Legges	Bromyard	www.leggesofbromyard.com
301. & 302.	Aldi	Atherstone	www.aldi.co.uk

7. Greetings pedant! I've been expecting you – I know what you're thinking! Whereas Derby is definitely Midlands, Bakewell and Chesterfield are more Yorkshire whilst Glossop feels more North West. I've put all the Derbyshire bakers in the Midlands here however to keep things gloriously and inconsistently consistent. Phew!

SOUTH EAST

4.	Percy Ingles	London	www.percy-ingle.co.uk
13.	Square Pie	London	www.squarepie.com
53.	Goddards	Greenwich	www.goddardsatgreenwich.co.uk
64.	Crown & Tuns	Banbury	www.puddingface.com
65.	Eagles Deli	Banbury	www.eaglesinfood.co.uk
77.	G.Kelly	London	www.gkellypieandmash.co.uk
78.	The Windmill	London	www.windmillmayfair.co.uk
88.	Laverstoke Farm	Basingstoke	www.laverstokepark.co.uk
99.	Manze	London	www.manze.co.uk

100.	West Cornwall Pasty Co	Buckinghamshire	westcornwallpasty.co.uk
121.	Plesteds	Southampton	2 Gordon Buildings, Shirley High Street, Southampton, Hampshire SO15 3LS
124.	Higgidy	Shoreham-by-Sea	www.higgidy.co.uk
134. & 273.	Tesco	Hertfordshire	www.tesco.com
140.	Charlie Bighams	London	www.bighams.com
142.	Turners	Bognor Regis	www.turnerspies.co.uk
143.	Bangers	Brighton	14 Baker Street, Brighton, East Sussex BN1 4JN
181.	Sainsburys	London	www.sainsburys.co.uk
205.	Sweeney & Todds	Reading	www.sweeneyandtodd.co.uk
225.	Cook Food	Sittingbourne	www.cookfood.net
226.	Stratton Bakery	Gerrards Cross	2A Station Road, Gerrards Cross, Buckinghamshire SL9 8EL
252.	Gunns Bakery	Sandy	www.gunns-bakery.co.uk
253. & 254.	BW Deacons	Buckinghamshire	www.bwdeacon.co.uk
255.	Childs	Toddington	22 High St, Toddington, Dunstable, LU5 6BY
261.	Elm Farm Country House	Norwich	www.elmfarmcountryhouse.co.uk
262.	Ruse & Sons	Long Melford	www.rusebutchers.co.uk
263. & 264.	The Pie Kitchen	Bury St Edmunds	www.the-pie-kitchen.co.uk
265.	Tudor Bakehouse	Harleston	www.tudorbakehouse.co.uk
266.	Brays Cottage	Holt	www.perfectpie.co.uk
267.	Metfield Bakery	Norwich	www.louisdeli.co.uk
268.	Pickerings	Norwich	www.sausageshop.co.uk
269.	Mr Kews	North Walsham	www.mrkewspies.com
270.	M.Newitt & Sons	Thame	www.newitt.co.uk
294. & 296. & 299.	Pauls Pies	Oxfordshire	www.paulspies.co.uk

SOUTH WEST

10.	Philip Baker	Exeter	www.philipbaker.org.uk
66.	The Dutch Oven	Yeovil	dutchovenyeovil.co.uk
67.	Sabins Deli	Sherborne	www.sabins.co.uk
68.	Bennetts	Poole	187 Lower Blandford Rd, Broadstone BH18 8DH
69.	Idahs Patisserie	Bournemouth	www.idahspatisserie.co.uk
70.	Bridport Gourmet Pies	Bridport	www.dorset-pies.co.uk
71.	Purbeck Smokey	Purbeck	No idea
72.	Michael Hart & Son	Cricklade	99 High Street, Cricklade, Wiltshire SN6 6AA
73.	Jessie Smiths	Cirencester	www.jessesmithbutchers.co.uk
120.	Pieminster	Bristol	www.pieminister.co.uk
135.	Tom's Pies	Devon	www.toms-pies.co.uk
141.	Farmer's Boy Inn	Gloucester	www.farmersboyinn.co.uk
144.	Philps	Hayle	www.philpspasties.co.uk
145.	Hampsons	Hayle	www.hampsonsofhayle.co.uk
146.	Warrens	Penzance	www.warrensbakery.co.uk
147.	The Cornish Pasty Co	St Ives	Harbour View, The Wharf, St. Ives, Cornwall
148.	Grumpies	Launceston	www.grumpiesofcornwall.co.uk
149.	Pengenna Pasties	Bude	www.pengennapasties.co.uk
150.	Martins	Exeter	www.martins-sandwiches.co.uk
151.	Ginsters	Callington	www.ginsters.co.uk
202.	Clarks	Bristol	www.clarkspies.net
203.	Halls	Stroud	www.hallsqualitybakers.co.uk
204.	Thomas Butchers	Malmesbury	www.thomasofmalmesbury.co.uk